INTERNATIONAL THEATRE FESTIVALS AND 21ST-CENTURY INTERCULTURALISM

Ric Knowles' study is a politically urgent, erudite intervention into the ecology of theatre and performance festivals in an international context. Since the 1990s there has been an exponential increase in the number and type of festivals taking place around the world. Events that used merely to be events are now 'festivalized': structured, marketed, and promoted in ways that stress urban centres as tourist destinations and 'creative cities' as targets of corporate enterprise. Ric Knowles examines the structure, content, and impact of international festivals that draw upon and represent multiple cultures and the roles they play in one of the most urgent processes of our times: inter-cultural negotiation and exchange. Covering a vast geographical sweep and exploring festival models both new and ancient, the work sets compelling new standards of practice for post-pandemic festivals.

RIC KNOWLES is University Professor Emeritus in the School of English and Theatre Studies at the University of Guelph, Ontario. He is the award-winning author of eight and editor of thirteen books on theatre and performance, as well as a former editor of *Theatre Journal*, *Modern Drama*, and *Canadian Theatre Review*. Among many book and essay prizes, he has won the Excellence in Editing (Sustained Achievement) award from the Association for Theatre in Higher Education, the Lifetime Achievement award from the Canadian Association for Theatre Research, and the Distinguished Scholar award from the American Society for Theatre Research. He is also a practising professional play devisor and dramaturg and a member of Literary Managers and Dramaturgs of the Americas.

T0384581

THEATRE AND PERFORMANCE THEORY

Series Editor
Tracy C. Davis *Northwestern University*

Each volume in the Theatre and Performance Theory series introduces a key issue about theatre's role in culture. Specially written for students and a wide readership, each book uses case studies to guide readers into today's pressing debates in theatre and performance studies. Topics include contemporary theatrical practices; historiography; interdisciplinary approaches to making theatre; and the choices and consequences of how theatre is studied; among other areas of investigation.

Books in the Series

JACKY BRATTON,
New Readings in Theatre History

TRACY C. DAVIS and THOMAS POSTLEWAIT (eds.),
Theatricality

SHANNON JACKSON,
Professing Performance: Theatre in the Academy from Philology to Performativity

RIC KNOWLES,
Reading the Material Theatre

NICHOLAS RIDOUT,
Stage Fright, Animals, and Other Theatrical Problems

D. SOYINI MADISON,
Acts of Activism: Human Rights as Radical Performance

DEREK MILLER,
Copyright and the Value of Performance, 1770–1911

PAUL RAE,
Real Theatre: Essays in Experience

MICHAEL MCKINNIE,
Theatre in Market Economies

RIC KNOWLES,
International Theatre Festivals and 21st-Century Interculturalism

INTERNATIONAL THEATRE FESTIVALS AND 21ST-CENTURY INTERCULTURALISM

RIC KNOWLES

University of Guelph, Ontario

CAMBRIDGE
UNIVERSITY PRESS

Shaftesbury Road, Cambridge CB2 8EA, United Kingdom

One Liberty Plaza, 20th Floor, New York, NY 10006, USA

477 Williamstown Road, Port Melbourne, VIC 3207, Australia

314–321, 3rd Floor, Plot 3, Splendor Forum, Jasola District Centre, New Delhi – 110025, India

103 Penang Road, #05–06/07, Visioncrest Commercial, Singapore 238467

Cambridge University Press is part of Cambridge University Press & Assessment, a department of the University of Cambridge.

We share the University's mission to contribute to society through the pursuit of education, learning and research at the highest international levels of excellence.

www.cambridge.org
Information on this title: www.cambridge.org/9781009044486

DOI: 10.1017/9781009043632

First published 2022
First paperback edition 2023

A catalogue record for this publication is available from the British Library

Library of Congress Cataloging-in-Publication data
NAMES: Knowles, Richard Paul, 1950– author.
TITLE: International theatre festivals and 21st-century interculturalism / Ric Knowles.
DESCRIPTION: New York : Cambridge University Press, 2022. | Series: Theatre and performance theory | Includes bibliographical references and index.
IDENTIFIERS: LCCN 2021026946 (print) | LCCN 2021026947 (ebook) |
ISBN 9781316517246 (hardback) | ISBN 9781009044486 (paperback) |
ISBN 9781009043632 (epub)
SUBJECTS: LCSH: Drama festivals. | Cultural relations. | Theater and society. |
BISAC: DRAMA / General
CLASSIFICATION: LCC PN1590.F47 K66 2022 (print) | LCC PN1590.F47 (ebook) |
DDC 790.2–dc23
LC record available at https://lccn.loc.gov/2021026946
LC ebook record available at https://lccn.loc.gov/2021026947

ISBN   978-1-316-51724-6   Hardback
ISBN   978-1-009-04448-6   Paperback

For
Christine

Contents

Preface

This book began as an examination of the role of contemporary theatre and performance festivals in the continuing project of intercultural encounter, negotiation, and exchange in the twenty-first century. The plan was to consider current contexts, conditions, and practices, asking how, and how well, they contributed, or failed to contribute, to intercultural negotiation and exchange in theatre, performance, and theatre and performance studies in the contemporary world. I planned to pick up where I left off in my work on international theatre festivals for my 2004 book, *Reading the Material Theatre*, integrate it with my subsequent work on theatrical interculturalism, and update both with an eye to current, and I presumed ongoing, conditions. But research doesn't always work out as planned.

My research was drawing to a close in March 2020 when, quietly at first, all hell broke loose. The globalized world became host to a new, globalized virus, people around the world were getting sick and dying or were forced into self-isolation, and theatre and performance festivals all over the world suspended operations. At the same time, the pandemic made visible and exacerbated existing inequalities and structural racisms that are deeply inscribed within an increasingly voracious global capitalist system, giving birth to waves of protests by Black and Indigenous people and people of colour and their supporters around the globe. It began to appear as though festivals and other public gatherings might never be the same again, and perhaps should not be. What began as an intervention into contemporary conditions was almost instantly transformed into a history book and its conclusion into a provisional guide on how to reinvent festivals under whatever new conditions might obtain in the remainder of the first century of this uncertain new millennium.

Whatever those conditions are, I hope and trust that live theatre and performance festivals return renewed, with a strengthened sense of their crucial role as intercultural mediators, sites at which the live negotiation of cultural values can take place in generative, genuinely transformative ways. And I hope that this book, in looking for new models of festivalization and festival epistemology, can contribute something to their reinvention and the creation of a more equitable world in which the traffic in cultures flows freely and respectfully in all directions.

Illustrations

xi

Acknowledgements

The research for this book has taken place on the traditional territories of countless Indigenous peoples around the world, ceded and unceded. The book was written in what is now Guelph, Ontario, Canada, on the treaty territory of the Mississaugas of the Credit (Between the Lakes Purchase, Treaty 3), where I acknowledge our responsibilities to the Dish with One Spoon Covenant and offer respect to Anishinaabe, Haudenosaunee, and Métis neighbours as well as to the many First Nations, Métis, and Inuit peoples for whom today this gathering place is home.

I would like to thank the diligence of my research assistants, Cynthia Ing and Nicole Carey, in helping me to navigate this project's vast research terrain.

I would also like to thank those literal fellow travellers on various research trips, including Erika Fischer-Lichte, Christel Weiler, Torsten Jost, Florian Thamer, Khahid Amine, and the delegation from the International Research Centre 'Interweaving Performance Cultures' for helping me navigate Theater der Welt in Mannheim and the Performing Tangier Festival in 2014; Majdi Bou-Matar, Pam Patel, and the MT Space Theater Company at the Journées théâtrales du Carthage in Tunisia in 2018; Beatriz Pizano, Trevor Schwellnus, and the Canadian delegation to Iberoamericano and FESTA in Bogotá in 2018; Rhoma Spencer, Michael Lashley, Joan Pierre, and the Canadian delegation to CARIFESTA in Trinidad in 2019; and especially Majdi Bou-Matar, again, for serving as my research assistant, cultural consultant, translator, social coordinator, and friend at the Arab Theatre Festival in Tunis in 2018.

Thanks to all those who helped and provided information about specific festivals, including Sue Balint, Beatriz Pizano, and Trevor Schwellnus (RUTAS Festival), Majdi Bou-Matar, Pam Patel, and Bó Bárdos (IMPACT Festival), Sue Balint (Fusebox Festival), Sue Balint (again) and Laura Nanni (Progress and SummerWorks Festivals), Yana Meerzon (Festival d'Avignon), Peter Dickinson (PuSh Festival), and David

O'Donnell for pointing me in the right direction around festival shows in Australia and, especially, Aotearoa, and for sending me one key review that I might have otherwise missed. Thanks, too, to Kirsty Johnston for her expert advice on disability arts festivals.

Thanks to my research assistant Kim Davids Mandar and to people all over the world who have helped me acquiring tickets, illustrations, and permissions: Christine Achampong, Matthew Austin, Art Babayants, Sue Balint, Stephen Bevis, Chelsea Carlson, Daniel Jelani Ellis, Emily Galdes, Fabian Hammerl, Buddy Hayward, Emma Henderson, Tamara Jones, Héctor Flores Komatsu, Chaima L'abidi, Alexandra Lauck, Mikhail Logvinov, Joanna Manavopoulou, Michelle Mangan, Tess Marshall, Charli Mathews, Muriel Miguel, Natasha Abd Muin, Joy Parkinson, Rayshawan Pierre, Carolina Rojas, Nina Rupena, Jonathan Russell, Joe Sidek, Remy Siu, Santee Smith, Sophie Speer, Liam Upton, Marijke Vandersmissen, Rachel Williamson, and Corey Zerna.

Claire McKendrick (University of Glasgow Special Collections), Thomas Engel (Managing Director, German Centre of the International Theatre Institute, ITI), and Theo Wittenbecher (archivist, German Centre of the ITI) were generous in helping me to acquire information about the Edinburgh Festivals, Theater der Welt, the ITI, and Théâtre des Nations, and I am grateful to Basma Hamed (*Taha*) and Man Yan Ip (*Hong Kong Three Sisters*) for help and feedback on their Edinburgh Fringe shows.

I am grateful to Margaret Werry for sharing with me her formal response to the panel on Festivals at the American Society for Theatre Research in 2016, and to Bryan Schmidt, Emily Sahakian, and members of the American Society for Theatre Research and the Canadian Association for Theatre Research who provided feedback on early drafts of Chapters 1 and 5.

I am greatly indebted to the contributors to the special issue of *Theatre Research in Canada* on Festivals and *The Cambridge Companion to International Theatre Festivals* that I edited as part of this project, all of whom shaped my thinking here, and especially Natalie Alvarez, T.L. Cowan, Erika Fischer-Lichte, Julia Goldstein, Jean Graham-Jones, Jen Harvie, Carol Martin, Alexandra Portmann, Emily Sahakian, Sarah Thomasson, and Keren Zaiontz on whose work I have shamelessly, but with acknowledgement, relied.

Isaiah Wooden and Patrick Maley at *Theatre Journal* and Kim MacLeod, Heather Davis-Fisch, and Jenn Cole at *Canadian Theatre Review* provided edits and feedback on various festival reviews and articles that have had a direct impact on this volume.

Finally, deep thanks to Tracy C. Davis, who has supported my work for decades and who as series editor has had a direct impact on this volume, to the anonymous readers for the press, and to Emily Hockley, George Paul Laver, Sharon McCann, and everyone at Cambridge University Press for their help and support.

The opening and closing sections of Chapter 1, 'Indigeneity, Festivals, and Indigenous Festivals', were first published as 'Indigenous Festivals' in *The Cambridge Companion to International Theatre Festivals*, ed. Ric Knowles (Cambridge University Press, 2020).

Research for this book was generously supported by an Insight Grant from the Social Sciences and Humanities Research Council of Canada, and by a Fellowship at the International Research Centre 'Interweaving Performance Cultures' in Berlin.

My deepest debts are to my always inspiring partner, supporter, best reader, and fiercest critic, Christine Bold, to whom this volume is dedicated.

Introduction

It's 4 p.m. on a hot, humid Saturday afternoon in August 2018 and I'm sitting with other guests at a table in the air-conditioned ballroom of the Bayview George Town Hotel in Penang, Malaysia. The room is decorated for a wedding reception, which it presumably hosts with some regularity on Saturday afternoons, and this event has all the trappings of one. But it is in fact a production at the International George Town Theatre Festival by an intercultural collective of sixty women from Malaysia, Indonesia, and Australia, featuring twenty-six women-identified performers of various races, ethnicities, religious affiliations, sexualities, ages, abilities, and national identities. The women parade into the room among the assembled guests in a grand entry to open the show. Many are dressed as bridesmaids – except that one lovely dress sports a dozen or so outsized cockroaches, another woman wears rubber gloves, curlers under her fascinator, and an apron, and another is in military camouflage gear. After the parade a woman crawls from her wheelchair onto one of four platform stages on each side of the hall and sings, beautifully, a song about love and marriage before telling her story: her father had beaten her mother when she was pregnant with her, and she was born legless. Others have various autism spectrum and developmental disorders. One 'proud Muslim woman' wearing a hijab and both signing for and performing in the show, is, she tells us, Deaf.

Say No More (Figure 1a), a devised show, addressed the women's personal experiences of gendered violence, marriage ('family is important; marriage is not'), sex ('they say we shouldn't talk about sex but fuck it! I'm going to talk about sex'), body shaming, and domestic labour. Most of the performers were amateur and the show was unrelentingly testimonial, but that was its point. It was also multilingual: almost everything was delivered in English and one other language. Multilingual, transcultural, transnational, trans-ability, feminist, and normalizing the act of women visibly helping women. And despite how harrowing much of the subject matter was, the tone, overwhelmingly, was mutually celebratory.

Figure 1   *Say No More* (1a) exceeded the national promotion mandate represented by the photography exhibit, *Stripes and Strokes,* by Mooreyameen Mohamad (1b), in which Malaysians of various genders, races, ethnicities, and ages were variously draped in 'the flag that unites them'. Photograph of *Say No More* by Sam Oster, courtesy of Tutti Arts; photograph of images from Mooreyameen Mohamad's *Stripes and Strokes* exhibition by Ric Knowles

Say No More, presented by Tutti Arts, Australia, in collaboration with Perspektif, Indonesia, and ACS Stepping Stone, Malaysia[1] – billed as '26 Women, 3 Countries, One Wedding' – was not typical fare for the George Town or any other International Theatre Festival, but it did make apparent the kinds of opportunities for intercultural collaboration, solidarity, negotiation, and exchange that such festivals can enable in spite of sometimes overwhelming pressures to the contrary. The month-long George Town Festival was founded in 2010 explicitly to celebrate George Town's position (population ca 800,000) as a UNESCO designated World Heritage Zone. Its ideological role within an English-speaking former British colony with a mixed population of Malay (mostly Muslim), ethnic Chinese (mostly Buddhist), ethnic Indian (mostly Hindu), and Indigenous peoples is to promote an overarching governing vision of 'one Malaysia', a country with an elected monarchy operating under a British parliamentary system in which there are fraught racial, ethnic, and religious tensions, press censorship is broadly exercised, homosexuality is prohibited by law, and a married woman's legal rights to 'maintenance' are conditional on her obedience to her husband.

The festival's intended purpose is to bring this fractured postcolonial nation-state together, literally, under one flag as a single 'imagined community' (B. Anderson). The festival's featured opening show in 2018, *Kelantan: A Living Heritage*, was framed by a lobby display, part of the festival's exhibition series, entitled *Stripes and Strokes* (Figure 1b), a series of photographs by Mooreyameen Mohamad of Malaysians of various genders, races, ethnicities, and ages variously draped in 'the flag that unites them' (George Town 64). The opening show itself celebrated the northeastern state of peninsular Malaysia as 'an ancient and traditional stronghold of Malay culture' (George Town 16) and featured a cornucopia of 'authentic' symbols of Malaysian nationhood: giant traditional drums (*rebana ubi*), dance (*Aysik*), dance-drama (*mak yong*), group trance song and movement (*dikir barat*), shadow puppetry (*wayang kulit*), and shimmering handwoven *songket* fabrics. Another exhibition at the festival, *Grit and Grace: The Grandeur of Monochrome Malaysia*, by S.C. Shekar, featured huge, high-resolution, and loving black-and-white photographs celebrating the beauty of Malaysian landscapes and peoples. As the programme indicated, *Grit and Grace* was 'a reminder that Malaysia has much to offer, be it her rich natural resources, environment, or the diversity of its people' (George Town 65). Nevertheless, by virtue of it's *being* international and a festival, George Town, like many other festivals, has often inadvertently exceeded the mandates and intentions of its sponsors and hosts; *Say No More* was, perhaps, one of those occasions.[2]

Festivals, the New Interculturalism, and the Definitional Field

From the 1990s to 2020 there has been an exponential increase in the number and type of festivals taking place around the world. Events that used merely to be events have become 'festivalized': structured, marketed, and promoted in ways that stress brand identities, urban centres as tourist destinations, and the corporate attractiveness of 'creative cities', all participating in the so-called 'eventification' of culture. These corporate, municipal, and state practices and the critical literature surrounding them have paid little attention to the actual content and impact of international festivals that draw from and represent multiple cultures, and what roles they play in one of the most urgent processes of the times: intercultural communication and exchange. This is the goal, and challenge, of this book: how, and how well, have international theatre, performance, live and combined arts festivals contributed to and shaped intercultural conversation, representation, and negotiation in the first two decades of the twenty-first century? Are there models of festivalization that might do these things more effectively? And how, in the wake of the COVID-19 pandemic that shut down festivals and other gatherings in early 2020, revealing and intensifying systemic inequalities and injustices based on racial and cultural differences globally, can such festivals learn from and build upon their record to date when they resume operations in however modified a form?

Once before, in the mid twentieth century, festivals resurfaced in the Global West and North in the wake of disaster after the Second World War as repositories of European high culture. They subsequently developed as what I here call 'élite' or 'destination' festivals in the second half of the century as the seemingly natural homes of the work of the great European directors, exemplifying what those festivals and their mandates have promoted as 'excellence'. Many of those directors – Peter Brook, Ariane Mnouchkine, Robert Wilson, and others – were also key theatrical players in the 'intercultural turn' in theatrical practice in the 1980s and 1990s, in which charismatic westerners, lamenting the moribund state of Euro-American theatre, raided the performance forms of other cultures, usually in the Global South and East,[3] appropriating and decontextualizing them in search of a vibrant, 'primitive' universalism that was thought to precede and transcend cultural difference. This work has been rightly criticized as colonialist, but many destination festivals have proceeded apace with what I think of as a global trafficking in cultures.

It is the purpose of this book, however, not simply to critique the cultural colonialism of festivals past and present, but to try to find other paradigms, exploring ways in which festivals can and have begun to engage more closely and critically with multiple cultures in context and in conversation with one another. Are there twenty-first-century festival models that eschew universalist aspirations in favour of what I have elsewhere called

> a new kind of rhizomatic (multiple, non-hierarchical, horizontal) intercultural performance-from-below that is emerging globally, that no longer retains a west and the rest binary, that is no longer dominated by charismatic white men or performed before audiences assumed to be monochromatic, that no longer involves the urban centres (in the west or elsewhere) raiding traditional forms seen to be preserved in more primitive or 'authentic' rural settings, and that no longer focuses on the individual performances or projects of a single artist or group[?] The new interculturalism ... involves collaborations and solidarities across real and respected material differences within local, urban, national, and global intercultural performance ecologies. (Knowles, *Theatre & Interculturalism* 59)

This new interculturalism is no longer necessarily tied to cooperation (or diplomatic relations) between nation-states but is 'increasingly drawn from intercultural creativity and located in multicultural milieux' such as global, festival cities (Um 1). And it is increasingly intersectionalist, considering the inter-imbrication of ethnicity, gender, sexuality, and ability as well as globalized, immigration, and diasporic considerations. The 'new intercul-turalism', according to Charlotte McIvor, 'is directed almost entirely towards investigating culture's individual and collective multiplicities, as mediated through performance in both local and global contexts' (2). This book's project is to contribute to the emerging sub-field of scholarship on the new interculturalism by examining the role of international theatre, performance, and live-arts festivals as key sites where that media-tion can occur.[4]

But first, what is an international theatre festival? At a moment in history when everything from aardvarks to zorillas has been 'festivalized',[5] when the discipline of performance studies has taught us to treat every-thing as performance, and when there have been increasing attempts to sever 'nation' from 'nation-state', it is necessary to provide some parameters.

This book concerns itself with international theatre festivals understood as 'meta-event[s]' (Schoenmakers 28) in which a larger, multifaceted cultural performance has embedded within it other instances and genres of performance that might otherwise have been free-standing; in which the individual performances it incorporates are set apart from everyday life as theatre, dance, live art, or aesthetic performance broadly understood; and in which performances derive from or represent more than one nation (with 'nation' understood to mean a more-or-less stable community based on shared culture). Briefly, to unpack the terms of my title, 'theatre', for my purposes, refers to public artistic events in which a separate performance space/time is demarcated, along with a distinction of some sort between performers and audiences, both local and visiting. 'Festival' refers to an event that is durational – though its duration can be measured in days, weeks, or very occasionally months – and takes place in an identifiable festival space, be it a venue, city, or geographical region.[6] 'International' is more complex. I use it in my title as a kind of catch-all around which festivals that cross various types of border come together in common parlance or in their own names and promotional discourses. Elsewhere, however, I use it in a more precise way in reference to traffic and diplomatic relations between post-nineteenth-century nation-states that are naturalized as autonomous. 'International', then, is distinct from terms such as 'global' and 'transnational' in tending to respect and reify the borders between states that are understood to be sovereign. 'Global' invokes globalization and refers to a late twentieth-century neoliberal development associated with economic measures and bodies such as the World Bank and International Monetary Fund, bodies that have eroded national sovereignties and supported the unrestrained circulation of global capital in a world understood to be postnational. 'Transnational', however, I use to refer to cultural forces that transcend rather than reify national borders in ways that are resistant to globalization *and* to the suturing of culture, legislation, and geography effected by the concept of the nation-state that underlies nationalisms of various kinds.[7] 'Interculturalism', my key term, exists in the contested, often unequal spaces between cultures that are variously understood as differently homogeneous communities – sometimes nations, sometimes not – within, between, or transcending nation-states.

These thumbnail definitions are practical, and roughly workable, but it is necessary to acknowledge that they do not apply equally to everything I consider in this volume: in the case of some festivals, for example, that present only in the evenings over a period of several weeks in venues spread across major metropolitain areas targeting primarily local audiences, the durational experience for festivalgoers, and especially performers, is weakened. Some festivals present live arts that can can only loosely be called theatre even in my capacious defnintion, and which often blur the distinction between actors and audiences. Some of the events staged by festivals, particularly curated live-arts festivals, now happen or have an impact outside of 'festival time'. Some events are organized across other than national borders, rendering the understanding of festivals as international events dubious. Indeed, each type of meta-event that is discussed here under the heading of 'festival' constitutes the terms 'international', 'intercultural', 'theatre', and 'festival' somewhat differently, and one of the main goals of this volume is to explicate the mutually constitutive nature of the forces that play themselves out around the assemblage of live events that my book systematically classifies for the first time, and that coalesce around the contestable, if practical phrase, 'international theatre festival'.

Liminality, Transformation, and Critical Cosmopolitanism

Scholars differ on the key characteristics of festivals, and their arguments circulate most relevantly, for the purposes of this book, on their potential transformational qualities at both the individual and social levels, and on the degree and kind of their cosmopolitanism.

Theatre scholar Erika Fischer-Lichte identifies 'four dimensions that are characteristic of festivals' (*Routledge* 174). The first two interdependent dimensions are the *liminal*, which she characterizes as 'the unique temporality that constitutes a festival as an in-between time' (174), and the *transformative*, in which 'new identities can be tried out or adopted or an existing identity can be strengthened'. This, in turn, produces 'a strengthening of the feeling of *communitas* and sense of belonging among participants' (175). I am most interested, not in festivals' transformational functions at the level of individual or even individual community identities, but in the potential for such events to contribute to the formation and transformation of newly intercultural communities across acknowledged and celebrated differences. And significantly, Fischer-Lichte notes that 'a liminal and transformative dimension might be particularly strong in international theatre festivals, when during the course of the performance a community between the spectators and actors from another culture may come into being' (*Tragedy's* 355). The liminality of festivals, however, is more variable across different types, sizes, and configurations of festivals, and the degree to which they can constitute liminal space has a direct bearing on their potential to be transformative: the liminal, the destabilizing, the unsettling, create the conditions in which transformation is possible. That possibility depends, in turn, on such things as the relationship between a festival's duration and its immersive experience (how long the festival lasts and how intensely festivalgoers are removed from their quotidian routines), and the degree to which the individual performances cohere or clash in constituting the festival as meta-event.

Some festivals require travel for most visitors to unfamiliar locations; some involve intensive immersive experiences that have the potential to challenge taken-for-granted ways of thinking and being, and to unsettle even settler societies. Some, on the other hand, offering evening and weekend performances dispersed throughout a large city over the space of a month or more, are unlikely to be experienced in any material way, especially by that city's residents, as moving them into a liminal zone very far outside of their regular routines, and are less likely to be experienced in any immersive or durational way by visitors or to place artists from different cultural locations and theatrical cultures into productive conversation. Still more important, for my purposes, is the degree to which the festival experience is liminal insofar as it shifts the normative ground under audiences' feet and moves them outside of their comfort zone. This is less a question of scheduling than of programming, and particularly the programming of difference. This book will be concerned with how and to what degree festival organizational structures, planning, procedures, and programming enable festivals to function as generatively unsettling meta-events, but also with how specific works within those festivals help to constitute them as genuinely transformative spaces. Most festival scholarship deals effectively with festivalization, festivalscapes, and festivals as meta-events at the expense of the cumulative, show-by-show experience that actually constitutes the event for most festivalgoers, and at the expense of detailed attention to the cultural work performed by individual performances within that larger context. It is, I propose, the push, pull, and tension between individual shows and between each show and the festival 'as a whole' that constitutes the experience of most theatre and live-arts festivals for most audience members, and most importantly for my purposes constitutes that experience's interculturalism.

For Fischer-Lichte the third and fourth dimensions of a festival are also interdependent, consisting of a *conventional* dimension in which the festival's regulatory system is imposed and, in a *cathartic* dimension, disrupted. The temporality of festivals consists, in part, of rigid scheduling, in which audience members prepare by poring over sometimes extensive and complex festival programmes, timing the space between events, and curating their personal festival timetables, while, particularly at the world's busy fringe festivals, theatre companies adhere to rigid set-up, run, and strike times to accommodate other shows in shared venues. On the other hand, festivals, in their cathartic, festive dimension, especially when they involve an intense, immersive durational experience, can consist of a temporal break from daily routines, a carnivalesque release from habits and hierarchies that generally regulate lives. Whether this release is ultimately culturally transgressive or reproductive, dangerously discharging chaotic energies or providing safe outlets for such energies within strict temporal and spatial boundaries prior to a return to regulatory norms, has been a matter of debate for decades. Fischer-Lichte herself sees these functions as sequential, 'first destabilizing and then reaffirming collective identity' (*Tragedy's* 108). Michelle Duffy, however, argues that 'th[e] capacity to transform arises out of affective relations facilitated by the festival between people and place' (229) in ways that exceed the festival's temporal and physical boundaries 'through memories, emotion, and personal relations. In this way', she argues, 'belonging is mobile – it moves from place to place, it moves in time – and at the same time is immobile, as it is attached to particular bodies, to our actions, feelings, and our experiences' (245). In other words, a festival's 'time-out-of-time'-ness (Falassi), rooted in the local, can potentially create transformations that endure, transcending both place and time. The different festivals and types of festival explored in this volume have different festival temporalities, some effectively setting themselves temporarily apart from daily life (often through opening and closing ceremonies), and ultimately invoking a kind of closure, while some stage events outside of festival time and/or aim to have long-term, year-round social impact. In any case, while it endures 'the festival', as Fischer-Lichte says, 'seeks to prevent the intrusion of the mundane' (*Routledge* 174).

Among the features of festivals that resist 'the intrusion of the mundane' are what Motti Regev, discussing the capacity for festival audiences as 'cosmopolitan omnivores' to 'engage in practices of cultural consumption that transgress the conventional boundaries of their own ethnic or national cultures' (111), calls their 'isomorphic rites' (118). These include, following Alessandro Falassi (4–5), rites of purification, rites of passage, of reversal, of conspicuous display and consumption, ritual dramas, rites of exchange, and rites of competition. Regev focuses in particular on rites of conspicuous display (the sheer number and range of events available, 118–19), rites of conspicuous consumption (the number of events each spectator attends, 119), ritual dramas ('special events just for the festival', 119–20), rites of exchange and reversal (the juxtapositioning and revaluating of 'masterpieces' and their challengers, 120–1), and rites of competition (the awarding of prizes, 121–2). Regev is less expansive about rites of passage, which strike me as having a greater capacity for transformation than the more consumerist rites of conspicuous consumption and competition, neither of which is inherently cosmopolitan and both of which adhere to the most conventional and culturally reproductive models of festival. Regev, however, does find in the intensity of programming at international festivals the potential for an aesthetic, border-crossing cosmopolitanism that doesn't exist in the 'occasional, unfocused pattern of cultural consumption or pro- duction' that obtains in the 'unorchestrated' day-to-day world of most national cultures (113), and it is perhaps this purposeful border-crossing that constitutes the rites of passage to which he refers. Many of the most genera- tively intercultural festivals examined in this volume have at their roots a distrust of the boundaries, borders, and barriers between disciplines, cultures, and epistemologies by which society routinely regulates itself. And it is this type of mistrustful, border-crossing, critical cosmopolitanism that the most interesting festivals in the twenty-first century seem to be moving towards.[8]

Gerard Delanty, writing in 2011 about 'the cultural significance of arts festivals' (190), perceptively identified a shift 'from internationalism to cosmopolitanism in the cultural logic of the festival' (196) that I would suggest began around the turn of the twenty-first century. Delanty argued that 'internationalism is increasingly being reworked as a cosmopolitan condition in which the national context is of diminished importance, and in place of being an organic experience the festival is rather a sphere in which a multiplicity of voices seek to be heard' (190). I would question how 'organic' the national context might be but the experience and recognition of 'a multiplicity of voices' – both intra- and internationally – can certainly denaturalize the nation-state as a stable 'organic' or imagined community in potentially generative ways. There is little doubt that the shift from internationalism, which has historically reified the status of the nation-state as a unit coercively suturing the cultural, legislative, and geographical, towards a new, critical cosmopolitanism at events that con- tinue to be called 'international theatre festivals' can only be enabling of a more fluid, multiplicitous, and equitable interculturalism. In any case, it is true that many festivals during the past two decades, as intercultural collaborations and partnerships have increased, have tended to eschew what had previously been common practice in their programmes and publicity, the identification of shows by nation as well as by discipline, and have thereby opened up the potential for a more critically cosmopol- itan consciousness while helping to undermine the role of the festival as a site of mutually reificatory diplomacy between sovereign nation-states.

Finally, in 2014 Jasper Chalcraft, Gerard Delanty, and Monica Sassatelli usefully identified four generative 'cosmopolitan relationships' that can occur at festivals and potentially bring about social change: 'the relativization of one's own identity', 'the positive recognition of the Other', 'the mutual evaluation of cultures and identities', and 'a shared normative culture in which self-Other relations are mediated through an orientation toward world consciousness' (110–11). These cosmopolitan relationships, particularly the first two, are central to any inquiry about the potential of international festivals to generate intercultural encounter, conciliation, and, ideally, understanding and exchange. I do, however, question Chalcraft, Delanty, and Sassatelli's focus on evaluation, and in particular their promotion of 'a shared normative culture' and movement 'toward world consciousness'. On the contrary, I hope to explore the ways in which festivals can move away from the kinds of evaluative context that have been traced to their supposed origins in ancient Greece and that sometimes manifest as competition, sometimes for prizes, and at other times as the futile and culturally exclusionist search for universalist 'excellence'. What I am in search of at international festivals is not a single normative culture, unified world consciousness, or pan-cultural standard of excellence; rather I wish to find and advance a festival culture and paradigm in which difference is relativized, valued, and actively promoted.

This is so in part because, for better and, especially, for worse, festivals can also, as James F. English argues, have a 'consecratory function'. 'Festivals', he argues, 'help to constitute publics by organizing their strug-gles over cultural values and canons of taste by means of which publics come to know themselves' (63).

> Festivals contribute importantly to the structuring of public reception and debate, producing consensus regarding 'the masters' and 'masterpieces' of a given cultural field, as well as the equally vital forms of dissent – scandal, outrage, controversy – over new, heterodox works or styles. (63)

Again, this consecratory function, on the one hand, can highlight or help to shape a supposed international consensus over values, canons, and heterodoxies that may, in fact, represent the coercive globalization of culture from the perspective of an artistic, cultural, or economic élite (see Waterman); or, alternatively, it can stage generative struggles over values, foreground inequities, and focus on contested histories and decolonial or (counter)cultural disruptions.

Eventification, Festivalization, and Creative City Discourse

Whether in the interests of coercive globalization or countercultural disruption, festivals can serve as sites where works and debates become 'eventified', 'where the everyday *life event* (performing a play, a concerto, a dance ...) is turned into a significant *Cultural Event* ... which in turn *eventifies* elements and issues of the particular society in which it is taking place' (Hauptfleisch, 'Festivals' 39, emphasis in original).[9] And if particular elements, issues, and performances of culture, on the one hand, become eventified through the work of festivals, the cultures hosting festivals themselves become 'festivalized'. According to Maurice Roche, '"festivalization" can be taken to refer to the role and influence of festivals on the societies that host and stage them – both direct and indirect, and in both the shorter and the longer term' (127). It is one of the purposes of this book to consider the extent to which the eventification and festivalization of culture, depending on the scale, ambition, sponsorship, mandate, location, and sheer *cost* of a festival – to organizers, sponsors, and audiences – has been productive in providing focus on exchange between nation-states (international), within cultural communities (intranational), or between and among relativized cultures (intercultural), or has privileged high, mass, or global tourist culture over either intercultural negotiation or 'elements and issues of the particular society in which it is taking place'.

At its best, as Jasper Chalcraft and Paolo Magaudda have argued, '"festivalizing" ... represents a shift away from the élite/popular cultural axis towards an idealized, but nonetheless not entirely imaginary, new democratic space where the performance of culture requires the interaction of artists, audience and locality' (175). Following Arjun Appadurai, they coined the term 'festivalscapes' to characterize festivals as 'the terrain on which ... a variety of "-scapes" (ethnoscapes, mediascapes, technoscapes and ideoscapes) are constantly at play' (174):

> Festivalscapes are a set of cultural, material and social flows, at both the local and global levels, both concrete and imagined, both deliberate and unintended, which emerge and are established during a specific festival. In this sense, festivals can be seen and analysed as terrains where different cultural, aesthetic, and political patterns and values temporarily converge and clash, constantly creating, stabilizing, and redefining the setting of festival interaction, and in doing so stressing the problems raised by the multiple articulations of global cultural flows, life and spatiality. (174)

Indeed, *as* festivalscapes, festivals can function as what Michel Foucault calls 'heterotopias', defined by Kevin Hetherington as 'places of alternate ordering' (9) – 'spaces where ideas and practices that represent the good life can come into being, from nowhere, even if they never actually achieve what they set out to achieve' (ix). Festivals, then, can potentially serve as sites for the 'renegotiation of communities' (Bradby and Delgado 3).

If festivalscapes are unpredictable and potentially productive sites of the convergence and clashing of different 'patterns and values', however, the forces that are brought to bear on them – political, economic, corporate, and cultural – are rarely equal, and the power differentials among community, municipal, national, and international stakeholders enmeshed in the vastly asymmetric flows and processes of globalization are vast. The pressures on festival organizers and sponsors that threaten to contain and limit possibilities for generative intercultural encounter and heterotopic new ordering within something resembling a level playing field are many and varied, ranging from differential access to international travel, visas, and other documentation for participating artists to differences in labour laws, safety standards, ticket prices, and audience amenities. But many are a result of efforts to instrumentalize festivals as players in a globalized economy. Festivals have long promoted themselves as 'bringing the world to our doorstep', while 'showcasing ourselves to the world'. But these aspirations, if not always this rhetoric, have shifted in the first two decades of the twenty-first century to something closer to 'bringing tourists and the corporate world to boost our economy', while 'branding ourselves as festival cities'.

In 2014 Nikolay Zherdev published an online working paper that examined how festivalization, working with 'creative city' policies and practices, had become a major part of development and urban planning strategies in contemporary cities. The phrase 'creative city' derives from two books by urban studies theorist Richard Florida, *The Rise of the Creative Class* (2002) and *Cities and the Creative Class* (2005), in which Florida promoted the revitalization of cities, not through traditional methods such as 'hard' infrastructure provision in the form of municipal services, tax breaks, transportation, and so on that would attract corporations, but through cultural strategies designed to attract their twenty-first-century workforce, a 'creative class' of young urban professionals – the 'soft' 'human capital or talent' that business increasingly requires (*Cities* 88). Prominent among these strategies, in Zherdev's view, was festivalization, which he defines as 'a specific way of organization and formation of urban space and social activities based on festivals' (6).

Florida identified the creative class by means of its diversity, which he measured by 'the Gay Index' (absurdly privileging 'coupled' gay men as an index of diversity) and by their attraction to 'cultural and nightlife amenities', which he equally absurdly measured by 'the Coolness Index' (*Cities* 88), privileging 'the experience economy'[10] and a vague and indeterminate sense of what is 'cool'. This is all, of course, highly problematic and more than a little silly. It has been rightly critiqued on the grounds of gender and race (McLean, 'Hos'; Parker), the production of urban inequality through the displacement and gentrification of culturally coherent neighborhoods (McLean, 'Cracks'), and 'the serial reproduction of an increasingly clichéd repertoire of favored policy interventions' globally (Peck 767; see also Finkel 20). But it has also been extremely influential: cities all over the world in the first two decades of the millennium rushed to implement creative city policies and engage in city branding intended to place them on the global 'cultural map' (Zherdev 8). Prominent among these were major 'festival cities' such as Edinburgh, Scotland, Adelaide, Australia, and Toronto, Canada, all of which prominently deployed creative city theories in their municipal and festival planning documents (see Thomasson, 'Producing' 168–9; M. Anderson 5, 33, and *passim*). Some of them, such as Toronto, where Florida is based, have hosted multiple festivals of one kind or another virtually every week of the year.

An example of how Florida's 'creative class' has invested in festival culture comes from Ontario, Canada's Kitchener-Waterloo region (KW), the so-called 'Silicon Valley of the North'. KW is home to one of North America's most culturally diverse small cities, and to the MT Space Theatre Company and its biennial IMPACT festival, one of the most adventuresome and highly respected small intercultural theatre festivals in the world. Rather than the familiar acts on the international touring circuit, in the ten years after its founding in 2009 IMPACT has biennially featured outstanding work, almost exclusively by Indigenous people and people of colour, from places such as Tunisia, Iran, Ecuador, Mexico, Aotearoa, Beirut, Bogotá, Chile, China, and Indigenous and immigrant communities across Turtle Island (North America). Nevertheless, Michael Litt, CEO of Vidyard, one of the area's countless tech companies, felt compelled, in an op-ed in Canada's national newspaper, *The Globe and Mail*, to call for KW to 'up level' its arts and culture scene to 'world class' in order to serve the tech workers of the innovation economy (Litt). In May 2018 Litt participated in the inaugural 'True North Festival', sponsored by Communitech and featuring a large corporate conference supplemented by a dominant-culture slate of performers, none of them local. 'Waterloo Region is about building cool things together', according to the festival's website (Communitech), scoring high on Florida's Coolness Index, but ignoring both local and transnational intercultures and, of course, not considering cultural difference among its measures of diversity.[11] Florida's creative city, it seems, succeeded for many in promoting a globalized and saccharine brand of creative city 'diversity' without appreciable difference.

In spite of the apparent ubiquity of festivalization, creative city discourses, city branding, the cultivation of 'place myths' (Thomasson, 'Producing' 111, citing Shields 60), 'festival tourism' (Quinn, 933), and other homogenizing and globalizing forces, the festivalscape in the early twenty-first century has not been entirely without disruptive fissures. Indeed, as Jorge Perez Falconi says, 'a Festivalscape is the constellation of contrasting trajectories and flows impelled by local, national, and transnational practices and discourses at a festival' (13), and as my opening example of the George Town festival suggests, it can rarely serve any unified agenda. Zherdev acknowledges that the 'top-down' dimension of urban planning within the context of festivalization is dependent on the 'bottom-up' participation of sometimes unruly artists (and others) who actually constitute the festivals. Designs for any festival as a meta-event, as at George Town, are often complicated or disrupted by the multiplicity of discrete events that make it up, and this tension is one of the things I will focus on throughout this volume. The experience economy, Zherdev notes, 'brings to life new actors, public-private partnerships, networks and interdependencies that result in new powerplay patterns fostering the production and consumption of experiences' (14). And chief among the 'new actors' he identifies are artists, local and otherwise. Other scholars have also focused on tensions between 'the instrumentalization of expressive culture' within 'a transnational festival geography' (Ronström 73–4), on the one hand, and 'localizing and diversifying forces' (76), on the other. For my purposes, 'diversifying forces' include those brought about by cultural difference, broadly understood, both within local host communities and among visitors, both artists and others. It is one of the unanticipated consequences of the shift to a neoliberal economy and its reliance (or insistence) upon individual entrepreneurialism that unruly artists, for whom that economy has created a new and frightening precarity, have also been led to enter into partnerships and transnational networks that compensate for decreased government support of artists and festivals alike. It has also, in some instances, placed artists in leadership positions as curators, co-curators, or guest curators, and while it has inappropriately downloaded administrative work and responsibility to them it has also better positioned them to create and constitute disruptive fissures in what was once a more uniformly top-down festival economy.

Festivals have not always been good at difference, partly because the festival context, through decontextualization, has often reduced work that is socially and politically powerful within its own communities to exoticism or pure formalism within the deterritorialized space of the festival.[12] In economic and environmental terms this can be compared to 'extractivism' in industries such as mining, forestry, and fossil fuel. As defined by Indigenous Michi Saagig Nishnaabeg artist and scholar Leanne Betasamosake Simpson, 'extractivism is a cornerstone of capitalism, colonialism, and settler colonialism. It's stealing. It's taking something, whether it is a process, an object, a gift, or a person, out of the relationships that give it meaning, and placing it in a nonrelational context for the purposes of accumulation' (*As We Have* 201–2). Timothy D. Taylor has similarly argued that one of the colonizing tasks that has been accomplished by festivals is 'domesticating the Other, keeping it at a safe distance and placing it in a capitalist framework of the consumption of commodities' (116, qtd in Ronström 78). Indeed, Julie Holledge and Joanne Tompkins, noting the 'lucrative drawcard' that 'exotic' intercultural theatre has been for international festivals (153), argue that 'onstage, culture as difference quickly becomes a commodity', while 'a culturally identified commodity product in performance sometimes comes to be recognized as a metonym for a culture' (157). 'Most arts festivals', they suggest, 'set out to present intercultural performance as a showcase of how cultures might intersect and interact, but the underlying financially driven structure of any festival and the resulting commodification of its art forms generally compromise the best intentions to promote interculturalism' (158–9). Such festivals – and Holledge and Tompkins are referring specifically to destination festivals in Australia – have historically been promoted and funded by local and national governments as economic engines, touring artists have often worn 'the ambassadorial and tourism mandates of their home country' (156), most festivals have relied on corporate funders who anticipate material returns, and all of this has tended to promote a 'checkmark', or 'sound-bite' approach to the cultures represented that can rapidly descend to meaninglessness (157–78). But not all festivals are the same, and in the early decades of the twenty-first century many festivals are adjusting to new realities and new types of festivals are emerging that address evolving social and economic conditions in potentially productive ways, and that, as I have suggested, also complicate the definitional field around the terms 'international', 'theatre', and 'festival'. It is this turning point in the life of festivals – the first two decades of the twenty-first century – that this book sets out to examine.

Partly because of a constant search for novelty, festivals have always tended to stress formal diversities – 'mixing, bricolage, eclecticism, crossover, blurring of genres and categories' (Ronström 80) – that can prove to be generatively disruptive in social as well as aesthetic ways. And according to sociologist Sharon Zukin, cities – including, presumably, festival cities – had begun by the end of the twentieth century to view the multi-ethnicity of their populations as a source of both cultural vitality and economic renewal (836). Festivals can be understood, then, as 'fields of tension' (Ronström 76), at once sites of the cultural reproduction of global capitalism *and* vehicles for communicative negotiation, diversification, resistance, and in the case of colonized cultures, decoloniality and resurgence.[13] And as management scholar Marjana Johansson has pointed out, 'apart from shaping cultural preferences festivals also shape patterns of inclusion and exclusion and can be mobilized to protect established boundaries as well as to transgress them. This organizing capacity of festivals means that they are political.' Festivals are evolving in the twenty-first century – or have the potential to evolve – in ways that could make their politics – including the politics of cultural inclusion, exclusion, and representation – visible and contestable.

Scope, Methods, and Theories

This book's goal is to interrogate the politics and practices of festivals in the first two decades of the twenty-first century as they related to the global traffic in cultures: the ways and degrees to which international theatre and multi-arts festivals stage, represent, exchange, market, and negotiate cultural difference, broadly understood to include ethnic, national, Indigenous, queer, disability, and other cultures. Festivals do function, perhaps first and foremost, as marketplaces, but as I have argued elsewhere following Peter Stallybrass and Allon White (Knowles, *Reading* 190), marketplaces are complex sites, both intensely local and 'only ever an *intersection* ... a conjunction of distribution entirely dependent upon remote processes of production and consumption, networks of communication, lines of economic force' (Stallybrass and White 27, emphasis in original). They are also places where different communities, categories, and cultures, both high and low, mix and mingle in unpredictable ways. Like, or as, marketplaces, festivals therefore become contested sites, spaces, as James Clifford says of museums, for negotiating 'the opportunities and constraints created by powerful and overlapping cultural, economic, political and historical forces and shifting political alignments', where 'the work of culture remains always political and relational, marking and mediating insides and outsides, imperfectly negotiating social factions' (qtd in Papastergiatis and Martin 53). Festivals, then, are the meeting points of multiple, distinct, and, crucially, unequal cultural forces that can be brought to bear upon each other and be experienced by artists and audiences in multiple and unanticipated ways. It is part of the purpose of this book to elucidate and evaluate the different ways in which different, and different kinds of international festivals in the early twenty-first century have enabled, enhanced, restricted, or resisted their potential to broker cultural exchange. This involves 'eschewing assumptions about the flat geo-political terrain of global multiculturalism', to borrow a phrase from Margaret Werry, and considering the relative merits of the different politics, and the different temporal, spatial, curatorial, financial, and organizational strategies of festivals as they play themselves out in different municipal, regional, and national settings.

Festivals are not the same the whole world over. François Campana has argued that western definitions of festivals that centre around 'a concentrated series of artistic and cultural offerings (grouped by theme or by art), with the participation of a wide audience' do not apply very well to festivals in Africa (50). They are equally inappropriate, I suggest, for festivals in the Caribbean, the Pacific, and across the trans-Indigenous world, where the events and the word that names them are constituted differently than at the cities that host the world's destination, fringe, and curated live-arts festivals. For this reason, in my discussion of festivals in these locations the definitional field I outline here will be applied with considerable elasticity, considering events that are certainly performative, but might otherwise be understood to be art markets, showcases, or cultural festivals, or to have elements of Carnival or ceremony that can challenge the very epistemology of festivals. There are also many events that refer to themselves as festivals but are beyond the remit of this book, and others that do fit my definitions but that I exclude for reasons of space. I do not consider the proliferation of Shakespeare festivals worldwide, for example, or the Shaw Festival in Ontario, Canada, events that call themselves festivals but in fact consist of extended repertory seasons; and I do not consider 'mega-events' such as the European City of Culture, Cultural Olympiads, or World Fairs except insofar as they relate to Chapter 1's discussion of Indigeneity and festivals. I also exclude from consideration series such as the Next Wave Festival at the Brooklyn Academy of Music (BAM), the Festival d'Automne à Paris, or the Berliner Festspiele that are called festivals but extend over many months and do not involve artists from different places being in the same location for a set-apart period, or audiences escaping in any durational way from their daily routines. Nor do I give extensive consideration in these pages to the many festivals devoted to specific performance forms such as puppetry, clown, circus, mime, physical theatre, solo performance, or street theatre where the focus is primarily on the form, and I do not look at amateur, university, educational, or online festivals, or the many festivals for young audiences that have flourished throughout the period. Finally, while I attempt to extend my discussion of festivals beyond the Euro-American festival circuits familiar to many in the Global North and West, my coverage is limited by the resources it takes to attend international festivals, and by my own linguistic limitations. I attended at least three of each type of festival considered in each of the following chapters, including festivals on six continents (albeit in very unequal proportions), but with the exception of the BeSeTo festival discussed in Chapter 5 I have only attempted to write about festivals whose primary languages of operation are English, French, German, Spanish, Portuguese, or Arabic (again, in unequal proportions), and I am grateful to those who have translated for me.[14]

It is said in much western theatre history that 'once upon a time, theatre and festivals were born simultaneously' – in Athens in the fifth century BCE (Maurin 8); that both were reborn in the medieval period; that they were revived, after the Greek model, by Wagner and his compatriots at Bayreuth in the 1870s and sustained by the likes of Peter Behrens and Georg Fuchs in Germany in 1901; and that they were reinvented at Edinburgh, Avignon, and elsewhere in the wake of the Second World War to shore up a bruised and battered European civilization. In most western scholarship this has been presented as a genealogy of the formation, reinvention, or reinvigoration of communities, usually understood as nation-states (see, e.g., Giorgi and Sassatelli; Fischer-Lichte, *Tragedy's* 82). It is still frequently argued that 'the close relation between festival and theatre in European history is striking. Festivals are almost inconceivable without theatre performances' (Fischer-Lichte, *Routledge* 175). But festivals long precede what the western academy understands to be theatre, and in the twenty-first century many festivals have evolved, other types of festival have emerged, and still others participate in a different genealogy entirely, one that, I suggest, demands a new festival historiography and makes possible a new festival cosmogony.

The approach of *International Theatre Festivals and 21st-Century Interculturalism* is not primarily historical, and although it is written by a white settler Canadian artist-scholar trained in the western academy, its focus is not exclusively on European festivals. Its primary critical and theoretical challenges are: (1) relationally to consider international theatre, performance, live arts, and combined arts festivals in the first two decades of the twenty-first century as sites of tension between the local and global and sites of unequal negotiation between cultures and cultural forms; (2) to analyse the impact of globalization, urban promotional discourses such as 'creative city' theory, and city branding on the ways in which inter-cultural negotiations are framed and practised at festivals; (3) to investigate ways in which festivals can be reconfigured to better enable cross-cultural understanding and a 'new interculturalism' 'from below' rather than through state intervention; and (4) to consider festival models, paradigms, and origin stories that offer generative alternatives to the élite, destination-festival model that has dominated the international circuit since the mid twentieth century. A final challenge is to acknowledge that, as Christine Nygren argues, festivals in different cultures require different theoretical and methodological approaches. This has led me, in addition to traditional research involving archival, print, and digital sources, to adapt an over-arching methodology that George E. Marcus calls 'multisited ethnography' (79): I have had different access to different festivals globally, participating as a board member, organizer, reviewer, or artist at some, attending others frequently and at length without formal participation, attending others only briefly with or without the aid of translators or cultural consultants, and visiting still others only virtually, through traditional forms of human-ities research, or not at all. Insofar as it is ethnographic my approach is based on my own participant-observation experience, and my research has been conducted, as Marcus articulates it, 'with a keen awareness of being within the landscape, and as the landscape changes across sites, the identity of the ethnographer requires renegotiation' (97).

The book is structured neither by chronology nor geography, but by a loose classification of festival type, each requiring different theoretical lenses. Festivals worldwide have existed in the twenty-first century for a variety of purposes and taken a variety of forms that have not in any systematic way been acknowledged in scholarship, and although classifica-tions and taxonomies are always in danger of reifying existing modes of understanding and, especially, valuation, when applied loosely and with a degree of self-consciousness they can also be useful. This book is therefore organized into chapters that provide a loose grouping of the different types of festival and genres of festivalization that, I suggest, have come to populate the global festivalscape in the first two decades of the twenty-first century. Although they share certain features and qualities, there is certainly overlap among the categories, and many shows have appeared at two or more different types of festival, I suggest that most festivals in this period can be categorized as one of the following: large, élite, or destination festivals programmed by organizers from an international menu of shows taking place in locations branded as 'festival cities' and marketed as tourist destinations; smaller, artist-run interdisciplinary live-arts festivals curated to put particular artists and live art forms into conversation with one another and with the urban geographies and populations that host them; anarchic, open-access fringe festivals that may or may not coincide with destination or artist-run festivals; socially activist festivals that exist to explore and promote political and/or aesthetic alternatives to dominant social and cultural formations; and what I call 'intracultural transnational' festivals bringing together work from a single cultural, regional, or language community that nevertheless transcend, transgress, or disregard national borders.

Although this volume aims to wear its theorization lightly, making itself available and accessible to festival organizers, funders, and general audiences as well as students and scholars, the overall theoretical frames that it employs are cultural materialism and the new interculturalism studies. The latter I have outlined above; the former pays attention primarily to the ways in which the mutually constitutive material conditions for production, reception, and 'performance text' (in this case, the individual shows *and* the festival as meta-event) determine in large part the cultural work performed by the festivals. This approach involves attentiveness to the ways in which the histories, politics, public discourses, reputations, mandates, organizational structures, publicity, ticketing, architecture, geographies, and neighborhoods that house the festivals, all ideologically coded, shape their meaning and impact (see Knowles, *Reading* 1–101). Within those frames I take cognate, but pragmatically different theoretical approaches to each festival and type of festival that I consider. These include:

— critical diaspora studies, which examines the relationships between diaspora and nation; transnationalism, localization, and globalization; territorialization and deterritorialization; and complex identity formations related to the migration and intermixing of cultures;
— critical cosmopolitanism, which attemps to circumvent the traps of universalism and state multiculturalism while imagining an attitudinal openness to cultural difference and a practice of navigating across cultural boundaries while redressing historical and extant power differentials among cultures;

- decolonial studies, which eschews the tendency of decolonization and postcolonial nationalisms to reify colonial binaries while undertaking the epistemological reconsideration of modernist and neocolonial structures, hierarchies, and practices in order to validate non-western cultural formations and the epistemic regimes that undergird them;
- and Indigenous resurgence studies, which focuses on cultural survivance and resurgence rather than merely resistance, building on Indigenous Nation-specific 'grounded normativity', the 'place-based foundation of Indigenous decolonial thought and practice' (Coulthard 13).

Beyond these, my consideration of curated, live-arts festivals employs the discourses of scholars such as Jen Harvie and Angela McRobbie who have studied the complicity of contemporary radical art with neoliberal economics; my reading of the open-access world of fringe festivals similarly invites analysis through the lens of neoliberal individualism and entrepreneurialism; while my discussion of what I have called 'intracultural transnational' festivals is illuminated by studies of global transnationalism.

Taxonomies, Paradigms, and Creation Stories

Although it focuses on the opening decades of the twenty-first century, *International Theatre Festivals and 21st-Century Interculturalism* opens by acknowledging a transnational, or rather trans-Indigenous tradition of what might be called festivals that predates western history. Chapter 1, 'Indigeneity, Festivals, and Indigenous Festivals', asks what it might mean to our understanding of festivals, and particularly of festivals as sites of intercultural negotiation, if we considered them to have originated, not with the Festival of Dionysus in Athens in the fifth century BCE – which was itself heavily influenced by similar festivals in societies Indigenous to Africa (see Zarrilli 59) – but with occasions of performative intercultural contact and negotiation among the world's First Peoples. What if we did not understand 'festival' to be, by definition, a western concept? What if our understandings of festival performance and performativity began with a different creation story?[15] Following from those questions and a brief account of events that might be understood to be Indigenous 'ur-festivals' that predate the Festival of Dionysus, the chapter traces a brief history of the relationship between Indigenous peoples, fairs, festivals, and mega-events in the west before turning to consider Indigenous-run festivals in the contemporary world that have brought together First Nations in ways that echo and revive ancient routes of trade, exchange, and the ceremonial practice of trans-Indigenous negotiation. I place this chapter first in an attempt to problematize traditional festival epistemologies, frame subsequent chapters within different ways of thinking about the form and function of festivalization, and disrupt Eurocentric festival (his)stories. In this chapter my theoretical frame is drawn from decolonial and Indigenous Studies, wherever possible citing Indigenous sources and identifying scholars and theorists by their Indigenous nations as specifically as possible in an attempt to respect Nation-specific Indigenous epistemologies.

Chapter 2, 'Destination Festivals and the International Festival Circuit', begins with what has often been considered the revival of international festivals in the west in the wake of the Second World War, when Edinburgh and Avignon were founded in 1947 to help salvage European high culture. These festivals and their international 'hallmark arts festival' descendants (Varney et al. 208) incorporated into their original purpose national identity reification, international cultural diplomacy, and in some cases peacekeeping, and then shifted to the more globalized economic functions of festivalization, eventification, and city branding early in the twenty-first century. They remain, problematically, I suggest, the dominant festival model globally, though some of them are adapting to changing realities and other types of festivals have emerged to challenge their preeminence. This chapter considers how festival programmers, for the most part selecting shows from a menu of touring productions and thereby constituting an international festival circuit, have formed a globalized marketplace that has threatened to erase cultural difference through decontextualization and commodification. Destination festivals throughout their histories have tended to participate in discourses of universalism, excellence, and the (post)modernist avant garde, and to constitute their audiences socially as élite arbiters of taste. They are seen by their municipal and national hosts, who are seeking to attract tourist dollars and corporate headquarters, as the gold standard to which all festivals should aspire. This chapter tries to find models and practices that might allow these destination festivals and their host cities to enable and celebrate rather than fetishize difference and to stage meaningful cross-cultural encounters despite global pressures to the contrary.

Many of the élite, destination festivals that were founded in the mid twentieth century, which have traced their origins to ancient Greece, having adapted to a changing sociopolitical landscape, nevertheless retain deeply embedded traces of their moment of birth; they remain, as Keren Zaiontz has argued, 'indivisible from the statecraft of Nations'

('From Post-War' 15). By the early years of the twenty-first century, however, the world was no longer populated by autonomous nation-states constituting national communities that were 'imagined', in Benedict Anderson's coinage, to be culturally homogeneous. Nor, after the decolonization movements of the mid twentieth century[16] and the late twentieth-century development of globalized capitalism, was it still dominated by the European imperial powers who had once colonized most of the Americas, Africa, and Asia. The élite, destination festival circuit that was founded in Edinburgh and Avignon, at Paris's Théâtre des Nations, and elsewhere not long after the founding of the United Nations in 1945, initially served internationalist purposes not dissimilar, in the cultural realm, to the diplomatic and peacekeeping ones for which that august body was established. Festivals founded since, many of them in reaction to the destination festivals I discuss in Chapter 2, have taken a different form.

The origins of the festivals considered in Chapter 3, 'The Curated Live-Arts Festival', are more recent. Beginning in the 1980s with LiFT (London International Festival of Theatre) and other festivals mainly based in continental Europe, and expanding in the 2000s to include North America, a new form of curated, interdisciplinary, artist-run festival responded both for better and for worse to neoliberal shifts in the globalized economy, challenged the cafeteria-style programming of 'the circuit', and began designing programmes with specific artistic and aesthetic goals that purposefully brought like-minded artists together in generative juxtapositions or collaborations rather than as signal representatives of their respective nations. Downloading managerial responsibilities and financial risks to artists-as-entrepreneurs, this festival model has nevertheless also transformed festival programming into a creative rather than merely administrative activity, while also often imagining new roles for festivalgoers as participants. While these curated, live-arts festivals often tend towards formalist experimentation and develop their own networks, they also often enable social as well as artistic experimentation to cross political and cultural as well as disciplinary boundaries, and they find ways of exploring, however problematically, the inter-imbrication of the work of international guests and the life of the host city both within and outside of traditional theatrical spaces. They tend to address local rather than tourist audiences, to engage directly with local issues and neighborhoods, and they often exceed traditional festival temporalities.

If festivals, including mushroom festivals,[17] sprang up like mushrooms all over the world in the late twentieth and early twenty-first centuries, nowhere is this more true than on the international fringe circuit, which, together with other kinds of festival alternatives, is the focus of Chapter 4. 'Open-access' fringe festivals, beginning in 1947 with the now mammoth Edinburgh Fringe as a genuine aesthetic and political alternative to the exclusions and élitisms of the Edinburgh International Festival, evolved by the twenty-first century into exemplary models of the neoliberal free market with all the inequities, precarities, and exclusions such markets inevitably encompass, constituting their artists as entrepreneurs and their audiences as experience collectors. Many fringes emerged, moreover, with no relationship to a centre: with no mainstage to be alternative to, such festivals – the only shows in town – have taken on broad representational mandates that have led to modifications and adjustments to their open-access principles and allow them to privilege certain types of difference. In addition to the official fringe circuit organized and promoted through various international networks, this chapter also looks at fringes of fringes, counterfestivals, 'alternativos', and 'manifestivals' that have emerged in the twenty-first century with more explicitly political, intersectional, identity-politic, and social-action mandates, and these have often staged or promoted generative dialogues, contestations, and confrontations across various kinds of difference. These politically alternative festivals at their best shift away from the dominant model of understanding their shows as spectacles and their audiences as consumers and move closer to the Indigenous festival model in which artists and audiences are understood to be participants or witnesses.

Chapter 5, which focuses on 'The Intracultural Transnational', concerns itself with a different type of festival that brings together an identifiable cultural, regional, or linguistic community across continental, hemispheric, or international borders. These festivals, I suggest, represent an emerging new decolonial paradigm that has much in common with the one I have identified as developing from an Indigenous tradition, with festivals often serving as sites at which generative debates internal to their specific communities can cross latter-day or enforced borders and forge transnational solidarities while acknowledging, celebrating, or mediating intracultural and historical differences. Indeed, these festivals of intracultural encounter, however vexed, might serve as alternative models of the kinds of negotiation and exchange that this book sets out to track down. They work to bring audiences together across their differences, most often to address historical divisions brought about by colonialisms and neocolonialisms of various kinds, to constitute trans- rather than international communities, and to ally with the Indigenous festival paradigm in compatible ways.

Taken together, these chapters, and this book, constitute a new and hopefully useful classification of twenty-first century festivals for future researchers, while also, crucially, assembling and analysing a documentation of effective practices and policies for festival organizers, funders, artists, audiences, and other stakeholders globally who wish to make future international theatre, multi-arts, and live-art festivals more than globalized sites of neoliberal capitalist circulation, and more conducive to real and open negotiation and exchange across acknowledged and celebrated cultural and other difference. The book (in)tends, that is, to displace the destination festival as the gold standard, and the fringe as the only alternative, proposing new festival genealogies and epistemologies that privilege trans- and intranational exchange over consumption, and the intercultural over the international. The Conclusion makes recommendations for 'Festival Futures'. It consists, in part, of a summary and compendium of 'wise practices'[18] in hopes that it might ease the way at festivals to come for the kinds of transnational, intercultural, multilingual, and intersectional work performed by the production of *Say No More* at Malaysia's George Town Festival with which this introduction began. The book itself also ends where it began, reiterating its proposal of an alternative creation story for international theatre festivals in the communal, performative, inter-nation gatherings that predate the Festival of Dionysus and model a different kind of festival experience.

CHAPTER I

Indigeneity, Festivals, and Indigenous Festivals

It's late July 2017, and I'm sitting at Toronto's Fleck Dance Theatre next to Muriel Miguel (Guna and Rappahannock Nations) and Deborah Ratelle, both of New York's Spiderwoman Theater and director and project manager, respectively, of Material Witness, *the show we're watching. The production is a collaboration between Spiderwoman and Aanmitaagzi, of Nippissing First Nation, Ontario, onstage as part of the Living Ritual Festival hosted by Kaha:wi Dance Theatre at Toronto's Harbourfront Centre. It is a searing revisiting of the serious subject matter of Spiderwoman's first show,* Woman and Violence, *in 1977, and yet Miguel is laughing uproariously from the audience as her nonagenarian sister (and Spiderwoman co-founder), Gloria Miguel, mugs shamelessly (Figure 2) and members of the cast don sparkling outer bras, aviation goggles, and ostrich feathers. This is not the sort of event where the audience, and especially the show's director, observes traditional theatrical decorum. It is a show and a ceremony honouring the women who, in a 'Pulling Threads' workshop, literally wove their stories into the large quilt that hangs upstage like a fabric cyclorama, gendered female, in a materialization of Spiderwoman's 'storyweaving' technique.[1] And as the closing event of this festival of Indigenous performing arts there is a celebratory feel to the evening, which is partly about witnessing. Like the Living Ritual Festival at which it was presented,* Material Witness *faces difficult truths head on, but does so as part of an 'inter-nation' gathering,[2] an affirmation and celebration of Indigenous resurgence globally. 'Because it's a ritual, and we're living', as Muriel Miguel asserted. 'We're living and sending things out into the world' (qtd in Commanda).*

From long before recorded western history to the present the Indigenous peoples of the world have engaged in ceremonies and communal perfor-mance activities that could not without diminishment be called 'theatre',[3] but might, from a western perspective, be called festivals, in ways that might productively unsettle western understandings of that term's defini-tional field. Settler scholar Shawn Huffman opens his 2003 article on

Figure 2   Nonagenarian actor Gloria Miguel mugs shamelessly in *Material Witness*, by
Spiderwoman Theater and Aanmitaagzi at the Living Ritual Festival in
Toronto in 2017. Photograph by Théo Coté

theatre festivals in what are now Canada and the United States with an
account of the birch-bark 'White Earth scroll', which he considers to be a
'pre-contact' Midĕ'wiwin record of a 'theatre festival' in Anishinaabe
territories on Turtle Island (North America). Depicting 'the different
stages of a theatrical initiation festival', the scroll, he argues, 'is no mere
illustration; it contains rather the coded inscription for a ritual performance, readable only by the *Midewiwin*, the initiated protectors of the
information it contains' (57).[4] As a settler scholar myself, I do not have
access to that protected information, nor can I know whether it is appropriate to consider the initiation ceremony recorded in the White Earth
Scroll to constitute a festival in any contemporary western sense. But given
that all accounts of the origins of festivals that I have considered in my
research trace them to some kinds of ritual or ceremony, usually western,
and usually understood to have their origins in fifth-century Athens,
I wonder whether Huffman has identified an alternative starting point –
a different festival creation story – that might reshape, in a foundational
way, scholarly understandings of festivals and their potential social
functions. Like that of *Material Witness*, the social function of the Living

Ritual Festival that hosted it was in part ceremonial: it was an internation gathering that required participation and witnessing rather than the passive spectatorship that is characteristic of western festivals, and the spirit of the event was less competitive, as at many festivals deriving from the Greek model, than mutually celebratory. As a trans-Indigenous gathering, it also enacted the kinds of generative decoloniality of many of the 'intracultural transnational' festivals that I analyse in Chapter 5, offering a related paradigm shift in the epistemology of festivals, particularly those that operate outside of western brokerage.[5]

In Australia, as on Turtle Island, Indigenous performative forms of exchange and negotiation that might now be called festivals existed long before they were witnessed, then popularized as 'corroborees', then banned or tightly controlled and commodified for western touristic consumption in the twentieth century. But as settler scholar Peter Phipps has argued,

> among the many functions of Aboriginal ceremonial life is to bring different clan groups together to perform and renew the law at significant times and places in the presence of related peoples. It has been common for people entering one another's country (in the Aboriginal sense of ancestral domain, not nation-state) to engage in ritual and ceremonial exchanges, frequently exchanging songs, dances and stories with people from far away. ('Indigenous' 685)

On the northwest coast of Turtle Island, similarly, there was the potlatch, a gifting ceremony described by Keren Zaiontz as 'a multifaceted festival that is core to the social order of many Pacific Northwest Peoples and encompasses public ceremonies, the marking of family celebrations, the passing down of history, and the enactment of law' (*Theatre & Festivals* 59). Tseshaht writer, artist, and actor George Clutesi, in a book-length account of what he calls 'the last Tloo-qwah-nah' (potlatch),[6] which he witnessed as a child, refers to the fourteen- to twenty-eight-day event in terms that align very closely with most contemporary definitions of a theatre festival (9): he talks frequently of the overarching meta-event as 'this great play, the Tloo-qwah-nah' (71), and refers throughout to the many individual performances that constitute the event as 'plays' (19, 88, and *passim*). He also refers to the location at which the performances took place as a 'theatre' (26). And certainly, the events he describes are both theatrical and festive, demarcating a 'time-out-of-time' (Falassi) in which both traditional and innovative performances, sacred and profane, were rehearsed and presented to the larger community as both participants and witnesses. Clutesi's account of the Tloo-qua-nah in his own community describes it, moreover, very much as an occasion for inter- and *intra*cultural exchange and solidarity, accounting for its purpose as the confirmation of alliances between visitors and hosts among the tribes that constitute the Nuu-chah-nulth on the west coast of Vancouver Island, solidifying common cause, and generally serving the purpose of 'getting to know each other' (136).

Like the corroboree in Australia, the potlatch was particularly threatening to colonialist, proto-capitalist regulators on Turtle Island, not only because of its role in forging internation alliances among Indigenous peoples, but also because it conferred social status, not on the accumulation, but the dispersion of wealth. And like the corroboree in Australia, the potlatch, along with other ceremonial activity and performance, was banned in Canada in 1885, and the ban was not lifted until 1951. But the existence of the Midē'wiwin records, the corroboree, the potlatch, and other ceremonial practices among the Indigenous peoples of the world, as Huffman argues, 'provides an expanded paradigm for the understanding of the modern theatre festival' (57).

What, then, would it mean to see theatre and performance festivals, not as having begun within the competitive framework of ancient Greece but among the *relational* frameworks of Indigenous communities globally?[7] What would it mean to understand festivals as conferring cultural capital through the dispersion rather than accumulation of worldly goods? To consider festivals as sites of the exchange rather than the commodification of cultures? To consider them as being grounded in the land and in Indigenous knowledge systems rather than in deterritorializing and decontextualizing programming practices? What would it mean to read Indigenous festivals as *living* practices rather than as having ended with the potlatch ban and other prohibitions? The reconsideration of festival origin stories might constitute an epistemological process of decoloniality, rewriting western definitions and understandings of festivalization itself to consider festivals, potentially, as performances of what Opaskwayak Cree scholar Shawn Wilson calls 'relational accountability' (77).

I have argued elsewhere that for thousands of years the world's Indigenous peoples have negotiated difference and facilitated trade in part through performance in ways that might be considered to be trans-Indigenous, and that might speak to a reconsidered role for international festivals in the future (*Theatre & Interculturalism* 6). The term 'trans-Indigenous' is used by Chadwick Allen, of Chickasaw ancestry, to indicate a critical methodology for considering a single Indigenous work from a globally Indigenous perspective (in addition to equally valuable but more narrowly nation-specific ones): 'The point', he says, 'is to invite specific studies into different kinds of conversations, and acknowledge the mobility and multiple interactions of Indigenous peoples, cultures, histories, and texts' (*Trans-Indigenous* xiv) by 'creating *purposeful* Indigenous juxtapositions' (xviii, emphasis in original), and employing 'multiperspectivism' (xxii). I suggest that international, transnational, and especially trans-Indigenous festivals provide unique opportunities for creating such purposeful juxtapositions, for enabling such multiperspectivism within the context of the festival event, not just for the purposes of analysis, but for those of the artists themselves and the cultures at large. As part of the ongoing process of decoloniality, understood as a decentering of European colonialist perspectives, it might, I suggest, prove useful to think about theatre festivals, not within the originary contexts of the competitions and judgements of ancient Greece and the detached eye of the civic *theoros* (see Zaiontz, *Theatre & Festivals* 6–7; Nightingale); not within the cathartic context of the medieval or Caribbean carnivalesque; and not within the context of international diplomacy and national identity (re)construction provided by the so-called 'founding' post-Second World War festivals such as Edinburgh and Avignon; but within those of ancient and contemporary trans-Indigenous negotiation and exchange, and what Michi Saagiig Nishnaabeg artist and scholar Leanne Betasamosake Simpson calls 'Indigenous internationalism' (*As We Have* 55).[8] Unlike most festivals in the western world having to do with nation-building, competition, and exoticist display, Indigenous 'festivals', it seems, have always been about learning how to share territory and resources – how to live together 'in a good way'.[9]

Western Festivals, Fairs, and Mega-events

It's no secret that Indigenous peoples have not been well treated in western festivals, fairs, and mega-events, though they have featured in them prominently and consistently, and continue to do so. On Turtle Island, at events such as the 1893 World's Columbian Exhibition (Chicago World's Fair), held to celebrate the 400th anniversary of the arrival of Christopher Columbus in the 'new world', Indigenous peoples from around the world were displayed as 'savages' benefiting from the civilizing influence of colonization in what amounted to an extensive 'human zoo' (Shahriari). At the Louisiana Purchase Exhibition (St Louis World's Fair) in 1904, 'Anthropology Days' displays scientized racial hierarchies while, adjacent to the fair, Buffalo Bill's Wild West Show featured reenactments by Native performers of the Battle of Little Bighorn ('Custer's Last Stand'),

as well as 'Indian' attacks on settlers' cabins, wagon trains, and the pony
express (Moses). Indeed, according to Nancy Egan,

> more than 25,000 indigenous people were brought to fairs around the
> world between 1880 and 1930. These people struggled under harsh and
> changing conditions. Many of them had to change their hair, their clothes,
> their entire appearance to fit the expectations of the organizers and the
> audiences they were supposed to perform for. Some people were the targets
> of racist violence while they were on display, while others experienced more
> subtle forms of violence and were used as subjects of scientific study on
> racial differences during the exhibition. And ... many people died during
> these exhibitions. (qtd in Shahriari)

An unintended consequence of the displays, however – and one that the
fairs' organizers attempted to prohibit – was the after-hours mingling of
Indigenous peoples from around the world, and, perhaps, the early formation of global trans-Indigenous conversations, partnerships, and solidarities. Festivals of various kinds have continued to facilitate such encounters
throughout their history, and despite their early participation in a racist
and genocidal colonial project, this may be considered one of their most
significant beneficial side effects.

These exhibitions faded after the 1930s, but there seems to have been an
almost seamless transition from world fairs to athletic competitions such as
the Olympic and Commonwealth Games. This transition began in
1904 by virtue of the Louisiana exhibition's coinciding in St Louis with
the Olympic Games and staging sporting events that paralleled them,
'featuring non-European boys and men of colour competing against one
another in archery, tug of war, discus, racing, and other [European
sporting] events' for which they had no training (Zaiontz, *Theatre &
Festivals* 58). Such unequally weighted competitions seemed to demonstrate to western audiences, according to Zaiontz, 'that there was a "natural" racial hierarchy in which the fittest athletes were also the whitest'.
They actively constructed 'irreconcilable racial differences as part of the
very apparatus of modern mega-events' (*Theatre & Festivals* 58).

Mega-events such as the Olympic Games and their attendant cultural
and arts festivals continued to be sites of struggle, sometimes negotiation,
and sometimes intervention for Indigenous people in settler states
throughout the twentieth century and into the twenty-first. In Canada,
Christine M. O'Bonsawin (Abenaki, Odanak Nation) has traced in detail
the evolving struggle between Olympic organizers and the Indigenous
peoples they wish to incorporate as national emblems. At the 1976
Montréal Summer Olympics, in spite of the closing ceremonies being

organized without Indigenous involvement, the Mohawk of Kahnawá:ke took the opportunity to put their proud history of showmanship on display and make themselves, their survival, and their resistance – what Anishinaabe scholar Gerald Vizenor famously calls their 'survivance' – visible. The Calgary Winter Olympics in 1988 served as the occasion for the tiny Lubicon Cree community in Northern Alberta (population 500), historically excluded from treaty agreements apparently by accident, to bring international attention to the exploitation and expropriation of their territories and subsequently gain broad international support for their struggle. By 2010 and the Vancouver Winter Olympics, the organizers recognized the need to partner with the Four Host First Nations (FHFN) early on.[10] And in spite of considerable criticism of the organizing committee's appropriation of Indigenous symbols, FHFN did convince the Vancouver Olympic Committee (VANOC) to include Indigenous participation in the official 2006 handover ceremony from Turin to Vancouver, in which the FHFN chiefs welcomed the world to their (therefore acknowledged) territory in a traditional Northwest Coast U'tsam (witness) ceremony. There were many failures on the part of VANOC to adequately dialogue with Indigenous peoples about their own aims and aspirations for the event, but the diligence and acuity of Indigenous partners did mean that the Vancouver Games achieved its goal of then 'unprecedented Aboriginal participation' in any Olympic event in Canada (O'Bonsawin 58).

In Australia, the 2000 Sydney Olympiad has been seen as a kind of landmark in the relationship between Aboriginal and settler Australians. The Games, and in particular The Festival of the Dreaming, the first in a series of annual Olympic Arts Festivals beginning in 1997 that led up to the Games, have received considerable scholarly attention. And the programme, along with the opening ceremony of the Olympics themselves, has received its share of criticism. Beatriz García makes the now familiar case that the arts festivals served up Australia's cultural diversity as exotic entertainment for visitors and (white) tourists, while Helen Gilbert and Jacqueline Lo note that 'indigenous involvement in the Olympics was susceptible to being incorporated into a narrative of reconciliation that would redeem the [Australian] nation's vexed self-image and enact a "national catharsis" of sorts' (71, citing Neilson 20). Nevertheless – and in spite of the fact that 'the Aboriginal peoples who became a focus in the international media spotlight and were the delight of the Opening Ceremonies were suffering Third World levels of poverty, poor-health and premature death rates' (Higgins-Desbiolles 37) – the organizers *did* collaborate. In fact, The Festival of the Dreaming itself was curated by Koori performer and director Rhoda Roberts (Bundjalung Nation), who agreed to serve as Festival Director only on condition that the event would remain under Indigenous control, and who delivered an address in Bundjalung at the Olympics' opening ceremonies, along with a history of the land on which they were held. The Festival's Project Coordinators, Lydia Miller (Kuki Yalanji) and Toni Janke (Wuthathi and Meriam) were also Indigenous.

And 'there is much evidence', according to Gilbert and Lo, 'to suggest that the Festival of the Dreaming managed to fulfil its brief as an Olympic event while also serving the interests of Indigenous peoples' (68). Roberts consciously used the event, housed in mainstream venues in Sydney including the flagship Sydney Opera House, to address ignorance about Aboriginal cultures, redress stereotypes, promote Indigenous languages, and create ongoing opportunities for Aboriginal people in the arts (Roberts). The festival included both traditional and contemporary Indigenous cultures, featured Indigenous performances ranging from 'high culture' (Shakespeare and opera) to street theatre, addressed political and social issues directly, and focused on the diversity within and among Indigenous cultures. Official documents of this, the first public face of the Sydney Olympics, included an official 'guideline of Authorship and Control' that promised Indigenous control 'where possible', particularly in programme content. The Indigenous team also produced a Protocol Manual to be used by staff when engaging with Indigenous communities (Roberts 9). Indigenous performances, moreover, were not ghettoized to this festival, but were also a feature of subsequent festivals leading up to the Games, and performances at the festival led to several tours beyond Sydney in its immediate wake.[11]

The Festival of the Dreaming was potentially destabilizingly hybrid, in that it included individual performances, such as *The Edge of the Sacred*, that were collaborative, in this case between the Aboriginal and Islander Dance Theatre and the Sydney Symphony Orchestra, and in that as a meta-event it functioned in a manner that combined elements of western and Indigenous festival epistemologies. The overarching structuring of promotion, ticketing, and presentation followed western models, but the opening Awakening Ceremony at the Sydney Opera House framed the festival as ritual: 'for me', said Roberts, 'it was a religious ceremony' (12). Indigenous groups gathered from great distances within Australia as well as from Aotearoa, Greenland, and Turtle Island for a kind of relational, trans-Indigenous gathering, one that, as Roberts says, 'reinforced our cultural community, our ties, and our languages' (5). It also, with a uniquely Indigenous emphasis, 'began a journey for Australians to hear the real humor, rhythm and music of the Australian landscape' (14). In ceding programming control to Indigenous artists, The Festival of the Dreaming opened an avenue for thinking differently about the potential meanings and social functions of festivals in the twenty-first century.

At the opening ceremonies for the Games themselves, Aboriginal participants were able to use ceremony, choreographed by the Yagambeh artistic director of Bangarra Dance Theatre, Stephen Page – later the first Indigenous artistic director of the 'destination' Adelaide International Festival – to cleanse the site. Page stated that his intention was to bring the clans together in a huge corroboree, 'not to send a glamorous postcard to the world, but to try to give a sense of the real spiritual experience of ceremony' (qtd in Gilbert and Lo 71). All Olympic events acknowledged twelve 'Gamarada Dignitaries'[12] as Indigenous hosts from the five land groups on which the games were held: Eora, Dharug, Ku-Ring-Gai, Tharawal, and Gandagarra (Hanna 60). The 2000 Sydney Olympics, then, not only served as a site of what Freya Higgins-Desbiolles calls (without apparent irony) 'reconciliation tourism',[13] but it 'cemented the indigenization of Australian performing arts even while generating a store of images of pride and success specifically for the Aboriginal community' (Gilbert and Lo 72). Finally, The Festival of the Dreaming also served as the inspiration for one of Turtle Island's most important twenty-first-century Indigenous arts and theatre festivals, Vancouver's 'Talking Stick Festival', discussed below.

It is important, then, to recognize the complexity of Indigenous participation in and use of mega-events such as the Olympic games. Despite a history of the exploitation of Indigenous peoples and cultures, on many occasions such events have been exploited *by* Indigenous peoples for their own purposes. And of course, many Indigenous communities have established their own events, some of them culturally specific (such as the Dene Games in Canada's Northwest territories), but many (such as the North American Indigenous Games and the World Indigenous Games) serving as productively trans-Indigenous 'examples', as Zaiontz says, 'of the indigenization of the *mega*' (*Theatre & Festivals* 61, emphasis in original). Zaiontz cites in particular the Arctic Winter Games, which bring together Indigenous athletes from Canada, Alaska, Greenland, Norway, and northern Russia. 'Unlike the viciously racist Anthropology Days', she argues, 'the Arctic and other contemporary Games are not proxies for the empirical display of savagery, but complex sites of solidarity, and modernity, by and for indigenous people' (61).

Indigeneity and/at Non-Indigenous Theatre and Arts Festivals

There have been many efforts to incorporate or represent Indigeneity at non-Indigenous festivals of theatre and performance, some of them more successful, or respectful, than others. In Europe, in particular, these have often involved exotic display, cultural appropriation, or patronizing forms of cultural preservationism. But many festivals have also provided Indigenous performers with opportunities to exercise autonomous agency, to achieve a degree of international visibility, and to engage in trans-Indigenous exchange.

In the late nineteenth and early twentieth centuries Indigenous entertainers in vaudeville and Varieté exerted a control over their working conditions and to some extent their representation that was unavailable to the performers in Buffalo Bill's Wild West Shows (see Bold 48), but they were nevertheless sometimes exhibited in actual zoos, such as the one in Dresden, Germany, where their appearances are memorialized even today on plaques and signboards. And even today, at the 'Karl-May-Spiele' (festivals) in Bad Segeberg and Bischofswerda, Germany, blond, blue-eyed men, women, and children hobbyists engaging in 'ethnic drag' impersonate tomahawk-wielding, scalp-taking 'Indians' in frenzies of romanticized nostalgia for a far-away wild west that never was (see Sieg 73–150).[14] Finally, in Wrocław, Poland, the well-meaning 'Brave Festival' still scours the world for cultures and people that are 'on the border of becoming extinct' (Brave Festival) – an unfortunate prerequisite for participation. It was founded by Grzegorz Bral after a trip to Mexico in which he attempted to follow in the footsteps of Antonin Artaud and visit the Tarahumara people, hoping, in a familiar exoticizing trope, to 'experience something, too' (Brave Festival). Bral returned to Poland and in 2005 founded a festival of 'authentic art ... which can save and protect thousands of forgotten, abandoned, lonely cultures and people'.

Most festivals incorporating Indigenous work have, to varying degrees, been less problematic than the exoticizing 'Brave Festival' with its discourse of dying races; indeed, some have been positively enabling. These range from the free-market passivity of open-access fringe festivals which 'permit', as Bruce Willems-Braun argues, Indigenous work such as Algonquin playwright Yvette Nolan's *Blade*, to 'appropriate space for a variety of purposes' (80); through small curated festivals such as Toronto's SummerWorks, which has often included new work by Indigenous playwrights and choreographers; to mega-festivals that have headlined international Indigenous superstars such as the Samoan director, designer, and choreographer Lemi Ponifasio. Ponifasio's work has appeared at many of the major destination festivals that are the subject of Chapter 2, including Festival d'Avignon, BAM, the Berliner Festspiele, the Edinburgh International Festival, Holland Festival, Toronto's Luminato, Ruhrtriennale, the New Zealand Festival of the Arts (where he was a guest curator in 2020), Chile's Santiago a Mil, Germany's Theater der Welt, and the Venice Biennale. Not all of Ponifasio's work focuses on Indigenous themes or employs Indigenous artists, though it was influenced by his own 'whakapapa' (qtd in Husband)[15] and by the ceremonial culture of the Kanaky, Kiribati, and Māori. In work such as *I AM: Mapuche* and *Ceremonia de Memorias*, moreover, he has engaged in trans-Indigenous collaboration, and in *Stones in Her Mouth* he assembled a team of ten Māori women in a powerful mélange of chant, song, dance, and oratory of rage and resilience (see Sykes). In all his work, as he says, 'I'm on the stage because I want to change the world' (qtd in Husband). And he has had the élite festival circuit as his global platform.

Élite festival circuits, however, have élite ticket prices, and access to them is limited in a way that it isn't for the world's fringes. The biggest of these and the twentieth-century progenitor of all the others is the Edinburgh Fringe, where Indigenous artists from various global sites have often been found hawking their shows on the Royal Mile, often in exoticist ways and displays. Occasionally, however, Indigenous and non-Indigenous theatre-makers have been able to seize the opportunity proffered by the fringe to stage genuine interventions, as when ARTICLE 11 and its co-artistic directors Tara Beagan (Ntlaka'pamux) and Andy Moro (Mushkegowuk Cree) presented their variable-content piece *DECLARATION* at Canada Hub in 2017.[16] The Edinburgh version, with the subtitle *Rematriation*, involved Beagan and Moro working with guest artists Kaha:wi Dance Theatre's artistic director Tekaronhiáhkhwa Santee Smith (Kahnyen'kehàka – Mohawk) and her daughter Semiah, together with Coast Salish poet and author Lee Maracle. The show began, the day I saw it, with a 2008 recording of then-Canadian prime minister Stephen Harper's apology to victims of Canada's abusive residential school system, followed by a tortured movement piece by Moro as a bureaucrat in whiteface charged with assessing abuse claims. Next came a dance piece by Smith, readings by Maracle, and an installation and ceremony remembering Canada's missing and murdered Indigenous women, all surrounded by Moro's assemblage of stereotypical dominant-culture 'images-of-Indians' video clips. The show functioned as its own mini festival after an Indigenous paradigm, bringing peoples together in performative dialogue and invoking ceremonial practices. But it was at the end and afterwards that *DECLARATION: Rematriation* made its most significant intervention. Audiences were encouraged to join the artists across town at the National Museum of Scotland as the company petitioned for the rematriation to their traditional territories in what is now Newfoundland of the remains of two Beothuk people, Demasduit and Nonosbawsut, stolen by the Scottish William Cormack in 1828, and stored at the museum in spite of an official request from the Newfoundland-Labrador House of Assembly and an in-person petition by Chief Mi'sel Joe, Mi'kmaq Grand Council, Miawpukek First Nation.[17]

Curated festivals are more complex and conflicted when inviting Indigenous work, particularly if the curator comes from the dominant cultures. As Joyce Rosario, former Director of Programming at Vancouver's PuSh festival, asks, 'How do you decolonize a curatorial practice that emphasizes prospecting? That idea that "you go out and discover!" I think that a whole generation of programmers . . . fashion themselves as *the discoverers*' (qtd in Zaiontz, 'Festival Sites'). It helps if the collaboration between curation and presentation does not involve dominant-culture brokerage, and if curation is thought of less as discovering than as putting in conversation, as at the IMPACT Festival, run by the MT Space Theatre in Kitchener, Ontario.[18] MT Space is dedicated to producing and presenting work from culturally diverse communities, and although it is run by its current artistic director, Gujarati Canadian Pam Patel, and the company's founder, Lebanese Canadian Majdi Bou-Matar, it consistently acknowledges the work of the traditional caretakers of the land and explores the relationship and potential for solidarity between Indigenous and arrivant populations.[19] IMPACT is the company's small-scale international festival and conference, running for one week every two years in the culturally diverse heart of downtown Kitchener. In its five incarnations over ten years the festival, which specializes in cutting-edge physical theatre,[20] has presented eighteen events from Indigenous artists and companies from Aotearoa/New Zealand and Australia as well as from Ecuador, Mexico, and different Indigenous Nations across Canada, including three works by Haudenosaunee artists, on whose (appropriated) land, the Haldimand tract, Kitchener sits. In its most recent incarnations Indigenous works have headlined the festival and constituted 25 per cent of its curated offerings. The festival's opening ceremonies always acknowledge and privilege Indigeneity, and Bou-Matar as festival director has invited Indigenous artists to serve on and chair conference committees that bring together 'culturally diverse and Indigenous artists' to address shared concerns.

IMPACT 17, in September 2017, was opened by Oneida elder George Kennedy, followed by an opening prayer, land acknowledgement, songs, and ceremonies. The featured opening night performance was *Mana Wahine*, by Aotearoa's Ōkāreka Dance Company, choreographed by Māori dancers Taiaroa Royal and Taane Mete in collaboration with Malia Johnston. It was extraordinary to see this show, inspired by a Māori story about a young woman captured in battle who returns years later to save her people from slaughter, take place on Haudenosaunee territory, and be there in conversation with ARTICLE 11's *DECLARATION*, Gwaandak Theatre's (Yukon Territory) *Map of the Land, Map of the Stars*, and perhaps especially Anishinaabe dancer Christine Friday's *Maggie and Me*, a one-woman show about women and healing. The powerful five-woman Māori show, weaving together gender and cultural identity while displaying the extraordinary skill and power of the women, spoke directly across trans-Indigenous differences in a way that is only possible at a a culturally intersectional festival such as IMPACT, and set a tone and context for the week's conversations as well as for future contacts and collaborations. And to see the late-night participation of the extraordinary Māori dancer and choreographer Taane Mete (Ngāti Kahungungu me Ngāti Koroki – Kahukura) with Cheri Maracle (Mohawk), Sophia Moussi (Lebanese, a member of the cast of *The Raft*, an MT Space/El Hamra Theatre, Tunisia collaboration at the festival), the ARTICLE 11 team, and others in generative and exciting improvisation, was a model of the kind of cross-cultural, trans-Indigenous connecting that IMPACT does best and that constitutes the festival as a metaperformance that is more than the sum of its intersecting parts.

But perhaps the most appropriate and effective model for non-Indigenous festivals wishing to feature Indigenous performance in a good way is full-scale collaboration at the administrative level, again, across differently marginalized groups and organizations. This is what happened when Toronto's Aluna Theatre – founded as an intercultural, intermedial company dedicated to work from the Latinx diaspora in the Americas who run the also small-scale biennial RUTAS festival – initiated an ongoing partnership producing the festival with Native Earth Performing Arts – Canada's largest and longest-standing Indigenous theatre company – beginning with the festival's second iteration in 2014.[21] The two-week 2018 festival placed *Réquiem para un alcarván*, by Lukas Avendaño (Zapotec) into conversation with the Mayan *Del Manantial del Corazón (The Heart of Spring)*, with *Los Materiales de la ira y el amor* by the founder of contemporary Indigenous dance in Ecuador, Wilson Pico, and with

Amal, by Kitchener, Ontario's MT Space, a devised show that explores, in part, what it means for Syrian refugees to arrive in Canada 'as settlers in a land that is not ours' (MT Space).[22] Taken together, on the stage, in the festival's conference component, and in late-night conversations at the festival cabaret, these shows served as occasions for exchange and analysis of mourning, celebration, ceremony, and resurgence that served as the bases for trans-Indigenous and transcultural solidarities that far exceeded issues of representation and visibility.

One performance at RUTAS 2016 raises several questions that are central to this inquiry. How might trans-Indigenous relational practices reshape the way festival protocols are understood? What might it mean for Indigenous peoples, whose very identity is tied to their relationship to their lands and waters and their human and non-human inhabitants, to perform at festivals that take place far from their traditional territories? My case study is a performance of Māori playwright Regan Taylor's *SolOthello* by Te Rēhia, a theatre company from Aotearoa/New Zealand at the Aki Studio as part of RUTAS 2016. Māori cultures, even more than most Indigenous cultures around the world, are deeply invested in protocol, and their protocols for reciprocal welcomes to lands and territories are particularly crucial and clearly developed. Also like many Indigenous peoples, the Māori are acutely conscious of the relationship between language and land; indeed, this is a key part of the mandate of Te Rēhia, which is 'to honour, revitalize, and transmit Te Reo Māori [the Māori language] through theatre to Aotearoa and the world'.

Before the show came to Tkaronto/Toronto,[23] many of the earliest performances of *SolOthello* took place in various *marae* (meeting grounds) throughout Aotearoa, where the company would have been welcomed to the space, the *wharenui* (central meeting house), and the *iwi* (people, nation, tribe) through the traditional welcoming ceremony known as a *pōwhiri*. In Toronto the performance was nested among several layers of welcome, in several languages. The general welcome to RUTAS was extended in English and Spanish (with a sprinkling of Indigenous languages) to all festival attendees and participants by the organizers at Aluna and Native Earth. Secondly, every workshop, panel, performance, and screening at the event was preceded by an acknowledgement, in English and one or more Indigenous languages, of the Huron-Wendat, Haudenosaunee, and Anishinaabe (particularly Mississauga of the Credit) as traditional caretakers of the land on which the event was held. Each event also included a welcome to Aki Studio, the home of Native Earth, which is a participant in a trans-Indigenous network of companies, festivals, and funders in Canada, Australia, and Aotearoa.[24] In addition, the Māori company was invited to the Six Nations (Haudenosaunee confederacy) territory just west of Toronto on the Grand River, where they would have participated in the edge-of-the-woods ceremony, been welcomed into the acknowledged land of the hosts through song, speeches, and smudging ceremonies, and been invited to reciprocate by offering their own ceremonial songs, speeches, and greetings. The Māori performer of *SolOthello*, Tainui Tukiwaho, told me that to be welcomed to Haudenosaunee land and hear there, for the first time, some of the Indigenous languages of Turtle Island, was a highlight of his visit; it served as an important basis for the kinds of trans-Indigenous exchange that Indigenous festivals uniquely enable.

In the final welcome in this nest of welcomes, as the audience gathered outside the theatre for the performance of Te Rēhia's *SolOthello*, we were invited, by variations on a traditional pōwhiri, into a space that the ceremony itself, together with a Māori roofing structure outlined in light above the stage, *constituted* as a wharenui, also constituting the audience as guests. In a symbolic sense the company had brought the hearts of their home territories with them to Toronto, where they engaged their hosts in mutual hospitality. The Māori understand the marae of their iwi as *tūrangawaewae* – a place to stand and belong that is used by the iwi for important tribal events. A pōwhiri is a ceremony by which outsiders are welcomed to the marae. This sometimes begins with a *wiri, wero,* or *taki,* a ritual challenge in which the visitors are identified, or constituted, as friends. But once so identified the *manuhiri* (guests), gathered in the *marae ātea* (courtyard), don't enter the marae until summoned by a *karanga* (call to enter) performed in Te Reo by the *kaikaranga,* women of the *tangata whenua* (host community). Once everyone has entered there is a round of *whaikōrero* (speeches), *waiata* (songs), and sometimes *haka* (a dance/challenge) for which protocol varies, at the end of which there are *harirū* (handshakes) and *hongi,* the ceremonial touching of noses that signifies the mingling together of the sacred breath of life, after which the manuhiri and tangata whenua (guests and host community) become one, and there is a sharing of food.

For *SolOthello* the pōwhiri was performed with variations. The audience-as-manuhiri were called into the space by a karanga performed by the show's Māori producer, Amber Curreen. As we entered, we were greeted by performer Tainui Tukiwaho, who introduced himself and shook each audience member by the hand in a variation on the harirū. Once everyone was assembled in the space-as-wharenui, Tukiwaho, wearing cargo pants, a

'Maid of the Mist' tourist sweatshirt from nearby Niagara Falls, a backward baseball cap, and bare feet, addressed us in a lengthy whaikōrero, delivered in Te Reo, followed by a 'support song' in Te Reo about 'remembering where you're from', performed by two women, one of them Amber Curreen. The only language we heard for the first more than twelve minutes was Te Reo, which Tukiwaho then genially translated for us, explaining the significance of the welcome we had received. He also identified (as whaikōrero do), the *kaupapa* (purpose of the occasion), to which I'll return. The welcome, the various acknowledgements and explanations, in both Te Reo and English, took twenty-five minutes and also served as a kind of charismatic audience warmup. The show itself, of course, was the feast.

I dwell on this, and have introduced so many words in Te Reo, first, to support the company's mandate of honouring and transmitting Te Reo beyond Aotearoa. Ethical Indigenous research, as Māori scholar Linda Tuhiwai Smith was among the first to argue, is mandated to serve the interests of the community with which it engages, and researchers are understood to be accountable to that community. But the second reason is the pivotal importance of welcoming, and not simply as courtesy. Stó:lō scholar Dylan Robinson, from Turtle Island's Pacific Northwest, has made the simple but brilliant point that a welcome is also and always a declaration of sovereignty ('Welcoming' 16). I am using 'sovereignty' as it is understood by many Indigenous scholars to mean more than western legal definitions,[25] which have to do with property, legal documents, ownership, and power over others, as opposed, for example, to 'self-government', broadly understood to include self-determination, control over one's own culture, 'spheres of autonomy' (Anaya 79), 'a regime of respect' (Alfred 471), and what the Māori call '*mana*', one meaning of which is 'one's standing in one's own eyes'.[26] The welcoming ceremonies I have been describing, like most 'Indigenous protocols of welcome', Robinson points out, 'remind guests that they are guests':

> To welcome presumes the authority and right to determine the proceedings that occur within the space. We welcome people into our homes, onto Indigenous lands, into countries, and to events we have organized. To welcome guests into each of these places is, to varying degrees, to signal sovereign control over the rules of the space and the authority under which such rules are enforced. ('Welcoming' 16)

'How', he asks his settler readers in Canada and elsewhere, 'are *you* accountable for the welcome you have overstayed?' (30).

This question, I believe, underlies the kaupapa, or purpose of the occasion, that Tukiwaho's address identified, genially and humorously, immediately after his opening whaikōrero and before proceeding to his performance of the 'play proper'. Issuing what might be understood as a displaced wiri (challenge to the visitors), 'Shakespeare', he said bluntly, 'was a thief' (*SolOthello*). Students of Shakespeare with some knowledge of his treatment of his source material know this. Residents of Canada, particularly anglophone Canada, also know that 'Shakespeare' – as a primary cultural technology of colonization – has in many ways outstayed his welcome throughout the now English-speaking world, including both Canada and Aotearoa. But Tukiwaho went on to deliver a very funny travel narrative of exactly how it came about that the Māori stories that it was apparent to him provided the plots for Shakespeare's plays arrived in early modern Europe. Finally, he introduced the solo production that followed by telling the Māori 'source' story for *Othello*, as passed down through his 'great great great great great great great ... great grandfather', demonstrating wittily how Shakespeare derived the (to him) clearly Māori names of the characters, pointing out the Māori derivations of the plot, and occasionally commenting, 'Coincidence? I think not.'

What was this adaptation of Shakespeare about? I have observed elsewhere that as a verb 'adapt' can be transitive or intransitive: you can adapt something, you can adapt *to* something – or you can engage in *adaptation* (the process) as a way of both adapting *and* adapting to' (Knowles, 'Adapting' vi). I would argue that this last is what *SolOthello* did in Toronto. As the Indigenous hosts of the colonizing Europeans for whom 'Shakespeare' has been a cultural and educational agent, themselves hosted in Toronto by the peoples of the dish-with-one-spoon wampum,[27] the Māori creators and producers of this adaptation were adapting *to* Shakespeare, and to his seeming inevitability – he has perhaps outstayed his welcome in both Aotearoa and Canada, but he doesn't appear to be going away anytime soon. With *SolOthello* this Māori theatre company was welcoming *and using* Shakespeare, at this festival, with considerable grace and humour, to speak to their own culture *and* to trans-Indigenous cultures around the world. And throughout the show, within Native Earth Performing Arts's Aki studio, the protective roofline of the 'home' marae into which we had been welcomed at the outset hovered above the performance space.

What, then, does it mean for Indigenous peoples to perform at a festival in a land that is not theirs? How can contemporary Indigenous theatre productively perform trans-Indigeneity in the context of a theatre festival?

Leanne Betasamosake Simpson, citing Anishinaabe scholar Gerald Vizenor's concept of 'transmotion' (Vizenor 15), talks about continuities between traditional and contemporary understandings of territory, identity, and sovereignty through an emphasis on Indigenous patterns of circulation in space. Simpson writes: 'In Precolonial daily life of Nishnaabeg people, movement, change and fluidity were a reality' (*Dancing* 89), neither, as in many western theorizations, a metaphor nor a choice. In many Indigenous peoples' understandings, moreover, territory is defined, not by physical borders but by language, philosophy, way of life, and political structure, while territorial 'boundaries' constitute relationships and institute negotiations that at the RUTAS festival were played out through a nest of welcomes and mutual acknowledgements of sovereign ground. Simpson argues that the circulations of the traditional Anishinaabe did not consist of wandering, but of moving outward from a territorial centre, not to a border, but to a place of encounter – perhaps, in the contemporary as in the pre-contact Indigenous world, a place like a festival – 'where one needs to practice good relations with neighboring nations' (*Dancing* 89). To perform at a festival, then – at least one with an Indigenous mandate and location – is to travel to a trans-Indigenous place of encounter, to constitute new relationships, and to institute negotiations through reciprocal and respectful protocols of welcome: to at once acknowledge, and declare, sovereignties. The production of Te Rēhia's *SolOthello* and its surrounding protocols of welcome at the RUTAS festival, within the context of Native Earth's Aki Studio, carved out a trans-Indigenous space of encounter. That encounter can perhaps serve as a model of ways and practices through which a festival not exclusively devoted to Indigenous work but organized in collaboration with Indigenous communities can function productively to facilitate exchange. It also, perhaps, provides a model of reciprocal relationships that can apply to festivals beyond the trans-Indigenous world.

Indigeneity and Destination Festivals

Destination festivals, as discussed in Chapter 2, provide the anti-, or counter-model to the Indigenous festival paradigm that this chapter proposes, and in general tend to represent the festivalization and display of Indigenous cultures stereotyped for spectatorial consumption. But there are degrees to which destination festivals in different national sites have attempted in the twenty-first century to acknowledge or accommodate Indigeneity for different purposes and with different degrees of success, and Indigenous artists have been strategic in their use of such festivals as occasions for cultural promotion and internation exchange.

In Australia, a settler society struggling to come to terms with its genocidal colonial past and work towards Indigenous–settler 'reconciliation',[28] attempts by non-Indigenous festivals to incorporate Aboriginal content have seemed urgent. They have taken place primarily at the 'élite' and very visible level of what Sarah Thomasson calls 'the Australian Festival Circuit', which, she argues, functions as the country's dispersed national theatre ('Australian' 133). As Gilbert and Lo note, 'at international festivals [in Australia] Aboriginality functions as a metonym for the "authentic"' (18), and often, as at the Indigenous Arts Showcase in Perth in 2003, festivals have featured packaged Aboriginality: 'High quality cultural product, ready for the international and national markets' (74). That these productions and their Indigenous creators 'have found strategies not only to manage the deleterious effects of commodity relations in the global market, but also to mobilize market interest in indigeneity to garner international support of Aboriginal political and social struggles' (Gilbert and Lo 74) is perhaps a marker of Indigenous ingenuity. That Aboriginal Australians have used international festivals abroad as occasions for trans-Indigenous exchange is a mark of strategic trans-Indigeneity. In the late twentieth and first two decades of the twenty-first century, Indigenous artists have used international festivals as occasions to get together, even as they had, more surreptitiously, in the 'Anthropology Days' of international world fairs.

Within the country, festivals have struggled to include Indigenous 'cultural markers' (Malone) – acknowledgements that they take place on Indigenous lands and *dis*place Indigenous peoples. The Adelaide Festival, 'the nation's premiere arts event' (Gilbert and Lo 112), might serve as an example. In an essay on cultural markers of Indigeneity in Adelaide since the 1960s – prior to which 'there was an almost complete absence of Indigenous public representations in Adelaide (and elsewhere in Australia)' (Malone 159) – Gavin Malone notes that the first major public artwork in Adelaide specifically to acknowledge Kaurna people and Kaurna land on which the festival sits – *Kaurna meyunna, Kaurna yerta tampendi*, by Kaurna artists Darren Siwes and Eileen Karpany and non-Indigenous artist Tony Rosella – was unveiled at the Adelaide Festival Centre as recently as 2002 (163). But Malone also notes that, for the Kaurna, the land, without monumental impositions, is itself a 'cultural marker', and among the recommendations with which he concludes his essay is a key one that applies to the festival itself: giving Indigenous peoples greater control over public space, and over 'both the commissioning and the creative process' (165). The issue of Indigenous creative control, as modelled by Rhoda Roberts's leadership of The Festival of the Dreaming, has been key to the degree of success achieved by destination festivals in Australia ever since.

Some attempt to cede control is what American star director Peter Sellars perhaps clumsily tried to do when he was appointed artistic director at Adelaide in 2002. But he started something that has been central to the (uneven) development of the Australian circuit. Sellars's appointment and his curation of the festival were controversial. He has been celebrated for his vision and denigrated for his management style. Contemporary coverage of the festival included headlines such as 'A Festival in Disarray' (Caust) and 'Festival Fractured by Chaos' (Bramwell). But crucially, as Jo Caust argues,

> Sellars wanted to have a different kind of festival that was not focused on major events imported from elsewhere. He wanted to have a festival organized to achieve very different kinds of goals from traditional festivals. He wanted the festival to operate within an organizational model that allowed for wide participation and consultation. He also wanted a festival that focused on communities not normally embraced by major arts festivals. (113)

He wanted, that is, a new, ancient festival paradigm. In attempting to address three key festival themes – the 'Right to Cultural Diversity', 'Truth and Reconciliation', and 'Ecological Sustainability' – Sellars introduced a new programming model that included a team of nine associate directors and several advisory committees in addition to the existing festival staff. The associate directors notably included two young Kaurna arts professionals, Karl Telfer and Waiata Telfer (Higgins-Desbiolles 41).

This collaborative, power-sharing model was designed to recentre the festival on the local rather than the flashily international, and explicitly to embrace Indigenous, social-justice, and community arts practice. Sellars persevered with a controversial plan

> to turn the civic Victoria Square into Tarndanyangga ['red kangaroo dreaming'], the gathering place for the Kaurna people, and the centre for the festival's Indigenous program. For more than ten days Aboriginal artists from all over Australia gathered to perform and share their culture with visiting companies from New Mexico, South Africa and Aotearoa New Zealand. They also walked the streets of a capital city as welcome guests in a major festival. (Bramwell)

The festival's opening ceremony, the *Kaurna Palti Meyunna*, itself a mini-festival under an Indigenous paradigm and Indigenous control, 'was conceptualized through Kaurna spirituality as the spirit of the dreaming ancestor, Tjilbruke, was invoked to bring peace and compassion, while all of the indigenous peoples visiting from near and far were called upon to carry out seven days of ceremonies prior to the opening and to which the non-indigenous were asked to respectfully stay away' (Higgins-Desbiolles 41).

The ceremony – 'the first major Kaurna corroboree in a century', according to Gilbert and Lo (123) – was, by all accounts, 'spectacular and moving':

> It ... brought together indigenous communities from around Australia, New Zealand, South Africa, New Mexico, and Tibet. Starting from the four squares of the city of Adelaide, processions of indigenous people, school children, and local communities walked to the central main square, or *Tarndanyangga*, lit a huge fire, and celebrated in dance, music, and storytelling. (Caust 111)

But Kaurna and other Indigenous people were not just brought out to decorate an opening ceremony. The festival itself featured newly commissioned Indigenous films and work from several leading Aboriginal dance and theatre companies, as well as a free series of events showcasing local, regional, national, and international Indigenous performers at Tarndanyangga, 'who used the event to communicate with each other as well as perform for the non-indigenous in the audiences' (Higgins-Desbiolles 41). In a determinedly trans-Indigenous event, Gyuto monks from Tibet were accompanied by Aboriginal dancers from Anangu Ptjantjatjara (South Australia), a children's choir from Cambodia, Zuni dancers from New Mexico, and an African new music star (Gilbert and Lo 123).

Sellars resigned or was dismissed from his position in November 2001, months before the festival's 1 March opening, and while his plans were reduced somewhat, they were not abandoned, and most agreed that in the end the festival 'reminded festival-goers that indigenous Australia should be central to all things Australian. Perhaps part of the controversy that dogged this festival', Freya Higgins-Desbiolles suggests, 'grew from resentment against this message' (41). Nevertheless, Sellars had opened the door for more Indigenous participation at the leadership level at Adelaide, and his focus on Indigeneity probably led, more or less directly, to the appointment, as his successor, of Stephen Page (Yugambeh), the artistic director of the Indigenous Bangarra Dance Theatre, as the first Indigenous director of the festival, or, as far as I am aware, of any of the world's recurring élite, flagship, or destination festivals.

Using the catchphrase 'the medicine of art' (qtd in Gilbert and Lo 126), Page in 2004 quietly maintained the festival's Indigenous content and succeeded with considerable grace and diplomacy in normalizing Aboriginal and Torres Strait Islander work as an ongoing and necessary feature of subsequent festivals, and indeed as foundational to Australian culture. 'Rather than being displayed as exotica, Aboriginal art forms were presented as diverse and dynamic expressions of mainstream contemporary Australia', reterritorializing the festival's hitherto European frames of reference by 'framing it within a distinctly Aboriginal sensibility and spirituality' (Gilbert and Lo 127). The show's opening, the Awakening Ceremony, assembled 500 members of the Kaurna, Narrungga, and Nagarrindjeri peoples to light a fire on the riverbank 'designed to reawaken the spirit ancestors, ignite the energies of contemporary indigenous groups and cleanse the site to shape a healthier future for generations to come' (127), and again, perhaps, to model an Indigenous festival paradigm grounded in ceremony and witnessing and operating in tension with the dominant one of the destination festival.

The alternative, Indigenous paradigm did not take permanent hold at Adelaide, an aging and overwhelmingly white city with an only 1.4 per cent Indigenous population and with a proud 'free settler' history.[29] In the early 2010s, Indigenous performances featured prominently at the festival, often featuring commissions and co-productions with other Australian festivals, often with the support of the Major Festivals Initiative that was instituted by the Australian government's Ministry for the Arts in 2006 (see Chapter 2). These included *Bloodland*, by Bangarra Dance Theatre in 2012, a ceremonial dance with a cast of twelve Indigenous performers directed by Stephen Page and performed in Yolŋu Matha (the Yolŋu language); *The Shadow King*, by Malthouse Theatre in 2014, an Indigenous adaptation and interpretation of *King Lear* directed by Michael Kantor in English and several Aboriginal languages; and *Black Diggers* in 2015, the stories of Indigenous soldiers in the First World War written by Tom Wright and directed by Wesley Enoch (Noonuccal-Nughi). And in its 2014–19 strategic plan, *A Culturally Ambitious Nation*, the Australian Council for the Arts articulated an ambitious set of strategies for investing in the arts based on the diversity of Australia's culture. The final goal of the plan was to at once naturalize Indigenous cultures within Australian arts, support the intergenerational transfer of Indigenous knowledge, and increase engagement with Indigenous cultural production. Together with the Major Festivals Initiative this five-year plan suggested that Indigenous presence at festivals would receive a funding boost. But governments change quickly in Australia, and with them, plans. The year after the Arts Council's five-year plan was to have ended, and without Indigenous leadership, Adelaide reverted to either tokenistic, exoticist, or minimal representation of the Kaurna people on whose land the festival was held. When I attended in 2020, the festival, under the leadership of non-Indigenous Australian Artistic Directors Neil Armfield and Rachel Healy, had no Kaurna presence on the programme. Indeed, it presented only one Indigenous show, *Buŋgul* from far-away North East Arnhem Land, a complex recreation of Yolŋu multi-instrumentalist and singer Gurrumul Yunupiṇju's final album, *Djarimirri (Child of the Rainbow)*, supported by the Major Festivals Initiative and shared on the circuit with the Perth, Sydney, and Darwin Festivals.

Subtitled or credited 'Gurrumul's Mother's Buŋgul, Gurrumul's Grandmother's Buŋgul, [and] Gurrumul's Manikay [ancestral song series]', *Buŋgul* was performed by nine male family members dancing, singing, and playing *bilma* (clapsticks) and *yidaki* (didjeridu) backed by the Adelaide Festival orchestra, all under the direction of the show's co-creators, Yolŋu elder Don Wininba Ganambarr and white settler Australian Nigel Jamieson. The downstage area had been transformed into a recreation of the sand, water, and bark ceremonial space at the Gulkula grounds on Gumatj clan country in North East Arnhem Land in Australia's Northern Territory, where the Garma Festival is held (see below); upstage was the thirty-three-piece orchestra. Backing the stage was a large screen onto which were projected live images of the dancers, sometimes from above, intercut with prerecorded images of Yolŋu arts and home country. Some parts of the performance were traditional, some were accompanied by the orchestra, and some were orchestral only, playing Gurrumul's music. The performers risked self-exoticization, their bare upper bodies smeared with ochre and their faces painted in traditional patterns, performing in front of the orchestra in their European black formal dress and before the festival gaze of an almost exclusively Balanda (white settler) audience (Figure 3). But they also staked their claim to be taken with equal seriousness as art to western orchestral music, and greater seriousness in terms of their art's relational connection to the land, plants, animals, spirits, ancestors, and people's way of life. The twelve different manikays performed in Adelaide addressed the crocodile, crow, and octopus, the fresh water, sunsets, and dark clouds, as well as man-made ship's masts, calico fabrics, and musical instruments from the madhukin and djoliŋ to the electric guitar. But crucially, the songs were not just pieces of music; they were, as Wininba Ganambarr said in his programme note, 'our maps, our law books, our title deeds, and our family history'.

Figure 3   The performers in *Buŋgul* at the Adelaide Festival in 2020 risked self-exoticization, but also staked their claim to be taken with equal seriousness as art to western orchestral music, and greater seriousness in terms of their art's connection to the land. Photograph by Toni Wilkinson

This was a remarkable show, intercultural in its outreach and form and performed on their own terms by the Yolŋu as cultural ambassadors of Indigenous Australia, offering cultural context – partly through detailed programme notes on the manikays – for the understanding of Gurrumul's music. But there were only two performances of the show at Adelaide and they were located in the relatively seedy Thebarton Theatre in the city's relatively insalubrious Torrensville suburb, close to Aboriginal Community Services but outside of the city's famous central grid and surrounding park system, and far from the upscale Festival Centre where most of the headline European events had longer runs.

Buŋgul had been better placed a few weeks earlier at the Perth Festival in an isolated Western Australian city with a large English and Irish, and only 1.6 per cent reported Indigenous population, where it had three performances at the physically and symbolically central Perth Concert Hall and took part in an opening week dedicated to Indigenous work. The show shared the week with a thirtieth-anniversary revival of the iconic first Aboriginal Australian musical, *Bran Nue Dae*, by Jimmy Chi (Bardi,

Figure 4　Yirra Yaakin Theatre Company's *Hecate*, an adaptation of Shakespeare's *Macbeth*, performed at the Perth Festival in 2020, served as an effective assertion of the strength, complexity, and value of Noongar culture and language. Photograph by Dana Weeks

Nyulnyul Chinese Japanese, and Scottish), which premiered at Perth in 1990 and is set there but is no longer so nue. It has been revived frequently and was made into a film in 2009, and the revival, like the film, was fundamentally a reproduction of the original, the optimism of which seemed a little less inspiring in 2020 and its question, 'Is this the end of our people?' a little more urgent.

Also sharing opening week at Perth in 2020, however, was *Hecate*, another Perth Festival commission and world premiere (Figure 4). *Hecate* was an adaptation of Shakespeare's *Macbeth* by its director, Kylie Braknell (Kaarljilba Kaardn), performed by the Yirra Yaakin Theatre Company based in the Subiaco suburb of Perth and run by the Noongar peoples. Adaptations of classics have been frequent at the world's destination festivals and have been most interculturally effective when they have involved minoritized groups claiming the cultural authority of western 'masters'. *Hecate*, performed without surtitles entirely in Nyungar (the endangered language of the Noongar), recentred the play around a titular character who is usually cut from productions of the classic text. This version's Hecate was an ancestral matriarch who, according to reviewer Laura Money, 'emerges from the very heart of the earth as she feels her land is dying. She laments the withering of her trees, her bushland, her water beds, her animals, and her people ..., a silent figure striving to restore balance to Country.' Hecate was a constant presence, working throughout in consort with three 'mischief makers' (Shakespeare's witches), a revenant Banquo, the voiced sounds of bushland nature, and a glorious projected cosmos to restore health to a land 'in disarray' – a result, of course, of colonization, a context not likely to have been lost on the show's overwhelmingly wedjela (white) audience. That the show relied on audiences' familiarity with the Shakespeare 'original' for their full understanding spoke to the continuing cultural authority of the classical text; that it asserted the equal cultural authority, expressiveness, and value of the Nyungar language spoke to Indigenous resurgence in Western Australia. Importantly, the festival presented *Hecate Kambarnap* in association with the show, an honouring of the Noongar people at which the audience shared a cleansing smoke as well as stories and speeches in Nyungar.

But the high point of Perth's opening week in 2020 was the exquisitely crafted *Bennelong*, created by Stephen Page for Bangarra Dance Theatre (Barangaroo, New South Wales), about the legacy of eighteenth-century Eora leader and British captive Woollarawarre Bennelong. *Bennelong* was collaborative insofar as its dramaturg, composer, and lighting designer were the non-Indigenous Alana Valentine, Steve Francis, and Nick Schlieper, respectively,[30] while creative control was firmly in the hands of the company's choreographer and director, Stephen Page (Yagumbeh), its resident designer, Jacob Nash (Murri), and its cultural consultant, Matthew Doyle (Muruwari and Irish). *Bennelong* had premiered in 2017 at the Sydney Opera House on Bennelong point, where its central character had lived. *Bennelong* was in part an historical revisiting and revisioning of the beginnings of the European invasion of Australia, which is typically identified with the arrival of the First Fleet under Governor Arthur Phillip in January 1788 (a date which loomed blood red over the show). Phillip, having been ordered to 'open dialogue with the natives' ('Bangarra'), kidnapped the show's central character, the young Woollarawarre Bennelong, who learned English and served as an intermediary between his people and the settlers, was taken to England and presented to King George III, and finally returned to his home country and way of life to die.

As the show opened in pre-1788 Australia, men and women assembled on the bare ground and moved in curvilinear patterns beneath a large, earth-coloured ring to resonant surround sound and powerful Indigenous song. The audience bore witness to Bennelong's birth and early years among his Wangal clan before the colonizers came bringing stiff salutes, ragged rhythms, and angular patterns into a space that had hitherto been all stomping feet and swaying bodies. The easy flow of communal life was interrupted, permanently, by the rigid uniformity of military jackets and inflexible routines, as Bennelong awkwardly donned a uniform and a new, equally ill-fitting identity as a British subject. With the British came disease, and some of the production's most powerful moments occurred as writhing, convulsing bodies emerged through a doorway between life and death-by-smallpox. The show was not without humour, and certainly not without great beauty, but what lingers is its sometimes graphic, blood-spattered depiction of colonial cruelty and the profound sadness of Bennelong's life and death, never more powerfully than in the depiction of Bennelong's tortured final days. Rejected by his former allies as well as his own people and trapped within his cottage, the mirrored walls converging on him, Bennelong died at Kissing Point on 3 January 1813, and was buried on the banks of the Parramatta River where he was born.

Bennelong was an accomplished piece of work, *representing* the brutality of colonization and the recalcitrance of conciliation between the Global North and South, but *enacting* the power and beauty of Indigenous artistry and the promise of resurgence (Figure 5). Matching the charismatic virtuosity of Beau Dean Riley Smith (Wiradjuri) as Bennelong and the depth, intricacy, and maturity of senior Torres Strait Island dancer Elma Kris (Wagadagam, Kaurareg, Sipingur, Gebbara, and Kai Dangal Buai), was a flawless ensemble of seventeen dancers enacting a powerful trans-Indigenous collaboration – Stephen Page touted the show's 'wonderful mix of Indigenous theatrical elements coming together' (qtd in 'Bangarra') – as well as collaborations between Indigenous and settler artists under Indigenous leadership. Kris, playing 'Psychopomp', evoked a future for Indigenous peoples in Australia that involved prisons and abuse, but also protests, demonstrations, and hope; Steve Francis, whose score blended Indigenous and European influences, saw the show, ultimately if somewhat optimistically, as a story of reconciliation: 'we could live side by side ... understanding each other's culture, or cultural way of life, having respect for one another', he said. 'Really, that's what it comes down to' (qtd in 'Bangarra').

Figure 5   *Bennelong*, created by Stephen Page for Bangarra Dance Theatre and performed
at the Perth Festival and elsewhere in 2020, enacted the power and beauty of Indigenous
artistry and the promise of resurgence. Photograph by Daniel Boud

Perth's experiment in 2020, the inaugural year of non-Indigenous
artistic director Iain Grandage's tenure, dedicating the first week of the
festival exclusively to four featured works from Indigenous Australia, risked
ghettoizing Indigenous work, but two of the featured shows extended into
the second week, when a fifth joined them on the programme, and the
festival film series featured two works by Indigenous filmmakers, one of
them Noongar. The featured work, moreover, consisted of a wide diversity
of Indigenous shows in different performance genres. There is no question,
in any case, that the critical mass of highly visible Indigenous performance
at Perth's main stages in 2020, in counterdistinction to the isolated staging
of *Buŋgul* in Adelaide, constituted the festival's first week, at least, as a
meta-event of major significance for Indigenous Australia.

The production that opened in the second week at Perth featured a
perhaps problematic, but historic collaboration, *BLACK TIES*, the first
between Indigenous theatre companies in Australia and Aotearoa, and
another commission by the Perth Festival funded by the Major Festivals
Initiative. Co-created by John Harvey (Torres Strait Islands) and Tainui

Tukiwaho (Māori), co-produced by Te Rēhia Theatre Company in Auckland and ILBIJERRI Theatre Company in Melbourne, and programmed at the Sydney, Perth, New Zealand, and Auckland Festivals, the large-scale show, with a cast of thirteen including the band, was billed as an 'hilarious and heartwarming' musical rom com about intercultural marriage between a Māori woman and Aboriginal man. It dealt with their two families attempting to reconcile their prejudices and preconceptions while audience members, seated at tables as guests at the wedding reception, looked on. *BLACK TIES* was popular, it exhibited the considerable skill and dexterity of the Indigenous cast and creative team, and it raised important questions, if lightly, about vexed intercultural issues. But it was also subject to criticism by many, including Tokelauan (Te Kaiga o Fagatiale, Nukunonu, Te Kaiga o Koloi, Uea) and Fijian (Kaideuba) reviewer Emele Ugavule, for failing to honour details in the tribe-specific history of treaty negotiations, for its 'comic' use of racial slurs, for the harmful representation of *takatāpui* (gay, lesbian, or transgender people), and for the damaging reinforcement of stereotypes about Blak (Indigenous) men and 'angry Blak women'. Ugavule left the theatre 'feeling hurt and ashamed'. The destination festival stage can be a fraught and very public site for the representation and negotiation of unresolved cultural difference within and between Indigenous communities.

Stephen Page, at Adelaide in 2004, was the first but has not been the only Aboriginal director of a major festival in Australia. Since 2017 Noonuccal-Nughi playwright Wesley Enoch has run the Sydney Festival, his hiring perhaps being one inspired response to the festival's forward-looking 'Reconciliation Action Plan 2015–2017', launched in 2013 with four major goals: 'respecting Aboriginal and Torres Strait Islander people and cultures, offering employment to Aboriginal and Torres Strait Islander people, offering development and presentation opportunities to Aboriginal and Torres Strait Islander artists and art workers, and building cultural awareness among our staff, our stakeholders and audiences of the diversity of Aboriginal and Torres Strait Islander stories' (Sydney Festival, 'Innovate'). Enoch has used the position to champion the interrelated issues of the use of Indigenous languages and the preservation of land, both within and beyond Australia.[31] In 2018 he addressed the British Council and the Edinburgh Festival's International Culture Summit, advocating deep knowledge of the landscape through the languages that emerged from it and emphasizing the inter-imbricated issues of the preservation of land and language (Enoch, 'If You').

In his first two festivals, Enoch strengthened these commitments. In 2017, in fact, he introduced an Aboriginal language course series, 'Bayala', and commissioned one of the series conveners, Aunty Jacinta Tobin (Dharug), and others to write a song 'in language' to be performed at the WugulOra ('one mob') morning ceremony on Australia Day (26 January) near the end of the festival. He also supported emerging Indigenous writers by incorporating in the festival's closing days Moogahlin Performing Arts's Yellamundie National First Peoples Playwriting Festival, an important development initiative which continued into the 2020 festival. Indigenous work on the programme proper in 2017 included a broad range of trans-Indigenous performances such as *Which Way Home* and *Blood on the Dance Floor*, both by Melbourne's leading Aboriginal ILBIJERRI Theatre Company, the former about an Aboriginal girl and her aging father on a trip to his birthplace, the latter a blood-based physical theatre piece featuring Narangga/Kaurna dancer and writer Jacob Boehme trying to come to terms culturally with his HIV-positive diagnosis. Also included were *Burrbgaja Yalirra* (Dancing Forwards), a triple bill of spoken word and animated video, solo dance, and dance/violin by the extraordinary Marrugeku company, based in remote Broome in the north of Western Australia, and the harrowing solo work, *Huff*, by Cree actor/writer Cliff Cardinal, produced by Native Earth Performing Arts in Toronto. In 2017 Enoch also introduced the Blak Out programme, 'excavating hope from a bleak political landscape' in Australia and in the world (Enoch, 'That's a Wrap').[32] The programme, which included music, dance, and visual art as well as theatre by Indigenous peoples, was designed to represent the *diversity* of First Peoples and to avoid burdening any one or two shows with what Enoch calls 'the responsibility of representation' (qtd in Boon). 'When you have more than a single show from First Nations artists', Enoch says, 'you immediately relieve that show from trying to represent the whole of that community' (Enoch, 'That's a Wrap'). The sheer variety of Indigenous and non-Indigenous performances in 2017 created a festival experience throughout Australia's financial capital and most populous and diverse city (population ca 5.5 million, almost 45 per cent immigrant) that was at once international in the traditional sense, 'internation' in the Indigenous sense, and actively intercultural. For Indigenous artists and audiences it was affirming; for settler Australians beneficially unsettling.

But perhaps the 2017 festival's most festive and most affirmative event was *1967: Music in the Key of Yes*, in which Aboriginal and Indigenous singers took the stage of the prestigious Sydney Opera

House to celebrate the fiftieth anniversary of the referendum in which Australians voted overwhelmingly to remove passages in their constitution that discriminated against Aboriginal people. Yolŋu artist Yirrmal both opened and closed the show, his 'soaring vocals in language let[ting] us all know', according to Murri reviewer Emily Nicole, 'that despite continued oppression, Indigenous culture is enduring, resilient, and very much alive'.

Enoch's appointment was extended, and as I write he has completed his fourth season as Sydney's Artistic Director in January 2020, a season in which a full third of the events listed in the festival programme were Indigenous, some of them carrying a very high profile. These included *Bungul* prior to its tour to Perth and Adelaide; *BLACK TIES* mounted in collaboration with the Auckland Festival; and the revival of *Bran Nue Dae*, all part of the Australian circuit in 2020 and all discussed above. It also included two world premieres that involved Indigenous and settler artists collaborating in the lead creative roles of playwright and director. *Black Cockatoo,* by settler playwright Geoffrey Atherden, was directed by Enoch himself; *Black Drop Effect*, by Yuwaalaraay playwright Nardi Simpson, was directed by the Trinidad-born Felix Cross. The former, focusing on the retrieval from the depths of the archives of the story of Jarwadjali cricketer Johnny Mullagh's 1868 tour of England with an all-Indigenous team, consisted of a commentary on shifting and differing perspectives on history. It employed Wergaia language within a dominant English text, and a cast of six doubling in Blak and white roles. It focused, often powerfully, on the historical injustices and contemporary neglect suffered by Australia's first Indigenous sports hero. The latter show accepted Enoch's challenge to Aboriginal and Torres Strait Island artists to be ready for the 250th anniversary in April 2020 of the arrival of Captain Cook at Kamay (Botany Bay). Staging debates around the possibilities and problems of reconciliation through cultural enactment and encounter, *Black Drop Effect* used five Indigenous and two settler actors, an inventive choreography, swirling projections, and an evocatively eclectic sound score to clock Indigenous reactions over time to various official commemorations of Cook's landing. The titular black drop effect refers to the optical illusion that occurs during the Transit of Venus when two opposing shapes seem to merge, appearing to produce a teardrop on the lip of the sun. It was the attempt to measure the Transit of Venus that was the official excuse for Captain Cook's voyage of 'exploration' in 1770, and the effect served as an apt metaphor for Australia's diverging national narratives and the tears they continue to produce.

Finally, the 2020 edition of the Sydney Festival under Enoch extended the festival's trans-Indigenous outreach once again to what is now Canada, including performances by the musical sensation Jeremy Dutcher (Wolastoqiyik (Maliseet) of the Tobique First Nation). But perhaps as important as the featured performances were the festival's efforts to engage in critical conversations about Indigeneity. These included 'Warra Warra What?' at the State Library, a consideration of the first words James Cook and his men heard ('Go away!') when they arrived on the coast of what is now Australia, and more importantly of Dharawal history and language in what is now New South Wales. They also included, closing the festival, *Procession*, a cleansing ceremony, song, and dance led by Aboriginal Elders through the streets of Sydney, and *The Vigil*, an all-night-long experience of performance and reflection at the Barangaroo Reserve waterfront park, both held on the eve of Australia day. These events, the opening and closing ceremonies, and many of the individual Indigenous events framed the 2020 Sydney festival within a decolonial Indigenous festival paradigm constituting its audiences, as often as not, as participants and witnesses to events that straddled the line between theatre and ceremony.

The evolution of the Adelaide, Perth, and Sydney Festivals, particularly under Indigenous leadership, demonstrates that destination festivals in the early twenty-first century have had the fragile capacity to broker conversations across Indigenous–settler differences and to showcase powerful Indigenous performances before local, national, and visiting audiences. Nevertheless, the overarching purpose of most such festivals necessarily remained nation, state, and city branding, and Indigenous work was always in danger of co-option, commodification, or even disappearance, even as it was exposed to the global festival marketplace. To consider the full potential of Indigeneity to shift the ways we think about festivals and the cultural work they perform, it's necessary to look at a model more fully under Indigenous control.

Indigenous Cultural Festivals: 'Irreconcilable Spaces of Aboriginality'

Cultural festivals organized by Indigenous peoples themselves vary in focus, size, and purpose and are rarely only about theatre or the arts as such, though they are certainly performative, and it's not difficult to trace their lineage to festivals that predate contact with the western world, western history, and the festival culture of ancient Greece. Perhaps more directly than any others, these festivals provide what can be understood to be a decolonial festival paradigm that for western understandings can be profoundly unsettling. Some, such as the large-scale (1 million visitors in five years) Festival Internacional de la Cultura Maya (Yucatán, Mexico), are recognizably destination festivals in their appeal to visitors, but are focused on a single, in this case Mayan, culture. FICMAYA, as it is called, has broad ambitions, as signalled by the title of the festival and the conference that it hosted in its sixth incarnation in 2017: 'Cosmogony and the Preservation of the Planet'. The preservation and celebration of Mayan cultures, cosmologies, and cosmogonies (creation stories) are seen in this festival as invitations to the world to learn and heal. Other, smaller festivals, such as Riddu Riđđu ('small storm at the coast'), held in Gáivuotna (Kåfjord), Norway, whose mandate is 'to promote and develop the Sami coastal culture', are primarily local and focus on cultural preservation, survival, and renewal in the face of resistance, sometimes violent. At the very beginning of Riddu Riđđu the festival's young founders were ridiculed and spat upon.

Aboriginal cultural festivals, almost all of them in traditional, remote territories in far northern Queensland or the Northern Territory in Australia, have been among the most successful in at once negotiating Indigenous–settler political relationships *and* maintaining what Métis scholar David Garneau, from Turtle Island, calls 'irreconcilable spaces of Aboriginality' (27), and they are, of course, under the exclusive leadership of Indigenous people.[33]

Australia

In Australia's far north the Mapoon Indigenous Festival in Cape York was founded in 2007 as an assertion of the 'historical continuity, social legitimacy, autonomy and sovereignty' (Slater, 'Our Spirit' 134) of the small Tjungundi community of Mapoon, forcibly removed from their homes in 1963 by the Queensland police who burned their houses to the ground to prevent their return. The 2017 festival celebrated fifty years of resurgence. Other of the more than 100 Aboriginal festivals in Australia each year as of 2010 (Phipps, 'Indigenous' 683), such as the Yeperenye Federation Festival (Alice Springs), the Barunga Festival (Barunga), and the Laura Aboriginal Dance Festival (Cape York), operate as 'a means of entering into intercultural dialogue, a testimony to ongoing political struggles and, for both Indigenous performers and their audience, provide an important context for the contemporary negotiation and transmission of Indigenous people's identities (Slater, 'Our Spirit' 130–1).

The Garma Festival of Traditional Cultures (North East Arnhem Land) is exemplary, part of what Peter Phipps calls 'An effervescence of local indigenous cultural festivals [that] is one manifestation of [a] subtle shift toward a globalizing indigenous identity that emphasizes the specifically local' ('Performances' 220). Garma is an annual, four-day festival held by the Yolŋu people at the Gulkula grounds, a sand-covered ceremonial site on Gumatj clan country. It is, as Phipps says, 'an intercultural gathering of [Australian] national significance, and simultaneously is a local gathering of Yolngu [sic] clans on Yolngu land for Yolngu political, ceremonial and recreational purposes' ('Performing' 110). The Yolŋu peoples have been prominent in Aboriginal rights movements in Australia, in part because of their late colonization and their having maintained strong connections to their ancestral lands, laws, language, and performance forms.[34] 'Our ancient sovereignty is here', said Djunga Djunga Yunupiŋgu at a ceremonial welcome to Garma 2018 (Davidson), and the festival both grounds itself in that sovereignty and engages Balanda (non-Indigenous visitors) with Yolŋu cultural practices, language, and cosmology. Central to the festival is the buŋgul, a dance that encodes Yolŋu history, sovereignty, and law, is performed every evening on the festival grounds, and has in a mediated form been taken on tour to Australia's major destination festivals, as discussed above. In its manifestation on home country, it teaches Yolŋu youth languages and cultural practices while also making Yolŋu epistemologies and ontologies – together with their capacity for intercultural, international negotiation, diplomacy, and trade – visible to visiting Balanda politicians and dignitaries. 'Yolngu dance', as anthropologist Franca Tamisari says, 'because they hold the law' (qtd in Phipps, 'Performing' 152). As a festival requiring 'complex inter-clan political negotiations on a number of levels, from the sacred ritual and religious to the economic' (Phipps, 'Performing' 118), Garma promotes and models Yolŋu Matha (language) on the land from which it emerged, and it encodes Yolŋu understandings of interdependence and relationality with other peoples as well as with the natural and spirit worlds. And in doing so it hails non-Indigenous Australians, including invited political leaders, to enter into reciprocal, nation-to-nation relationships with the people to whose land they have been welcomed *as guests*.

Garma, then, like other Indigenous cultural festivals in Australia, exists in a complex, deeply intercultural world, its goal being, as Lisa Slater argues, 'to compose anti-colonial relations' ('Sovereign' 132) or, I would argue, more generatively decolonial ones. 'Indigenous cultural festivals', she says, constitute 'innovative responses to keeping culture alive –

meaningful lifeworlds comprised [of] local networks of production, circulation, exchange, sociality, and law, embedded in settler, liberal modernity'. (134). Also, however, as 'expressions and generation of, as well as experiments in, Indigenous modernity' (138), they enact what she calls 'relational ontologies' (137).

> Cultural festivals are one ... *route* for reinvigorating significant relationships and social identities, with the express purpose of strengthening young people's capacity to navigate the demands of a deeply intercultural world, and to be innovators and agents of the new roles and possibilities generated by our shared present ... I am arguing that cultural festivals are peaceful weapons in a continuing ontological political contest. (144, emphasis in original)

This, for me, constitutes a paradigmatically different role for festivals than that enshrined in canonical histories of western theatre and festivalization, a direct and affective public assertion of the ongoing and independent value of cultures, epistemologies, cosmogonies, and cosmologies of peoples whose rights remain unrecognized in the Australian constitution.[35]

Trans-Indigeneity in the Pacific

Festivals of Pacific peoples negotiate less with single national settler governments, as in Australia, than with the oceanic vastness of the region that they attempt to connect. Phipps's essay on Indigenous cultural festivals as 'Performances of Power' compares Garma to Hawai'i's Merrie Monarch Festival, which, however, focusing on the hula as a bridge between traditional culture and Indigenous modernities, brings together performances from across the Pacific, including Aotearoa and Tahiti. In this, the Merrie Monarch Festival is representative of festivals of Pacific peoples, which tend to operate on a more explicitly trans-Indigenous level than do Garma and other more culturally specific events. These festivals serve in part to forge solidarities across Oceanic cultures, including those of what French cartographer/'explorer' Jules Dumont d'Urville labelled Micronesia, Melanesia, and Polynesia in 1832, each fragmented by its own complex colonial histories and contemporary realities in which the UK, Spain, France, Germany, Holland, Australia, Japan, Chile, and the United States have controlled, ravaged, and exchanged islands. The interventions performed by these festivals, then, function not at a national but a transnational level, creating trans-Indigenous solidarities, supporting cultural resurgence, and, like the festivals discussed in Chapter 5, forging links across latter-day national borders.

The Festival of the Pacific Arts (FESTPAC), founded in 1972 in Fiji, takes place every four years hosted by a different country and nation, thereby avoiding co-option by the agendas of national governments. FESTPAC is not designed for tourists. Its function is to bring Pacific peoples together in a spirit of regeneration. Its ambitious and wide-ranging guiding principles are as follows:

> We, the indigenous peoples of the Pacific, assert our cultural identity, rights and dignity. We do so, mindful of our spiritual and environmental origins, through our dynamic art forms and artistic history and traditions. As indigenous peoples we share the following objectives:
>
> – Encourage awareness of a collective voice
> – Foster the protection of cultural heritage
> – Explore the creation of dynamic new arts
> – Cultivate global awareness and appreciation for Pacific arts and cultures
> – Promote our traditional languages
> – Value the wisdom of our elders
> – Support the aspiration of our youth
> – Advocate a cultural peace through dialogue with the cultures of the Pacific
> – Promote cultural development within the social, economic and political development of our countries
> – Encourage the indigenous peoples of the Pacific to continue their efforts for recognition. (Stevenson 4–5)

Although the initial goals of the festival were preservationist and functioned on the level of cultural exchange, it has developed in the twenty-first century into a site where young artists and contemporary arts – music, design, film, dance, and theatre – build on traditional forms and practices to forge new and forward-looking trans-Indigenous, trans-Pacific modernisms and form transnational political alliances. The 2016 festival, held in Guam with 2,700 artists and performers from 27 Pacific Island countries and territories – some arriving in a dozen handcrafted vessels guided by traditional navigators – also hosted a meeting of the Pacific Ministers of Culture to discuss a regional approach to the 2005 UNESCO Convention on the Protection and Promotion of the Diversity of Cultural Expressions, as well as a Forum on Culture, Arts and Sustainable Development in the Pacific.

But FESTPAC is only one of many festivals forging solidarities across the Pacific islands and their diaspora. In Aotearoa alone there are Pacific festivals in every major urban area, ranging from Northland through the central North Island and Wellington all the way down the east coast of the

South Island to Invercargill on the southern tip. These festivals forge and express pan-Pacific solidarities, celebrate Aotearoa as a new, rather than ancestral Pacific homeland, and establish relationships of trans-Indigenous solidarity between Pacific peoples and the Māori. The largest of these festivals, and the largest Pacific festivals in the world, take place in Auckland: the original, student-focused Polyfest (there are now sixteen) and the original, community-based Pasifika[36] Festival (there are now fourteen). In addition to these are the Tu Fa'atasi '(stand together') festival in Wellington, and the grandmother of them all, the Polynesian Festival in Rotorua founded in 1972, originally a Māori event but renamed Te Matatini o te Rā in 2004 to indicate its broadened scope (matatini in this context meaning 'many faces').

Auckland is now known as 'the biggest Polynesian city in the world' (Mackley-Crump, 'Pacific'), and its Pasifika Festival is the largest of its kind globally. The festival is a free, family-friendly event held over two days in late March in, as of 2019, eleven different 'villages' in Western Springs Park representing, respectively, the Cook Islands, Fiji, Niue, Aotearoa, Hawai'i, Kiribati, Samoa, Tahiti, Tuvalu, Tonga, and Tokelau. The festival's opening night concert involves each Pacific nation presenting a short performance that recognizes and draws upon the knowledge and experience of community elders. Along with honouring elders, the festival hires and mentors young Pacific people in roles within the organization and management of the festival. Finally, the festival focuses on differences between and diversity among the Pacific communities it represents and brings together. In a key essay that focuses on the Pasifika festival in Auckland, Jared Mackley-Crump argues that the festivalization of Pacific cultures 'creates notions of diasporic identity and belonging', with the festivals functioning as 'complex transcultural contact zones' that at once provide opportunities for exchange and solidarities among Pacific peoples and for the display of Pacific cultures to outsiders ('Festivalization' 59). Pacific festivals, he argues,

> are transcultural spaces. They are in that they are meeting places of different Pacific cultures, diverse in their differences, unified by commonalities, and they are also where these different Pacific cultures and peoples meet others. Furthermore, Pacific festivals are transcultural because they are spaces through which Pacific pasts meet contemporary urban Pacific presents, a terrain upon which what it means to be of the Pacific in the twenty-first century can be contested. (28)

Mackley-Crump identifies (28–9) four types of 'contact parties' that occur within the context of the festival – the Intergenerational, Intra-Pacific, Intra-national, and International – which cumulatively provide a site for what he calls 'a multi-local mapping of place' (34), a reterritorialization of Aotearoa as a place, a 'sea of islands' that, drawing on James Clifford, 'blend[s] together routes and roots to construct alternative public spheres' (34, citing Clifford).

Pacific festivals are perhaps unique in constructing what Mackley-Crump calls 'urban Oceanic spaces' (31) in which diasporic Pacific peoples can forge identities that are no longer neither here nor there, but *both* here *and* there, at once based on traditional relationships to the land and, especially, the water, and grounded in newly forged trans-Indigenous modernities. Such festivals, then, as complex spaces of multiple belongings, function as sites of both the negotiation and consolidation of intercultural, trans-Indigenous diasporic subjectivities.

Indigenous-run Theatre and Performance Festivals

Indigenous cultural festivals such as those I have been examining have been important sites for the performative negotiation and constitution of identities within individual, intranational, and trans-Indigenous communities. (Trans-)Indigenous festivals dedicated to contemporary theatre and performance have taken on the extra role of negotiating across aesthetic and formal differences and the derivation of contemporary forms from the languages, territories, and traditional cultural texts and practices of different Indigenous nations. They play the mediating role, in the contemporary world and the aesthetic realm, played by ceremonial types of Indigenous performative encounter – ur-festivals – that predated contact with European colonizers; at their best they provide alternative ways of thinking about festivals in the twenty-first century in constituting festivalgoers, particularly Indigenous ones, as participants and witnesses. Insofar as they also attract settler and arrivant audience members, however, they do not constitute communities in the way that non-Indigenous festivals are said to do. The audience experience at most Indigenous theatre festivals is a divided one that consists of Indigenous people as hosts and relations, together with non-Indigenous attendees who are welcomed as guests and encouraged to experience the festival as real or potential allies.

Indigenous festivals dedicated to contemporary live art are relatively rare, but tend to come in three forms: play development festivals (represented here by Native Earth Performing Arts's Weesageechak Begins to

Dance in Toronto); intra-National festivals (represented here by Full Circle's Talking Stick Festival in Vancouver);[37] and transnational, trans-Indigenous festivals (represented here by the Living Ritual International Indigenous Performing Arts Festival in Toronto in 2017, with which this chapter opened).[38]

Weesageechak Begins to Dance completed its thirty-first annual edition over two weeks in November 2018, featuring new works and works in progress in theatre, dance, and opera.[39] It also featured work by emerging Indigenous artists who were part of the festival's Animaking Creators Unit dedicated to the diversity of new Indigenous voices, and (since 2017) a two-spirit Cabaret produced in conjunction with Buddies in Bad Times (queer) theatre.[40] Weesageechak is extraordinary in its intergenerational and interdisciplinary assemblage of developing work from First Nations across the land that is now called Canada, and increasingly over the past decade, from Aotearoa and Aboriginal Australia as well, in instances of trans-Indigenous outreach and collaboration. Weesageechak 2016, for example, hosted the first showing of *Waka/Ciimaan/Vaka*, a collaboration among Native Earth Performing Arts, Raven Spirit Dance (British Columbia), and Tawata Productions (Aotearoa), involving artists from Canada, Aotearoa, and the Cook Islands whimsically exploring 'the effects of climate change and environmental capitalism on the people and animals of the northern and southern hemispheres' (Dickinson, 'Waka'). Its title means 'canoe' in the production's three languages.[41]

Weesageechak's focus on development is crucial in allowing it to support the exploration of new, or newly hybrid forms (such as Indigenous opera, which has featured several times at the festival), and of new relationships across Indigenous nations within and beyond Turtle Island, without the pressures or expenses of full production. The focus, moreover, is on relationships *within the room* – between artists, directors, dramaturgs, and local audiences from different Indigenous cultures, rather than on the festivalization of the space or the eventification and marketing of the festival for international or tourist consumption. Weesageechak is able to take risks. And far from the competitive frenzy of many fringe festivals, the atmosphere at Weesageechak is one of mutual celebration. It is, in short, festive.

Vancouver's Talking Stick Festival, presented annually by Full Circle: First Nations Performance, is a two-week interdisciplinary internation festival featuring traditional and contemporary visual arts, dance, theatre, music, pow wow, and film by Indigenous artists from across what is now Canada. It was founded in 2001 in the wake of the experience of Full

Circle founder and artistic director Margo Kane (Cree/Salteaux) performing her solo show, *Moonlodge*, at The Festival of the Dreaming in the lead-
up to the Sydney Olympics, an example of the beneficial effects of trans-
Indigenous exchange (See Lachance and Couture; La Flamme). Organized
on the horizontal principles of radical Indigenous democracy signalled by
its name, the festival models ancient 'talking stick' protocols, in which only
the holder of the talking stick (or in some cultures the eagle feather, pipe,
shell, or wampum belt) has the right to speak, and everyone else is required
to listen with attention and respect before the stick is passed to the next
person in the 'talking circle' (see Indigenous Corporate Training).
A festival modelled on these principles exhibits appropriate behaviour for
audiences who are constituted as active, attentive participants engaged in
meaningful exchange rather than as passive spectators or consumers
of entertainment.

In 2018 Talking Stick featured, as 'headliners', *Scháyilhen (Salmon
Going Up the River)*, an exhibition curated by mixed-race Cree artist
Richard Heikkilä-Sawan; *Sokalo*, by Québec's [ZØGMA], a percussive
dance company, in collaboration with Vancouver's Louis Riel Métis
Dancers; *Map of the Land, Map of the Stars*, a collective creation by the
Yukon's Gwaandak Theatre in Whitehorse, combining theatre, dance, and
music; and 'Reel Reservations', a 'cinematic Indigenous sovereignty series'
(Full Circle, 'Headliners'). In addition, the festival offered a 'family fun'
series consisting of Axis Theatre Company's *Th'owxiya: The Hungry Feast
Dish*, a TYA show written by Joseph Dandurand (Kwantlen First Nation);
Raven Spirit Dance's *Salmon Girl*, directed by Quelemia Sparrow
(Musqueam) and choreographed by Michelle Olson (Tr'ondëk
Hwëch'in); a Métis kitchen party; and a pow wow. There was also
'Nightlife', which included *Heartbeatz!* and *Indigi Groove* (a performance
series featuring Tuthchone/Tinglit, Métis, Squamish, and other musicians); *Indigifemme*, a burlesque performance exploring contemporary
Indigenous sexualities; and a closing Kw'iyilshswit dance party.
Finally, the festival hosted the four-day Scháyilhen Industry Series for
presenters, artists, scholars, and audience members interested in the development of Indigenous arts. It was, in short, an extraordinarily eclectic
and trans-Indigenous meta-event fulfilling the festival's mandate to
'to showcase and celebrate Indigenous art and performance to a
wider audience' (Full Circle, 'About') while enabling wide-ranging
conversations across Indigenous nations, ages, sexualities, and
performance genres.

But Talking Stick is more than simply a showcase. It is also, as Lindsay Lachance (Algonquin Anishinaabe) and settler scholar Selena Couture have argued, a nurturing space of embodying 'Indigenous ideas of transformational love, "grounded normativity" and kin relations that cross earthly boundaries' (11). Lachance and Couture draw upon the work of Karyn Recollet (Cree) on 'kinestellary relations', Glen Coulthard (Dene) on 'grounded normativity', and Leanne Betasamosake Simpson on 'decolonial love' to discuss the ways in which the festival 'activate[s] the territorial, radical relationalities that are bringing what is traditional into the future' (Carter, Recollet, and Robinson 215–16). 'Kinestellary relations' are modelled on the movement and circulation of the constellations and constitute 'reciprocal relationalities of kinship across the human and other-than-human worlds to open up multiscalar flows of Indigenous being and thinking' (Lachance and Couture 13). 'Grounded normativity', according to Coulthard, is a 'place-based foundation of Indigenous decolonial thought and practice ..., the modalities of Indigenous land-connected practices that inform and structure our ethical engagements with the world and our relationships with human and nonhuman others over time' (13). And 'decolonial love' is a transformational process of joining together 'in a rebellion of love, persistence and profound caring' (Simpson, 'decolonial'). According to Lachance and Couture, the Talking Stick Festival's flexible, decentred, non-hierarchical organizational principles and practices model these Indigenous and deeply ethical and relational concepts in structuring 'an event that honours and builds relationships and resiliency through deep love that aims to transform' (18) – offering a profound Indigenous variation on the transformational properties and potential of festivals discussed in this book's Introduction, and an actively decolonial festival paradigm. In my experience, the festival offers a profoundly moving and welcoming coming together of artists and audience/participants over ten days each February, powerfully modelling internation encounter and Indigenous cultural resurgence.

While Weesageechak Begins to Dance and Talking Stick are long-standing annual events, the small-scale Living Ritual Festival with which I opened this chapter has only happened twice in a little over a decade, but in spite of its size is an example of a widely transnational, trans-Indigenous event based on sharing and exchange rather than on competition or spectacle.[42] The first festival in 2006, organized by Kaha:wi Dance Theatre's Kahnyen'kehàka (Mohawk) Artistic Director Tekaronhiáhkhwa Santee Smith from Six Nations of the Grand River, highlighted 'ritual', was subtitled 'World Indigenous Dance Festival', and featured traditional and community-based work. The second, in 2017, again organized by Smith (along with Kaha:wi's Mohawk then General Manager Cynthia Lickers-Sage), highlighted 'living', was subtitled 'International Indigenous Performing Arts Festival', and featured contemporary, interdisciplinary, and experimental work.

Living Ritual was in many ways exemplary in grounding its international trans-Indigeneity in the local and programming meaningful encounters among all participants in the form of workshops, panels, and keynote 'provocations' rather than the often-underachieved aspirational rhetoric of festivals that are not so carefully curated. The 2017 iteration of the festival provided an opportunity for precisely the kinds of trans-Indigenous analysis that Chadwick Allen calls for by juxtaposing performances at Toronto's Harbourfront 'synchronically and globally' (*Trans-Indigenous* xxvi) over three intensive days in July 2017. It was presented as a forum for dialogue on decoloniality and artistic exploration, promoting trans-Indigenous creative cross-pollination. Living Ritual in 2017 was exemplary for also being deeply grounded in the cultures and practices of the Haudenosaunee (primarily Mohawk), who hosted artists from Turtle Island, Aotearoa, and Australia as well as arrivant and white settler participants. The event opened outdoors by the waters of Lake Ontario with an Onkwehon:we Edge of the Woods ceremony, in which visitors, having affirmed that they came in peace, were welcomed into the acknowledged territory of the Onkwehon:we, Anishinaabe (Mississaugas of the Credit River), and Huron-Wendat. In addition to songs, speeches, and smudging, each visitor was presented with a feather and a cup of water with which to clear the dust of travel from our eyes and ears and clear our throats in preparation to see, hear, and speak 'in a good way'. The hour-long ceremony – a living ritual – was powerful and gracious, and like the nest of welcomes surrounding Te Rēhia Theatre's *SolOthello* at the RUTAS festival, and like every welcome (as Robinson reminds us), it was also a declaration and acknowledgement of sovereignties. Indigenous visitors from Aotearoa and Australia also offered songs and greetings from their home territories before the ceremony concluded with an inclusive Round Dance.

The brevity and scale of Living Ritual 2017 meant that all participants were there for the duration, and in addition to sharing six eclectic dance, theatre, and dance-theatre performances in the evenings (open to a general public), they shared techniques and strategies throughout each day in a series of intensive workshops, shared positions in keynote provocations, and shared information and strategies at participatory panels on such things as Indigenous 'Process and Methodologies', 'Documentation', 'Platforms and Presence', Collaboration', 'Protocols for Consent', and 'Ensemble and Sovereignty'. The evening performances, two per evening, ranged from Indigenous variations on contemporary dance and documentary through Kapa Haka and a mashup of 'hip hop, physical percussion, and rhythmic cultural pattern' (Living Ritual), to theatricalized Inuit storytelling and, of course, the Spiderwoman-styled 'storyweaving' with which I began this chapter.

But one of the strengths of the festival was that the artists not only saw one another's work, but they participated in intensive workshops that allowed for deeper aesthetic, technical, political, and cultural exchange than is available at most festivals. These workshops provided some of the most invigorating moments of the festival, as when Kalaallit artist Laakkuluk Williamson Bathory, from Iqaluit, Nunavut, orchestrated a participatory full-body workshop on the Greenlandic mask dance, *uaajeer-neq*. Participants from various Indigenous and non-Indigenous cultures around the world smeared our faces with black greasepaint (for humility) and then added white (to evoke the ancestors' bones) and red (for female genitalia). Mouths were stuffed, grotesquely, with bits of apple and carrot (for male genitalia). ('In our language', Williamson Bathory said, 'the word for "art" is "the making of eccentric things".') We were instructed to squat, keeping our genitals close to the ground so there would be a connection between our sexual beings and the earth; to move our eyes around; and to explore, in an orgy of improvisation, our animal, glutton, sexual, male and/ or female, scary and suggestive selves – a very visceral and earthy kind of transcultural, interpersonal exchange.

From the other side of the world, the Māori Hawaiki TŪ Productions' Kapa Haka warrior dance/theatre production of *Hononga* was complemented by a vigorous Kapa Haka workshop led by Beez Ngarino Watt, but also balanced by a different side of Māori culture through a much gentler workshop and solo performance, *Manawa*, by Taane Mete (Ngāti Kahungungu me Ngāti Koroki – Kahukura). Mete's performative lecture and workshop was a highlight of the festival. Less demonstration than sharing, it began with a moving account of serving Mete's mother by helping transport her to the other side, then shifted into a fluid solo dance-demonstration based on that experience, before concluding with a workshop in which he choreographed all of us, as participant-performers, in a delicate exercise of connecting sky and earth worlds through a bucket and a cloud. Simple, evocative, and empowering, it felt exemplary of the trans-Indigenous sharing that the festival set out to enable.

The festival *was* limited in many ways. It was a small, physically and temporally contained one-off event without the pressures of long-term sustainability. Although well-funded by the colonialist Canadian government's settler nationalist 'Canada 150' programme, apart from the evening performances it was not broadly advertised, in part, I assume, because it was intended to be dominated by the participating Indigenous artists and performers rather than curious onlookers. And the conference and work-shop components mostly took place in the intimate space of the Fleck Dance Theatre's lobby area, where Euro/Mushkegowuk Cree designer Andy Moro, of ARTICLE 11, had designed and installed a welcoming and flexible modular environment. This festival was not primarily meant for outsiders, and while visitors were made welcome, there were very few white settlers in evidence. But on its own terms, both physically and discursively, the festival enabled and modelled productive and empowering circles of conversation across latter-day artificial and divisive international boundaries, and it took care to situate itself on the land and to welcome visiting companies to bring their own land- and water-based epistemol-ogies and practices with them as guests. Living Ritual was a partial realization of Allen's vision of a trans-Indigeneity that 'will require reviving old networks of trade and exchange – and creating new networks of Indigenous interactions as yet unimagined' ('Decolonizing' 392).

What Would It Mean?

I began this chapter with a series of questions: what would it mean to see theatre and performance festivals, not as having begun within the compet-itive framework of ancient Greece but among the relational frameworks of Indigenous communities globally? The chapter has suggested that festivals can perhaps best function when they are genuinely 'internation'; when they feature Indigenous creative leadership and are grounded in the land, languages, creation stories, ceremonies, and knowledge systems that emerge from it rather than in the deterritorializing and decontextualizing programming practices of many international festivals; and when they constitute festivalgoers as guests, participants, and witnesses rather than consumers or voyeurs. As events participating in Indigenous resurgence globally, Indigenous festivals, in the words of Leanne Betasamosake Simpson about resurgent Indigenous organizing more generally, are 'necessarily place-based and local, but ... also necessarily networked and global' (*As We Have* 178). I hope, in subsequent chapters exploring various types of international festivals worldwide, implicitly to measure their relative success in promoting intercultural negotiation and exchange less against the founding model of ancient Greece, and more against the foundational Indigenous prototypes and practices explored here.

CHAPTER 2

Destination Festivals and the International Festival Circuit

I'm sitting alone in a small cubicle at the Church Hill Theatre Studio in Edinburgh in August 2017 wearing headphones and peering out of the darkness at small boxes of light that move slowly past me in a revolving diorama. The elaborate installation separates audiences into individual booths to tell the story sequentially, through miniature, hand-crafted story-board models and pre-recorded voices, of the two-year, four-thousand-mile 'flight', as refugees, of two Afghan brothers, aged eight and fourteen, from Kabul to London. Flight, by the Scottish company Vox Modus, is based on journalist Caroline Brothers's politically charged novel, Hinterland, *and it is being presented as part of the Edinburgh International Festival (EIF), one of the progenitors of the post-Second World War European destination festivals.[1] The venue has been modified, at considerable expense, to accommodate the large carousel, and the craftsmanship of the modelling of the figures and environments through which the story is told – like a three-dimensional graphic novel, with overhead shots, close-ups, long shots, blackouts, and the kinds of forced perspectives characteristic of that form – is painstaking. But sitting alone in the dark peering at inevitably cute little figurines posed to enact a story about exploitation, perilous crossings, enforced child labour, hunger, tear gas, confinement, arrest, rape (by 'the smiling man'), and ultimately the death of the littlest boy, feels more than a little voyeuristic. The deliberate depoliticization of the source novel and the research on which it is based – the programme note boasts of having excised the politics to focus on 'the intimacy and humanity of the story about the two boys' (*Flight*) – and the removal of this story from its global political causes and contexts, reduce the experience to that of expensively produced refugee porn.*

Flight was billed as 'a modern odyssey', implicitly claiming a classical lineage and universal immutability (*Flight*). Never mind that this was not the story of a king returning home from a rapacious war of revenge but that of disempowered young boys forced from their home by global social, political, and economic actors far beyond their control. Without these contexts the story was reduced to sentimentality, at best, while the cuteness factor of the figurines – there were no live bodies or voices with which to interact, and no actual Afghans or refugees (no physical 'others') to return the gaze – severely diminished its larger impact and significance. There was nothing about *why* this story happened, and no challenge to the global community, as presented by the source novel, to take responsibility. Why, indeed, were tiny and cute and the restriction to private individual spectatorship in which audience members neither shared a space nor saw the show at the same time – as opposed to communal witnessing – the right choices for the telling of this story?[2]

Over the course of the 2017 Edinburgh International Festival, in addition to *Flight*, I saw a powerfully cathartic adaptation of the *Oresteia* by Zinnie Harris that nevertheless reduced Aeschylus's epic trilogy to an explication of Freudian psychoanalysis; a pretentious game-show/mind-reading act in chicken suits, *Real Magic*, by England's Forced Entertainment that made hollow (and seemingly insincere) claims for depth; a reverential but ultimately empty Irish reproduction of the Beckett classic *Krapp's Last Tape*, presented as a bromance between now-disgraced director Michael Colgan and actor Barry McGovern; and an appallingly self-indulgent, politically reactionary, and homophobic new two-part play, *The Divide*, by Alan Ayckbourn. I came to wonder if the Festival was of necessity only about depoliticized aesthetics, individual psychology, fluff, feathers, reverential reproductions, and reactionary politics. Is the type of decontextualization, depoliticization, and liberalist universalism represented by *Flight* and these other shows inevitable within the deterritorializing context of the international festival circuit?[3]

Most of the élite, destination, or 'hallmark' festivals (Varney et al. 208) studied in this chapter have drawn their inspiration, directly or indirectly, from the festivals founded in Edinburgh and Avignon in 1947 in the aftermath of the Second World War, just two years after the founding of the United Nations, to help shore up European (high) culture, civilization, and a revivified, 'civilized' nationhood, in the wake of the devastation caused by unbridled populist European nationalisms (see Zaiontz, 'From' 15–16).[4] In a special issue of *Contemporary Theatre Review* on festivals in 2004, David Bradby and Maria Delgado pointed to 'a general consensus that the festival as we think of it today has been shaped more powerfully than we might realise by the two great foundational post-war festivals – Edinburgh and Avignon' (2) – and indeed, many of the other types of festival studied elsewhere in this book arose in *reaction* to the élite festivals that were initially modelled on those two. In the decades after their founding, the Edinburgh and Avignon festivals and their imitators shifted, in a staggered way depending on their national locations, away from their original, 'civilizing' mission, including national identity reification and international cultural diplomacy, to serving primarily as international marketplaces for the exhibition and exchange of cultural capital in the late twentieth century. Around the turn of the twenty-first century there was another shift to the more globalized neoliberal economic functions of festivalization, eventification, creative city planning, and city branding. But these élite festivals have retained, deep in their DNA, the traces of their original reificatory internationalism and their 'high-culture' civilizing mission. Located in the capital city and the seat of a now nationalist Scottish government seeking independence from the UK based on the distinctiveness of Scottish culture, the Edinburgh International Festival remains a centrepiece at once of Scottish tourism and nation promotion. The streets of Edinburgh at festival time are alive with bagpipes, kilts, and thistles, and the saltire, the Scottish flag, is everywhere.

The festivals considered in this chapter are many and varied, but all tend to be 'top-down' organizations, as Kenneth Grundy says of the destination National Arts Festival in Grahamstown (now Makhanda), South Africa (409): conservative, Eurocentric, colonialist, and slow to respond to aesthetic experimentation or social change.[5] Most are programmed by a single artistic director, sometimes with the support of a programming committee, who travels the world, mostly to other festivals, trolling for shows. Artists are invited, their fees, travel, accommodation, and technical costs are paid by the festivals, and the festivals retain the box office income. These festivals are usually registered charities, they tend to be sponsored by national and/or municipal governments, funded through public subsidies, foreign embassies, corporate sponsorships, and (increasingly) venture philanthropy (see Lin et al.), and are administered through boards of directors and corporate-style management structures. Their ticket prices are high, and their audiences tend to be 'cosmopolitan omnivores' (Regev 111) and arbiters of taste from society's upper and upper-middle classes for whom the experience of festivalization is as much about being seen as seeing, and more about cultural consumption than intercultural communication. They tend also, throughout the Global West and North and beyond, overwhelmingly to be white.

The structure, scale, and financial stakes of destination festivals might best be illuminated by examining a relatively modest, mid-sized festival that was purpose-built *as* a destination festival early in the twenty-first century. The Luminato Festival was launched in 2007 as part of Toronto, Canada's 'Creative City' initiative. It was the brainchild of two politically connected business leaders, David Pecaut and Tony Gagliano, and designed in part to lure visitors back to the city after the health and tourism crisis caused by the outbreak of SARS (Severe Acute Respiratory Syndrome) earlier in the decade (M. Anderson 5). As Laura Levin and Kim Solga argue, the festival's framework is 'resolutely . . . corporate first, arts second' (159). In addition to funding from various corporate sponsors, private donors, and other government funding sources, the festival controversially[6] received CAD $22 million in direct initial funding from the provincial government for its first two years, undercutting existing arts funding, including that for the city's many culturally specific and inter-cultural theatre companies (see Knowles, *Performing*), and bypassing the arm's-length Ontario Arts Council's juried assessment system (whose entire budget is under CAD $65 million). Luminato immediately established what appears to many to be a top-heavy corporate administrative structure and arranged multi-million-dollar partnerships with corporations that aspired to and did directly influence programming (see Zaiontz, 'From' 22). The operations of the festival have been scaled back considerably after those heady f(o)unding days, but as of 2018 it operated on an annual budget of almost CAD $8 million, which does not include funding raised by visiting artists from their own countries' ministries and embassies, or the contributions, largely in-kind, of the local co-producers of many of its events. The festival's webpage in 2019 listed its CEO, Anthony Sargent (above Artistic Director Naomi Campbell), at the top of an organizational chart that included two Vice Presidents, a Finance Manager, an Executive Assistant, twenty-one full-time employees on the Programming and Production Team, seventeen board members, most of them prominent business leaders, plus year-round staff, three-month seasonal contract positions, venue managers, and as many as 500 volunteers at festival time (M. Anderson 47). In addition to funding from thirteen 'Government Partners' at the national, provincial, and municipal levels, the festival is supported by nineteen 'Corporate Partners' (ranging from five major banks to newspapers including the *New York Times*), twenty Canadian and thirty international 'Programming Partners', plus individual donors ranked from 'founding luminaries', 'discovery fund' donors and 'Muses' through 'lodestar' and 'supernova' supporters to those in the 'Gold Patron Circle', the 'Patron Circle', the 'Limelight', and the 'Starlight'.[7] All donors receive name recognition from the festival and tax deductions from the Canadian government.

Budgets and administrative structures such as these are not unusual among destination festivals, but there is no doubt that they have a direct impact on what festival audiences experience. Michèle Anderson noted in 2009 that 'After giving so much money to an organization such as Luminato, which is not a government agency, the only oversight that dictates what Luminato does with these funds is that of the private and corporate funders, since they insist on specific returns for their investment' (23). 'The pitfalls of becoming too big, siphoning off too much government money, and taking too many directives from those who finance Luminato', Anderson argued, 'loom large' (64). The festival has retrenched in recent years, operating on a smaller budget than in its early days and focusing more on local work while also radically reducing or eliminating its previously signature free events along with its controversial initiatives targeting the city's marginalized neighbourhoods and housing projects.[8]

My experience of the festival in 2019, where I attended fifteen of the eighteen events in the evenings and weekends over seventeen days, was mixed. Half of the events were in some sense local, three of which were commissioned by the festival, one other being a world premiere, and the rest being work already in circulation or revived for the occasion.[9] Another half-dozen shows were from elsewhere in Canada, one of which was commissioned. The international shows included the Canadian premiere of *Flowers for Kazuo Ohno (and Leonard Cohen)*, a tribute to the Japanese Butoh master and Canadian poet/songwriter by the Colombian La Compañia del Cuerpo de Indias; the North American premiere of *Rite of Spring* by Yang Liping and her Peacock Contemporary Dance Company from China; the Canadian premiere of *Masquerade* by the Vakhtangov State Academic Theatre of Russia; and the Canadian premiere of *Triptych (Eyes of One Another)*, produced by New York's ArKtype/Thomas O. Kriegsmann. Most of the shows were presented or co-presented by individuals, foundations, or theatre companies in the city or, in the case of *Masquerade*, presented in conjunction with an already existing series, in this case the 'Stage Russia Series' by Show One Productions, which caters largely to a Russian émigré community in the city and would have included the show in its season with or without Luminato participation. *Rite of Spring* was produced for and by an international network of festivals in China, the UK, Australia, and the US.

The result was a festival that, apart from individual events that attracted specific Indigenous or expat communities, and apart from the participatory family basketball show *Monday Nights*, was not very festive, and certainly didn't seem to constitute festival attendees as a community. Indeed, the festival appeared, in my experience, to divide its audience, in a place that bills itself as 'the world's most multicultural city' and indeed is home to communities from almost every nation on earth, into the familiar silos of state multiculturalisms:[10] the turnout for *Masquerade* was overwhelmingly Russian Canadian, that for *Rite of Spring* about 50 per cent Asian, for Nicole Brooks's *Obeah Opera* Afro-Caribbean, and so on. And the co-producing companies from Toronto tended to bring their own discipline-based music, dance, or theatre audiences with them. The audience experience of the festival would seem to have been fragmented, with little geographical or temporal concentration, an audience base that was an overwhelmingly local one selecting individual shows rather than 'pilgrims' experiencing the festival as a coherent or inter-interrogative meta-event. Apart from festival organizers, I saw few of the same faces at more than one event, and artists, scheduled against one another in widely dispersed parts of the city over the festival's *longue durée*, had little opportunity to so much as see one another's work, much less engage in generative exchange. Indeed, in an interview with the online *Intermission* magazine, Toronto-based puppeteer Ronnie Burkett, a darling of the destination festival circuit whose *Forget Me Not* premiered at the 2019 Luminato as one of the festival's commissions, lamented, 'I'll be performing *Forget Me Not* for the entire duration of Luminato, so I won't be able to see other work' (Burkett).

Finally, although there were individual productions that engaged politically across cultural difference (of which more below), they were not programmed in such a way that they spoke to one another directly, and few of the shows could have ruffled even the most sensitive of corporate feathers. Mikhail Lermontov's Russian classic *Masquerade* at the cavernous and corporate Metro Convention Centre was a lavish and overwrought historical romance about jealousy in the snow; Burkett's *Forget Me Not* a perambulating, participatory puppet play about love that played, when I saw it, to an audience of primarily white seniors; and *Flowers for Kazuo Ohno (and Leonard Cohen)* a soothing meditation in music and dance about time and the creativity of old age. *The Full Light of Day*, the featured Canadian piece written by Daniel Brooks and directed by Kim Collier at the glitzy Bluma Appel Theatre, asked the audience to sympathize with a wealthy and corrupt white corporate family threatened by racialized bad guys while impressing spectators with a spectacular array of theatrical bells and whistles. Not much there to rock the boats of the funders or engage the majority white festival audience in anything beyond consumerist spectatorship.

Edinburgh, Interculturalism, and the Festival Circuit

> There is a kind of festival that's very prevalent now, it's arisen out of
> the combination of economic consideration and, I would say, lazy or
> sloppy curation, which is essentially shopping experiences, with the
> curator as personal shopper. They go around, they find stuff that they
> think you would like, they bring it to your doorstep, and that is their
> function. It has nothing to do with connecting artists with one
> another, it has nothing to do with connecting artists from other
> places with artists locally, and it may not even have to do with
> introducing new audiences to new work. Sometimes you go places
> and you feel like this festival audience was established years ago; it's x-
> thousand people, which is sufficient to sell the tickets and fill the
> venues, and that's the end of it. Those can be fun. I mean, I like
> seeing new work from other places, but if you see enough of those
> festivals they are really boring.
>
> (Frisch 52)

Most of the world's élite, or destination festivals in the twenty-first century
are programmed 'cafeteria-style' from a menu of itinerant shows, many of
which are, as Erika Fischer-Lichte observes, 'produced exclusively for the
global market without any local audience in mind' (*Routledge* 139). Such
shows tour from one festival to another in what has become constituted as
an 'international festival network' (Fricker 81), though commissioning and
co-producing within that network are also increasingly common (see
Portmann). Fischer-Lichte points to a 'festival aesthetic' that has developed
and is 'increasingly alienated from a local audience' (139), while Frédéric
Maurin suggests that 'the very existence of this [international festival]
circuit has given birth to highly marketable, pre-formatted productions
aiming to travel smoothly from one country to another, to please one
audience after another, yet running the risk of vapid blandness' (6).
Increasingly, moreover, in the early twenty-first century the global network
is constituted by a number of globally regional or continent-based festival
circuits or 'routes', as Owe Ronström calls them,

> a set of routes, both tangible and intangible, from simple paths to elaborate
> highways. Along these routes circulate artists, audiences, technicians, goods
> and services, but also ideas, economic models, forms of social behaviour
> (such as how to behave as artists and audience), representations (artefacts,
> images, props etc.), visibility, attention and recognition. Their interconnec-
> tedness and interdependence is a main source of the cultural energy that
> makes festivals attractive to so many. This makes access to the

interconnecting routes an important issue, which of course gives an espe-cially crucial role to the gatekeepers in festival organisations. (74)

Many of these routes, moreover, somewhat ominously reprise, or in Alvin Eng Hui Lim's phrase are 'haunted by' (63), earlier colonial trade and shipping routes and can now serve similar neocolonial functions and interests culturally, constituting what Yvette Hutchison calls 'circuits of empire' (158; see also Holledge, Thomasson, and Tompkins).

Edinburgh, Avignon, and their emulators have been 'destination' events for a very long time, but it was only in the early twenty-first century that the term was theorized in tourism and events management scholarship and in city planning in ways that have direct impact on the programming of the festivals and the experience of their audiences. The city of Edinburgh, for example, drew up its events strategies in order to consolidate its position specifically *as* a tourist destination in the early 2000s in a series of city planning documents focusing sequentially on the festival (2000), on tourism (2001), and on 'events strategy' (2002) (see Robertson and Wardrop 122–3). Bernadette Quinn, noting in 2005 that 'the use of the term "festival tourism" is increasing among tourism researchers' (933), teases out some of the causes and effects of this shift. She notes that in the context of globalization tourists have become increasingly mobile, and festivals are increasingly 'construed as entrepreneurial displays, as image creators capable of attracting significant flows of increasingly mobile capital, people, and services' (931). This has led, she argues, to a situation in which 'raising the city's international profile and attracting visitors seem to have become the *raison d'être* of the city festival' (932). And of course Edinburgh's festival strategy includes a concentration of festivals in August, when the EIF is joined, in the small city centre of what by world standards is a small, culturally homogeneous capital city (population ca 540,000, 92 per cent of which is white), by the Art, Tattoo, and Book Festivals as well as the mammoth Festival Fringe of which I write in Chapter 4. All of this taken together makes Edinburgh an irresistible draw for the cultural omnivores that make up the audience of the EIF, where according to Quinn, 'the emphasis is very much on the spectacular' (932). This in turn has led to a focus, in Edinburgh as elsewhere, on visitors rather than city residents, on the city's historic centre – the tourist neighbourhoods of the Old Town and New Town rather than its more diverse and downtrodden areas (Jamieson 72) – and on the increasing standardization of destination festivals following the same formulaic plan-ning models globally (see Doğan 78; Finkel 20). Ultimately it has led to

decreased artistic autonomy and a diminished capacity for challenge or
critique (see Quinn 934). By as early as 1996 George Steiner was calling
for the closing down of the EIF, which like other festivals, he argued, had
become 'a meaning free zone' (qtd in Martin, Seffrin, and Wissler 93).

What impact does all of this have on what Clive Barker calls 'the
possibilities and politics of intercultural penetration and exchange' at
festivals? Christina S. McMahon wrote in 2014 that 'international theatre
festivals epitomize the enhanced interconnectedness of cultures that characterizes our age of global circulation' while also posing 'significant obstacles to meaningful intercultural exchange' (2–3), and that is one of the
tensions this chapter explores. In practice, at the level of the destination
festivals, at least – although as Julie Holledge and Joanne Tompkins point
out, 'Intercultural theatre is a lucrative drawcard for international arts
festivals, particularly when one of the intercultural partners can claim
'exotic' background' (153) – real cultural difference tends not to be very
prominently on display, and when it is, it tends very much to be for the
purpose of display rather than dialogue. Helen Gilbert and Jacqueline Lo
observed in 2007 that 'cross-cultural theatre increasingly functions as a
signifier of the cosmopolitan credentials of international arts festivals'
(105) – signs of their sophisticated pluralism that are often little more
than empty signifiers. Many festivals, in fact, particularly those in the
English-speaking world, and most particularly the EIF, have significantly
retreated from even linguistic difference, intuiting or perhaps assuming
their audiences' aversion to surtitles, or worse, untranslated 'foreign'
languages, even European ones. When 'the foreign' appears at such festivals, moreover, it is most often taken out of the social, historical, and
cultural context for which it was created and within which it has meaning,
and is thereby reduced to having either a purely formalist or detached
exoticist interest (Knowles, *Reading* 182–8). Barker provides the example
of watching *Niugini-Niugini*, by New Guinea's Raun-Raun Theater,
which was designed to be played in the clearings of jungle villages, 'in a
cold church hall in Edinburgh, amid an elderly Scottish audience, at an
afternoon performance', leaving him with 'a sense of numbed culture
shock which deadened any understanding that might have been possible.
In this as in other cases', he says, 'there was no shared context which would
allow any meeting or meaningful exchange' (249–50). He concludes that
'what works best in festivals ... is either what is very close to the homegrown production style or some work of exotic beauty which can be
appreciated visually, with little or no regard given to its content or cultural
significance' (250).

Holledge and Tompkins have usefully pointed to three different cultural contexts that are at play and in conversation (or tension) within the destination festival circuit: (1) 'cultural milieu': 'the cultural milieu or social sphere in which the festival is located' (153), including local participating or non-participating populations (the latter usually non-white or working-class) that are impacted or displaced by the event; (2) 'culture': the 'dominant cultural heritage' of the host country (154), including its national borders and dominant ethnic categories; and (3) 'Culture', or 'high culture': the art forms 'perceived to be artistically superior to more populist genres' (154). Festivals, they argue, 'are often assumed to be celebrations of culture (and Culture)': they 'isolate, frame, translate, and market culture as exoticized difference by producing, re-distributing, and selling performance' in a marketplace where 'a culturally identified commodity product in performance sometimes comes to be recognized as a metonym for a culture' (157). Thus Culture comes to represent culture, and national 'high-culture' artefacts come to stand in for essentialized differences at a national level: *kathakali* quickly becomes 'Indian dance', becomes India; *wayang kulit* becomes Balinese dance, becomes Bali, or even Asia; and so on, as cafeteria-style programming from an international 'best-of' menu morphs into the display and reification of supposed cultural 'essences' for tourist consumption or for expatriate communities in diaspora who tend to turn out in full force out of a sense of compensatory nostalgia for a homeland that never was. Meanwhile, Culture displaces or marginalizes cultural milieu: the cultural differences celebrated by the festival, as Kirstie Jamieson argues of the EIF, 'privilege the dominant interests of the wealthy cultural pilgrims who seek the palatable and traditional otherness', while the diversity that constitutes the local in many festival cities is obscured or disregarded and 'those *communities* identified by their peripheral housing estate rather than their cultural tastes are written off the map of the City of Festivals' (72, emphasis in original). 'Most arts festivals', Holledge and Tompkins conclude, 'set out to present intercultural performance as a showcase of how cultures might intersect and interact, but the underlying financially driven structure of any festival and the resulting commodification of its art forms generally compromises the best intentions to promote interculturalism' (158–9).

But must it be this way? Is it always? Writing in 2003 and 2005 Jen Harvie has twice examined charges against the EIF for being élitist, once concerning the festival's founding and early history ('Cultural Effects') and once regarding its more recent relationship to globalization (*Staging*

74–111). Part of her argument in both writings is that the festival *has* been élitist in its programing from the outset, but she posits that early on its élitism allowed it the privilege of presenting European plays untranslated in their original languages, thereby presenting and promoting a crucial type of cultural difference, however geographically limited ('Cultural Effects' 20). Later in its history, Harvie contends, the festival's 'European elitism' allowed it to fend off American-style globalization understood as 'Disneyfication' or 'McDonaldization' (*Staging* 81–2, 90–4). Neither of these arguments has continued to hold true: as I write even surtitles are rare at the EIF,[11] much less untranslated European or other languages, and while, if the stereotypically worst effects of globalization may be somewhat held at bay, the festival's participation in the globalized festivalization of culture proceeds apace. Harvie does, however, point to the possibilities that the EIF might 'also provide the opportunity for artists to develop their work in ways that are not encouraged in their domestic contexts', including international co-productions, given the festival's wealth (*Staging* 99–100). But the examples she gives are intercultural only among white-identified artists within the UK and Europe, and recent festivals have extended that reach primarily only as far as the United States, also among white artists.[12] When the Festival does include subtitled, non-European shows, it is often in smaller spaces for limited runs, as when *Voicelessness*, an intricate dystopian show by Iranian director, writer, and performer Azade Shahmiri, was performed only twice during the three-week duration of the 2017 festival, in Farsi with English surtitles, at the Festival Theatre's 'intimate' – meaning low-capacity – space, The Studio. And in the same year the 'New and Now' series of International Plays from the Royal Court Theatre in London was limited to a week of hour-long, low-profile morning readings in translation, also at The Studio.

But for the most part the situation described by David Graver and Loren Kruger in 1993, in one of the few essays to have been devoted to the question of interculturalism at the Edinburgh festivals or any of the destination festivals, remains more or less in place almost thirty years later. They depicted both Edinburgh festivals (the EIF and the Fringe) as dominated by 'crude parochialism', on the one hand, and 'bland multicultural mist', on the other, with only a few exceptions in which 'successful integrations of regional and international concerns recognized their specific locality (both theatrical and social) . . . as a forum where local interests can meet foreign influences on an equitable footing' (71). Among their most evocative examples was a production of *Yo tengo un tío en América* in which audiences were invited, in the context of a psychiatric clinic, to imagine the life of Indigenous peoples in the Americas before the arrival of Columbus. It was created, however, by a company from Catalonia and spoke most directly, if allegorically, to European (Catalan) concerns (see 83–4). A still more evocative example was performed on the huge proscenium stage of the Lyric Theatre at the 2014 festival. *Ganesh Versus the Third Reich*, by Australia's Back to Back Theatre (including actors from disability cultures), featured the elephant-headed god Ganesh travelling through Nazi Germany to reclaim the Swastika as an ancient Hindu symbol. This epic intercultural metadrama probed risky cross-cultural issues touching on disability culture ('freak porn'), anti-semitism ('the Jew stuff'), the appropriation of cultural and religious symbols, and the ethics of theatrical representation (Waterfield 237–8). As *Guardian* reviewer Brigid Delaney remarked, 'it's not a cozy production'. But it toured to festivals around the world and is an example of provocative intercultural work that even destination festivals such as the EIF can productively host in the globalized twenty-first century.[13]

But does the simple one-off presentation of complex intercultural productions suffice to move festivals *as meta-events* beyond the dictates of the neoliberal marketplace and initiate meaningful dialogue and exchange across significant difference? For audiences, the experience of the EIF itself is of the very occasional 'unfamiliar' show amidst a festival experience overwhelmingly dominated by European high culture, classical music, opera, and dance at upscale venues mixed, for most visitors, with 'slumming' at the free-market Fringe, as discussed in Chapter 4. And for artists, unfortunately, scheduling at the EIF as at most destination festivals ensures that most shows arrive, set up, perform, strike, and leave without the artists ever having had the opportunity to see the rest of the work at the festival, much less engage with performers from other cultures working in other styles or grounded in other epistemologies or cosmologies. There are rarely public or private sessions scheduled at the EIF or other élite festivals in which artists compare notes or exchange ideas and insights, and opportunities for local artists and audiences to engage with visitors beyond the promotional or press conference level are rare. In 2019, however, the EIF in partnership with the British Council and the University of Edinburgh's Futures Institute, staged the 'You Are Here' programme, which not only involved productions by eight companies representing Scottish, Irish, Nigerian, Malian, Lebanese, Canadian, Indigenous, and disability cultures, but engaged them in 'behind-the-scenes' professional programmes about 'what local, national, and international citizenship might mean in the twenty-first century' (Edinburgh International Festival 35). There was also a public component to this series, including 'breaking bread' conversations with artists, 'Saturday sessions' to discuss issues facing artists, and a 'morning manifesto' that was up, at least notionally, for public debate. Developments such as this have the potential to begin to move the destination festivals beyond the serial representation of exotic, othered cultures towards a more genuinely new critical cosmopolitanism.

The Festival d'Avignon, too, in spite of an enduring Eurocentrism, a failure through most of its history adequately or appropriately to represent work from its former colonies (as I discuss in Chapter 5), and, as the *New York Times* complained in 2018, an overwhelming masculinism (Capelle), has made recent efforts under the directorship of Olivier Py to diversify its interests. Within France, ever since its purposefully ex-centric founding outside of the Parisian metropole, Avignon has always had a reputation for being 'un festival résolument politique' (Loyer and de Baecque 587), and it has periodically dedicated itself to a 'renewed cosmopolitanism' (Turk 279). In 2006 it explicitly set out to examine 'the enduring worldwide impact of colonialism' (Turk 298), and since Py took over leadership in 2014 has turned away from what had become an emphasis on formalist experimentation by star European directors and returned to a more political focus. In 2019 it dedicated much of its programme to hot political issues such as conflict between the artist and the state (*OUTSIDE*, by Russian dissident director Kirill Serebrennikov), migration, and rising ethnic and other nationalisms within the new Europe. But the small provincial city of Avignon (population ca 95,000), unlike Paris, is overwhelmingly white, as are the preponderance of visitors who attend the festival, and while it is perhaps ex-centric geographically within France, its focus remains largely national.

In addition to work by immigrants from former French colonies in Africa, however, as discussed in Chapter 5, the 2019 programme at Avignon featured British Bangladeshi choreographer Akram Khan's *Outwitting the Devil* at the prestigious Palais des Papes venue. The show was based on a fragment of *The Epic of Gilgamesh* discovered in Iraq in 2011, in which an elderly Gilgamesh, confronting his own mortality, watches himself as an arrogant young man destroying a cedar forest and the habitat that it shelters. Khan's choreography adroitly and beautifully blended contemporary western dance styles with those of Kathak and Bharatanatyam from India, but the show's political focus was softened by its mythical frame and in any case had more to do with environmental than intercultural issues and read as exotic in the medieval environs of central Avignon. More directly representing and enacting encounters across cultures within France were *MAHMOUND & NINI*, written and directed by Henri Jules Julien, and *Place*, by Iraqi-born playwright Tamara Al Saadi. The former was designed, according to its director, as 'an experiment in prejudices' (qtd in Meerzon), in which a Black, gay Egyptian man speaking Arabic and a white French woman speaking French aired their received opinions about one another's cultures to the audience, interacting only occasionally when they rose from their chairs to perform short dance sequences. The latter told the story of a young French-speaking woman, Yasmine, who suddenly finds herself emerging from the Métro in Paris unable to comprehend the signs that surround her. She is aided by a mysterious girl who translates for her and leads her through scenes from her childhood in Iraq, where she encounters her double, who only speaks Arabic. Both these shows addressed directly the increasing racial tensions and confusions within France in the century's second decade that have occasionally surfaced in horrific events such as the Charlie Hebdo shootings in January 2015, which was explicitly cited in *MAHMOUD & NINI* – and both shows did so directly through the evocation of language barriers. Perhaps it is cultural tensions and negotiations within France itself rather than across national borders that the Festival d'Avignon is best positioned to address, if only from its privileged position outside of the multiracial metropole.

The Adelaide Festival

The destination festival, founded in 1960, that was most directly modelled on the Edinburgh International Festival takes place half a world away, in Adelaide, South Australia. Adelaide (population ca 1.4 million) is larger than Edinburgh, and unlike its northern-hemispheric counterpart is a determinedly regular, planned city, but it is also predominantly white, its population being of almost 90 per cent European ancestry, and it boasts, as I've indicated in Chapter 1, a proudly 'free settler' heritage. Like Edinburgh's, too, its festival takes place in a month crowded with others, including Adelaide Writer's Week, the 'Garden of Unearthly Delights' amusement park, WOMADelaide music festival, and the Adelaide Fringe discussed in Chapter 4. Unlike the EIF and its Fringe, however, the Adelaide Festival and Fringe do not together constitute a hectic round for theatregoers, in that they compete with one another for evening and weekend time slots, leaving residents' working hours intact and visitors' weekday schedules open for other forms of tourism. The Adelaide Festival participates every February–March in the international festival network and is considered to be 'the jewel in the crown' of the Australian circuit (Thomasson, 'Jewel') – what Helen Gilbert and Jacqueline Lo call its 'capital city festival loop' (90). Australia is of interest here in part because of its significant Indigenous population – all of its festivals take place on occupied Indigenous territory – and in part because it was the second country in the world, after Canada, to adopt an official policy of multi-culturalism, though successive conservative governments since the 1970s have shifted their emphasis away from that term towards a more indeter-minate emphasis on 'diversity' (see Thomasson, 'Producing' 253–61). The Australian government has a nation-reifying stake in the support and promotion of the country's festival network, which Sarah Thomasson argues constitutes a de facto decentralized Australian national theatre ('Australian' 133). In 2006 the government launched its ongoing 'Major Festivals Initiative' through the Australia Council for the Arts, explicitly designed to support 'the commissioning, development and showcasing of new Australian performing arts productions of scale for Australia's major international arts festivals' (Australian Government 3). That this initiative has precisely to do with the nation-building and branding potential of 'major' festivals operating at 'scale' is clear from its stated goal to 'strengthen Australia's reputation as a sophisticated and artistic nation with a confident, outward-focused arts sector' (3). Its purpose is also clear from an assessment and delivery system operated through the Confederation of Australian International Arts Festivals, which includes the Adelaide, Brisbane, Darwin, Melbourne, Perth, Sydney, and Ten Days on the Island Festivals that are the initiative's direct beneficiaries.[14] It does not include any of the many smaller festivals, excluding culturally specific or intercultural ones such as Adelaide's OzAsia Festival, which focuses on the Asian presence within Australia. Hosted by the capital city of South Australia, the so-called 'festival state', and the most globally prominent of the Australian festivals, the Adelaide Festival may be considered to be representative of the Australian circuit.[15]

Writing of the Adelaide Festival at the time of its founding in 1960, I.I. Kavass identified the formula for successful international festivals that had developed by that time, and that Adelaide followed: attractive location, a multi-arts programme combining the conventional with the 'challenging', a generous sprinkling of international celebrity, and the co-operation of local artists and support people to do the grunt work (8). This formula has remained essentially in place at Adelaide as at many destination festivals, though an extra element – an appetizing sampling of the exotic – was added early on. Like those of most of the Australian festivals, Adelaide's most direct engagements with the intercultural have traditionally come through productions from Asian or Aboriginal and Torres Strait Island peoples and most often have to do with the negotiation of distinct Australian national identities. I have discussed efforts to Indigenize the Adelaide, Sydney, and Perth Festivals in Chapter 1, so I will focus here on interactions between Adelaide, Asia, and Adelaide's own Asian population at a time when Australia had, however intermittently, shifted its global economic policy away from Europe towards its neighbours in the Asia-Pacific region. In 2007 Helen Gilbert and Jacqueline Lo described moments at which key Asian forms and methods were introduced to Australian festival audiences through the Adelaide Festival – Japanese *bunraku* puppetry in 1972 (91); Vietnamese water puppetry in 1988 (94); *wayang kulit* (Indonesian shadow puppetry) and its sister form *wayang golek* (three-dimensional puppetry) in 1988 (95–6); and the Suzuki Method of acting in 1992 (155). Asian shows programmed in the festival's early decades, however, tended to be framed within what Gilbert and Lo call 'the well-worn vocabularies of pictorial orientalism', while towards the end of the twentieth century Asian work was interpreted, recontextualized, and decoded according to an 'assimilationist' agenda (115) and the city's 9.4 per cent Asian population has never been significantly in evidence at the festival. Gilbert and Lo focus their analysis on the 1994 so-called 'Asia' festival at Adelaide, where 50 per cent of the programming was from East Asia and the Western Pacific, blending traditional and avant-garde works but eschewing text-based modern productions and risking 'authorizing the image of Asia as *spectacle*' (119, emphasis in original). The festival's 'showcasing' of Asia in its first four decades, then, 'was not conducive to deeper forms of cross-cultural communication' (119), and in subsequent years, as the Australian government's Asian initiatives were redirected, the festival's Asian focus declined.

In the first two decades of the twenty-first century those shows that did appear at the festival were often generative examples of either the representation of cultural difference through culturally specific formal elements, or the productive practice of cross-cultural collaboration. In 2007 and 2012, for example, the Cloud Gate Dance Theatre of Taiwan presented choreographer Lin Hwai-min's dance pieces, *Cursive 1* and *Water Stains on the Wall*, respectively, that explored movement patterns based on the culturally specific embodied rhythms of the creation of Chinese calligraphy (see Tonkin). In 2013, *Doku Rai* exemplified the virtues of cross-cultural collaboration between Australia's Whaling Firm and Black Lung Theatre and the Timor-Leste collectives Liurai Fo'er and Galaxy. The show opened the festival with an energetic and visually stunning presentation in English and Tetum about family, culture, and competition that was created collaboratively by twenty members of the companies during an immersive retreat in remote Timor (see House).

But such work was not common at the festivals in this period, in spite of one of the four goals of the Australian Council for the Arts' 2014–19 plan being the promotion of cultural diversity in the arts. This may be in part because Adelaide Festival audiences are the most uniformly white of any festival I have attended, the city's population is aging, and the organizers have felt the need appeal to that audience. More charitably, it may have to do with the fact that since 2007 the Adelaide Festival Centre has also presented, over two weeks in the spring season, the important annual OzAsia Festival, explicitly dedicated to fostering cultural exchange, which presumably siphoned off shows that might otherwise have appeared at the Adelaide Festival itself as well as audiences that might have attended them. The 2019 programme at OzAsia, which, however, is not part of the Confederation of Australian International Arts Festivals and therefore has played no role in the selection of projects funded by the Major Festivals Initiative, consisted of nine shows plus art exhibitions and installations. The shows included the commissioned world premiere of *Light*, by Thomas Henning and TerryandTheCuz, co-produced with Malaysia's George Town Festival, which was unfortunately performed without its set (which was quarantined in Malaysia) and with only one technical rehearsal. But the show was an appropriately collaborative, appropriately 'unsettling' revisionist history of Francis Light, the British father who claimed Penang for Britain, his unrecognized wife Martina Rozells, and their so-called illegitimate 'Eurasian' son William, who later founded and mapped out the ever-so-regular city of Adelaide's central grid, square, and park system that organizes festivalgoers' experiences to this day. Other shows included Indian theatre-maker Abhishek Thapar's genuinely intercultural *Surpassing the Beeline*, an immersive performance/conversation involving food and the role of cultural traditions; Jaha Koo's quirky anti-capitalist show, *Cuckoo*, described at length in Chapter 3; and the clever but not notably Asian board-game-inspired £¥€$ *(Lies)*, an immersive, interactive piece about the global financial system by Belgium's Ontroerend Goed, marketed at OzAsia as a Belgium/Hong Kong collaboration. Ironically, however, given explicit attacks on global neoliberalism marshalled by shows such as *Cuckoo* and £¥€$, the festival forfeited the opportunity to prioritize meaningful conversations and negotiations across real and pressing issues around interculturalism and immigration in an

Australia whose official policies are often xenophobic, by aligning the festival in 2019 with the inaugural Asia-Pacific 'Creative Cities' conference, with all of the neoliberal baggage that term carries.

Asian presence at the Adelaide Festival itself when I attended in 2020 was limited to the transnational collaboration *Between Tiny Cities* រវាងទីក្រុងតូច, choreographed by Australia's Nick Power, which offered an inspiring model and image of intercultural negotiation through the mediation of international b*boy culture. Dancers Aaron Lim, from Darwin in Australia's Northern Territory, and Erak Mith, from Phnom Penh, Cambodia, wearing jeans, t-shirts, and sneakers, occupied a taped-out circle in a converted factory space. Surrounded by a standing audience crowding the edge of the circle, they began tentatively, with delicate movements unusual in the b*boy genre, as they tested one another, seeking common ground before building to the more familiar energy of competitive hip-hop, albeit with considerable humour and grace as they grew in admiration for each other's skill. This phase of the performance culminated in a long, suspended moment in which the dancers stood side-by side, perspiring and breathing heavily from exertion as they perused one another with sideways glances. The dance then moved into a phase that felt like real, embodied negotiation across difference, as they moved supplely to text spoken by Mith in Khmer with rhythms resembling nursery rhyme, and finally danced together, in constant contact through the backs of their hands, in what registered as a close and even tender friendship. 'Much of the dance', as reviewer Michael Jarque wrote of a performance of the show in Sydney, 'is an exploration of how two very different dancers in build and style – one dancer significantly taller and broader than the Cambodian hip hopper – try to engage with each other as they seek to bridge the fundamental cultural and geographical gap through the universal language of hip hop' (see Figure 6). Exhibiting impressive athleticism, the show also seemed to use what is now a transnational movement vocabulary joyously to celebrate what I read as friendship across real but negotiated difference. And in fact, the show was the productive culmination of a four-year dance exchange between Darwin's D*City Rockers and Cambodia's Tiny Toones youth programme, and it toured internationally to the Darwin, George Town, Hong Kong, Noorderzon (Groningen, Netherlands), and Sziget (Budapest) Festivals and beyond. The afternoon I saw the performance in Adelaide standing among a class of teenaged students it served as an animated, youthful break from classical European choral music in staid local churches and high-profile international shows at the Festival Centre, where backpacks were not permitted in

Figure 6   Between *Tiny Cities* រាង ទី ក្រ ង ក្ម ច offered an inspiring model and image of
intercultural negotiation through the mediation of international
b*boy culture. Photograph by Pippa Simaya.

the fashionable venues, cash was not accepted at the bars, and polite
festival protocols prevailed.

The Shows of the Destination Festival Circuit

Any theatre or other type of festival is experienced by audiences in large
part as the accumulation of individual shows that constitute it. It may,
then, be worth considering what *kinds* of intercultural performance the
world's élite festival circuits enable, what kinds of interplay among those
performances they facilitate, what kind of meta-event they cumulatively
constitute, and what the components are of a destination festival that
successfully enables intercultural exchange. Three of the most common
strategies used on the circuit are the production, translation, or adaptation
of canonical works, the eschewing of spoken text and the subsequent need
for surtitles in favour of wordless spectacle or dance, and the presentation
of international or cross-cultural collaborations and co-productions.

The most familiar inter-, or more often cross-cultural work at festivals of
all kinds has since the earliest post-war festivals been productions of

western classics, often Shakespeare, by non-western directors such as Tadashi Suzuki and On Keng Sen, or productions of 'Eastern' classics such as *The Mahabharata* by western directors such as Peter Brook. Most of these shows have been celebrated in the west, many have been critiqued as appropriative during the 'interculture wars' of the 1980s and 1990s (Knowles, *Theatre & Interculturalism* 23), and most constitute what Daphne Lei has call 'HIT' (hegemonic intercultural theatre) – 'a specific artistic genre and state of mind that combines First World Capital and brainpower with Third World raw material and labor, and Western classical texts with Eastern performance traditions' (571).

Problematic 'intercultural' productions helmed by dominant-culture directors and creative teams have not, of course, disappeared from the destination festival circuit, and many of their problematics now revolve around ill-conceived variations on non-traditional, colour-blind, or what Brandi Wilkins Catanese prefers to call 'nonconforming' casting (18). An epic, five-and-a-half-hour revival at the Perth Festival in 2020 of *Cloudstreet*, Nick Enright and Justin Monjo's 1998 adaptation of a modern Australian classic, the 1991 Tim Winton novel, and an earlier destination festival success, might serve as a current example. The original production of the show was widely read as a local story *and* national allegory, with its two central families inhabiting #1 Cloud Street, Perth, representing two (white) Australian archetypes, the hardworking battler and the lazy but loveable larrikin, and the house – a former Anglican mission for Aboriginal girls – standing in for the nation. The original show was criticized, also widely, for its relegation of Indigenous presence within the allegory to a kind of guilt haunting the presumptively white nation, a haunting that is ultimately exorcised by the birth of a (white) child that brings the families – the nation – together (see Thomasson, 'Australian' 140–1). The revival, as reviewer Zoe Barron wrote, was 'spruced with diversity' by director Matthew Lutton, whose solution when I saw it in Perth in 2020 was to decorate the production with bits of Nyungar (the Noongar language), amplify the presence of the 'others' that haunt the eponymous house, and cast one of the families as mixed race.[16] Unfortunately, but perhaps not surprisingly, it was not the humble but respectable battler figure, Lester Lamb, but Sam, the indolent patriarch of the Pickles family, who was cast as Blak (Indigenous), as were his troublemaking progeny – all except his daughter Rose, the play's most empathetic character who gives birth to the redemptive child. The revisioning, presumably intended to redress the earlier production's problems and strengthen the synecdoche of the house-as-nation, both reinforced harmful stereotypes and caused confusion. As reviewer Tim Byrne observed when the show opened in Melbourne, the amplified Indigenous presence haunting the inhabitants of the house 'cuts against the racial diversity inside that house', making the haunting puzzling. None of the creative team apart from two cast members in minor roles identified as Indigenous, and there was no cultural consultant indicated in the show's programme. On the opening night when I saw the show, few of Perth's ca 32,000 Indigenous residents appeared to be in attendance at what felt like a gathering of the city's social élite, turned out in all their finery at the Edwardian His Majesty's Theatre on a street named after the nineteenth-century Permanent Secretary for the Colonies, Robert William Hay.

A perhaps more damaging example, working against genuine intercultural understanding while seeming to promote it, was the casting of *The Doctor*, the Almeida Theatre, London adaptation of Arthur Schnitzler's 1912 Austrian classic, *Professor Bernhardi*, which was featured as a headliner at the Adelaide Festival in 2020 and requires some careful unpacking. English director Robert Icke practised what might best be called 'surreptitious nonconforming casting' in ways that were surprising, innovative, and, in their application, insidious. The show, generically a problem play, relied on its audience initially reading characters according to the traditional semiotics of gender and skin colour, and later being 'surprised' – and in one key instance not being informed at all – with revelations that characters had been purposefully cast against such readings.

The Schnitzler source text begins with a male, Jewish doctor refusing a Catholic priest access to a patient after she has received an abortion, on the grounds that it will cause the patient undue suffering to realize that she is dying. *The Doctor* begins the same way, except that the title character, Ruth Wolff, is now a secular Jew and is played brilliantly and sympathetically by star-power white actor Juliet Stevenson as a woman. The audience sees her refuse access to a white male priest. Only later in the play, after Dr. Wolff has been viciously accused of racism, is it 'revealed' that the priest, whom we have experienced as white, is Black, bolstering the doctor's defense that she doesn't 'see colour' (see Figure 7). The audience hadn't either. Similarly, two colleagues who take her side in the play's debates are played by Black actors who are later revealed to be white, and in one case, Jewish. Meanwhile, a hiring process is underway at the clinic run by Wolff, who champions excellence in the form of a Jewish female applicant over a demonstrably inferior Catholic favoured by Wolff's denigrators, who argue that his hiring will defuse an escalating controversy and save the clinic's funding. That the audience is clearly meant to understand

Figure 7   In *The Doctor*, presented at the Adelaide Festival in 2020, the audience
encountered the play's Catholic priest as played by white actor Jamie Parker, only later
learning that the character was Black. Photograph by Tony Lewis.

that the candidate promoted by the play's tragic heroine is 'just a better
doctor' who happens also to be a Jewish woman, again prejudices the
debate. As Brandi Catanese has demonstrated, the ideals of not seeing
colour, and the transcendence of race, particularly when promoted
through non-traditional, nonconforming, or colour-blind casting, are dangerous chimeras: 'asking (usually nonwhite) people to transcend racial
consciousness' – to not see colour – 'is usually just a more polite way of
demanding that they "get over it"' (Catanese 21). Representing a key
character in the play as heroic *because* she supposedly doesn't see colour
and casting the show in such a way that the audience is tricked into
being similarly colourblind, is dangerously, and surreptitiously, to imbal-
ance the scales. It is, indeed, to practise what Ju Yon Kim calls 'colour-
blind racism' (141).

  Reviewers of the show when it first opened in London observed that the
non-traditional casting was both pervasive and random – Ruth Saville in
Time Out saying that 'each actor is deliberately cast outside their identity'
('Doctor'). But not all actors in fact *were* so cast; the casting was much

more selective and more covertly purposeful than Saville would suggest.[17] Two roles that were not cross-cast, for example, were those of Ruth Wolff's clearly excessive and unsympathetic accusers at a television debate, women of colour played by women of colour who came across as stereotypically angry and imbalanced, viciously and unfairly attacking a flawed – she was arrogant – but fundamentally good character (also not cast against phenotype) and aligning themselves as fellow panellists with anti-vaccinators and the fundamentalist religious right. One Black interrogator was introduced as a postcolonialist sociologist, eliciting immediate guffaws from audience members in Adelaide the night I attended. A final straw in this camel's back was the casting of Ruth Wolff's life partner, whom we saw throughout as a younger Black woman named 'Charlie', seeming to deflect any suggestion that Wolff has prejudices based on gender, sexuality, or skin colour. But there was no 'reveal' about the actual gender, race, or sexuality of Charlie, as there were of those of other characters, and the audience was left uncertain, if they considered the question at all. The theatrical deck here was clearly stacked to present a case for 'excellence' against the supposed excesses of the 'politically correct' in what was carefully constructed as the tragedy of a woman more sinned against than sinning.

And it worked. Predominantly white critics with the cultural authority of Michael Billington stated without equivocation that the play's competing arguments were 'handled with exemplary fairness' – a view the show invited, which, of course, is what made the casting strategies so insidious. That the play, directed by a white Englishman with a white creative team, was brought to the prime, upscale venue of a major international festival by its two white artistic directors where it was well received by an overwhelmingly white audience and press corps is not surprising, but it does, perhaps, suggest that plays exploring contemporary issues around race, gender, sexuality, and representation require a less imbalanced representation of artists in positions of creative control if they wish genuinely to present more balanced arguments.[18]

Adaptations of classics have most often been interculturally effective when they have involved minoritized groups claiming the cultural authority of western 'masters'. I discussed a recent example in Chapter 1, Yirra Yaakin Theatre Company's *Hecate*, an adaptation of Shakespeare's *Macbeth* that served as an effective assertion of the strength, complexity, and value of Noongar culture and language. As I write in March 2020, *Hecate* has been performed only at the Perth Festival in Noongar territory before an overwhelmingly wedjela (white) audience. Another recent large-scale and high-profile example from the 2018 Shanghai International Arts

Festival, however, toured in 2019 to the Edinburgh International Festival, the Luminato, Brisbane, and Melbourne Festivals, and beyond. Yang Liping's *Rite of Spring*, by the Peacock Contemporary Dance Company, is at once an Asian adaptation of a western classic, a show created specifically for the destination festival circuit, and a powerful, wordless dance/spectacle that in Toronto attracted white settler and Asian Canadian audiences, when I saw it, in about equal proportions. The show was both a remarkably beautiful spectacle employing familiar exoticist tropes and a coherent inter- and intracultural intellectual and aesthetic reinterpretation of the Stravinsky classic.

When I first entered the Macmillan Theatre at the University of Toronto's Faculty of Music at the Luminato Festival in June 2019 and saw twelve dancer/deities seated in the lotus position wearing colourful costumes and headdresses and seeming to observe the audience with outsized eyes painted on their closed eyelids, while a Buddhist 'Lama' carefully arranged large golden Chinese ideograms in blocks around the stage, I was tempted to vacate the premises before the show had properly started. Undeniably beautiful, this seemed like a familiar kind of orientalist exoticization. As the show developed, however, it became apparent that it was a fully thought-through and redemptive Buddhist overwriting of the sacrificial narrative of the Stravinsky–Nijinsky original. The show was created and directed by ethnic-minority Chinese Bai choreographer Yang Liping from Dali in China's Yunnan province, whose dance traditions mingle in the production with echoes of Pina Bausch. The Stravinsky score was bookended by entirely contemporary music by internationally award-winning composer Xuntian He, inspired by Tibetan traditions. He, a professor at Shanghai Conservatory of Music, is accredited with being the creator of new musical languages and methods of composition ('Xuntian'), but his score seamlessly complemented and completed the original Stravinsky composition. The stunning visual iconography by award-winning scenic artist Tim Yip was drawn from traditional Buddhist and contemporary Chinese art (see Figure 8).[19] As a whole, the Peacock Contemporary Dance Company production engaged intellectually, emotionally, and aesthetically with intracultural strands within China as well as with Stravinsky's western modernist classic to create something that to me and to Toronto's culturally diverse audiences, was entirely new. No claims were made to static authenticities or even syncretic hybridities, and there were no reifying gestures towards 'pure' forms; rather, the show entered into dynamic conversations between living and changing traditions and artistic practices. It was a costly show to mount and tour, it required

Figure 8   Yang Liping's *Rite of Spring* is at once an Asian adaptation of a western classic, a show created specifically for the destination festival circuit, and a powerful, wordless dance/ spectacle. Photograph by Mikhail Logvinov.

large and well-equipped venues, and was the kind of show that only a large and well-funded festival on the destination circuit could support.

The ubiquitous intercultural productions of classics, usually western, at destination festivals – some of them individually culturally productive, some reproductive – are, I suggest, cumulatively experienced by festival-goers primarily as reflections of their 'universal' status and adaptability. When such productions form a critical mass of the intercultural work at the premium venues (with premium ticket prices) at any festival as meta-event, as they most often do at the world's élite festivals, they can only be experienced as the standard-bearers of (colonialist) western high culture.

Also familiar at destination festivals are shows that eschew text in favour what is often understood to be the universal language of dance, which can, of course, function in purely formalist ways or can devolve into mere spectacle, often as the folkloric or exoticist display of the 'ethnic' other. But it would be a mistake to dismiss the efficacy of the multiple languages and embodiments of dance as flexible and effective tools for cross-cultural encounter. I have already discussed the ways in which Nick Power's

Between Tiny Cities រាឯទីក្រុងតូច used dance to model intercultural negotiation in exemplary ways at Adelaide in 2020. Another example from the same festival, *Black Velvet*, by Shamel Pitts and Mirelle Martins, however, was equally compelling but perhaps more complex at the level of reception. Pitts, an African American dancer and choreographer from Brooklyn, trained in Israel in the Gaga method with the Batsheva Dance Company and danced with Batsheva for six years; Martins, a performance artist from Brazil, trained in New York City with Pitts. Together they created a compelling piece that appeared at first to be purely formalist – Martins standing at an impossible height above the stage, a fifteen-foot skirt draping from her waist to the floor below, her otherwise nude body sculpted by side light and anointed with gold as she rocked her arms gently to the sound of tinkling bells, as if cradling a baby. When she descended and joined Pitts on floor level, however, the dance developed into an intricate exploration of the nuances of the creators' cross-cultural relationship, veering between interdependence and rejection, pleasure and pain, the intimate and the inscrutable. But the nudity, the luminescence of the golden makeup on Black skin performed in Adelaide before a predominantly white audience (I saw one young Black woman in the house) lent the show more than a whiff of voyeuristic exoticism; festival reviewers, white and male, riffed rhapsodically on 'the gleaming muscular bodies of co-creators Shamel Pitts and Mirelle Martins ... dressed alike in short skirts, topless' (Brissenden). And as one of the few representations of the 'other' at the festival it was, like the Yolŋu show *Buŋgal*, discussed in Chapter 1, performed well outside of Adelaide's central grid at the Odeon Theatre in the suburb of Norwood, far from the Festival's geographical and symbolic Centre.

Dance and physical theatre at destination festivals, then, do have the capacity to bypass linguistic silos and 'speak' across difference. But when performed by racialized and ethnic 'others' they are often also experienced by dominant-culture festival audiences as exoticized spectacle, ethnic or even folkloric display by the stereotypically silenced: enjoyable, even titillating on occasion, they can serve to spice up a festival but rarely to occasion serious dialogue or negotiation across cultural difference.

A final familiar element of the destination festival circuit that has lent festivals a certain cachet while promising productive cross-cultural encounter is the international co-production, made appealing to organizers because their costs can be amortized across two or more festivals. Indeed, Alexandra Portmann argues that scholars need to recognize 'an emerging model of festival production that ... is increasingly involved in dynamic

networks of global co-production among festivals, artists and other institutions' (51). Portmann provides a case study of the embeddedness within
an international festival co-production network of Philippines-based performing artist Eisa Jocson's *Happyland* trilogy. Jocson's work, which
'investigates the role of Philippine labour in a migratory context, the
production and commercialization of happiness, and the role of gender
and racial stereotypes in entertainment industries' (Portmann 43), was
generated through partnerships with curators in Singapore, Hong Kong,
Belgium, and Zürich. It has appeared at the Zürcher Theater Spektakel, La
Bâtie-Festival (Geneva), and Internationales Sommerfestival Kampnagel
(Hamburg), among other festivals, mainly in Europe.

But co-production in itself does not guarantee smooth intercultural
communication and exchange. In Chapter 1 I discussed the historic co-
production of *BLACK TIES*, the first collaboration between Indigenous
theatre companies in Aotearoa and Australia, from which at least one
Indigenous reviewer left feeling hurt and ashamed. Holledge and
Tompkins (120–7) provide a rare look inside the rehearsal hall dynamics
of another difficult co-production, *Masterkey*, an Australian/Japanese show
adapted and directed by Mary Moore from Masakoi Togawa's thriller, *Oi
Naru Genei*, and presented at the Adelaide Festival in 1998 with a mixed
and intergenerational cast of Australian and Japanese actresses. The performers came from mixed performance disciplines: butoh, shingeki,
Stanislavski, Brecht, and 1990s-style physical theatre. The production
assigned each woman an individual space, or 'wardrobe', allowing them
to interact with one another while grounding their performances in their
different expressive modes and interiorities and associating their diverse
performance codes with individual character rather than generic cultural
difference. Nevertheless, the process became conflicted, ostensibly over
issues of costuming that were, however, symptomatic of deeper questions
about the suppression of the older Japanese actors' corporeal realities and
silenced memories. Despite its best intentions, the production's interculturalism did not constitute equitable exchange.

One of the most successful examples of generative intercultural encoun-
ter comes from the less ambitious model of collaboration (rather than co-
production) offered by a show that appeared in 2019 at both Toronto's
Luminato and the EIF's 'You Are Here' series, and at other festivals since.
The Buddies in Bad Times Theatre (Toronto) production of *Kiinalik:
These Sharp Tools* was created by Evalyn Parry, Laakkuluk Williamson
Bathory, Erin Brubacher, and Elysha Poirier with Cris Derksen. It was
performed by Parry, the Toronto-based queer white settler artistic director

of Buddies, and Bathory, the Iqaluit-based Kalaaleq (Greenlandic Inuk) performance artist, spoken word poet, and storyteller, with live music by two-spirit Cree cellist Derksen and direction by white settler actor/director Brubacher. It constituted, for me, one of the most powerful explorations, demonstrations, and representations of cross-cultural encounter in the creation process, on the stage, and in the audience that I have encountered at festivals anywhere. On a set fronted with blocks of melting ice, the show explored – in English, Inuktitut, eloquent cello music, traditional (white) folk and Inuit throat singing (katajjaq) – the relationship between Parry and Williamson Bathory, the South and the North, settler and Inuit peoples, Canada's past and present. Through the story of a friendship between the two women that began on a research expedition ship mapping the Davis Strait en route to Greenland – a ship populated overwhelmingly by settler scientists and tourists, with a very few Inuit aboard – the show both confronted settler Canadians and others from the (ironically) 'Global North' with their ignorance and neocolonial complicity and presented the possibility of collaboration and conciliation. It explored with audiences in participatory sequences their experiences of the North, probed their attitudes to and knowledges of the lives and cultures of the peoples there, and critiqued the colonialist, extractivist, and environmentally destructive politics of successive Canadian governments, all the while genially modelling a respectful and mutually supportive relationship across acknowledged differences. The climax of the show was a harrowing but stimulating performance by Williamson Bathory of the Greenlandic mask dance, *uaajeerneq*, in which she paints her face black with slashes of red and white, stuffs her cheeks with small balls to distort her features, and heads off into the audience, barefoot and dangerous, to confront individuals up close and personally with her sexually aggressive and suggestive side, flicking her tongue, grinding her hips, and producing guttural grunts and groans from deep in her core. Using the set's melting ice to clean off her make-up, she later explained the function of the dance: to help people confront their fears and express their powerful, playful, and essential sexual selves. Part theatre, part concert, part performance, part demonstration, part celebration of the beauty of the northern landscape, the show modelled the kinds of transgressive, transformative intercultural work that even the most conservative and careful of festivals can enable when they stage genuine and carefully considered collaboration, and when they are created, as *Kiinalik* was, not for the generalized audiences of any festival circuit, but for specific, targeted ones, in this case the expansively queer Canadian audience base of Buddies in Bad Times Theatre. A programme note, signed by all the creators, articulated the show's goals, largely, in my view, achieved:

> Let it be the beginning of a conversation
> Let it be a meeting place and a reckoning
> Let it live radically in a feminine paradigm
> Let it be complex
> Let it be unresolved
>
> (*Kiinalik* programme)[20]

Alternative Destinations

In the twenty-first century many of the festivals that have or aspire to having élite status have adjusted or adopted the traditional festival formula as articulated by Kavass, or have negotiated between the local and global in ways that have accommodated more meaningful interculturalism than others, and some of these, responding to emerging neoliberal realities, have moved towards something more closely resembling the 'curated' festival model analysed in Chapter 3 that Keren Zaiontz has identified as 'second-wave' ('From Post-War').

The biggest theatre and dance festival in North America, Le Festival TransAmérique (FTA – formerly Festival du théâtre des Amériques[21]), is clearly a destination event, but from its founding in the bilingual, multi-cultural city of Montréal in 1985 by Marie-Hélène Falcon and Jacques Vézina has been distinct from the post-war festivals and their imitators. It was founded, as its name suggests, as a hemispheric event, fostering globally South-to-North as well as North-to-South cultural dialogue and influence. Early on it featured 'plays of resistance from Argentina, Brazil, Colombia, Cuba, the United States, Mexico, Uruguay, Venezuela, Canada, Québec and even northern Québec (Inukjuak) ... featuring multiple languages, aesthetics and different generations of artists' (FTA, my translation). And from the outset the festival was curated in ways that reflected the personal vision of Falcon as artistic director, productively invoking what French philosopher Jacques Rancière has called 'dissensus' – 'a dissensual re-configuration of the common experience of the sensible' that provokes cognitive-sensual dissonance (140):

> We never sought consensus. In our opinion, that was a dead end that empties art of its poetic and political charge. From the get-go, we were interested in aspects that create rupture: marginality, difference, racial and cultural mixing, illegitimacy, the fly in the ointment. To paraphrase John

Cage, if something disturbs you, listen to it. We kept our ears open to what was unique, dissonant, discordant, radical, to artists who question their art and their era, who seek new forms of expression, other ways of experiencing theatre, of encountering the audience. What do we need to see? What is important and should be shown today? What should we resist? The Festival was a huge worksite, constantly evolving. (Falcon, qtd in FTA)

The statement takes part in a familiar modernist aesthetic discourse that has often valorized the appropriation and decontextualization of the cultural and performance forms of 'othered' cultures as a way of introducing the thrill of the new. But it can also, in the ways promoted by Rancière and on some occasions realized at the FTA, be read as producing a genuine and generative gap between the world as cognitively 'managed' prior to the theatrical experience and the experience of cognitive dissonance and disrupted complacency when represented worlds or performance forms are experienced affectively through unsettling or disturbingly unfamiliar performances that, presented without the mediation of the famously problematic receptor-adaptors of Patrice Pavis's 'target cultures' (4), resist such appropriation.

The festival quickly expanded from the Americas to the world, and like other destination festivals it has hosted the biggest modernist and postmodernist names on the international circuit, from Peter Brook, Frank Castorf, Tadeusz Kantor, Elizabeth LeCompte and the Wooster Group, Christoph Marthaler, Ariane Mnouchkine, Meredith Monk, Anatoli Vassiliev, and Robert Wilson to the homegrown Marie Brassard, Robert Lepage, Gilles Maheu, Denis Marleau, and Wajdi Mouawad. But it has not lost its edge, it has increasingly taken on the role of co-producer rather than simply presenter, and it has continued to stage unmediated, dissensual difference, and to call itself 'trans-cultural, trans-disciplinary, [and] transnational' rather than simply 'international' (Falcon, qtd in FTA). It was at FTA that I first encountered the startlingly beautiful Indigenous modernist work of Huron-Wendat artist Yves Sioui Durand, for example, and his company Ondinnok, the first Indigenous theatre company in Québec and now one of the most recognized on the international circuit. At the very first FTA in 1985 Falcon took a risk on the virtually unknown company in an outdoor show, *Le Porteur des peines du monde*, that subsequently toured the world. I was introduced to their work at the FTA in 1999, when *Iwouskea and Tawiskaron* reenacted a Huron-Iroquois creation story in and around a longhouse/tent for forty audience members at a time in the basement of Montréal's Monument National, on the traditional territory of the Kanien'kehá:ka (Iroquoian Mohawk)

Nation. This was the Nation, and the territory, that had been involved in an armed resistance to the appropriation of its sacred territory for a golf course less than ten years earlier in what has become known as 'the Oka crisis', in which the Sûreté du Québec police force and the Canadian Armed Forces responded to the protestors with rifles, tear gas canisters, and concussion grenades in a violent standoff that lasted seventy-eight days.

The staging of *Iwouskea and Tawiskaron* was intimate, as cast members touched audience participants gently on the shoulder, arm, or back, escorting us individually into the space, involved us in the ritual placing of small stones on the body of one of our number, and always worked within inches of us inside the enclosed space. The ritual involved sweet-grass and stones, skulls, feathers, and bones as totems, and the performers, sometimes wearing evocative outsized masks, conjured the spirits of the ancestors, engaged in rites of purification and atonement, and enacted the story of enemy twin brothers born of Sky Woman after her fall from the Sky World. But the central character of the evening was the tent itself, constructed almost as the living carcass of an animal, with its canvas skin and birch-bough ribs. The tent served as both theatre and set, an intimate gathering place, a screen for shadow play, a frame for acrobatics, turtle's back, and, at one powerful moment, a living and breathing body, expanding and contracting like the belly of the woman who emerged from its apex.

But this production was no merely anthropological resuscitation and presentation of an ancient rite for our festive consumption; rather, the company was putting the Saint Lawrence Iroquoian culture into practice in the present and making it visible in a society that has not always been willing to acknowledge its existence. At one point, the audience emerged from the confines of the tent to be confronted by a high-tech, space-walking sound machine that produced some of the show's powerful electronic soundscape, the most effective place at which the merging of past, present, and future occurred in the production and the place where the show acknowledged, through the use of urban sounds and rhythms, its location at the heart of a contemporary festival city on Indigenous land. *Iwouskea and Tawiskaron* was groundbreaking, and importantly, it was not alone on the programme. As in 1985, when Ondinnock's work was paired with the Inuit throat-singing show, *Katajjak*, in 1999 it was relieved of the burden of representation by being matched, in the same space, with the intimate *Trial of Kicking Bear*, by the then Chief of the Cree Fox Lake First Nation in Manitoba, Michael Lawrenchuk.

Falcon retained her position as artistic director at FTA through to 2013. Her curatorial practice notably involved an exemplary combination of the cultivation of local and regional connections with travel, not only to other festivals in the recursive loop that generates and sustains a reproductive economy of festive uniformity, but to less predictable places in which performance most actively engages with the social. And, crucially, like many festival curators in continental Europe but unlike most in the anglophone world, she was never afraid of linguistic difference. Over her nearly thirty years as director, she regularly introduced Montréalers and international attendees to formally cutting-edge and politically provocative work from around the world, the familiar stars from the international circuit mixing with outstanding local performers and surprising shows from unexpected places. Falcon was succeeded by her protégé Martin Faucher, who has continued the tradition she established, his first season in 2015 including such work as *Dancing Grandmothers* by the South Korean choreographer Eun-Me Ahn, in which a dozen grand-mothers shared the stage with nine young performers in an uplifting, infectious dance. The 2020 FTA was interrupted by the global COVID-19 pandemic, but its announced programme was to include work such as *J'ai pleuré avec les chiens*, by the emerging local Euro-Cree-Métis star choreographer Daina Ashbee in conversation with provocative work from Chile, Egypt, Zimbabwe, and Nunavik, the northern, Inuit region of Québec.[22]

As we have seen, festivals in Australia and Aotearoa/New Zealand function for the most part as cogs in a festival circuit in which featured shows travel from city to city, whose festivals lodge competitive claims to world or national premieres. In 2020, however, the New Zealand Festival of the Arts in Wellington experimented with a new format, with mixed success. Wellington is a medium-sized city (population ca 425,000) with a young, 23 per cent Indigenous Māori and Pacific peoples and 15 per cent Asian population. It is the capital city of a nation-state that, unlike most settler societies, acknowledges its First Peoples, the Māori, through the (unevenly applied) Treaty of Waitangi (1840), the use of the bilingual 'Aotearoa/New Zealand' national name, and the inclusion of Te Reo Māori (along with English and New Zealand Sign Language) as an official language. The Festival and its associated Fringe occur simultaneously, and festival and fringe venues are located in close proximity to one another in the city centre, most near the city's tourist-friendly waterfront area.[23] Festival venues include traditional theatre spaces as well as the Soundings Theatre on the fourth, Māori-focused floor of the waterfront Te Papa

Tongarewa Museum, the Opera House, and various galleries around the city.

In 2020 the three-week festival appointed three all-star 'guest curators' – Lemi Ponifasio, Laurie Anderson, and Bret McKenzie – who worked together with the festival's 'creative director' Marnie Karmelita in successive weeks to programme one week each. In practice, this meant that the guest directors, globally prominent festival artists in their own right, invited about half of each week's schedule, some of it their own work, which was supplemented by a 'festival programme' curated centrally, presumably to provide balance. Following a pōwhiri (Māori welcoming ceremony – see Chapter 1) hosted by the Te Āti Awa / Taranaki Whānui Iwi (tribe), Samoan multidisciplinary artist Lemi Ponifasio opened the festival with the culturally eclectic *Chosen and Beloved*, centring around a performance of Polish composer Henryk Górecki's 1976 *Symphony #3: Symphony of Sorrowful Songs*, the third movement of which uses the text of a Silesian folk song describing the pain of a mother searching for her lost son killed in an uprising. The evening brought together the MAU Wāhine (the Indigenous women members of Ponifasio's company), the New Zealand Symphony Orchestra conducted by Estonian American conductor Kristjan Järvi, and Syrian soprano Racha Riszk, in an 'orchestral art experience' that commemorated the Christchurch mosque shootings on 15 March 2019 and focused thematically on the suffering of women. The MAU Wāhine, in mourning black and white, opened the evening moving to a simple choreography on a rock-filled proscenium, pouring buckets of blood onto the stage and speaking in untranslated Te Reo, Riszk sang beautifully from isolated positions in the space, and the show resolved into a cascading waterfall of light.

Ponifasio also brought difference and intercultural encounter to the festival through the premiere of his own opera/theatre/dance/ceremony, القدس *Jerusalem*, inspired by the epic Concerto al-Quds by the Syrian poet Adonis (Ali Ahmad Said Esber) and delivered in large part, again, in untranslated Te Reo; through an installation at the Te Papa Tongarewa Museum that animated the archive of thirty years of the work of his company while inviting the public to contribute; and through the presentation of *In Search of Dinozard*, a challenging, resolutely decolonizing theatre creation by Faustin Linyekula and Studios Kabako from the Democratic Republic of the Congo, performed in whiteface. Presented in a multiplicity of African languages including English, French, Swahili, and Zulu, *Dinozard* was alternately tender, defiant, and agonizing, confronting an overwhelmingly dominant-culture audience with uncomfortable truths. Finally, and crucially, Ponifasio's curatorial week included 'Te Ata', billed as a festival within a festival, which brought artists from Aotearoa and around the world into contact with young New Zealanders for two weeks of creative development and presentation. Among the intercultural assemblage of artists were the likes of South African protest musician Neo Muyanga, US Youth Poet Laureate Kara Jackson, Germany's Der Faust prize-winner for dance Aloalii Tapu, 2019 New Zealand Arts Laureate Coco Solid (aka Jessica Hansell), Grammy Award-winning opera singer Jonathan Lemalu, baritone Kawiti Waetford, and the New Zealand Sinfonia for Hope orchestra.

Ponifasio's curation brought more experimental, and more diverse work to the festival than many of its patrons are used to, and many audience members and reviewers expressed confusion or even contempt for some of the offerings – especially the Peter Sellars production of Claude Vivier's opera, *Kopernicus*, which they found inscrutable. But as one reviewer also noted, Ponifasio was 'breaking new ground by inviting a fresh audience into a theatre that is usually a bastion of high European performance art' (Pringle), and that can only be a good thing.

Beyond the opening week, however, the experiment with multiple curators in Wellington floundered somewhat, at least as it applied to opening the festival to difference. Laurie Anderson's own work was challenging and provocative, including her collaboration with Taiwanese new media creator Hsin-Chien Huang on the virtual reality installation *To the Moon*. But if some of the work she programmed pushed artistic boundaries, there was little that was explicitly or generatively intercultural, a gap that was left to be filled through the festival programme's presentation of the touring Māori/Indigenous Australian collaboration, *BLACK TIES*, discussed in Chapter 1. The third week, curated by returning New Zealander Bret McKenzie, was largely populist fluff, redeemed somewhat, again, by festival programming that among some strong but not intercultural European offerings[24] featured the collaboration *Hōkoi me te Vwōhali: From Spirit Eagles Land* by Aotearoa's Ōkāreka Dance Company (Māori) with the problematically named non-Indigenous Cincinnati-based Exhale Dance Tribe in the US, performed with many Māori visibly in attendance the night I saw it on the floor dedicated to Māori life and history at the Te Papa Tongerewa Museum. Ōkāreka is a young company from Auckland that purports to 'present a powerful fusion of contemporary dance and Māori muscle memory' (Okareka); Exhale 'integrates earth-based philosophies into our movement practices' and operates 'very much like a tribe' (Exhale). The show's first half included some powerful Māori movement sequences incorporating embodiments, *wiri* (hand movements) and facial expressions, staged to resonant surround-sound text and song in Te Reo, and it clearly and cleverly staged moments of both conflict and negotiation. But the show seemed to become less and less informed by Māori cultural texts as it progressed, and apart from a brief, haka-inflected epilogue it ended with jazz dance that was pure Americana. As a white settler Canadian, I was unable to detect any Cherokee influence in the music or choreography.

The curatorial experiment at the New Zealand Festival, then, was a mixed success, and the audience experience was different depending on which of the three weeks anyone attended, how much of the earnest but largely amateur, largely local fringe festival they participated in, and how they spent their performance-free weekday hours in late summer in Wellington. As is so often the case, though, the experiment demonstrated that intercultural encounter, at destination festivals as elsewhere, is best and most effectively brokered by the historically disempowered placed in positions of creative leadership.

Moving outside of festivals grounded in European culture and cultural forms or hosted in settler societies, Denise Varney, Peter Eckersall, Chris Hudson, and Barbara Hatley have written about the role of arts festivals in the creation of newly 'liquid modernities' and the de- and recentring of cultural power in Asia, formulating a 'new half-Western, half-Asian modernity', developing 'culturally hybrid works', and purportedly promoting 'a discourse of openness and racial tolerance' (211). Their examples of Rajat Kapoor's *Hamlet: The Clown Prince* and Robert Lepage's *The Blue Dragon* at the Shanghai International Arts Festival in 2007, however, do not strike this viewer as moving far beyond shows typical of the global festival circuit over many decades, the Lepage, in particular, serving, as much of his work on the festival circuit does, as an almost archetypal example of the appropriative HIT interculturalist orientalism identified by Daphne Lei.[25] Their discussion of the 'strategic management of culture' at the Singapore International Festival of the Arts, moreover, sounds precariously close to city- and nation-branding, with an unhealthy degree of large-scale intervention in the arts by a government that is generally understood to be repressive.

One iteration of FIBA (Festival Internacional de Buenos Aires), however, does offer an example of what can happen at a destination festival when it is sufficiently flexible and purposefully decentred. According to Jean Graham-Jones, the 2009 festival broke from a long tradition of Eurocentric globalism at the festival, which has in previous and subsequent iterations relied on support from the Alliance Française, the British Arts Council, and the Goethe-Institut, selected work from the global touring circuit, and concentrated its programming on England, France, Germany, Israel, Italy, and Spain (233–4). But FIBA relies primarily on the sponsorship of the large (population ca 15 million), theatrically hyper-active, but not notably culturally mixed city of Buenos Aires itself, which frees it from too heavy a dependence on support from embassies and NGOs elsewhere and allows its directors a certain flexibility. The 2009 directors, Rubén Szuchmacher and Alberto Ligaluppi, made the conscious decision to decentre the festival and to reimagine it outside of the international marketplace and the world of city branding. 'There was no Mnouchkine, Wilson, Castellucci, or Marthaler' – European luminaries (or "rehashed figures") who dominate the international circuit (Juan José Santillan, qtd in Graham-Jones 234) – but there were twenty-four shows from Buenos Aires and other Argentinian cities, three shows from companies in neighbouring Santiago, Chile that had never before been invited to the festival, and an international menu featuring work from cities not usually seen at such events: Ajaccio, Cochabamba, Córdoba, Ghent, Maputo, Palermo, Poznań, Rosario, Tucumán, and Wrocław. The festival also avoided the pernicious competing diplomatic nationalisms of many stops on the destination festival circuit by listing shows alphabetically, not by nation, but by city of origin. The festival was complemented by workshops, colloquia, film, music, and reading series, and by the presentations of books and awards.[26]

The fourth edition of the biennial Interferences International Theatre Festival, held in the medium-sized East European city of Cluj-Napoca, Romania (population ca 400,000) over twelve days in November–December 2014, also modelled a number of good practices. Although it hosted work from fourteen countries, Interferences is not a destination festival on the same scale as many of those under discussion here, and this fact alone helps facilitate exchange. It allows, for example, the organizers to avoid parallel programming, and therefore for all participants to see, discuss, and compare the same shows over the course of the event. And as Jozefina Komporaly says, 'Transcending borders – ethnic, cultural, linguistic, and generic – has emerged as a dominant focus of the festival' (550). The festival's success in this regard is accomplished by focusing intercultural dialogue through daily post-performance discussions and, crucially, through attention to language and translation that exceeds the often-hurried accommodation of linguistic difference through surtitling – though all events indeed either had simultaneous translation or were surtitled in three languages. According to Komporaly, 'There was no such thing as a primary language for this festival: translation, to put it differently, was not a subsidiary facet, but its central focus' (551). Moreover, she argues, 'in addition to privileging translation among languages, the festival offer[ed] a platform for *showcasing* instances of cultural translation. It attract[ed] performances that operate as a vital mode of cultural representation and a dynamic social practice, addressing questions of heritage and belonging in a transnational context' (552, emphasis added). In part this was accomplished through a combination of full cultural contextualization, and in part through a willingness to go beyond representations of static cultural authenticities. Komporaly offers the example, among others, of Jaram Lee's *Sacheon-Ga* at the 2014 festival, a loose adaptation of Brecht's *The Good Person of Szechwan* rooted in traditional Korean *pansori* music theatre interwoven with Brechtian Epic Theatre technique in ways that fundamentally reinvented the *pansori* form. The production, however, was made legible, not through the 'reception-adaptors' provided by the 'cultural modeling' of any target cultures (as in Patrice Pavis's famously problematic 'hourglass' model of intercultural performative exchange – Pavis 4), but through a well-attended *pansori* workshop run at the festival by the composer and performer herself. Interferences, finally, taking place in a post-communist state with a fraught political history that includes tension between the dominant ethnic Romanian population (ca 81 per cent) and the ethnic Hungarian minority (16 per cent),[27] does not revel in familiar humanist intercultural tropes of shared common humanity, but is willing to tackle more difficult and conflicted relationships across difference, including, in its 2018 incarnation, war (see Interferences).

Even Germany's august Theater der Welt, which has a somewhat different origin story than those festivals that trace their beginnings to Edinburgh and Avignon and operates using a different model from the international standard, has proven in recent years to also have more intercultural flexibility. Recent festivals have modelled a shift from diplomatic internationalism and neoliberal globalization to a more socially productive interrogative transnationalism, and from a 'top-down' programming model towards an artist-driven curatorial one. Theater der Welt traces its origins to the International Theatre Institute (ITI), which remains its governing body, and to its predecessor, the Théâtre des Nations, from which it emerged in 1979. Both the ITI and Théâtre des Nations, founded in 1948 and 1957 respectively, were post-war internationalist, UNESCO-suppported initiatives advancing the goals of mutual understanding between nation-states understood to be sovereign. Erika

Fischer-Lichte traces the evolution of programming at both festivals explicitly, like the UN, 'to serve peace' (Fischer-Lichte, 'European' 93). Throughout its history,[28] Théâtre des Nations focused on the work of the major European directors, the experimental work emerging from Europe and the United States, and on 'authentic' (exotic) traditional performances from Japan, India, Sri Lanka, and Bali. The early years of Theater der Welt continued to feature the European 'masters' and western experimental works but added to these productions that became known as 'intercultural' theatre, consisting of 'HIT' work by Peter Brook, Robert Wilson, Tadashi Suzuki and others that blended eastern and western traditions. As the festival has evolved into the twenty-first century, however, perhaps because of certain features of its design, Theater der Welt has been more flexible than many of the large destination festivals in responding to and reflecting both global developments in theatre and performance and the immediate specificities of its location, while also avoiding both the kinds of stultification that can settle in among august institutions and the 'decline' stage in 'the destination lifecycle' that Martin Robertson and Kenneth MacMillan Wardrop identify in their study of the marketing of Edinburgh as a festival city (118).

There are three features of Theater der Welt that now distinguish it among destination festivals: it is (now) triennial, each iteration takes place in a different city or region within Germany, and artistic directors are appointed for only one iteration of the festival. This has meant that, since 1999 when it was held in Berlin as the once and future capital of a reunited Germany, the festival has engaged in real material ways with its host city to the point that each festival has been largely *about* the city in which it takes place – its space, its people, and its history. In a once-divided Berlin that remained under reconstruction, this meant engaging audiences and others in over two dozen theatrical and non-theatrical spaces throughout the city and making 'locality and spatiality . . . perhaps the most interesting underlying themes of the festival as a whole' (Irmer 124). By 2014, Matthias Liliental, that year's director of the festival in Mannheim, argued in an interview entitled 'A Change Has Totally Taken Place', that rather than simply bringing 'big productions from all over the world', he was able to ask: 'what is the relationship between the city where I'm showing these performances and the things I am bringing and adding to it? And I think', he remarked, 'this change is really enormous' (Sellar, 'A Change' 73). Liliental associated the change with a reconceptualization of the role of festival director itself in the preceding years from *programmer* to *curator* (74), perhaps beginning to align the festival more closely with the curated,

artist-run 'second-wave' festivals discussed in Chapter 3 than with other
large destination festivals. In any case, the Mannheim festival and its
2017 successor in Hamburg were at once transnational, in their connect-
edness to global events and politics, and determinedly local. I experienced
the city of Mannheim and the 2014 Theater der Welt in part by staying
with my partner in one of the twenty-two pop-up rooms of 'Hotel Shabby
Shabby' that were designed as festival installations by architecture students
worldwide using found or recycled materials and dispersed in parks and
markets, on riversides and rooftops throughout the city (see 'Hotel Shabby
Shabby').

The Hamburg Theater der Welt in 2017, presenting in its main
programme forty-four shows from all habitable continents, was nevertheless true to its motto, 'think global, act local' (Remshardt 229). 'The city',
according to Ralf Remshardt, 'was the most remarkable spectacle of all',
and its harbour was 'at once its organizing trope and location', though
there were at least sixteen venues throughout Hamburg (229). The harbour in Hamburg, as the festival programme proclaimed, is 'a place of early
colonial and current globalization, a place of transit and transition, of
hope, fleeing, and migration' (qtd in Fischer-Lichte, 'European' 97), and
the festival engaged fully with its historical and contemporary realities at a
time when Germany, and in particular its Chancellor Angela Merkel, was
controversially providing strong leadership in what was known as the
European Migrant Crisis concerning refugees from Syria, Afghanistan,
and Iraq. The festival centre was located at the former 'Africa Terminal'
from which German soldiers embarked to South West Africa (Namibia) in
1903–4 to quell the Herero revolt and carry out the twentieth century's
first genocide. It housed Lemi Ponifasio's *Children of Gods*, commissioned
and created for the space as a 'rite of transformation' focusing on the
sufferings of children caught in the world's conflict zones and contemporary genocides (See Fischer-Lichte, 'European' 97; Remshardt 229).
A large warehouse at the end of the harbour served up South African artist
Brett Bailey's *Sanctuary*, addressing the global refugee crisis to seven
perambulatory spectators at a time (Remshardt 232). A container suspended from a waterfront crane literally contained recent immigrants to
the city who recounted their stories; another show consisted of a boat trip
on the Alster and Elbe rivers during which audience members met the
harbour's working people (see Fischer-Lichte, 'European' 98). With half of
its presentations world premieres or commissioned works, with a determined concentration on the links between the historical and contemporary
local and global, and with curation that privileged immigrant and refugee

stories, the Hamburg Theater der Welt was a far cry from the familiar and formulaic globalized marketplace for shows programmed from a standardized international menu, and its engagement with 'performing the intercultural city' (see Knowles, *Performing*) delved much more deeply into the city's intercultural histories and contemporary complexities than any neoliberal 'creative city' or city branding strategies.

Towards a Curatorial Turn

Large élite and destination festivals do not exist primarily for the purposes of intercultural exchange. They are supported by municipal and national governments as ways of attracting attention, tourism, and corporate investment, they are supported by corporate sponsors as a way of associating their products and services with 'the best' that the art world has to offer, and they are supported by audiences in part because of their cultural cachet. Nevertheless, by virtue of their *being* international events dedicated to expressive culture that bring artists from around the world to a single location for a fixed period of time, they provide opportunities for generative exchange that it would be foolish to waste.

This chapter has revealed some of the structural problems inhibiting destination festivals from realizing their potential as *trans*national, cross-*cultural* crucibles. It has also explored some movement in the destination festival circuit away from a model in which festival programmers either promote the canonical or experimental 'best' of (usually) western art to a global public or scour the world for culturally transcendent spectacles that can be extracted from the social context within which they derive their meaning and presented as novelties or exotica for flaneurs, voyeurs, or, as Regev says, 'cosmopolitan omnivores' (111). Many of the festivals' attempts to evolve have derived in part from a response to a shift away from the twentieth-century welfare state attitude to arts funding towards a neoliberal faith in individual entrepreneurialism. This has had myriad negative effects, of course, which have been explored and exposed in work such as Jen Harvie's *Fair Play* and Angela McRobbie's *Be Creative*. It has also led to experiments, such as those described here by FIBA, Interferences, the New Zealand Festival of the Arts, and increasingly Theater der Welt, that might best be understood as part of 'the curatorial turn' in festival administration to which I will turn in Chapter 3.

CHAPTER 3

The Curated Live-Arts Festival

It's a Sunday morning in January 2018, and I'm standing at the top of the 550-foot-high Lookout Tower at Vancouver's Harbour Centre, over-looking the city and the waters that surround it. I'm in a prescribed position above the harbour listening on the headphones provided as a young girl, Lily, describes a future, utopian Vancouver with gas-free cars that run on underground roads, robots in the sea who clean up all the garbage, football fields on the tops of buildings, free clean water distri-bution, lots of places for homeless people to live, and most of all lots of places where phones aren't allowed so that people can 'communicate with one-another in person'. I'm approached by a ten-year-old Asian Canadian girl who introduces herself as Savannah, asks me my name, age, and other general questions, and offers to answer any questions I have about her. We have time to exchange pleasantries before I'm instructed to replace my headphones and listen to another young voice offering a very different, dystopian vision of a future Vancouver overcome by floods, fires, and other environmental disasters, after which Savannah returns and politely asks me more pointed questions: my vision of what's in store for the city in the decades ahead, my hopes, my message to the future. What, after all, have I done for Vancouver? When Savannah leaves, I hear her voice mixed with those of fifteen of her friends and classmates from Hastings Elementary Community School pretending to be 100 years of age and describing what life in the city is like 'now'. The utopian view prevails.

Lookout, part of Vancouver's PuSh Festival, was created by British artist Andy Field and originally co-commissioned by London's The Arches and the Unicorn Theatre. It has been adapted and is performed by local schoolchildren, as it has been in Auckland, Cairo, Guangzhou, Madrid, Riga, Salzburg, São Paulo, Shanghai, and at least half a dozen cities around the UK (see 'Lookout'). It is characteristic of a type of flexible, socially engaged, what I call 'transnational/local' performance that is the trademark of globally touring companies such as Rimini Protokoll (Berlin) and the

Gob Squad (Nottingham and Berlin), and that proliferates at festivals such as PuSh, festivals that Keren Zaiontz has called 'second-wave' ('From').[1]

For Zaiontz, the second-wave festival emerged with the turn of the millennium both in compliance and in critical engagement with the upsurge in neoliberal policies and practices, the advent of a postnational world, the death of the welfare state and widespread government support for the arts, and the emergence of 'creative city' politics and practices inspired by the work of urban studies theorist Richard Florida. For Zaiontz, second-wave festivals are central to a developing international network of co-producing organizations that co-commission work by an increasingly mobile circuit of global artrepreneurs. The network now includes some of the post-war destination festivals discussed in Chapter 2 that have evolved with the economic and political times to address changing circumstances. But while Zaiontz points to a new relationship with performance space and with local host cities as the central defining feature of the festivals she calls second-wave, socially and locally engaged shows, while certainly enabled by this new type of festival, are not definitive of them. Many so-called second-wave festivals also stage works that would not be out of place at, and indeed often also appear at, destination and fringe festivals around the world. I suggest that the related, but more fundamental characteristic of such festivals is a conceptual shift in the twenty-first century away from festival *programming* (from an international touring menu) to an emerging model of *curation* that derives from the visual arts – what Tom Sellar calls 'the curatorial turn' in the performing arts – and from a fundamental and generative disregard of disciplinary distinctions ('Curatorial'). I will, then, attempting to avoid resonating with second-wave feminism and any teleological implications of series of waves, refer to this type of artist-run interdisciplinary festival as curated live-arts festivals.

Defining the curator as 'one who generates connections and structures formats around new work' (7), Bertie Ferdman has argued that the rise of interdisciplinary live-arts festivals has amplified the role of the curator, who unlike a festival programmer is required to conceptualize 'how, where, when, why, and for whom such events are structured and presented' (7). In the curated festivals of the twenty-first century the programmer or presenter who travels to festivals around the world to choose 'the best' of what is on offer has been replaced by the artist-curator who travels to make connections, sometimes to unexpected locations and not only to other festivals, but who also 'questions preconceived assumptions that shape performance, as well as his or her own role in shaping that discourse'

(17). '[P]erformance curators', as Sellar argues, 'are ideally invested, simultaneously, in critical discourses of cultural politics, social engagement, the history of art, dramaturgy, and performance studies' ('Curatorial' 22).

> They have been embraced as an essential link between theory and praxis, able to join separately developed disciplinary strands; they have been hailed as a possible negotiator of institutional and genre categories at a time when institutions are rethinking their limitations, artists are blurring forms with unprecedented fluidity, and discourses ... are resolutely, and freely, interdisciplinary. ('Curatorial' 22)

The rise of the festival curator leads to festivals in which contexts and opportunities for communication across difference – among artists, between artists and audiences – can be foregrounded, not only on the level of content, or even of the forms and structures of shows, but of modes of festival selection and presentation themselves – of festival epistemologies. Considering curation as 'both cultural and financial strategy' (Ferdman 10), for example, Ferdman intriguingly points to a new model of festival touring that applies to shows such as *Lookout* and other transnational/local performances that Zaiontz discusses, in which *concepts*, rather than individual productions or artists, tour. Rather than bringing casts, sets, and costumes to a festival, curators invite fully developed concepts that are restaged and adapted to local contexts using local performers (such as Savannah and her classmates in my opening vignette) and local performance spaces, and allocating money to local labour in support of local artists and economies (see Ferdman 16–17). Ferdman offers as the prototype the mini-festival *Ciudades Paralelas (Parallel Cities)*, conceived by Argentinian Lola Arias and German Stefan Kaegi (of Rimini Protokoll), first staged by Rimini Protokoll at the HAU (Hebbel am Ufer) in Berlin in 2010, in which eight artists were invited to create performances for a city's 'functional places' – a train station, factory, hotel, courtroom, and library – which could then be 'relocalized' each time the mini-festival toured (16–17; see also Rimini Protokoll). Arias explains:

> The pieces were genuinely portable, in the sense that the only thing we are transporting are concepts. The concept for each piece would be fully developed, and each piece would be restaged in the context of each city with different performers, different spaces, and so on. The only person travelling was the artist and his or her idea, recontextualized at every site. (qtd in Ferdman 17)

The idea of the 'portable concept' can, of course, buy into neoliberal festival economics and problematically privilege the individual artrepreneur while also replacing attempts to solve specific social problems locally with imported ideas that are merely applied, adapted, and interpreted rather than created in response to local conditions. And because it is interlinked, the curated festival network that is a prime market for such shows can serve, not only as a potential market for artists' work, but also a restrictive gate that brokers access. As Alex Lazardis Ferguson argues, the curator can serve, not only as 'a cultural agent providing a platform for cultural exchange', but also as a 'gate-keeper regulating access' to symbolic capital and transformational aesthetic experience for performers and audiences alike (Ferguson 97).[2] But festival curation can also create a generative context of denaturalization and contestation in which everything is open to question. As Ferdman says, festival curation of this kind can involve 'paying attention to the context of the theatrical event and rethinking the norms of participation in the realm of the live, prompting everyone to ask, *what is this?*' (6).

If the curated live-arts festival model differs from that of the destination festival in its programming model, it also differs in audience address and experience. Destination festivals exist, by definition, primarily to attract visitors to host cities that they constitute as tourist destinations. Everything they do – their 'universalist', 'world-class' programming, their fundraising, their relationship with local amenities ranging from hotels, restaurants, and bars to international travel and municipal transit – is geared towards attracting visitors and facilitating their tourist experiences, which includes forging alliances and sharing resources with other tourist organizations. The live-arts festivals of the twenty-first century, on the other hand, while they welcome visitors, primarily target local audiences, address local concerns, stage site-specific work in which local geographies play starring roles, and aspire to have lingering social impact outside of formal festival 'time-out-of-time' temporalities, in part by creating 'permanent structures to sustain artists and audiences from one festival to the next' (Frisch 51; see also Zaiontz, 'From' 31–3). They set out to make local festivalgoers see their cities differently, while forging strategic, locally relevant and impactful transnational networks. They can, then, bring local (inter)cultures within culturally diverse cities into direct conversation with other, transnationally intercultural ones in unique, performative ways. Finally, 'curators', as Alexandra Portmann says, unlike destination festival programmers, 'establish long-term relationships between festivals and artists in order to facilitate the production of performances within a larger network of co-producers and to support working relationships over more than one production period' (Portmann 41).

For my purposes, of course, the key question is whether the turn to a curated model of festival organization does or can facilitate festivals' capacity to enable and stage intercultural as well as interdisciplinary encounters in generative ways. 'Will they transform their institutions to look more like the city they're located in, or will they invite in guests, to create the *appearance* of diversity', Norman Frisch asks? 'Generally speaking', he answers himself sardonically, 'they'll always opt for the second' (59), but the question is worth pursuing.

The Predecessors

Zaiontz identifies her 'second wave' as emerging in the early twenty-first century, but there were late twentieth-century predecessors who paved the way and remain important. These include, among others, the Festival aan de Werf, founded in Utrecht, the Netherlands, in 1986; High Performance Rodeo, founded in Calgary, Alberta in 1987 as 'One Yellow Rabbit Secret Elevator Experimental Performance Festival'; the Malta Festival, rooted in social change when founded in Poznań, Poland, in 1991, of which more below; the Carrefour international de théâtre de Québec, founded in Québec City in 1991 and conceived as a cultural and creative crossroads; the biennial Theaterfestival SPIELART, founded in Munich in 1995; and the prestigious Baltic Circle Festival, founded in Helsinki in 1996, one of thirteen members of the FIT (Festivals in Transition) network in Europe and Egypt.[3]

Baltic Circle is exemplary, presenting itself as 'an artwork', 'a contemporary theatre festival, a community, a network, and a performing arts laboratory' dedicated to contributing to and participating in social change, creating 'active ties to decision-makers and opinion leaders in society. We stir up situations and spaces where these figures can meet arts professionals and search together for new interactions' (Baltic Circle, 'About'). Helsinki (population 650,000) is Finland's broadly multicultural capital city and gateway, hosting the country's largest immigrant population. It is home to people from over one hundred nations of origin, including, prominently, Russia, Estonia, and Somalia, foreign citizens make up almost 10 per cent of the population, and there is also a significant Indigenous (Sámi) presence. Baltic Circle is a small festival with only two full-time and four seasonal employees, that nevertheless takes its role as cultural mediator seriously. The festival focuses on the Baltic and Nordic countries, but also includes work from places such as Brazil, Japan, and Canada. In six days each November the festival mounts a concentrated series of performances, including plays newly translated, transnational co-productions and cultural collaborations, as well as artist exchanges, seminars, and encounters that always address local and global social issues including 'the potential of social and political agency of performance' (Baltic Circle). And it often does so across significant cultural and other differences. The 2019 edition included, for example, a live-streamed film and seminar, *Halt Colonial Powers!* that featured the history and contemporary resistance and resilience of the Sámi peoples – the First Peoples of Northern Europe – as discussed by Sámi artists, activists, and scholars.[4] But its programme also productively pushed the boundaries of the intercultural by featuring a series that included a performance, *Posthuman Theatre*, a *Panel on Non-human Performance*, and a participatory session that invited audiences to engage in *Conversations with Objects*, shifting the ground away from the focus, typical of western festivals, on human display closer towards an Indigenous festival paradigm.

But the grandmother of the curated live-arts festival is the alive and still kicking biennial LiFT (London International Festival of Theatre), founded in 1981 by Rose Fenton and Lucy Neal with the intention to 'challenge British theatre and open a window on the world' (Fenton and Neal 19).[5]

LiFT, London

LiFT is a large-scale biennial festival that runs for seven weeks in June and July. Over almost 40 years it has presented work from 66 countries and commissioned 40 new productions and events, and in 2018 alone it hosted 1,000 artists and 160,000 audience members at venues across London, one of the most diverse and culturally complex cities in the world with a large and varied Black (14 per cent) and Asian population (18 per cent). It is supported by a full-time staff of seven (half of whom are currently people of colour) and a twenty-person board of directors (mostly from the corporate or tourism sectors or local council). Its overall budget in 2018 was approximately £2 million, and its major funders are the Arts Council of England and (at least prior to Brexit) the Creative Europe programme of the European Union. It also relies heavily on corporate sponsors and a tiered list of donors ranging from an 'Artistic Director's Circle' (£5,000/year) through LIFT Originals (£2,500), Commissioners+ (£1,000), and Commissioners (£500) to Young Commissioners (£300) and LIFTees (£120). LiFT participates in four European networks with other festivals and arts organizations, including House on Fire (supporting arts creations contributing to political and social debates); Imagine 2020 (supporting work exploring climate change); Be SpectACTive! (supporting active spectatorship); and Festivals in Transition (FIT), for whom it is leading the Urban Heat project supporting artists working with urban communities.

From the beginning Fenton and Neal brought work to the festival from places like Malaysia, Poland, Brazil, and Japan that was political, socially engaged, experimental, and never previously seen in the UK, and it has continued that tradition. 'Rejecting the kind of superficial relationship between visitor and site often produced through international touring's usual economy of brief runs and quick turnover', Jen Harvie observes, 'LIFT's directors present dialogues between visiting and local artists, hold after-show discussions for audiences and visiting companies, develop site-specific work, and create opportunities for local artists and audiences to collaborate with visiting artists' (*Staging* 126). What's more, as Harvie points out, they ask questions such as 'How many different cultures co-exist in London? What is their relationship with their countries of origin? And how do we make connections between London and the rest of the world?' (126). As David Binder, guest director of the Festival in 2018 says, '[The] collision of culture', in London as an intercultural city, '[is] what LIFT has always embraced and celebrated' (Massie-Blomfeld, qtd in Zaiontz, 'From' 35n21), and the audience experience at the festival is at once rich, varied, and challenging.

LiFT stages events all over the city in theatrical and non-theatrical spaces, engaging with the city as place in ways that are archetypally 'second-wave' in Zaiontz's terminology. Over the years they have built a replica Bastille out of concrete blocks on London's South Bank to celebrate the bicentenary of the French Revolution, 'unleash[ed] a party of Catalan pyromaniacs on the usually sober reaches of Battersea Park' (Johansson 65), and, in 2018, released a flock of 1,500 glow-in-the-dark pigeons into the night sky over London in tribute to their ancestors' role in the First World War. The 2018 edition also saw an interactive children's show by Punchdrunk theatre staged in a flat in North London's broadly multi-ethnic Tottenham district, and a 150-dancer mashup at the Tower of London (see J. Thompson). Directly addressing cultural difference in the 2018 edition were a new verbatim work by Anna Deavere Smith, *Notes from the Field*, addressing the trajectory of American youth from poverty to prison, and Faustin Linyekula's *In Search of Dinozard*, exploring the impact that decades of war, trauma, and economic uncertainty have had on the people of the Democratic Republic of the Congo as a result of European (Belgian) colonization. Finally, in partnership with Battersea

Arts Centre, LiFT sponsored Poetra Asantewa and Kwame Boafo from Ghana as artists in residence in 2018 as part of the festival's New International Voices programme.

Typically of contemporary curated live-arts festivals, LiFT's work and impact extend beyond festival time. Perhaps the best example of this is the partnership, established in 2015, between the festival and Mammalian Diving Reflex, a Toronto-based company that creates 'site and social-specific performance events, theatre productions, participatory gallery installations, videos, art objects and theoretical texts to foster dialogue and dismantle barriers between individuals of all backgrounds by bringing people together in new and unusual ways' (Mammalian).[6] Among their performances are *Haircuts by Children*, performed at LiFT in 2010, in which children of various ethnic backgrounds between the ages of nine and twelve offer free haircuts to festivalgoers. Some of the children who performed in the first iteration of the show in Toronto remained with the company and eventually formed 'Young Mammals' in training eventually to take over the company. It is the idea of the youth collective that is the basis of the Mammalian Diving Reflex long-term, six-year residency at LiFT, whose local London participants are called 'upLIFTers'. Most of the work of the upLIFTers is community-based, focused on social issues, and timed, not according to festival scheduling, but to the school year, thus challenging traditional festival temporalities. Within the festival schedule in 2018 the Young Mammals, upLIFTers, and Mit Ohne Alles – a similar group formed during a Mammalian residency at the also curated Ruhrtriennale festival in Duisburg, Germany – performed *Nightwalks with Teenagers*, 'a guided tour by youth for adults' through the culturally mixed, but predominantly South Asian Mile End neighborhood in East London at dusk (Zaiontz, 'From' 32). In 2019, an off year for the festival, the upLIFTers also created a locally based game, *Your Tottenham – If These Streets Could Talk*, in which they gathered stories in advance from audiences that were incorporated into an online map taking participants on a free immersive, augmented-reality experience to sites throughout the Ghanaian, Colombian, Congolese, Albanian, Kurdish, Greek, Turkish, Somalian, Filipino, Zimbabwean, and largely Afro-Carribbean Tottenham neighbourhood, one that has a history of tension between the police and the area's racialized communities. Throughout its existence, in ways such as these, LiFT has served as a prototype for artist-curated festivals throughout Europe and North America. And although the festival experience over the *longue durée* of LiFT is somewhat attenuated, its goal, prototypically, is civic engagement rather than cultural tourism.

Europe

In the first decade of the twenty-first century the artist-curated festival proliferated in Europe, including the founding of such notable examples as ANTI Contemporary Art Festival in Kuopio, Finland and the Ruhrtriennale in Duisburg, Germany, both in 2002, and both dedicated to works that 'explore and explode urban space' in innovative ways (ANTI); the Manchester International Festival of new work in Manchester, UK, in 2007; and the 'playfully disruptive, seriously curious' Wunderbar in Newcastle, UK, in 2009 (Wunderbar). Each of these festivals has its special features. The Ruhrtriennale maintains its flexibility by appointing its artistic directors for three-year limited terms and carves out its distinction largely through its relationship to the city of Duisburg and the surrounding Ruhr region, the third largest urban area in the European Union, the driver of Germany's post-war economic miracle in the 1950s and 1960s, and the area hardest hit by the economic crisis of the early 1970s. The festival, logically, focuses its performances on and in the city of Duisburg's former industrial buildings, as artists seek to dialogue with these spectacular industrial spaces. Its manifest interculturalism, however, does not notably represent Duisburg's large Turkish community, which represents almost 20 per cent of the city's population but tends, as in the rest of Germany, to be marginalized or resented (see Smith and Eckardt). Scheduled for September 2020 alongside collaborative interdisciplinary work by festival circuit stars such as South Africa's William Kentridge (with Kyle Shepherd and Nhlanhla Mahlangu) and Germany's Christoph Marthaler (with Peter Rundel and Anna Viebrock), was Argentinian Lola Arias's characteristically transcultural, characteristically topical *Futureland*, a show, in the form of a video game, about teenage refugees who have come alone to Germany from Afghanistan, Syria, Somalia, Guinea, and Bangladesh and are caught between cultures and generations. But the Ruhrtriennale is also more directly involved in conventional politics in ways that are characteristic of the European network, in 2018 opening in the Duisburg-Nord Landscape Park with a lecture by Indian atomic physicist, activist, and Nobel Prize winner Vandana Shiva entitled 'Earth Democracy Now'.

ANTI, notably and admirably, is free of charge, enabling broad access. It curates events throughout the year, and participates in the 'Future Divercities' collaboration, an initiative of ten partner cities, all but one of them in Europe, that 'explores new ways of collaboration and co-creation by using innovative co-design methodologies in artistic processes, incubating artwork that shuffles urban geographies, or explores new participative digital tools to creatively experience the city'. Its goal is 'to enable citizens to see things in a different way' (Future).[7] ANTI is also a participant in IN SITU, a European platform for creation in public space involving twenty partners in twelve European countries (see Metropolis, 'In Situ').[8] ANTI, moreover, remains flexible, responding tactically to artistic and municipal developments in the small culturally homgeneous city (population ca 120,000) known as the cultural centre of Eastern Finland. Keren Zaiontz has described the ways in which the 2015 edition reoriented itself around the Kuopio Marathon, 'shifting the date to coincide with the race, installing artworks at the start and finish lines, interleaving socially engaged events in and around the marathon, and hosting seminars on collective endurance' ('From' 26). The programme at ANTI ranges from the experimental to the inscrutable and tends to raise questions of cultural difference obliquely, as in 2019 when Montréal-based choreographer Dana Michel, in *Mercurial George*, performed a series of mysterious tasks, some of them culturally coded. A Black woman before a largely white audience representing nothing explicit, her performance was nevertheless cumulatively legible, as one reviewer wrote, as one 'that reveals the mundane daily struggle of life on the margins' (Rogers). In the same year Portuguese-Belgian performance artist and environmentalist Maria Lucia Cruz Correia's *Voice of Nature: The Trial* explored 'interbeing, intersectionality and restoration' by reconfiguring a courtroom to explore the difficulties of granting personhood to non-humans and thereby pushing the envelope of the intercultural (ANTI, 'Maria'), and, like Baltic Circle, approaching understandings of human-to-non-human relationality that also underpin many Indigenous festivals. Both shows are typical of the ex-centric and radically intercultural work regularly featured at the festival.

Metropolis, Copenhagen

Metropolis, founded in Copenhagen, Denmark in 2007, is not a festival. Its website calls it 'a meeting point for performance, art, and the city – an art-based metropolitan laboratory for the performative, site-specific, international art' (Metropolis). It stages a 'summer season' from May to September each year that has been discussed as an exemplary 'city festival' (Johansson 63–4), but that does not bring artists and audiences together for a delimited festive 'time out of time'. If not a festival, however, it is determinedly 'second-wave', in Zaiontz's sense. Metropolis is produced by Københavns Internationale Teater (Copenhagen International Theatre, or KIT), which, without its own dedicated theatre space, functions as a network and catalyst, using the entire city as its stage and subject matter. Prior to Metropolis KIT had produced such notable intercultural events as the Images of Africa Festival in 1991, 1993, and 1996.

Metropolis works across artistic disciplines and, as the title indicates, takes the modern metropolis as its laboratory. According to the website,

> Metropolis is in, for and with the city. Our space is the city space. We work to unravel the distance between art and reality by placing art in the midst of everyday life. We see art as an essential community-developing element, and through Metropolis, artists can engage with the city and its people, relate to the present and help create a future. (Metropolis)

In addition to its summer season of work walking (or dancing) through, staging, engaging with, redefining, and performing the city, Metropolis functions as an urban laboratory launching teaching projects; it offers residencies; like ANTI it is a partner in the EU-supported platform for art in public space, IN SITU; and it publishes articles 'by architects and city planners who work with cultural planning and temporariness; by artists who confront and expand possibilities and limitations in the city; [and] by academics contextualizing urban artistic practices' (Metropolis).

The 2019 programme was largely dedicated to various prominent European artists designing various ways for 'walking in the city' – backwards, within a mirrored cabinet, musically, hoist on acrobats' shoulders – but always engaged in walking 'as a democratic artform . . . where everyone creates their own experience' (Metropolis, 'About Metropolis'). But Metropolis's most characteristically intercultural presentation was a reprise and update of *100% FOREIGN?*, curated by Maja Nydal Eriksen, a show that began at Metropolis in 2017, collecting and displaying portraits and stories of Danish citizens with refugee backgrounds, after which it expanded its archive as it toured the country for two years. By 2019 it consisted of 250 portraits and 250 interviews with people who arrived in Denmark as refugees since 1956 and changed the face of the country. In a city that is one of the largest in the Nordic region, with almost 25 per cent of its ca 2 million population of immigrant background, in addition to its official internationalist mandate the festival takes seriously the interventions it can make into municipal inter- and intracultural encounter.

Malta Festival, Poznań

The Malta Festival was founded in Poznań, Poland in 1991 as the 'International Theatre Festival MALTA'. Because it is confined to a prescribed festival time of ten days Malta more accurately fits my working definition of a festival than Metropolis, and it has transformed in the twenty-first century into one of the most prominent artist-curated interdisciplinary live-arts festivals in Eastern Europe. The festival began in a tumultuous moment in Polish history as the country transitioned from its communist past under Soviet influence to democratic government and a market economy as the Republic of Poland. Its early years featured largely outdoor summertime performances around the artificial lake after which the festival was named, accessible to all and serving to create a collective community experience. In its second decade the festival expanded in scale and geographical footprint in the city, inviting big names from the international destination festival circuit such as Romeo Castellucci and Pippo Delbono, staging huge concerts by pop-music headliners from Leningrad Cowboys to Nine Inch Nails, and beginning to inhabit post-industrial and public buildings around the city. Late in the 2000s, however, the character of the festival shifted again, as small-scale site-specific and interactive performances in a New Situations series that was introduced in 2007 began to appear throughout the city, and discussions, workshops, and debates with artists, critics, sociologists, philosophers, literary scholars, and theoreticians were introduced.

In its third decade Malta assumed its new name and its new role as a curated, multidisciplinary, experimental, transnational festival grounded in its own communities and dedicated, in exemplary curatorial fashion, to the 'vigilant examination of its own mission' (Malta, 'Short'). Twenty years after its founding it introduced 'Idioms', a themed laboratory programme addressing urgent social issues, whose two-day Forum provides an intellectual context for its performances and issues in book publications. Notable iterations of Idioms that positioned it to work across cultural and other differences include the 2011 edition, entitled 'Excluded', which 'deliberated on the position of a human being in the world that is, on the one hand, overcrowded and suffering from privation, while on the other, marks individual human existence with loneliness and growing isolation' (Malta, 'Short'). In 2012, 'Akcje Azjatyckie/Asian Investments' hosted several projects that 'documented economic, historical and human relations' between Europe and Asia: 'Artists were asking if in the globalized world of capital, power and ideology flow there is a place for otherness, foreignness and individual perspective' (Malta, 'Short').

The recent, 2019 edition of Malta was curated by Belgium's multi-generational and interdisciplinary Needcompany (Grace Ellen Barkey, Jan Lauwers, and Maarten Seghers), who, based on the etymology of the word 'curator' (curo: to look after, attend to, or cure), understood their role to be one of healing (see Malta, 'Army'). They opened the festival, themed 'Leap of Faith', with a collective ceremonial cleansing action, building and then destroying a model of a controversial new keep recently added to Poznań's historic Royal Castle, and ended it with a singalong in the open space of Wieniawski Park near the city centre. In between, the Idiom programme rang variations on approaches to faith, from freedom to fanaticism; the festival presented outdoor performances and theatre premieres such as *Hańba*, based on John Maxwell Coetzee's Booker Prize-winning novel *Disgrace* (co-produced by Stefan Żeromski Theatre in Kielce, South Central Poland), dealing with sex and race in post-apartheid South Africa; and Generator Malta, a community arts programme initiated in 2013 in Liberty Square, continued to constitute Poznań, a Renaissance, university city, 'as an agora, space for dialogue, open meeting and exchange of experiences' (Malta, 'Short'). Generator serves as 'a platform for creativity, exchange of ideas, art and fun, and mostly for cooperation' in Wolności Square at the heart of the city, housing a large stage, the Silent Malta disco (in 2019 a queer night), a healthy eating habits zone, creativity workshops, a playground, and an area for active leisure activities. According to the festival website

> The Generator and its programme – deriving from the idea of culture understood as cultivation (Latin: cultus agri), being and creating together – is also an important gesture indicating the need for the positive evaluation of the 'festivalisation' of culture and life. If a festival remains a holiday, combines different art forms, maintains an open attitude towards the audience and artists who are ready for dialogue and the constant forming of new communities, then it is still worth thinking of it as a vital and needed manifestation of creativity and meaning in the world.[9]

The Malta Festival has had a direct influence on the year-round theatrical culture of its host city as the progenitor of a critical mass of alternative companies that constitue Poznań as the centre of the Polish 'off-theatre' movement.

Finally, like so many artist-driven festivals in Europe, Malta Festival Poznań has been part of a larger network, in this case House on Fire (HoF), which has attempted 'to claim a place in the public debate about social, environmental and political issues, arguing that artists have an active role to play in society and that artistic creation offers a valid source of knowledge and experience' (House on Fire). Its objectives are:

– Co-production and presentation of performing arts productions that have the ambition to make a contribution to the critical debate of issues on the political and social agenda (an artist-led approach);

- Organisation of multidisciplinary thematic projects, realized in close collaboration with Associated Partners from universities and civil society from all over Europe (a curator's approach);
- Publication of a series of five copy-books, dedicated to thematic approaches in the performing arts (a theoretic approach). (House on Fire)[10]

The cutting-edge curated live-arts festivals in Europe that emerged in the early twenty-first century, then, are resolutely urban and entrepreneurial and tend to focus on new and experimental performance, on local civic engagement, and on active and direct audience participation either individually or in groups, often in outdoor or site-specific settings. Their programmes rarely include plays as they are traditionally understood, or feature playwrights, and their engagement with the intercultural tends either to be specific to the host city or nation or focused on issues such as immigration or the rise of totalitarianism in ways that are topical in Europe at their moment of presentation. These European festivals also tend to participate in themed, continent-wide networks and beyond, involving co-commissioning, co-producing, training, research, and residencies that Keren Zaiontz argues have also developed new, alternative, often activist modes of sociality in the face of the fragmentation and precarity of neoliberalism's push for entrepreneurial individualism ('From' 24–5). And they have a key element to offer any emerging twenty-first-century festival paradigm: their engagement with intellectuals, politicians, and activists, using their position as live, public fora to engage festivalgoers in active and informed public debate about immediate local and globally relevant social, environmental, and political issues.

North America

North American festivals have evolved somewhat differently. In addition to the ongoing High Performance Rodeo in Calgary and Carrefour international de théâtre de Québec, there are five major twenty-first-century curated live-arts festivals in North America, each of which figures in its own ways in the transnational festival ecology. Taken together, however, they have a different flavour than their European counterparts, form a less formal network, tend to be smaller in scale, are often dominated by one-person shows performed by their creators,[11] and tend to be more successful at staging, representing, and negotiating cultural difference, especially around Indigeneity, beyond the level of locally current issues, if they are perhaps less good at collective mobilization. They do, however, as Joyce Rosario, former Associate Director of Vancouver's PuSh Festival, says, share a 'similar orientation' that from the beginning, like their European counterparts, has been self-reflexively 'about the relevance of the festival in society today', and 'about asking what role festivals can play in shaping the city' (qts in Zaiontz, 'Festivals' 162). Both concerns are central to the curatorial turn. TBA (Time-Based Arts),[12] in Portland, Oregon, and PuSh, in Vancouver, British Columbia, were founded in 2003, Fusebox in Austin, Texas and Under the Radar in New York City two years later, and Progress, in Toronto, Ontario not until 2015.

Under the Radar, New York

Although it is produced by and takes place at New York's Public Theater and is firmly grounded in its historic Greenwich Village, Astor Place neighbourhood (see Martin), Under the Radar is dedicated more to formal, aesthetic experimentation, including a more traditional understanding of 'the avant garde' (Brantley, Green, and Collins-Hughes), than to the exploration or renegotiation of urban space, and it continues, resolutely, to stage scripted plays in the recognizable spaces of theatres. The 2020 festival had no perambulatory performance, city walks, transnational/local shows, post-industrial sites, waterfront spectacles, or site-specific work, and indeed all but four of the twenty-five shows and events took place at venues within the Public Theater itself, which had the distinct virtue of enabling informal conversation and exchange among the festival's diverse participants.[13] As Oskar Eustis, Artistic Director of the Public, has said,

> for the two weeks of the Under the Radar Festival, The Public is a citizen of the world, part of a global community that crosses national boundaries and insists on the international character of culture. For two weeks, we welcome artists and presenters from all over the world and are allowed to participate in a vigorous, cantankerous, and joyous colloquium about where the world is heading. It's exhilarating, exhausting, and irreplaceable. (qtd in Martin 126)

Scheduled to coincide with the January meetings of the Association for Performing Arts Professionals, a US-based international presenters' organization, the festival functions in part as a kind of global avant-garde performing arts marketplace. Nevertheless, partly because New York is a broadly multicultural city with a 25 per cent Black and 14 per cent Asian population, and the now upscale Astor Place neighborhood historically an immigrant one (see Martin 120–3), Under the Radar also serves the Public Theater's mission to provide 'a high-visibility platform to support artists from diverse backgrounds who are redefining the act of making theater' (Public). That the diversity is not only disciplinary but cultural is clear from the programming for the 2020 edition, where, indeed, almost every show featured a non-dominant-culture creative team and explored one or more type of cultural difference. The shows were not identified by nation in the programme or positioned to fulfill any kind of diplomatic or representational role. The main programme included an American play performed in Mandarin, a show exploring the contemporary realities of Indigenous Mexico (of which more below), a Palestinian play performed by Israeli and West Bank actors, Samuel Beckett's *Not I* performed by an actor with Tourette syndrome exploring neurodiversity, an experimental Japanese play, a show in which five activists with intellectual disabilities hold a public meeting, three plays exploring Black histories and subjectivities, and a short virtual reality collaboration between Laurie Anderson and Taiwanese new media star Hsin-Chien Huang in which the audience is taken to the moon. The 'Incoming' series at the Shiva Theater was equally diverse and adventuresome, including six shows that together probed Black, 'Indigiqueer', and Asian American experience, identities, and cultural (mis)representations. An Under the Radar Late Night series, a Concert Series in Joe's Pub, an Open Circle series on 'Black Art, Black Liberation', and an Audience Accessibility Panel rounded out the 2020 programme. The audience experience at Under the Radar, then, is one of serial immersion over two intense weeks within a contained space in a global city and diverse upscale neighborhood in a multifaceted meta-performance of cultural difference.

A show typical of intercultural work on the curated, live-arts festival scene, but perhaps particularly representative of Under the Radar at its best, was *Andares*, by conceptual director Héctor Flores Komatsu and Mexico City's Makuyeika Colectivo Teatral. A naturalized US citizen, Komatsu is Mexican-born of Mexican and Japanese heritage, trained in the US in Theatre Directing with minors in Translation, World Theatre, and Ethnic Studies and working internationally with the likes of Peter Brook and Marie-Hélène Estienne in Paris as an awardee of the inaugural Julie Taymor World Theatre Fellowship. *Andares* ('pathways') would seem to have been influenced by Brook: it is, as reviewer Chris Jones has written, 'theatre at its most elemental' in at least two senses. It is minimalist in the

Figure 9   In 2020 *Andares* brought to Under the Radar festival audiences acute awareness
of the global impact of American corporate and political imperatives
and interferences. Photograph by Fabian Hammerl

current Brook manner: three actors largely playing themselves, few props,
some mask work, and minimal tech support (see Figure 9). And, also after
Brook, it is in part 'a poetic narrative about the lives, ancestral myths and
culture' of Indigenous people of, in this case, rural Mexico (Bishop). The
show was performed in Spanish, Mayan, Zapotec, Tzotzil, and Wixarika
with English surtitles, and if it began in familiar territory, with, as New
York reviewer Natalie Rine writes, 'fiestas and families', it quickly moved
into regions largely uncharted by Brook and other western interculturalists,
'expertly layering and painting story after story to turn traditional narratives about Mexico on their heads, and to pull back the curtain on present-
day struggles and strife' (Rine). It dealt with specific and local (to what is
now Mexico) Indigenous issues ranging from enforced land dispossession
through violent cultural repression, community resistance and renewal to
individual stories of growing up Muxe (a third gender in Zapotec culture),
ultimately also addressing Donald Trump, MAGA, and The Wall. All of
these issues were probed through revivified creation stories and other
culturally specific narratives.

Andares was performed with great skill and grace by three storytellers
(Josué Maychi, Domingo Mijangos, and Lupe de la Cruz) and one

musician (Raymundo Pavon Lozano), and it characteristically brought to Under the Radar audiences in the corporate capital of the US acute awareness of the global impact of American corporate and political imperatives and interferences. Arguably, Komatsu and his company reappropriated the work of western interculturalists, attracting New York audiences through familiar Brookian tropes but locating them in real-world contexts that addressed grounded Indigenous normativities in negotiation with western and Indigenous modernities.[14] Although its *form* was the familiar one used by many festivals in the Global West and North – the serial presentation of plays from different countries – the feel of Under the Radar was neither competitive nor spectacular, and its staging in a single location tended towards the creation of an experience closer to the communal, participatory, relational one modelled by the Indigenous festivals I discuss in Chapter 1 than to that of spectatorial objectification and consumption.

Carol Martin has argued, however, that in spite of relatively low ticket prices – USD $30 for most shows – 'an experimental theatre festival like Under the Radar can easily be accused of élitism' (129) in that it tends, she says, to attract an educated rather than a popular audience, a distinction that has a resonance that is perhaps peculiar to the United States in the early twenty-first century. More cogently, she points out that, because the festival relies in part (as many festivals do) on the shows' countries of origin to pay travel costs and artist fees, large parts of the world that can't pay such costs remain un- or underrepresented.[15] 'Can the phrase "under the radar" really apply to performances that are well-publicized, supported, and moving around the world?' she asks (129):

> What about performers from countries that do not or cannot provide support? What about performers from Sudan, Syria, Iraq, Chad, Iran, Libya, North Korea, Somalia, Venezuela, and Yemen – the countries listed by President Trump's travel ban?[16] A look at UTR's 'geographical reach' map of the world showing where the artists come from, reveals huge blanks for the Arabian Peninsula, sub-Saharan Africa (except for South Africa), the interior of central Asia, the western portion of South America, small portions of South-East Asia, and the Scandinavian countries . . . Are [these places] off the radar? No-fly zones? Still operating in post-colonial economies? Are these regions bereft of experimental performances? If so, why? Poverty, religion, political turmoil, lack of interest in experimental performance, or religious conviction? What does it mean to be global when UTR's global reach is not 'everywhere'? (129)

These are questions that could be asked of almost every festival discussed in this book.

Fusebox, Austin

The focus of Under the Radar, then, is on formal experimentation and its strengths are in the representation of difference and the bringing together of a community of difference among artists and audiences in a concentrated space in one of the world's most multicultural cities. Fusebox, in the smaller city of Austin, Texas (population ca 932,000) focuses its energies on liveness and serves its beleaguered progressive community largely as a celebration and validation of itself in a fundamentally hostile US state. Its strengths are its ability to draw from and on an already established local arts community, and, because of its 'Free Range Art' fundraising initiative, its ability to offer its full programme free of charge with first-come-first-served registration.[17] The festival both presents and commissions new work, and it operates year-round with a healthy slate of public events, workshops, advocacy, online blogs, and interviews keeping in touch with its artists. Without the concentration of venues that the Public Theater offers in New York, Fusebox events are spread across the city but concentrated into an intensive, five-day programme. Without the range of local cultures that constitute New York's arts scene, its capacity to constitute communities of difference is more limited, in spite of Austin's deserved reputation as an isolated pocket of liberalism in Texas. A large majority of the shows at the festival, almost exclusively interdisciplinary 'live art', are from the US, many of them from Austin itself. International shows in 2019 were from England, Chile, Mexico, Norway, and Scotland, and shows representing cultural difference, fittingly for a city with large Hispanic, Black, and LGBTQ populations, tended to concern Black, Latinx, or queer experience and to intervene productively into dominant-culture representations of those groups. And as the website for the 2019 festival says,

> The performances, the parties, the meals, the discussions, etc, leverage and celebrate the potential of the live situation. What does it mean to be in a space with other people and what kinds of things are only possible in this space?' ('Fusebox Festival 2019').

'For us', the website says, 'the act of putting on the festival is built on a deep belief in creating space for the unexpected, for disruption, for discovery, and experimentation. It's also a powerful moment to connect, imagine new things together, and build community.'

In 2019 this meant such things as Justin Favela, in a work entitled *¿Quihúbole?* ('What's happening?'), wrapping the Festival Hub in piñata-like papier-mâché including text from a conversation with his mother and grand-mother in Guatemala, a significant origin of asylum seekers to the US, many by way of Texas, who are controversially subject to abuse and deportation without being allowed either to register asylum claims in the US or to access effective protection in Guatemala (see 'Deportation'). Other featured shows in 2019 included Michael J. Love's *GON HEAD AND PUT YOUR RECORDS ON!*, an 'aural/visual mixtape' exploration and celebration of Blackness ('Fusebox Festival 2019'); or *ARAB.AMP*, an Arab futurist music experiment featuring Mike Koury replacing Palestinian multi-instrumentalist Dirar Kalash, who was denied an entry visa to perform at the festival. Exemplary of Fusebox's range and speaking to Austin's large environmentalist community was Chilean director/playwright Manuela Infante's solo show, *Estado Vegetal*, in which co-author and performer Marcela Salinas extended the intercultural into the interspecies and the interspecies beyond animals to vegetables. Emerging from Chile, the show arguably expanded the reach of an existing green movement in Austin, the capital city of an oil state with an abysmal environmental record. Structuring her story around a 'trunk' event and 'branching out' into the stories that grew from it, Infante privileged plant voices and ontologies, to the degree that the performer followed the light, as plants do, rather than being followed by it as in traditional theatre. Performed in Spanish with English surtitles, this absurd, sophisticated, complex, polit-ical, and very funny show was grounded, as it were, in developments in the new field of plant neurobiology, which affirms the fact that plants are cognitive organisms and asserts the presence of the vegetative within humans (who are partly made up of plant genomes). It also aligned with Indigenous understandings of the centrality of relations with non-human nations. With great versatility and virtuosity, the show returned the human, as it were, to its roots.[18]

PuSh, Vancouver

At the other side of the continent in the West-Coast Canadian city of Vancouver, the PuSh Festival is also premised on the building of commu-nity and on 'the conscious mix of local and global programming' (Dickinson, 'PuShing' 140) in a city whose population is made up of over 51 per cent visible minorities, mostly East Asian. PuSh also focuses on live art and, also without its own dedicated performance space, is staged in venues spread widely across the city (population ca 610,000). According to the festival website,

> The PuSh Festival highlights new ways of storytelling, new forms of staging, new approaches to combining disciplines, and new views on contemporary themes and issues. PuSh envisions its leadership role as a catalyst and animator. We foster connections between existing audiences and artists, while providing an occasion for dialogue and exchange between like-minded communities. (PuSh, 'About')

According to Peter Dickinson, an academic, artist, and former President of the festival's Board, 'some of the key principles' of PuSh, under its founding Artistic and Executive Director Norman Armour, are 'a lack of dogma and ideological hierarchies around performance aesthetics, fostering collaboration and partnerships inside and outside the studio, [and] understanding the relationship between one's practice and the overall social and cultural sustainability of one's city' ('PuShing' 139):

> From the beginning, PuSh sought to establish itself as a unique performance brand within the increasingly crowded landscape of regional festivals by being 1) curated; 2) multidisciplinary; and 3) local, national, and global, not just in terms of the scale and scope of the work and artists presented, but in terms of the critical conversations prompted in its audiences and the opportunities for creative exchange fostered among industry partners as a result . . . Finally, . . . PuSh is more than just an animator of the live arts; it is also an incubator, actively commissioning new work from local and international artists. (133)

According to Joyce Rosario in December 2017, then PuSh's Associate Director, the festival started, in part, because 'there simply weren't a lot of international works coming into the city, and therefore a kind of dialogue with the artists here [in Vancouver] was missing' (qtd in Zaiontz, 'Festival' 154). In response, founders Norman Armour and Katrina Dunn, both practising artists, initiated a modest series with Touchstone Theatre and Rumble Productions in 2003 that officially acquired festival status two years later. PuSh has grown since its lean early years to the point of having a budget, in 2018, of nearly CAD $1.8 million, almost half of which came from grants from municipal, provincial, and national governments, and over half of which was spent on artistic and curatorial expenses. With this budget a year-round staff of 9 plus 40 seasonal contract staff presented 150 performances and events at eighteen venues across the city over three weeks in January 2018, with the aid of 200 volunteers, and of venue managers not employed by the festival.

In an essay entitled 'PuShing Performance Brands in Vancouver', the festival serves Dickinson as an illuminating case study of the complex relationship between a curated live-arts festival 'that speaks to the diverse urban community [it] claims to represent' (132) and the venues and funders that it needs to enter into partnership with in order to establish and maintain its place in that community and serve its own and its communities' core values. Dickinson begins with an account of PuSh's attempts to establish as a flagship, anchoring venue the newly renovated Woodward's building at the edge, on one side, of Vancouver's and Canada's poorest neighborhood, the Downtown Eastside, and on the other of a developing and gentrifying 'cultural precinct' that it was hoped might come to serve as the core of festival activities (134). The historic building at the intersection of the Gastown and Chinatown neighbour-hoods had been associated with community service, including bringing cultures together, during periods of economic decline and recovery since its construction in 1903, but had been vacant since 1993. It was rein-vented in 2010 as the home of Simon Fraser University's (SFU) School for the Contemporary Arts and established as a PuSh partner with shared values. A year later the University approved a CAD $10 million donation from Goldcorp – a mining company with a human rights record that was questionable at best – that gave the corporation name-brand rights to the building as the Goldcorp Centre for the Arts but caused a flurry of controversy. Dickinson's analysis teases out, in this context, some of the cultural, economic, and urban semiotic resonances that subtend a pro-gramme tagline such as 'a PuSh presentation at the Goldcorp Centre for the Arts, SFU Woodwards' (132).

Goldcorp has never directly sponsored PuSh, and many local organiza-tions do sponsor work at the festival that directly engages with the city in socially conscious ways. Dickinson points, for example, to local artisanal bakery Terra Bread's support for Projet in Situ's *Do You See What I Mean?* in 2013, a blindfolded guided tour of the city that was also supported by the Canadian National Institute for the Blind. He also cites the local financial co-op Vancity's sponsorship of the festival's Aboriginal Performance series and its free community ticketing programme in 2011. But it is worth asking what the staging of such a series under local sponsorship means at the very moment when the festival was also associ-ated with a Vancouver-based multinational that in 2014 was making international news for brutally suppressing Indigenous protests against the environmental devastation caused by its mining operations in Guatemala (see Hill; Dakin and Moyles)?[19] What did it mean to open the festival in 2012 in the Goldcorp Centre, on the edge of the Downtown Eastside with its high Indigenous population and its grisly history of violence against Indigenous women,[20] with *Amarillo*, by Mexico's Teatro

Linea de Sombra? On opening night this show about the horrendous situation facing would-be immigrants attempting to cross into the US paused to address a letter to 'citizens of Vancouver', including the Simon Fraser University President seated in the front row, urging them 'to protest the damage wrought on the environment and local indigenous populations by mining companies' – including Goldcorp – 'operating in Mexico' (Dickinson, 'PuShing' 148). At the very least this raises questions about the many intersecting and competing resonances of sustainability – cultural, urban, economic, and environmental – for the festival, for a city built on the unceded territories of the Sḵwx̱wú7mesh (Squamish), Stó:lō and Səlílwətaʔ/Selilwitulh (Tsleil-Waututh) and xʷməθkʷəy̓əm (Musqueam) Nations, for its people (including both the hip *and* the homeless), for the various cultures it supports (including the Indigenous and the immigrant), and for the environment, both local and global.

The relationship between PuSh and the Goldcorp Centre at SFU has cooled in recent years, though the festival still retains ties with the SFU Faculty of Communication, Art and Technology which hosts the festival's 'Critical Ideas' series there (see Dickinson, 'PuSh'). And in 2020 the Centre staged the intercultural *Flying White –* 飞白 at its large, 400-plus-capacity Fei and Milton Wong Experimental Theatre. The anticipated 'cultural precinct' has not fully materialized, at least as a geographical base for the festival, which now extends from New Westminster in the southeast to the University of British Columbia campus in the west.

PuSh is representative of most curated live-arts festivals in its efforts to stage transnational/local shows such as *Lookout*, with which this chapter opened: shows that are locally produced but based on concepts that travel from festival to festival globally, purportedly engaging the concerns of host cities. But quite apart from difficult questions of sponsorships, partnerships, and sustainability that dog all small-scale festivals such as PuSh, it's worth asking how effectively these internationally designed, locally applied shows can exceed their neoliberal marketability and serve local communities in culturally specific and genuinely generative ways. *Lookout* certainly engaged with local schoolchildren in what must have been, for the children, a consciousness-raising exercise. But for festivalgoers such as myself, did standing at a tourist observation deck overlooking the picturesque Vancouver waterfront actually engage audiences with the specific social or ecological situation facing a socially and culturally striated Vancouver? (None of the observation stations used by the show was on the side of the tower overlooking the rest of the city, and both the show and the tower more figuratively overlooked most of the city's more impoverished neighbourhoods.) Was the overview with which spectators were provided sufficiently specific to address the local cultural or even geographic situation of Vancouver as anything other than a vaguely representative global, oceanside city?

The same questions apply to other PuSh imports that have cast locally but thought globally. Two of the progenitors of such shows on global circuits, the Berlin-based Rimini Protokoll and the Berlin-Nottingham collective Gob Squad, have each appeared at PuSh and raised such questions. Rimini Protokoll's *100% Vancouver* in 2011 (following *100% Berlin* and *100% Vienna*) cast 100 local Vancouverites (including recent immigrants) to provide a 'psychographic' portrait of the city of the kind used by marketers to develop arguably reductive algorithms allowing them to target their advertising (see Dickinson, 'PuShing' 145). Audiences were delighted to 'see themselves' in this way, but it is open to question whose interests the portrait ultimately served. Did including among the cast a very recent immigrant woman from Vietnam constitute the show as effectively or meaningfully intercultural? Did the show generate productive conversations across the city's many different communities? Did it constitute the city *as* a community of difference?

Karen Zaiontz has analyzed the PuSh appearance in 2014 of Gob Squad's globally peripatetic transnational/local *Super Night Shot*, in which the company give themselves the pre-show hour to record a nighttime film of their host city and their interactions with its inhabitants that is shown unedited on multiple screens, with the final minutes shot live in the theatre lobby. The show has purported to take on the anonymity of urban life in hundreds of host cities since 2003, and it all feels stylishly rebellious (see Zaiontz, 'Human Rights' 48). But given its time and other constraints (including the company's lack of in-depth knowledge of place), it can only, at best, remain superficial as a reflection of the city, most useful, perhaps, in reinforcing the agendas of city branding and tourism promotion. Zaiontz concludes that the success of the many local variants of *Super Night Shot* at festivals in Canada and elsewhere has been due to the fact that 'it was risky in appearance only. The production posed no significant challenge to existing institutions or sites of power' (49):

> Locking their gaze on the city, Gob Squad confirmed what PuSh and its audiences already knew about Vancouver. This confirmation of the familiar aspects of the city was shown to be as appealing to audiences as its transformation into an unpredictable, carnivalesque site.
>
> As long, that is, as that familiarity did not reveal what was undesirable about the city. Despite their proximity to Main and Hastings Street [at the

heart of the Downtown Eastside] – one of the most socially marginalized neighborhoods in Canada – Gob Squad screened a version of Vancouver that I can only describe as Vancouver *lite*. *Super Night Shot* avoided contact with the culture of homelessness, drug addiction, mental illness, and survival sex work that is a visible part of street life in parts of Gastown and Chinatown. (50–1, emphasis in original)

And, of course, it did not address the realities of, or reasons for, the urban inequalities that disproportionately assign such visible aspects of street life to some communities rather than others.

In addition to the transnational/local *Lookout*, programming at PuSh in 2018 included inventive immersive work such as Shannon Yee's *Reassembled, Slightly Askew*, from Northern Ireland, and Britt Hatzius's transnational/local *Blind Cinema*, from England and Germany. In the former, a maximum of eight audience members were 'admitted', hospital-style, with plastic wrist bands, to a clinical setting in which, replacing our shoes and jackets with sleep masks and headphones, we lay on hospital beds and experienced, through extraordinary 3D sound technology, the journey from admission through brain surgery to recovery of a survivor – the playwright – of a serious brain injury. In the latter immersive intergenerational experience, the audience was seated blindfolded in a movie theatre while a row of children behind us, some of them 'audible minorities', described in whispers what they saw projected onto the screen. These are familiar examples of the type of creative curation that frequents the curated live-arts festivals that are the subject of this chapter, and in spite of some of the shortcomings I've discussed, they did represent potentially generative provocations for lively discussions-across-differences – including in these cases generational differences and differences in ability and health – that followed the performances.

Vancouver is a broadly intercultural, environmentally conscious city on Canada's Pacific Coast with a large and relatively well-off Asian and a significant, largely indigent Indigenous population (officially 2.2 per cent in the 2016 census),[21] and the programming at the festival to some extent reflects and attempts to intervene in these realities. In 2018 the festival's Board President, Mira Oreck, praised the curatorial team for assiduously searching out artists who 'push boundaries, promote thinking, and initiate collaboration between and among cultures' (PuSh, 'Programme', 14). One member of that team, Filipina Canadian Joyce Rosario – one of the very few women-of-colour curators of international festivals I have encountered – has indicated that 'sometimes my very presence alone is a challenge to the dominant paradigm' (qtd in Zaiontz, 'Festival' 159), which, of course, tends to normalize whiteness.

In 2018, in addition to the stunningly complex and virtuosic *MDLSX* by gender-fluid artist Silvia Calderoni and Italy's Motus, drawing on Jeffrey Eugenides' novel *Middlesex*; the evocative puppet show *It's Dark Outside* by Australia's The Last Great Hunt, effectively addressing, for children, dementia among the elderly; and New World Theatre's transformative *King Arthur's Night*, by a mixed creative team of Down Syndrome and non-disability artists – each of which effectively took on different and currently urgent forms of cultural difference – PuSh addressed Asian and Indigenous cultures directly in three of its mainstage presentations and in many other aspects of the festival. In addition to the shows themselves, including choreographer Lin Lee-Chen's epic and elemental *The Eternal Tides*, from Taiwan, Euro-Cree-Métis choreographer Daina Ashbee's visceral and feminist *Pour*, from Québec, and a concert performance by two-spirit Euro-Cree cellist Cris Derksen, the 2018 festival included an important Critical Ideas session on Contemporary Indigenous Women's Performance featuring seven Indigenous panellists from First Nations in Turtle Island and Australia.[22] The PuSh artists-in-residence in that year, moreover, were the three members of Vancouver's own Hong Kong Exile, a diasporic performance collective founded by Natalie Tin Yin Gan, Milton Lim, and Remy Siu to explore cultural politics in interdisciplinary ways. In addition to leading the PuSh Youth programme and completing their own development work in the second year of their two-year residency, Hong Kong Exile's contribution to the mainstage series in 2018 was *Foxconn Frequency (No. 3): For Three Visibly Chinese Performers* (Figure 10), with Remy Siu taking the lead. The show exemplifies the ways in which a curated live-arts festival can nurture and support a local intercultural company exploring urgent transnational political concerns in intellectually sophisticated, aesthetically innovative, and provocatively interdisciplinary ways.

The performers in *Foxconn Frequency* – Natalie Tin Yin Gan, Andrei Chi Lok Koo, and internationally acclaimed pianist Vicky Chow – never spoke, and their repetitive, sometimes-frenzied piano playing was never heard by the audience but was competitively evaluated in various ways by the computers that were connected – along with a screen, speakers, and a live 3D colour printer keeping track of their progress – to their keyboards. On one level, the show was a commentary on the labour of artistic and other industrial production and the competitive culture of piano pedagogy. Another layer of significance, however, was signalled by the title's reference to Foxconn Technology Group, the Taiwan-based multinational electronics company that made the news early in the 2010s for its poor working

Figure 10   Resident arts company Hong Kong Exile's *Foxconn Frequency (No. 3): For Three Visibly Chinese Performers* brought a complex, political, sensory overload performance to Vancouver's PuSh Festival in 2018. Photograph by Samson Cheung Choi Sang 張才生

conditions and military-style surveillance that prompted a series of worker suicides executed by jumping from factory roofs in mainland China – suicides that continue to this day. The show included the projection of excerpts from poems by one of those workers, Xu Lizhi, who jumped to his death out of a window in a dormitory run by Foxconn in Shenzhen, China, in 2014. The 'visibly Chinese bodies' of the show's subtitle, then, referenced the living and dead bodies of Chinese workers. The complex, sensory-overload show played on the stereotype of the hypercompetitive Asian musical prodigy dressed in pristine white button-up shirts and black trousers, but it did much more than explode a stereotype. As reviewer Kelsey Blair wrote, 'the piece's final image – two visibly Chinese female performers onstage pounding piano keys that make no sound – [was] powerful, and the production's impressive technology, in combination with its complex intellectual underpinnings, [made] for thought-provoking avant-garde theatre'.

PuSh 2020 was equally compelling in its representation and exploration, in this case, of a wide range of cultural difference and the politics impacting it. The line-up is worth rehearsing at length to illustrate the kinds of wide-ranging, complex, and intersectional works the festival as meta-event placed in conversation:

– the opening weekend party, *Ikigai Machine*, offered what its subtitle called *A Disability-Arts Vaudeville Experience* by Deaf-culture curator, advocate, and artist Myles de Bastion, featuring DJ Deaf Wish;
– the Critical Ideas series included a session on disability and 'crip' arts featuring blind artivist Alex Bulmer in conversation with Keren Zaiontz;[23]
– *Anywhere But Here*, by Vancouver's Electric Company Theatre, told the 'reverse immigration' story of a family's attempt to return from Canada to Chile in 1979, exploring the condition of statelessness in ways charged with contemporary relevance;
– *Footnote Number 12*, by Norway's Spreafico Eckly and Vancouver's Theatre Replacement, probed the politics of language and the power of privilege in a deconstructive show that included a participatory reading experience for audiences;
– *Frontera*, a collaboration by Canada's Animals of Distinction and Fly Pan Am with the UK's United Visual Artists, used light, gestural movement, and music to challenge the impermeability of borders and the omnipresence of surveillance;
– *Gardens Speak*, an immersive sound installation, one of two shows at the festival by Lebanon's Tania El Khoury, exposed audiences in groups of ten to the dangerous and subversive burial practices of the families of those killed by the state in contemporary Syria;
– *Old Stock: A Refugee Love Story* by Hanna Moscovitch and Halifax, Nova Scotia's 2b theatre company told a raucous tale of Moscovitch's refugee grandparents' arrival in Canada from Romania in 1908;
– and finally, Toronto's Frank Theatre staged Jamaican Canadian powerhouse d'bi young anitafrika's *She, Mami Wata & The Pussy WitchHunt*, taking on gender, sexuality, religion, and the legacy of colonization in present-day Jamaica.

As a meta-event, then, PuSh in 2020 constituted a complex and far-reaching intersectional conversation about difference, ability, privilege, immigration, and state power. Local audiences experiencing the festival were exposed to a cornucopia of cultures in conversation, a conversation that was carefully curated and choreographed by the festival's 'Critical Ideas' series of public conversations with artists and activists.

Vancouver's significant eco-activist, Indigenous, and Asian communities, moreover, were not forgotten. Environmentalism was in evidence in the form of a featured, one-night-only workshop presentation by Toronto's Why Not Theatre of *What You Won't Do for Love*, featuring Canada's environmentalist icon, Japanese Canadian David Suzuki, and his life partner Tara Cullis. The show, under development by Why Not and PuSh, was scheduled to premiere in a full production at PuSh 2021. It is based on Suzuki and Cullis's life and activism together, asking what it would mean to love the planet with the same intensity and commitment that we love our partners, children, and friends. The show was used in 2020 publicity and fundraising materials to announce a commitment on the part of the festival under its then artistic director Franco Boni to 'creativity', 'political consciousness', and 'stewardship', as well as to what it is now calling a defining feature of the festival: 'relationships – between organizations, between people, between humanity and a global climate emergency' (PuSh, 'Fall Update').[24] In this focus on relationships and stewardship, PuSh under Boni was directly influenced by his work with Indigenous artists in consciously turning the festival towards an Indigenous model involving relationality, participation, and witnessing.[25]

Relationships, relationality, and what Opaskwayak Cree scholar Shawn Wilson calls 'relational accountability' – across the human and non-human world – are at the heart of most Indigenous worldviews (97–125). They were also at the heart of Skwxwu7mesh/Stó:Lō/Irish Métis/Hawaiʻian/ Swiss interdisciplinary artivist Tʼuyʼtʼtanat-Cease Wyss's 'Keynote Manifesto' at the festival's Industry series, which focused, among other things, on sustainability. And they were at the heart of that year's Critical Ideas series. Curated by Keren Zaiontz and Dylan Robinson (Stó:lō), Critical Ideas 2020 included sessions On Commitment, On Democracy, and On Gathering, this last featuring four Indigenous artists: choreographer/director Emily Johnson (Yupʼik), writer/artist Camille Georgeson-Usher (Coast Salish/Sahtu Dene/Scottish), choreographer/curator and researcher Satu Herrala of the Baltic Circle Festival in Helsinki, and Robinson. Finally, the PuSh Assembly series that incorporates Critical Ideas also included the weeklong Invasion Day – Foreshore Session. A week of public events informed by the ebb and flow of the tides, this series of sound, performance, discussion, exchange, talks, walks, and listening sessions was designed to link Vancouver's False Creek transnationally and trans-Indigenously with Sydney Harbour, Australia and to explore their parallel histories of colonization, settlement, and climate change.

There was, however, only one Indigenous show in the mainstage programming at PuSh 2020. *Skyborn: A Land Reclamation Odyssey*, by

Musqueam writer/performer Quelemia Sparrow, was a world premiere and part of the Femme series at its Vancouver East PuSh venue, The Cultch. In this show the burden of representation posed by being the only Indigenous mainstage show at the festival was eased somewhat by the cultural specificity of the work – what Coulthard would call its grounded normativity (13). *Skyborn* was grounded in Musqueam cosmology, and used Musqueam and Stó:lō visual and storytelling techniques to recount the journey of a granddaughter to reclaim her lost soul from the land of the dead. By extension, this story became the reclamation odyssey of the show's subtitle – the reclamation of land, culture, and self which built on the traditional form of the spirit-canoe voyage along a river of stars to carve out, in the science-fiction fantasy mode of Indigenous futurism,[26] the moving beyond mere survival to a thriving present and the prefigurative imagining-into-being of a flourishing future – in short, Indigenous resurgence. Using a traditional Coast Salish practice, the show-as-ceremony was performed before an invited witness (U'tsam) from the audience – and before the audience in general constituted as witnesses rather than spectators – who is charged with the responsibility of keeping the memory alive.[27] Sparrow, in a consensus-based trans-Indigenous creative collaboration with her director Kim Senklip Harvey (Syilx, Tsilhqot'in, Ktunaxa, and Dakelh) and a team of singers, puppeteers, mask-makers, visual artists, and designers, performed the central granddaughter character (who also appeared as a masked puppet), her grandmother, mother, father, and sister as they encounter a black hole, a hungry wolf, a rabbit, a dragonfly, and a cosmic cast of characters. The show participated in and contributed to an active movement in Vancouver, British Columbia, and Canada towards Indigenous cultural resurgence, itself an ongoing reclamation oddyssy. Its mixture of ceremony with representation, its explicit use of the U'tsam witness ceremony, and its assignment of the role of witnesses to all of its participants, model at the level of the individual show a new and ancient Indigenous performance paradigm.

Vancouver's significant East Asian community was reflected and constituted onstage *as* a community at PuSh 2020 in a variety of ways. *Monday Nights*, by Toronto's 6th Man Collective, was an obvious choice for PuSh. Originally produced by Toronto's The Theatre Centre under Franco Boni, the show engaged audience members of all ages in a self-reflexive, participatory reenactment of Monday night pick-up basketball games by an almost all-Asian group of young men. *Cuckoo*, part of Korean-Belgian multimedia artist Jaha Koo's *Hamartia Trilogy*, brought global *and* Korea-specific, anti-capitalist awareness to the festival in a performance that is discussed in more detail below as part of Toronto's Progress Festival. The large-scale, showcase production of the festival, however, explicitly intercultural, was the world premiere of *Flying White* – 飞白 at the Fei and Milton Wong Theatre at SFU, a collaboration between Vancouver's Wen Wei Dance and Turning Point [contemporary music] Ensemble, choreographed by Wen Wei, composed by Owen Underhill and Dorothy Chang, and evocatively designed by Linda Chow (costumes), Jonathan Kim (lights), and Mark Eugster (scenic consultancy). The show is named for a rare and particularly graceful type of traditional Chinese calligraphy consisting of wide, black, ribbon-like brush strokes on a white paper background that give the impression, appropriately as an inspiration for choreographic experimentation, of jumping or leaping on the surface without losing contact with the paper (see Beyond Calligraphy). But this was not in any sense a traditional dance piece to musical accompaniment. It gathered an intercultural ensemble of six dancers and twelve onstage musicians playing a mix of Chinese and western instruments who were integrated interactively into the choreography, with music, dance, and elements such as rice, paper, water, silk, and ink woven (metaphorically) together in a complex live tapestry. Chinese Canadian Wen Wei's chore-ography blended Chinese and Canadian elements from Tai Chi, Martial Arts, Peking Opera, and contemporary dance to 'explore cross-cultural links that are especially rich in the cultural ecology of Vancouver and are imbedded in unique ways in the work of the individual artists' in the production ('Turning Point'). The show attracted a large and culturally mixed audience from British Columbia's lower mainland, including a substantial Chinese Canadian component,[28] and arguably contributed to the sophisticated constitution of uniquely intercultural Chinese Canadian subjectivities.

PuSh, then, is mindful of the need to stage, and disrupt, stereotypical representations of difference, and to present work that exhibits cultural difference less as static and fixed in time than as vibrant and complex components of an intercultural urban performance ecology. The audience experience of PuSh consists primarily of local audiences actively engaging with their own city, bringing festivalgoers from different residential and ethnic neighbourhoods together over three weeks each (usually rainy) January at venues distributed throughout the city, in an extended live-arts exploration of aesthetic and cultural difference. Because of its geo-graphical and temporal dispersion, however, and in spite of a stellar and intellectually challenging Critical Ideas series, PuSh has to date been less good at bringing people, particularly artists from outside of the city, together in the same space across their differences for meaningful exchange. TBA (Time-Based Arts) Festival, only 500 kilometres south of Vancouver in Portland, Oregon, occurs in a more concentrated space.

Time-Based Arts (TBA), Portland

Just down the coast from Vancouver is the culturally rich and politically left-leaning, racially mixed, and LGBTQ-friendly[29] US city of Portland, Oregon (population ca 650,000), which became a national flashpoint around Black Lives Matter protests and American electoral politics in the summer of 2020. Over ten days each September Portland's Time-Based Arts (TBA), which has used a rotating guest curator model since the departure of its founder Kristy Edmunds in 2006, is carefully designed to foreground cross-disciplinary encounters with and between artists. Indeed, Norman Frisch of the Yale School of Drama, has argued that TBA

> encompasses installation work, all kinds of media work, new media work, site-specific performance, dance, theater, and so on. It's creating a context in which all these different kinds of artists are seeing and connecting with one another, and it's opening up the possibilities of these various art forms to one another. Over and over again I've met artists at that festival who began as one kind of artist and became another kind of artist because their eyes and senses were opened by encountering other artists at this festival over many years. That's a great contribution.
> That's a festival that happens one month a year but has a year-round impact on its community. One of the reasons it's been able to do that is that Portland is a very manageably sized community. It's possible for most of the artists and much of the audience to really know one another. It's a small enough city that they can find one another, see one another, keep in touch with one another ... Festivals that are spread over a large area are much more difficult to curate, as anyone will tell you. (Frisch 51–2)

Indeed, in 2019, almost half the programme's forty-nine events consisted of panels, workshops, creative exchanges, meet-the-artist events, an opening block party, a pancake breakfast, a functioning festival Corner Store, and especially 'conversations', of which there were no less than eleven officially scheduled. Almost every show, film, and installation at the 2019 edition of the festival, moreover, involved staging or working across difference of one or more kinds – ability, culture, race, gender, or sexuality. Many of the performances and events were free, and few ticket prices exceeded USD $25.

The featured artist at TBA 2019 was Japanese American Eiko Otake. Performing *A Body in Places* in and around the Center for Contemporary

Art and Culture as part of the festival's opening reception, she also presented *The Duet Project: The Distance Is Malleable*, which explicitly explored 'the different ways individuals encounter and converse . . .; how we grapple with cross-generational provocation; environmental and nuclear disaster; the malleability of distances between locations, individuals, and events; and what the dead left us' (Portland). She also presented *A Body in Fukushima: Reflections on the Nuclear in Everyday Life* at the festival, her film about the desolate and radiation-soaked landscapes of Fukushima, Japan in the wake of the 2011 earthquake, tsunami, and nuclear meltdown there.

> Throughout the film, Eiko is in constant dialogue with a post-apocalyptic environment, a changing terrain – seas rage, 1-ton bags of contaminated soil stand still, and more lately, an irradiated ancient burial ground and shrines become the only places of visual memory amidst of 'recovery'. The series of costumes add a distinctive color palette to the environment. A large swath of red cloth, sewn from the lining of her grandmother's kimono, accompanies her on her trek and becomes tattered. Superficial attempts at decontamination and normalization are made by workers lacking appropriate protective gear. (Portland)

The festival's other shows, conversations, and events covered as broad a range of differences as at PuSh. And again, I offer a sampling of them here to illustrate the type of cumulative, intercultural meta-event typically experienced by adventuresome TBA audiences:

- the Noche Libre Collective – DJ La Cósmica (Dez Ramirez, Chicanx), DJ Lapaushi (Inés Paulina Ramírez, Ecuadorian), and DJ Mami Miami (Emmily Prado, Chicana) set out to create space for Black, Brown, and Indigenous woman by celebrating their families' roots and rituals in the tradition of puro pinche pari (which loosely translates as 'party 'til you fucking drop');
- Miguel Gutierrez, in *This Bridge Called My Ass*, choreographed a group of Latinx dancers in a formal negotiation between his own queer Latinx identity and the traditions of the white American avant garde;
- Leilah Weinraub presented her film, *SHAKEDOWN*, a celebratory history of Los Angeles' black lesbian strip club scene;
- Adela Demetja and collaborators presented *NEXUS 1*, a transnational collaboration between artists from and/or working out of Albania, Austria, Bosnia and Herzegovina, Germany, Montenegro, the Netherlands, Romania, and Portland exploring interlinked social and political issues in Europe and the US;

— Myles de Bastion, who also appeared at PuSh in 2020, curated with Portland's CymaSpace collaborative a night of experimental music and sound that centred Deaf and Hard-of-Hearing artists and audiences, using visual, vibrational, light-based, and other immersive and multi-sensory interpretations and displays of sound;
— and drag clown Carla Rossi (Anthony Hudson, Confederated Tribes of Grande Ronde), in *Looking for Tiger Lily*, used song, dance, drag, and video to ask what it means for a queer, mixed Indigenous person to experience their heritage through white normative culture in the form of the 1960 production of *Peter Pan*, featuring Sondra Lee's blonde, blue-eyed, 'Indian Princess'.

All of these performances were accompanied by conversations or workshops with the artists involved, allowing artists access to one another, and audiences access to their processes of production; none of them exoticized the performers as objects of a dominant-culture gaze, and all of them intervened in dominant-culture representations of the disabled, queer people, people of colour, and especially queer people of colour, making significant space for their intersectional cultural expression and conversation.

But perhaps the clearest embodiment of TBA's interculturalism, in 2019 appropriately grounded in Indigeneity, came from New Mexico-based multidisciplinary and ceramic artist Cannupa Hanska Luger, raised on the Standing Rock Reservation in North Dakota – site of the controversial Dakota Access Pipeline protests – and himself of Mandan, Hidatsa, Arikara, Lakota, Austrian, and Norwegian descent. Luger presented a solo exhibition and related performance, *A Frayed Knot* and *AFRAID NOT*, respectively, which also included *The One Who Checks and the One Who Balances*, an Indigenous futurism exhibition of regalia designed to be worn in performative actions of resistance and protest in support of communities whose land and culture are impacted by resource extraction and other threats to Indigenous land and water rights. The best way to capture the tenor of the installation is to quote from the artist's statement:

> There is a line, that spans across time in a continuum. This line is the record of our existence and is woven into the very fabric of being. But this line, through tension or abrasion or brute force, has been cut. The edge of this line is broken and unravelling. In order to connect to our past we must take up that line in both hands and tie it to our present in order to guide us into the future. Our stories are a long worn line and the effort to maintain them has left an artifact of that care in the form of A Frayed Knot. (Portland)

The best way to evoke the performance, which involved tying a physical line from the tools of decolonization to their extracitivist tasks, is to quote this performative poem:

> These are not ancient artifacts.
> These are not culturally specific artifacts.
> These will not be found in the historical record.
> These do not shine light on a lost civilization.
> These were not dug from pits by devoted scholars.
> These were not stolen from burial grounds.
> These were not gifts from a fascinated collector.
> These are not donations from friends of the museum.
> These are trapped tools for our current battle.
> These are made of earth to slay our earth eating monsters.
> These fit in our hands. These rest on our shoulders.
> The instructions for use are embedded in our genetic memory.
> These are needed now and so are we.
> In this time we must remember our belonging to the earth.
> We must re-establish reverence for our land, rather than resource.
> We must recall the fact that we are this place.
> We must fight. We must survive.
>
>   (Portland)

This show and others insisting on a response from festival audiences that went beyond passive spectatorship would not have been out of place at an Indigenous festival in the alternative, participatory festival paradigm this book, as meta-performance, is in part proposing.

Progress, Toronto

The neighbourhood city of Toronto, Canada's largest city and the fourth largest in North America with a population in the Greater Toronto Area approaching 7 million, represents itself in its publicity materials as 'the world's most multicultural city', with 52 per cent of its population reporting as members of a visible minority and with residents from almost every country on the globe.[30] It is also one of the world's most active festival cities, not, like Edinburgh and Adelaide, in a single month, but throughout the calendar year. And it is the home of creative city theorist Richard Florida, whose work has heavily influenced its urban planning. The city's Progress International Festival of Performance and Ideas, in its fifth annual edition in 2020, is the youngest of the North American curated live-arts festivals and is unique in at least three ways. First, Progress is the small-scale wintertime international offshoot of the city's long-standing annual

SummerWorks festival, the latter a kind of curated fringe festival of mostly new, mostly local work proposed in response to an open submissions call.[31] Uniquely, the 'fringe' preceded the international festival, and the two happen six months apart, but the festivals share a fringe aesthetic, with most shows using small casts and minimal sets and technical support. Second, the Progress curatorial model pushes to extremes an international trend that, as Zaiontz says, 'increasingly manifests itself ... through a redistribution of curatorial power in which the core curator or artistic director works laterally with a larger network of community members and arts workers that result in initiatives such as long-term collaborations, artist residencies, or the production of a "festival within a festival", that is both of, and apart, from the larger festival programme' ('From' 30).

The redistribution of curatorial power in the case of Progress takes the form of serial curation *within* each festival – what one participant in 2019 called 'curatorial potluck' – all under the organizational aegis of SummerWorks and its co-presenting partner and venue, Toronto's The Theatre Centre. Artistic and Managing Director Laura Nanni and her staff, in effect, curate the curators without necessarily even having seen all of the shows, as each is presented by a different arts organization within the city with different disciplinary expertise. Final programming decisions are made collectively by the full curatorial team, taking into consideration how the works 'speak' to each other and constitute the overall festival as meta-event. As a kind of umbrella organization running both the summer and winter festivals, the mandate of SummerWorks is to provide resources and support as a platform for artists. 'Progress', then, according to Nanni, 'is in part a platform for curators. We create the infrastructure and provide professional development for them' (Nanni). In 2019, for example, Aboriginal (Narangga/Kaurna) performer Jacob Boehme's *Blood on the Dance Floor*, from Australia, about being 'blak, gay, and poz [HIV positive]' (*Blood*), was co-curated by The Theatre Centre and Native Earth Performing Arts, Canada's leading Indigenous theatre company; *real real*, by Brazilian-born singer-songwriter Bruno Capinan, was curated by Toronto's global music hub, Uma Nota Culture; New York-based performance and installation artist Autumn Knight's *Documents* was curated by the nomadic contemporary arts organization FADO Performance Art Centre; Okwui Okpokwasili's *Poor People's TV Room SOLO* performance installation, also from New York, was curated by the Power Plant Contemporary Art Gallery; and so on. In a sense, then, the festival is less *inter*disciplinary, on a show-by-show basis, than serially multidisciplinary, less *inter*cultural than serially multicultural, placing shows from different disciplines and cultures in conversation with one another over the course of the festival, and doing so within the comfortable confines of Toronto's most socially conscious arts incubator, The Theatre Centre, where audiences inevitably engage one another as well as festival artists in conversation before, between, and after shows in the congenial and centrally located café/bar.

This curatorial model does, however, risk segmenting the festival audience, as each organization brings its own following (dance audiences coming for dance, theatre audiences for theatre, and so on). But this segmentation is only occasionally evident,[32] and overall the model has the effect of bringing together a kind of meta-community of arts organizations, each with its own local, national, and international connections and areas of expertise, but together constituting an active, cooperating live-arts network in the city. The redistribution of curatorial powers also allows for such things as, in 2016, the programming of a 'microfestival' curated by Edinburgh's Forest Fringe (see Chapter 4), in which 'storage rooms and outdoors spaces were converted into pop-up, one-on-one performance and installation sites' and a 'buddy system' was set up in which Forest Fringe artists consulted with Toronto artists presenting new work at Progress (Zaiontz, *Theatre & Festivals* 77).

Progress is a modest, small-scale festival in a big city, presenting ten or eleven shows plus 'ancillary events' (such as opening and closing parties, community meals, talkbacks, and, in 2019, a Performance Bus to and from the opening of the Rhubarb Festival across town,[33]) all in the city's accessible arts incubator, The Theatre Centre, in the city's hip, economically and culturally mixed Queen Street West/Parkdale neighbourhood over two-and-a-half weeks. Its mandate is to assemble 'a dynamic group of curatorial companies and progressive performance work from across the globe that is urgent and reflective of contemporary approaches to form' (Progress). The festival is funded largely through the municipal, provincial, and federal arts councils and the federal Canadian Heritage fund,[34] plus box office revenue, each guest curator acquiring funding to pay its own artists, with SummerWorks and The Theatre Centre, who also curate specific shows, providing technical and marketing support as well as curatorial mentoring and 'in-kind' support. Most tickets are CAD $25, less with a three-show pass, and some are less or even free.

The curation of Progress in 2020, according to a December 2019 press release, was 'rooted in interrogations of class structure, economic collapse, and climate crisis – dovetailing into explorations of inheritance and how we might navigate what we have been handed' (Progress). There were several issues raised by the ways the 2020 programme attempted to enable conversations – in two cases literally – across difference. There were outstanding culturally specific and cross-cultural shows that were at once explicitly political and formally experimental, such as bluemouth.inc's *Café Sarajevo*, an immersive multidisciplinary show about war, war tourism, civil disobedience, ethnicity, nationalism, justice, blame, revenge, and forgiveness in a still divided Bosnia. There were also shows using variations on the stand-up genre such as British performer Scottee's *Class*, about working-class experiences and sensibilities; and a purely stand-up night called *Comedy as a Second Language* performed by immigrants to Canada and primarily addressing immigrant issues and encounters. Some of these, such as *Class*, might be seen as variations on the transnational/local genre that I have discussed elsewhere: the show was adapted slightly from its UK origins to employ local names and brands, but the adaptations were more cosmetic than substantial and diminished the impact of a show that usefully introduced discourses around difference – class difference – that are increasingly brutal but are not often evident or acknowledged in North America.

Similar concerns, however, applied to the festival's two participatory workshops that were explicitly staged as conversations with audiences across difference. Gay male Londoner Scottee's *Working Class Dinner Party*, a kind of companion piece to *Class*, and self-professed 'working-class Afghan queer multidisciplinary artist' Shaista Latif's *How I Learned to Serve Tea*, were both designed to engage audience members directly in what were presented as 'difficult' discussions. Both involved food – the first, gruffly delivered pizza, the second, artfully arranged oranges, grapes, figs, and tea – and both involved audience members, hosted and orchestrated by the events' facilitators, sitting at tables discussing and giving their opinions on issues around social inequality. In *Working Class Dinner Party* we were asked to consider such things as working-class pride, shame, success, and joy: 'is anything about working class joy dangerous?' In *How I Learned to Serve Tea* we were divided into groups and asked to discuss and report on such things as desire, transparency, and who gets invited to the table. Both workshops were earnest but entertaining; both presenters relied on the authority of lived experience but claimed to have no answers; and both struggled with difficulties most events of this type face at curated live-arts festivals aspiring to foreground cultural difference: how can complex issues be delved into in any depth within the time constraints of a 60–90 minute performance; how can a work involving this type of audience participation avoid the almost inevitable trap of audience members' propensity for performative self-display; and how can the presenter and host know what their audience – usually one that is sophisticated around these sorts of issues – has already thought about and might understand at least as well as they do? The tone adopted by both works, as well as by *Class*, included Scottee's 'I know what you're think-ing' – he didn't – but is perhaps best represented by Latif's artist statement in the show's online house programme: 'look I'm not here to placate and support your complicity' (Latif). *How I Learned to Serve Tea* nevertheless foregrounded and brought to consciousness the different and complex ways in which the participants were or were not privileged and how their identity positions shaped their views, it carefully checked in with us on how comfortable or confused we were feeling throughout, and as reviewer S. Bear Bergman wrote of the performance I attended, it consistently asked 'what spoken or unspoken transactions, agreements, and coercions are happening right now?'

For me, a performance that was more successful at provoking thought and generating complex conversation was Jan Derbyshire's *Certified*, about Canada's mental health system and the performer's own diagnoses over several years as certifiably insane. That the show took place a mere two blocks away from CAMH, the country's largest research and clinical Centre for Addiction and Mental Health, in a neighbourhood in which the mentally challenged homeless population of the city is in frequent evidence, made the show all the more immediate and resonant. Derbyshire, who identifies as they/them and attracted a largely intersectional queer, feminist, and disability arts audience, and whose show benefited from expertly designed audio interpretation, is an experienced stand-up comic. The show was framed by an observation that the Chinese ideogram for 'crisis' is comprised of both 'danger' and 'opportunity'. It was structured as a hearing before the 'Mental Health Review Board'. The audience, constituted as the Board, was given the same fifty minutes to judge Derbyshire that an actual board has in which either to declare them sane or reincarcerate them. Standing before a large silver moon – for lunacy? – Derbyshire talked to us off-mic, 'performed' on-mic, and staged interviews with a series of psychiatrists represented by a rubber ball plopped atop the mic stand. Each doctor constructed a different story of their illness, each medicated them differently, and each worked from questions laden with assumptions: 'why', asked one, 'are you wearing boy's clothes?' The medications prescribed suspended their suicidal ideation, fended off the voices in their head, and killed their imagination. Derbyshire eventually learned through therapy and naturopathy to get off the meds and monitor their condition. The medical system, they determined, was good at handling the dangerous side of crisis, but also good at suppressing any opportunity it presents. The audience, inevitably, declared them sane.

But the most powerfully political show at the festival, intercultural or otherwise, was *Cuckoo*, part of multimedia artist and music maker Jaha Koo's *Hamartia Trilogy* and produced by CAMPO arts centre in Ghent with Bâtard live-arts festival in Brussels. The show at once participated in and critiqued the individually atomizing neoliberal market in which Toronto's stock exchange is Canada's leading participant while also speaking locally to Asian, and specifically Korean audiences in the city as it had earlier at Vancouver's PuSh and Adelaide's OzAsia Festivals. *Cuckoo* is worth discussing at some length as representative of the kinds of political, globally cross-cultural work that small-scale, carefully curated festivals such as these enable. It also provided a model for sur- and subtitling that improved upon the distracting, whip-lash-provoking one familiar at too many festivals at which surtitles are created as afterthoughts and located far above the stage.

The show opened before its human performer came onstage. On a rectangular table stage centre were three Cuckoo brand rice cookers, popular in Korea, one of them steaming and filling the space with the unmistakable smell of cooking rice. The large screen upstage exploded with a televised announcement from 21 November 1997, Korea's 'National Day of Humiliation', on which its economy was bailed out to the tune of USD $55 billion and placed under the administrative control of the International Monetary Fund (IMF), which instituted brutal austerity measures. This was followed by graphic images of public protests and their violent repression every year since, concluding with the image of a man unhesitatingly, and seemingly casually, jumping to his death.

Jaha Koo entered and walked slowly downstage. He told us in Hangugeo about *Good Morning Mr Orwell*, an installation created by Nam June Paik for satellite distribution on New Year's Day, 1984 – a rebuttal, according to Paik, of Orwell's dystopian novel about the oversight of Big Brother.[35] 'Twelve days later, I was born', Koo cooed, smiling – or indeed showing any emotion – for the only time in the show. When he retreated behind the table his co-stars, the Cuckoos, took over, literally leaving him in the dark. Koo had escaped from Korea accompanied only by his clothes and a rice cooker that was programmed to speak – 'Cuckoo is finished cooking rice. Please take me' – initiating a 'post-human friendship' to fill Koo's loneliness. But the Cuckoos – Hana, Duri, and

Seri – had much more to say, or at least two of them did, and they did so in Hangugeo with very effective and precise subtitles projected onto the front of the table, just beneath the charismatic cookers and well within the audiences' line of sight.

In a surreal sequence early on, the central rice cooker introduced itself and the older model Cuckoo – who had limited vocabulary – when the third, more sophisticated appliance with a fancy LED display interrupted, quite capable, it said, of introducing itself. The two high-end cookers traded insults, cursing magnificently, while the first cooked and kept its opinions to itself. The AI-enhanced Cuckoos were extraordinary and were given well deserved acting credits in a programme which, uniquely, included a credit (to Idella Craddock) for 'Cuckoo hacking' – not, apparently, an easy feat. Meanwhile, the audience came metaphorically to understand that, 'under the pressures of capitalism, we become more like our commodities, [and] our commodities have become more like us' (Gleaden).

Apparently, Koo doesn't agree with Nam June Paik's view of Orwell. Koo's Korea, whose Big Brother is the IMF, is distinctly dystopian: businesses are routinely liquidated, families destroyed, and every 37 minutes someone dies by suicide. The action of the play began with the suicide of a friend, its landscape was dominated by the inhuman determinates of global capitalism, and its atmosphere by an overwhelming sense of 'Golibmuwon' (고립무원), an untranslatable word expressing helplessness and isolation to which Koo returned throughout. And 'Koo himself', as reviewer Henry Gleaden notes, 'is a lonely figure', his friends lost to suicide, his emotions contained, his expression deadpan, deadened. After cradling a Cuckoo in his arms in mourning for the death of his friend, Koo told the story of a nineteen-year-old mechanic who was hit by a train and killed while trying to fix a malfunctioning door in the Seoul subway, working within an impossible pressure cooker in a disorienting rush of events.

In a startling juxtaposition, the screen then ignited with a clip of the professionally happy American self-help guru Gretchen Rubin rabbiting on about self-fulfillment, to which one Cuckoo responded, 'I'm so tired of this white bullshit.' Rubin, it turns out, is the wealthy daughter-in-law of Robert Rubin, US Secretary of the Treasury during the Clinton administration and architect of Korea's National Day of Humiliation. The Cuckoos sang a witty, rhyming song about Rubin senior and 'capitalist imperialist neo-colonialist disaster'.

Figure 11   Creator and performer Jaha Koo, his three co-stars, and effective subtitles in
Cuckoo, a powerful show exposing the human cost of rampant global
capitalism. Photograph by Radovan Dranga

In the end, this was a show about isolation, dehumanization, and death;
it communicated some of the real, material inequalities that are at play
when intercultural encounter goes global. (See Figure 11.) In the final
scene, Koo removed the sticky, sushi-grade rice from the silent cooker,
moulded it into blocks, and piled them into twin towers. The night
I attended one of the blocks crumbled, perhaps by accident, illustrating,
as reviewer Maria Rößler noted, 'the arduous yet meaningless labour of
continually building upward at the foreseeable risk of collapse'. Koo
fashioned the remaining rice into 'a small human figure' that, pathetically
and powerfully, tumbled, apparently of its own volition, 'from a tower of
steamed rice' (Rößler). Death by capitalism.

With one of the most diverse audiences of any festival I have attended,
Progress effectively draws on festivalgoers through site-specific and participatory work and work addressing specific elements of Toronto's cultural
communities to enhance its capacity for intercultural dialogue, negotiation, and exchange at The Theatre Centre's welcoming and centrally
located café/bar, within the city itself, and beyond. Progress doesn't
get everything right – it included, unusually, no Indigenous work in

2020 – and not all of its shows are equally successful. But it takes risks, helps create a cross-disciplinary, cross-cultural live-art community in Toronto, and brings a healthy international dose of experimentation to bleak midwinter in a city that may still be a bit staid, but is making progress.

Urban, Engaged

The phenomenon of curated, live-arts festivals that proliferated in the first two decades of the twentieth century in response, on the one hand, to what is widely seen as the stultification of the élite or destination festival circuit and its failure to address the local or social, and on the other to the pressures of neoliberal economics, was primarily a European and North American one – a creation of the Global West and North. Theatre and performance festivals in Asia, Australasia, India, and South America have tended to emulate the model of the destination festival, promoting civic and national brands, articulating national identities, and attracting tourism.[36]

Within Europe and North America, the curated, live-arts festivals have distinguished themselves from destination festivals and the other types I've discussed in this book by being overwhelmingly urban in location and sensibility, eschewing the destination myth of pilgrimage (and escape) first modelled by Wagner's Bayreuth and followed in Edinburgh, Avignon, and elsewhere. Unlike destination festivals, they tend for the most part to address local rather than visiting audiences, to constitute those audiences as participants and partners rather than tourists and consumers, and to stage for them the experience of denaturalized encounter with their own urban landscapes. They are far removed from the destination festival realm of international diplomacy, and tend to address interculturalism on the local level, focusing on such things, within Europe, as 'the migrant crisis', or in North America on the multiple cultural communities that exist in global cities such as Toronto, New York, and Vancouver, including mixed Indigenous ones.

Beyond the local, these festivals tend to form networks of like-minded artists and institutions based on shared artistic and political interests rather than festival circuits and neocolonial distribution 'routes' based on convenience, cost, and colonial histories. The temporality of the curated, live-arts festival, too, is one less set apart from the exigencies of daily life – less 'time out of time' – than engaged with its problems, issues, difficulties and debates, and determined to make an impact beyond festival time. Both of these characteristics – urban and engaged – lend themselves to the orchestration and staging of sometimes fraught intercultural encounter rather than the presentation of packaged exoticism or spectacle staged for an objectifying festival gaze. Closer to the Indigenous prototype discussed in Chapter 1 than to the destination festival modelled on Athens, Avignon, and Edinburgh, these festivals tend to engage audiences less as spectators than as witnesses or even participants, and often, for reasons that are both economic and political, employ non-actors, including local ones, as performers, reflecting the demographics as well as the concerns of local populations. And they tend, especially in Europe, to move outside of or to reconfigure traditional theatrical spaces as well as received dramatic structures.

As Keren Zaiontz argues, 'the artist run "second wave" was not formed to enhance the image of cities or speed urban growth and revitalization. The city remains important – as do the spatial possibilities that the city poses in terms of performance – but as a location of democratic assembly, a site of performance research, and a space of alternative solidarities' ('From' 24). It was the search for such alternatives that originally motivated the fringe festival movement, as discussed in Chapter 4, with mixed results.

CHAPTER 4

Fringe Festivals and Other Alternatives

It's the last day of February in the leap year of 2020, and I'm sitting in the Black Box Theatre adjacent to the luminous Rose Garden at the Botanic Garden in Adelaide, South Australia. My fellow audience members and I – all of us looking very white, most of us well past middle age, many of us cradling drinks from the festival bar – have just witnessed a late afternoon performance of Josephine, *billed as 'a burlesque cabaret dream play' about Josephine Baker, the legendary African American performer who took Paris by storm in the 1920s. Everything about the setting except the awkward, fringe-style stacking chairs contributes to our comfort. The solo show, exquisitely performed by its co-creator Tymisha Harris,[1] has been a hit at fringes around the world since 2018. It shows Baker as a consummate entertainer, spy for the French Resistance during World War II, and civil rights activist recruited by Martin Luther King to perform at the March on Washington in 1963, where in fact she was the only female speaker. In* Josephine *she instead sang a stirring rendition of Bob Dylan's 'The Time's They Are A'Changin'' – deftly altering lines to reflect current times: 'don't stand in the doorway, don't block up the hall', for example, became 'don't stand in the doorway, don't build up your walls', reflecting Donald Trump's isolationist America. The show has also touched lightly on racial politics, including a brief version of the story of Baker's nineteenth-century predecessor in Europe, the South African Saartje Baartman, which makes at least some of us feel a bit self-congratulatorily liberal.*

Harris has also, however, performed Baker's famous banana dance wearing only the iconic banana skirt and beaded necklace that Baker had flaunted at the Folies Bergère in 1927, and pasties. She has flirted shamelessly with the audience throughout – at one point inviting an older man in the second row to help reattach her bra (he joked comfortably that he had more experience removing them). And she has praised the warm, purportedly non-racist welcome Baker received from Parisian audiences in contradistinction to her reception in New York, making no reference to the racist signification of the banana belt then or now, happily tossing one of the bananas into a crowd that the performance constitutes as Parisian and welcoming. The sold-out show, in form a non-threatening, mildly titillating historical biopic, has been enthusiastically received by the audience at curtain call, and Harris is now silencing our applause and delivering a familiar fringe festival pitch: she invites us to tell our friends about it if we enjoyed ourselves, our enemies if we didn't. She encourages us, too, to purchase souvenir promotional buttons ('you can use them as pasties'), and souvenir plastic bananas from the box office by the bar.

Josephine is a solid and entertaining if never very challenging show; in another context it would be strong, but unexceptional. In the aging, conservative, and predominantly white university city of Adelaide (population ca 1.4 million), however, performed as part of a large and competitive fringe festival before an audience that appears to be almost all white, the show's coyness, its titillation, and its unremarked racist symbolism on display and on sale rendered it problematic. The Black female body, here, felt as though it was offered up, not by the actor, but by the festival, for display and consumption. Festival audiences, moreover, were constituted in this context as both consumers and voyeurs, and comfortably so, without a hint of challenge around the uninterrogated sources of our pleasure, and although Tymisha Harris made a great deal of eye contact, often with fluttering eyelashes, there was no challenging return of our festival gaze. What is it about the context provided by fringe festivals that can turn an unexceptional and potentially anti-racist show into questionable spectacle in this fashion? What are the alternatives?

Edinburgh Festival Fringe

Fringe festivals, beginning with the original Edinburgh Festival Fringe (EFF)[2] in 1947 and Avignon's 'Off' festival in 1969,[3] were the first to challenge the destination festivals, but by the turn of the twenty-first century had revelled in their self-proclaimed 'alternative' status long past its 'best by' date. During the seventieth anniversary of the Edinburgh Fringe in 2017 – '70 years of defying the norm', according to posters around the city – I saw prominent signs at Fringe Central proclaiming 'WE'RE AN ALLIANCE OF DEFIANCE', and 'WE WILL NOT BE SHOOSHED'. And in its earliest incarnations, like Avignon's 'Off', the Fringe at Edinburgh *was* an alternative, mounted in protest against the perceived élitism of the Edinburgh International Festival (EIF), which Jen Harvie says 'provoked' the founding of the fringe movement partly by ignoring local work and popular culture in its programming ('Cultural'

21). The same phenomenon happened at the Brighton Festival in England twenty years later, in Adelaide, Australia in the early 1970s, and elsewhere, as élite festivals worldwide sprouted what were billed as anarchic, experimental, populist, or local alternatives to their 'high-culture' international main stages. Part of the phenomenology of these fringe festivals, indeed, is the felt experience of participating at an unruly, affectively 'alternative' event taking place in grubby streets and downscale venues in counter-distinction to the more sedate ambience that prevails at their accompanying destination festivals. In the 1980s, however, famously in Edmonton, Alberta in 1982, fringes began to pop up all over the world in places with no mainstage in sight, and nothing to be alternative to, and many destination and live-art festivals had incorporated 'fringe', 'OFF', 'nouvelle scène', and 'club' scenes into their own 'in' programming and under their own sponsorship, as a way of featuring small, alternative, or local work.[4] By the twenty-first century, however, the fringe movement had succumbed to the pressures of the neoliberal marketplace, its rebellious artists were transformed into artrepreneurs, and their defiance into precarity.

The world's fringes vary in size, character, and geographical setting, but the dominant characteristic of most is some variation on non-juried open access.[5] At Edinburgh, which is the dominant fringe model worldwide, the largest, and the most international,[6] this means, in theory, that anyone from anywhere who can find a venue can be part of the festival, modelling the radical democracy for which the Fringe is famous. But if the élite festivals have programmers and 'second-wave' festivals curators, the Fringe has venues. Finding a venue means negotiating terms with venue managers, and if the Fringe itself is open access, the venues are not. Artists and companies wanting to attract audiences and have even a slim chance of breaking even financially are most likely to do so in carefully circumscribed ways at the corporate supervenues – the Pleasance, Assembly, C-Spaces, Underbelly, Gilded Balloon, Zoo, and others – each of which in effect curates its own programme, publishes its own brochure, and is in it for profit.[7] As Keren Zaiontz points out, moreover,

> These venues are typically organized around standardized time slots (one or two hours), standardized stage-audience arrangements (spectators are seated and facing the stage), and standardized scenography (back-to-back schedules limit set, costume, and lighting choices). Given that super venues tend to run multiple, mid-sized and large spaces with seating capacity ranging from 50–750, and produce the majority of the events, works that defy artistic convention can be hard sells to producers and mainstream audiences alike. (*Theatre & Festivals*, 70–1)

To make deals with small or independent venues, or to move very far outside of the standardized format, is to take considerable risk: in 2017 at one small independent venue in an insalubrious part of town I attended an early-Sunday-morning show that had travelled all the way from South Africa and I was the sole audience member. The viable alternatives to the corporate venues are the nation-based programmes – Big in Belgium, Canada Hub, Taiwan Season, Focus Korea, all of which are carefully curated and funded in the interests of national promotion in ways that echo the élite destination festivals – or to present as part of a curated series at a discipline-based venue or programme (Dance Base, Aurora Nova Celebration of Physical Theatre).

In addition to venue and series managers, fringe participants are almost inevitably influenced in terms of the work they perform by the presence of international presenters – over a thousand of them – who attend the festival annually trolling for shows. As Sam Friedman argues about the festival's comedy scouts, theatre presenters and agents serve as 'cultural brokers', 'hidden tastemakers' whose own instincts, guesses, and dispositions are projected onto imagined audiences and are often normalized according to unspoken categories of class, culture, and colour, 'constructing, reproducing, and intensifying' rather than merely reflecting supposed divisions in taste (38). Artists projecting potential success at the fringe and subsequent touring, then, are subject to self-policing according to standards, categories, and predilections that tend towards the familiar and avoid anything unsettling, unusual, or unpredictable.

But even setting aside the processes of pleasing presenters and negotiating terms with venue managers, to what degree the EFF remains 'alternative', how enabling its radical democracy is and for whom, have been called into question in the twenty-first century. Elspeth Frew and Jane Ali-Knight, writing about the increasing commercialization of the Edinburgh and Adelaide Fringes, have gone so far as to offer a new definition of a fringe festival, eschewing earlier definitional fields having to do with innovation, experimentation, creativity, and 'low-brow' accessibility, and redefining a fringe festival as 'an opt-in multi-arts festival, involving independent and managed artists creating high and low arts performances, supported by a strong nonprofit fringe organization via marketing and box office activities' (242). The most consistent and careful critic of the EFF, however, is Jen Harvie ('International'; see also *Staging* 82–9), who labels the EFF as a 'model neo-liberal capitalist market, with all of the collateral social damages that entails' ('International' 103):[8]

> The most serious risk I think the Fringe poses is normalizing, helping to globally disseminate, and serving to legitimate a neo-liberal capitalist market ideology, environment, and set of practices that is profoundly damaging – to theatre and performance, and therefore to audiences, but especially to artists/workers. ('International' 103)

Among the damages identified by Harvie and others as emerging from the EEF's lack of regulation are:

- its sometimes-appalling working conditions for exploited artists and venue employees who (unlike those invited to curated or destination festivals) pay their own expenses, work for free or below-minimum wage, and exercise what Zaiontz has called 'the art and sweat of self-subsidy' (*Theatre & Festivals* 71);
- unequal access for artists and audiences from minoritized groups and the consequent exacerbation of social inequalities;
- a culture of competitiveness;
- and domination by predatory corporate venues.

Ironically, a festival founded to counter the élitism and exclusivity of the Edinburgh International Festival has come to be marked by those very characteristics; indeed, in 2019 it was labelled by one self-identified working-class performer as 'the epicenter of elitism' (Rasmussen). And while the Fringe as international marketplace is becoming increasingly diverse and attracting shows from all around the world, its audiences, though they also come from almost every country in the world, are overwhelmingly drawn from the white and privileged classes, as are the critics who so directly determine how well a show will do in an over-saturated market in which 53,232 performances of 3,398 shows were on offer at 300 venues when I attended in 2017 – not including shows at the International or the three other festivals held in the city at the same time.[9] All of this, together with such things as the resources required for marketing, accommodation, and food, and the costs and bureaucracies of travel to and from the festival – artists participating in the Arab Arts Focus series, for example, are routinely denied visas – mean that the opportunities for meaningful or equitable cross-cultural communication, negotiation, and exchange are surprisingly limited and uni-directional: the festival tends to be dominated by scenarios in which white, middle-class audiences watch decontextualized, exoticized, or even self-exoticizing Others, or hear minoritized performers explain racism and white privilege to liberal dominant-culture sympathizers.

Playwright and performer Selina Thompson, in an article entitled 'Excerpts from the Diary of a Black Woman at the Edinburgh Fringe', describes being interviewed by an ill-informed journalist looking to her for 'the exotic' at the festival, points to several instances of overt racism, and gives an account of her own and other artists' experiences 'looking out into a white audience, and feeling horribly, horrifically alone, feeling like doing the show is going into battle'. Thompson ends her excerpts optimistically with an account of an 'Artist of Colour meetup' and increasing solidarity among such artists that has ameliorated somewhat her experience of isolation and loneliness. And, turning from the artists' experience to those of the audience, there are now record numbers of international works on offer and more opportunities to see shows by women, queer, non-binary people, and people of colour than there used to be, if one chooses to do so. Madani Younis – then artistic director of London's Bush Theatre, who writes about the EFF as regularly consisting of

> a harsh reminder to me of what privilege in British theatre looks like; of waiting to see what exotic cultural stereotypes are offered up as tepid forms of diversity from around the world; of the narrow mono-cultural lens through which work is critiqued; of economics and class, of tribalism and élitism; of waiting to count how many really good shows that involve a White brother behind a microphone I will sit through

– published a piece in 2017 entitled 'Black, Asian and Other Artists from Marginalised Groups Have Fought Their Way onto the Programmes of Edinburgh Festival Fringe and I Want to Shout about It'. But as Younis notes, audiences at the Fringe remain overwhelmingly monochromatic, 'the press is still a whitewash', and the dominant patterns persist. In 2017, for example, I saw *A Matter of Race* at the EFF, in which one white and one Black woman with otherwise identical biographies somewhat paternalistically instructed a predominantly white audience about racism in the UK. In the same year I attended *The Korean Tale of Princess Bari*, a family event in which an exotic Korea was offered up to western children, who left, having completed forms saying what they had learned from the show about Korean culture, with postcards with their names inscribed, beautifully, if inscrutably to most of them, in Hangul.

There were, however, other and better shows reflecting (and producing) difference, which for audience members who chose to follow them together constituted a more dynamically intercultural festival. These included, to give a sense of the Fringe's range of intercultural offerings:

- *Hong Kong Three Sisters*, a stunning production from Hong Kong about being an artist in that beleaguered intercultural city (which unfortunately ran for only three nights);
- the powerful intercultural dance collaboration *Together Alone*, by Zoltán Vakulya (Belgium) and Chen-Wei Lee (Taiwan);
- Natasha Marshall's delightful *Half Breed*, about growing up the only Black girl and budding artist in a small town in Wiltshire;
- *The Fall*, a collective creation by Black student activists at the Baxter Theatre Centre in Cape Town about the removal of a statue of Cecil Rhodes from their campus;
- *Tshepang* (hope), by Lara Foot, also from Cape Town, about the brutal rape of a nine-month-old baby and of the Black village where she lived;
- *Taha*, written and performed by Amer Hlehel, about the life of poet Taha Muhammed Ali in occupied Palestine;
- and, notably, Selina Thompson's own solo show, *Salt*.[10]

Thompson is a powerful, charismatic, charming, angry, sorrowful, and loving performer. Her play recounts her personal cross-cultural retracing at age twenty-five of the transatlantic slave triangle from the UK to the Elmina slave mansion on coastal Ghana, on to her parents' birthplace in Jamaica, and finally back to the UK by way of the alluring depths of the Atlantic. 'Europe', she realizes, 'is awash with blood, built on suffering'. Beautifully written and moving fluidly between the soft beauty of micro-phoned passages delivered almost as verse, charming and challenging direct address, sophisticated materialist analysis that was reinforced, literally, with a sledgehammer, and the simplicity of its two central and structuring metaphors of salt and triangles, the show was one of the very best of the 2017 Fringe. It has since become a regular at fringe and other festivals worldwide – I saw it at Toronto's Progress festival – where it has included a searing critique of racism at the EFF itself. As Younis says, 'there's still a shitload of inequality to deal with and we need to notice where represen-tation isn't happening'.[11]

Part of the problem of representation at the EFF and other festivals has to do with the ways in which, and degrees to which, festivals and festival space are purposefully regulated by the City Council and the Fringe Office. Kirstie Jamieson, in an essay on 'the festival gaze and its boundaries', argues that there is a gap between 'the differences of artistic expression' and 'the expression of [actual] social difference' that remains invisible at festival time in Edinburgh: 'Performed difference is staged during the festival season to be promoted, recognized, and celebrated, whereas those differences that would genuinely challenge and re-order social meaning are beyond the limits of the festival map' (72) – a map which is overwhelmingly limited to the UNESCO-designated Old and New Town tourist districts of the city, but not its high-density working-class, impoverished, and more culturally diverse neighbourhoods. However much artists – particularly street performers at the Fringe – deploy what Iain Munro and Silvia Jordan call 'spatial tactics' – 'embodied spatial practices that creative artists use to re-appropriate and re-socialize public spaces' (1500) – the fact remains that even the seemingly anarchic streets and 'saturated' public spaces of Edinburgh at festival time are carefully licensed and controlled (see Martin et al. 20). Festival space is *'made'*, as Bruce Willems-Braun argues about the Winnipeg and Vancouver fringes in Canada, 'with specific distinctions and relations' (76, emphasis in original), pointing to a

> particular configuration of discourses organized by dynamics of gender, race and class. The manner in which the fringes rework and reassert this configuration results in the production of 'public' spaces in a manner whereby access is unequal, even if the subjectivities they shape are necessarily ambivalent, with 'possibilities for plurality and contestation ... that are at once sustained and circumscribed by existing social and spatial-relations. (79)

Harvie points to recent efforts to mitigate some of the most serious problems at the EFF: its lack of attention to the provision of permanent theatrical infrastructure in Edinburgh; the mental health of its artists-under-pressure; mentoring, networking, and support, particularly of artists from minoritized communities; the regulation of working conditions and venue management; providing free or discounted access to underrepresented groups; and fostering a spirit of camaraderie rather than competition among artists. And she refreshingly makes her own positive recommendations for change ('International' 112–16).[12] And even as it stands the EFF does, however unequally and at whatever cost, provide the opportunity for new or emerging artists to develop their craft and any artist to have the experience of presenting work over an extended, three-week run, to be seen and perhaps selected by some of the over one thousand presenters that attend the festival every year, and to be reviewed by a national and international press corps that comes in droves and awards stars and prizes. Whatever its free-market and neoliberal limitations, moreover, the Fringe uniquely provides a genuine opportunity for creative exchange between artists, including artists from different countries and cultures. Most shows run at the same timeslot once a day for the festival's full twenty-five days among at least a dozen slots scheduled from early morning to late at night, so when they're not hustling for audiences, artists are watching, talking, and talking to one another about their work. In addition, Fringe Central (a relaxed space for fringe participants and media) offers dozens of events – 155 in 2017 – that provide advice, context, consultations, information, and strategies, including such things as an 'Asian Artists Gathering' and workshop sessions on 'Disability Equality Training' and 'Directing and Diversity' (Edinburgh Festival Fringe, 'Fringe Central').

Nevertheless, the degree to which any participant or spectator experiences the Fringe as a cross- or intercultural, or even international meta-event, depends largely on their own choices and their own self-curation of the massive Fringe experience at which no one person can see more than a tiny percentage of what's on offer. Many audience members, however, undergo the Fringe as experience collectors, sprinting from one show to another adding steps on their pedometer, and attending up to half a dozen shows per day in frenetic rites of conspicuous consumption that leave litte time for contemplation even if they have chosen to attend some of the festival's more culturally challenging encounters. Conversations in Edinburgh bars at fringe time are as likely to be about how many shows one has seen as what those shows dealt with. In any case, like other oversaturated free-market economies, and like social media, the EFF can too easily operate as a bubble in which audiences only encounter what they already know. Difference at the Edinburgh Festival Fringe needs to be sought out, and time has to be taken by more discerning festivalgoers to digest the experience.

Adelaide Fringe Festival

Unlike its Edinburgh counterpart but in a city three times its size, the Adelaide Fringe receives significant public funding,[13] but the festivals are comparable in being the largest in the northern and southern hemispheres, respectively – Adelaide's fringe hosting 3.3 million people and featuring 7,000 artists at 1,326 events across 517 venues in 2019 (Adelaide Fringe, 'Annual Review 2019') – and being at the heart of a month – August in Edinburgh, 'Mad March' in Adelaide – crowded with festivals in their respective 'festival cities'.[14] The Adelaide Fringe is in fact modelled on the EFF and shares many of its strengths and weaknesses. Like the EFF it is non-juried and open-access; like the EFF its shows take place – in addition to theatres and the ubiquitous church, community, and lecture halls – in a 'Garden of Unearthly Delights' amusement park where festival venues share the grounds with beer tents, fifteen-minute comedy show booths, and a 'freak show', as well as in tents, restaurants, bars, boats, bathrooms, attics, swimming pools, shopfronts, and shipping crates throughout the city; like the EFF it is regarded by artists as providing the opportunity for artrepreneurs 'to build their identity as artists, to practice their craft, to experiment, and to generate further work opportunities' (Caust and Glow 4); like the EFF it is dominated by corporate venues (see Thomasson, 'Too Big' 46–7); and like the EFF it has been criticized for 'perpetuating the logic of neoliberalism by promoting free-market competition, relying on precarious labour practices, and requiring artists to become artrepreneurs while taking advantage of what Lauren Berlant terms the 'cruel optimism' of artists' aspirations for success' (Thomasson, 'Too Big' 40; Berlant). Also like the EFF but in my experience to a more extreme degree, and in spite of its stated commitment to 'cultural diversity, inclusivity, acceptance' (Adelaide Fringe, 'Manifesto'), the Adelaide Fringe Festival is largely the preserve of the white, middle-class, and non-disabled, both onstage and off. In part, perhaps, because the festival is marketed to Adelaide first rather than to international tourists (Frew and Ali-Knight 239), whatever diversity the fringe serves, as for Richard Florida's creative class, is 'a diversity of elites' (Florida, *Rise* 79). Finally, Adelaide offers fewer opportunities for extended runs, and apart from weekends there are few time slots offered during the day, with the result that, while the festival as a whole is less of a marathon for audience members, the shows themselves more directly compete with one another and with presentations at the Adelaide Festival proper, and artists have fewer opportunities to see and talk about one another's work.

When I attended in 2020 there were also few opportunities to see shows that staged, probed, or questioned the diversity of Australia's population, and fewer, apart from *Josephine* with which I opened this chapter, that explored difference internationally. I did see the charmingly acrobatic outdoor family show *1000 Cranes* by the Gemini Collective, which took place near the Himeji Japanese Gardens in one of the municipal parks on the edge of the city's central grid system and told the familiar story of the twelve-year-old girl, Sadako Sasaki, who succumbed tragically to leukaemia in the generational wake of the bombing of Hiroshima. And I saw *Tales of an Urban Indian*, a fringe regular by Darrell Dennis from the Secwepemc First Nation in British Columbia, Canada, which dissonantly took place on a bus touring Adelaide's suburbs with its (so far) third actor in the solo role. *Frankenstein: How to Make a Monster*, from BAC Beatbox Academy at London, England's Battersea Arts Centre, in spite of being framed by some off-putting fringe and competitive hip-hop hype, was one of the best. A mixed cast of highly skilled young beat-box vocalists, three men and three women, three white folx, three Black, recast Mary Shelley's *Frankenstein*, remarkably faithfully in theme if not in narrative, in five smart 'chapters': The Power of Knowledge, How to Make a Monster, Growing Pains, The World Uncensored, and The Descent. Finally, *The Nights, by Henry Naylor*, also produced by Redbeard Theatre & Gilded Balloon Productions in the UK (the latter one of the EFF's corporate venues), was inspired by the story of Shamima Begum, a fifteen-year-old schoolgirl from the multicultural Bethnal Green in London's East End, who ran away to Syria to become a jihadi bride, was lost for three years, and finally found unrepentant in a refugee camp asking to come home. She was, unsurprisingly, excoriated by the British press, and Naylor's play probes, somewhat moralistically, how and why that might have happened, along with the impact and consequences more broadly of a criminal war and a xenophobic society. Both actors, appropriately, were white. But this Fringe was not, in my experience, the place to go for any very serious intercultural exchange.

Toronto Fringe and Next Stage Festivals

The Edinburgh Fringe has inspired fringe festivals around the world, but not all of them follow precisely the same format. While at the EFF and Adelaide Fringe open access means that anyone who can acquire a venue is admitted to the festival, many of the world's over 300 fringes run 'unbiased' lotteries in which artists who pay small application fees are randomly selected and assigned a space centrally, while others run bring-your-own or rent-your-own venue systems or other similar schemes. The Toronto Fringe Festival was founded in 1989 with, unlike the EFF and Adelaide Fringe but like most fringe festivals in North America and many around the world, no 'main' festival to be alternative to, which makes its fringe status questionable. After all, as Richard Demarco, a founder of the EFF, has said, 'A fringe means a curtain, and you cannot have a curtain going up and going down when all you have is a fringe' (qtd in Frew and Ali-Knight 237). The Toronto Fringe is a member of the Canadian Association of Fringe Festivals (CAFF), with twenty-one member festivals in Canada and eleven in the United States.[15] As such it is required to adhere to that Association's 'Ideals':

- Participants will be selected on a non-juried basis, through a first-come, first served process, a lottery, or other method approved by the Association.
- The audience must have the option to pay a ticket price, 100% of which goes directly to the artists.[16]
- Fringe Festival producers have no control over the artistic content of each performance. The artistic freedom of the participants is unrestrained.
- Festivals must provide an easily accessible opportunity for all audiences and all artists to participate in Fringe Festivals.
- Festivals will promote and model inclusivity, diversity and multi-culturalism, and will endeavor to incorporate them into all aspects of our organizations. (Fringe Festivals)

These guiding ideals are not just aspirational: both 'Fringe' and 'Fringe Festival' are registered by CAFF as trademarks in Canada, and all festivals who use these terms must legally adhere to the association's ideals, which in themselves serve to contain some of the excesses and abuses that obtain at Edinburgh, Adelaide, and elsewhere. The Toronto Fringe mandates that participants have a reasonable opportunity to earn back their investment and compensate themselves appropriately, while also maintaining the principle that audiences can see a variety of theatrical styles and genres at an affordable price. Since 1989 the Fringe has grown to become Toronto's largest theatre festival, with over 90,000 patrons and over 1,200 artists annually and producing over CAD $6 million in box office revenue that has been returned to artists as of 2019.

The city of Toronto promotes itself – accurately or not – as both the world's most multicultural city, as discussed in Chapter 3, and the third most active theatre centre in the English-speaking world,[17] and the Toronto Fringe takes seriously the last of CAFF's principles having to do with inclusivity and diversity, not simply in its administrative stream but in its adaptation of the 'open access' model. The festival's operations are funded through (steadily diminishing) arts and tourism grants and actively solicited private donations (the festival is a registered charity). Its venues – downtown theatres – are rented by the Fringe at discounted rates, and artists receive 100 per cent of their box office. Artists are admitted through an open system in which prospective participants, having paid a CAD $29 registration fee, are selected by lottery. According to its outreach coordinator in 2017, Kevin Wong, however, this system tends to produce, as it does elsewhere, a festival dominated by white male artists (cited in Budde and Samur 91). To correct this imbalance and attract both artists and audiences that more closely reflect the diversity of the city, the festival engages in what Antje Budde and Sebastian Samur call 'a form of counter-curation' (91). There are now eleven lottery categories, including the Teen category, the Senior category, the Site-Specific category, the Culturally Diverse Artists Project Lottery for those who self-identify as culturally diverse, and the Accessible Lottery for those who identify as artists with a disability.[18] In these last two categories the festival's normal registration fee is waived.[19]

The festival's efforts have paid off to some degree both within and beyond the special categories. Although a significant majority of the shows – particularly comedies and musicals – continue to be by dominant-culture artists, the festival regularly features productions from Indigenous, immigrant, and disability cultures, sometimes intersectionally in the same shows, and while the 'fringe binge' experience of audiences is not unlike that of Edinburgh, if at a smaller scale, audience line-ups outside the festival's main venues evince a broader range of cultures and languages in conversation with one another. In 2019, Andrea Malpili and Byron Abalos's Filipino family fantasy *Through the Bamboo*, for example, sold out Factory Theatre's main space to a mixed, multicultural audience throughout its run; Rita Shelton Deverell's *Who You Callin' Black Eh?* successfully probed the biracial, multiracial, 'postracial' experience in Canada at the same theatre's Studio space and was able to speak in sophisticated ways to an audience for whom this was not an unfamiliar one; Morgan Frey's *Young and the Limbless* set out at the accessible Robert Gill Theatre at the University of Toronto to subvert the sitcom format by casting and representing its central character as a person with a disability; and Kaho Koda's Japanese 'immigrant experience' play *Decaying Tongue* was well received by diverse audiences and reviewers at the Randolph Theatre.

But perhaps the best example of the kind of work enabled by the festival, featured at the 2017 fringe, is the devised piece, *In Sundry Languages* (Figure 12), by Toronto Laboratory Theatre under the direction of Armenian Canadian Art Babayants at the Theatre Passe Muraille main space. The show consisted of mainly comic or poignant scenes involving misunderstanding, miscommunication, or cultural gaps. A casting director tries to get a Russian-speaking actor to sound more (stereotypically) Russian, a multilingual taxi driver and his multilingual customer can't find a common language, an Arabic-speaking Muslim can't find the words to rent a room from a white landlord, a Chinese woman apologizes for speaking Cantonese but not Mandarin, and so on. But the show's most striking feature was not simply that it was multilingual, or even that it used

Figure 12   In *Sundry Languages* at the Toronto Fringe Festival in 2017: is it possible to develop a dramaturgy that doesn't always yearn for translation?. Photograph by Mathew Sarookanian

six different languages – Arabic, Cantonese, English, Portuguese, Russian, and Spanish – but that it left those languages untranslated. As the characters struggled to understand one another – often relying on gesture, intonation, embodiment, imagination, and good will – the audience, from a variety of linguistic backgrounds, struggled along with them. Laughter erupted from different linguistic contingents in different pockets of the house at different moments while performers struggled to communicate using their own and other languages, and everyone experienced what it feels like to not understand or be fully understood. 'It started as a creative experiment', explains Babayants:

> Is it possible to develop a dramaturgy that doesn't always yearn for translation? Translation gives you direct access to meaning but that meaning is always skewed, it's never the same as it is in the original language or culture. In a way, translation gives one an illusion of full access. But what happens when we don't hide the fact that things are not really translatable? What strategies would the audience develop to still understand what is happening on stage? ... Those who speak languages other than English, specifically non-native English speakers, which make up roughly half of the Toronto population, are given more access to meaning than those who speak English

only. In a way, theatre becomes a utopian space where the power (in this case the power of the official language) is subverted. (qtd in Karas)

It was an experiment that the Toronto Fringe's adaptations of the EFF models of open access and artist imbursement made more possible, as did the linguistic multiplicity of the city. The Fringe in this way also serves to create work for what in the case of *In Sundry Languages* was a relatively large cast of skilled immigrant actors, most of whom otherwise have difficulty getting cast because they speak heavily accented English. The multilingual, intercultural conversations the production staged and prompted continued outside the theatre and on social media, for me and many others, long after the show ended. It has toured widely since.

The Toronto Fringe, which takes place in July, extends its reach by also producing the Next Stage Theatre Festival for two weeks in the chill of January, supported by a heated hospitality tent adjacent to the two-venue Factory Theatre that hosts all the shows.[20] Next Stage is a small, curated festival of work by artists who have performed successfully at fringe festivals and are, notionally at least, ready for the next stage in their development. It does not charge an application fee and returns 70 per cent of box office to the artists. Although Next Stage resembles fringe festivals in some ways – low production budgets, minimal design elements, tight time slots and turnarounds – the fact of curation makes it easier to programme diversity. The twelve shows featured in 2020, which saw the highest audience turnout in the festival's history to date, included one by South Asian Canadian trans performer, Bilal Baig; one by self-professed 'drag tragicomedienne', Pearle Harbour; one by queer Chinese-Vietnamese Canadian actor and spoken-word poet, athena kaitlin trinh; one by disabled artist Ophira Calof; one by Iranian Canadian playwright Mohammad Yaghoubi; one by the Tita Collective of Filipina Canadian women; and one by Tallboyz, a collective of young men of colour. Of the remaining five shows, four were by women and one by a white man writing for a diverse cast and working with a female director. The quality of the work was mixed, but my experience of the festival as a native of the city was the pleasantly unsettling one of having my expectations exceeded, and my taken-for-granteds challenged.

Winter of 88, written and directed by Mohammad Yaghoubi, a metatheatrical and autobiographical play about a family living precariously and in fear during the missile barrage on Tehran near the end of the Iran-Iraq war, was particularly timely. This, the play's first staging in English translation, coincided precisely in January 2020 with a period of heightened tension between the US and Iran, the targeted killing of Iranian General Qassem Soleimani, the bombing of US military bases in Iraq, and Iran's accidental shooting down of Ukraine International Airlines flight 752 killing 176 people, 138 of whom were en route to a Canada that continues to mark the event as a national tragedy. The play's central couple were played by an Iraqi man and an Iranian woman, and the festival's multicultural audience responded with enthusiasm and, in many cases, tears.

The Toronto and other CAFF festivals have clearly and valuably found ways of intervening in a notionally democratic but rampantly free-market, open-access international fringe system by formulating various affirmative action mechanisms that help to balance the social scales. Other festivals have entirely rejected the open-access model and found ways of staging more thoroughgoingly alternative, pro-active, and socially conscious festivals.

Other Alternatives: Counterfestivals, Microfestivals, and Manifestivals

It's March 2018, and I am in Bogotá, Colombia as part of a delegation of artists and presenters from Canada led by Aluna Theatre's Beatriz Pizano and Trevor Schwellnus.[21] I'm here to attend the destination Festival Iberoamericano de Teatro de Bogotá (FITB), and alongside it, FESTA, the Festival de Teatro Alternativo Bogotá. The former, once a leading player on the Latin American and indeed international destination festival circuit (see Menza and Lapierre; Graham-Jones 226), in spite of some spirited offerings in widely dispersed venues around the vast expanse of the city (population ca 8 million), has seen better days,[22] and along with my colleagues I find myself gravitating towards the much more dynamic Alternativo, concentrated for the most part in the La Candaleria district in the city's historic centre, with its plethora of thirty mostly small stages within easy walking distance of one another.

At show after show, I can't help remarking the presence of a charismatic woman in her late sixties or early seventies who seems to be everywhere, animating the entire festival (including the important 'programmación acádemica') with her unrelenting focus and unbounded energy. This turns out to be legendary poet and activist Patricia Ariza, a founder in 1966 and now artistic director of Bogotá's Teatro La Candelaria, Colombia's first and preeminent politically alternative theatre, and the artistic director, since 1994, of FESTA itself. Although FESTA runs concurrently with

FITB, it is in no traditional sense a fringe. Rather, it presents itself as a genuine alternative, unapologetically political, interventionist, and radical. Of its 105 shows in 2018, 85 are from Colombia, most of them from Bogotá itself, many of them large-cast collective creations, and all of them addressing urgent social issues. No less than five of those are expertly directed by Ariza, one show, from Medellin, is inspired by her work, and another is dedicated to her. The international component of FESTA consists of twenty shows, also socially and politically engaged, from Argentina, Bolivia, Brazil, Ecuador, Venezuela, and the US, and a number of transnational collaborations. The festival has plenty of room – it makes room – for work by and about Indigenous communities, communities of formerly enslaved peoples, women, and other communities of resistance and resurgence. It forges solidarities among them, and its praxis is the activist one that Walter Mignolo, for whom the concept of 'Latin America' is a colonialist European invention (see Mignolo), has called 'decoloniality' – an epistemic reconsideration of the structures of knowledge and subject formation that were implanted by the former colonizers that I will revisit in Chapter 5 (see Mignolo and Walsh). As Natalie Alvarez has argued, FESTA is

> more than just 'window shopping': FESTA ... is a destination point for artists interested in politically committed works that advance new modes of expression and stylistic vocabularies ... Ariza expects a commitment from festival attendees: she wants the festival attendee to be *there*, seeing all the shows and engaging in conversations – not only about the performances but also about the urgent political issues of the moment. ('Roots' 31, emphasis in original)

And Ariza herself models the behaviour she expects by being there – and here, and seemingly everywhere at once, at a festival at which my colleagues and I joined 18,000 others breathlessly navigating the steep hills and valleys of this high-altitude city (at 2,640 metres above sea level the largest city in the world at its elevation) to attend three to five shows a day over the festival's twelve intensive days.

FESTA is unique, as are most of the festivals discussed in the remainder of this chapter. Genuine alternatives tend not to form templates or build networks, though they do forge solidarities across their differences. What FESTA does share with the other alternatives under consideration is the political consciousness of the social activist and a refusal of any variation on the free-market open-access principles that dominate the fringe world. These festivals are resolutely purposeful.

Edinburgh's Counterfestivals

The EFF, the Adelaide Fringe, and other open-access fringes tend to be dominated by stand-up comedy at corporate venues, and by shows that are billed and flyered as 'whacky' or 'outrageous', but are so in almost entirely normative ways. For genuine alternatives, alternative models are needed. Frew and Ali-Knight have argued that the commercialism bred from the free-market, artrepreneurial atmosphere of hustling for audiences blunts the fringes' capacities for experimentation, or indeed their capacity to be alternative in any meaningful political or aesthetic sense. It is not surprising, then, that if the historic fringe festivals no longer maintain their anarchic energy or alternative status, others have emerged – some of them in association with the fringes themselves – to take their place. Even at Edinburgh there are, for example, the Free Fringe and the now suspended Forest Fringe, not to mention the buskers and street performers that constitute a kind of fringe-of-the-fringe. 'Fringes', as Keren Zaiontz says, 'have spawned their own counterfestivals' (*Theatre & Festivals*, 10). Some of these counterfestivals have managed the inclusion and representation of difference better than others.

Perhaps the most iconic images of the Edinburgh Fringe, symbolizing the chaotic and unbridled energy of festival time, are of actors and buskers hustling on the High Street, constituting, if not a counterfestival, a fringe-of-the-fringe (Figure 13). But in fact, as Iain Munro and Silvia Jordan have demonstrated, the street artists performing throughout the city are forced to deploy 'spatial tactics' to negotiate a host of regulatory systems in order 'appropriately' (vs appropriatively) to occupy and socialize public space. The street festival, described by the Fringe Office's Director of Street Events as 'the single biggest venue of the Fringe' (qtd in Munro and Jordan 1504), is officially sanctioned and regulated by the Fringe Office and the Edinburgh City Council. There is a 'draw' for designated locations each morning, timeslots and the tidiness of pitches are controlled, and a steward at each act monitors such things as noise regulation. There's a booklet listing the performance conditions that must be adhered to and another, *Fringesafe*, on health and safety. There's a 'Director of Street Events', and even regulations on where you may or may not play bagpipes. The tactics used by performers to negotiate all this and 'own the space' (1522) are instructive, as they form 'the Street' and 'the pitch' as flexible spaces (1503–4), sculpt 'the edge' (1504–5) and 'height' (1506) of their allotment, manipulate their props and their audiences (1506–7), and build

Figure 13   Hundreds of buskers expertly negotiate the regulations and control their allotted space at the Edinburgh Fringe Festival. Photograph by Ric Knowles

climaxes and finales towards 'the hat' (1508). The ingenuity, skill, and resiliency of many of the performers is impressive, but this is not a space that is notably welcoming of difference, cultural or otherwise, the buskers seem to be overwhelmingly white, and most of what difference *is* on display consists of what appears to be self-exoticizing exhibitions by Asian, African, and Other Fringe performers promoting their Fringe shows before curious dominant-culture *flâneurs*.[23]

Also in Edinburgh, the Free Fringe, which began its operations in 2004 and by 2019 ran 9,053 performances of 410 shows (Free Festival, 'August 6–30'), attempts to offer 'something for everyone' (Free Festival, 'Theatre Shows') and bills itself, oddly, as 'an open but curated free festival' within the EFF itself: 'we do not restrict performers in any way' but 'we decide which shows best fit our programming' (Free Festival, 'Perform with Us'). The festival is organized by Laughing Horse, however, a comedy promoter, and the shows that best fit their programming are largely stand-up and sketch comedies taking place mostly in bars and nightclubs who stand to benefit from hosting shows through increased liquor sales. All performances are free, and performers are not charged for participation nor are they paid, relying on voluntary donations to pay their expenses. The Free Fringe, then, offers a different kind of open access – for audiences – and 'aims to create the "old" values of financial accessibility alongside creativity' (Frew and Ali-Knight 238), but its curation in no sense privileges diversity, difference, or, apart from free admission, access.

The festival that was run by Forest Fringe from 2007 to 2017 in conjunction with the EFF offered a different alternative. Founded by Deborah Pearson, initially at the request of the Forest Café, 'an anarchist vegetarian café in Edinburgh', Forest Fringe developed into an 'artist-run curatorial collective' led by Pearson, Andy Field, and Ira Brand (Pearson, qtd in Zaiontz, 'Festival' 159, 153). Together, Pearson, Field, and Brand 'create festivals, host residencies and occasionally commission new work as a way of helping support a large and diverse community of independent artists working across and between theatre, dance, and live art' (Forest Fringe). According to Lyn Gardner, however, Forest Fringe is also and in the best sense a 'messy, badly behaved and sometimes simply astonishing theatrical outfit that broke the [Edinburgh Fringe] festival's mould' and 'reinvented Edinburgh'. It started with 'a few caveats' from the manager of the Forest Café, who offered his space as a venue: 'One caveat was that he wanted it to be all experimental work. Another caveat was that he wanted it to be free for everyone, artists and audience members. And he wanted it to be all volunteer-run' (Pearson in Zaiontz, 'Festival' 159). All of these became fundamental to the Forest Fringe mandate, as Pearson, Field, and Brand responded to the free-market Edinburgh Fringe system, 'which is efficient and profitable, rather than creatively adventurous, socially responsible, and artistically supportive':

> The free labour that sustains Forest Fringe is a response to these conditions. It is a collective choice and an act of political and economic defiance. Forest Fringe is a free space held open by artists, for artists; a space in which we can resist the restrictions of this free market and imagine something more beautiful in its place. (Andy Field, in Field et al.)

The Forest Fringe raised funds throughout the year to provide accommodation, logistical, technical, and promotional support for artists during the festival's two-week run, initially at the Out of the Blue Drill Hall in the city's working-class, if now gentrifying Leith neighbourhood, and again in various spaces, forms, and venues after they lost their space in 2011. The Forest Fringe festival was run independently of institutional or governmental support or subsidy; it explicitly attempted 'to provide artists with agency and community and to imagine new ways of existing together under capitalism' (Forest Fringe); and, crucially, it existed as part of an artists' collective with a larger mandate than simply to stage a festival, sell some shows, or promote a city as a tourist destination.

As a curated event, the Forest Fringe festival was able to make space, not only for new work, but for experimentation with different ways of doing things – a different festival paradigm – and with 'the structural frameworks that distribute and make that work happen' (Ferdman 15). They incorporated into their programme shows such as Rosana Cade's *Walking:Holding*, in which one audience member at a time is taken on a walk through the city, holding hands along the way with six different strangers who range in age, gender, race, sexuality, and background (see Cade); and Search Party's *Growing Old with You*, which documents in real time, a decade at a time, the experience of aging (see Search Party). Neither show would be likely to be programmed or to succeed at the EFF's corporate venues, but both welcomed difference and made significant critical and, arguably, social impact.

One of Forest Fringe's most important and for my purposes most intriguing enterprises, however, was its collaboration with playwright/director David Greig and London's Gate Theatre on the 'Welcome to the Fringe' initiative, which enabled Palestinian artists and Israeli artists who reject Israeli state funds and the baggage they carry with them to come to the Edinburgh Fringe in 2015. The twelve visiting artists were partnered with UK artists attending the EFF, and Forest Fringe hosted a day-long multidisciplinary showcase of their work. Forest Fringe's involvement stemmed from the question: 'How can artists of limited financial means, and who live in areas of great conflict or political repression, get access to the world's largest and most diverse arts festival?' (Forest Fringe 2015, 'Welcome to the Fringe', qtd in Zaiontz, *Theatre & Festivals* 76). Andy Field has described the effort involved in orchestrating the event, and its impact:

> For Forest Fringe, Welcome to The Fringe was not an easy project. We worked very hard and very late into the night. With the help of the artists themselves we bent the spaces we had to fit shows that shouldn't have been able to fit in them. We squeezed an entire miniature festival into the space of a day. We did everything we could to support those artists and realise their work in the way they wanted, even when it meant stripping out and completely rebuilding our main theatre space in under 24 hours. And our experience was only one fraction of the effort by David Greig, [writer and editor] Henry Bell, the British Council, the Al-Qattan Foundation [a not-for-profit development organization based in Ramallah], friends, supporters and the artists themselves that enabled this whole project to happen. What did happen was in the end something truly wonderful – a day of

unexpected joy and collective reflection, of incredible variety and unpre-
dictability, a day rich in conversation and possibility. A day of welcoming.
(Field et al.)

As Keren Zaiontz has argued, Welcome to the Fringe 'resulted in a vital
intercultural exchange, a redistribution of art capital to artists in precarious
political circumstances, and the chance to acquire new perspectives on a
complex region all too often reduced to jarring images and sound bites in
compressed news cycles' (*Theatre & Festivals* 76). Welcome to the Fringe was a
one-off, but it models the kind of interventionist initiative that seems to be
necessary if international fringe festivals are to become genuinely and
generatively intercultural.

Forest Fringe ceased running a festival at Edinburgh in 2017, at least
temporarily, in part out of exhaustion and the problematics of unpaid labour,
but it was never exclusively about the festival anyway, and that has been part of
its flexibility and its strength. 'As practicing artists', says Pearson, 'we're constantly trying to think through different ways of curating our work and the work
of our contemporaries, and those in our communities' (qtd in Zaiontz, 'Festival'
153). In addition to running the festival in Edinburgh this has meant:

– organizing 'microfestivals' including performances, intercultural pair-
  ings, and conversations in old cinemas, warehouses, and found spaces
  within the context of already-existing festivals in places like Bankgok,
  Lisbon, London, Reykjavík, Toronto, and Yokohoma;[24]
– producing 'Paper Stages' in 2012, 'a festival of performance contained
  within the pages of a beautifully designed book with each page containing a completely new work by a different artist' that others were
  invited to perform in various locations around Edinburgh (Forest
  Fringe, 'Paper Stages');
– producing an experimental feature film as part of a company residency
  at ArtHouse Jersey on the British Channel Island;
– and organizing 'The Amateurs Club' at Somerset House in London,
  'sort of like an after-school club for adults and artists' (Pearson in
  Zaiontz, 'Festival' 160).

It may be that a successful, socially conscious, and truly intercultural
festival has, after all, to be more than just a festival.

Alternative Identities

'More-than-just-a-festival' characterizes many of the events discussed in
the remainder of this chapter. Many of these have to do with a larger, but

often very specific identity-politic or social justice mandate. Among these are the world's many gay, lesbian, queer, or LGBTQ theatre festivals in places ranging from Antwerp, Belfast, Dublin, and New Delhi to New York City, Paris, Seoul, Toronto, Vancouver BC, and Washington DC, with names ranging from 'Jerk Off' through 'Outburst' to 'Fresh Fruit' and 'Homotopia' (see Arestis; Paré). And many of these go beyond the promotion or celebration of LGBTQ rights and cultures, crucial as that may be in places such as India and Korea.

Edgy and Hysteria
The genesis and history of, and relationship between, companion festivals in two Canadian cities demonstrate some of the potential for festivals to engage the complexities of the performance of fluid genders and sexualities in the contemporary world and to constitute communities of difference – communities, that is, that are not characterized by their sameness but by their solidarities across internal differences. In a recent special issue of *Theatre Research in Canada/Recherches théâtrales au Canada*, Montréal's Edgy Women Festival (Edgy) and Toronto's Hysteria: A Festival of Women (Hysteria) are discussed together by their curators, Miriam Ginestier and Moynan King, in a way that features their shared efforts to stage queer, multidisciplinary, 'undisciplined' (Cowan et al. 126) events that hail and constitute queer women and lesbian audiences while resisting the perceived tendency of such performance to be 'earnest' (130).[25] Edgy had its genesis in a series of cabarets curated by Ginestier beginning in 1994 that coalesced into a festival when it received Canada Council funding in 2006. It ran until 2017. Hysteria began as a full-fledged festival at Toronto's Buddies in Bad Times, North America's largest queer theatre, in 2003, and ran there for six years. The festivals shared sensibilities, goals, and many of the same performers, and the cooperation and collaboration between them have fostered relationships and legacies that persist into the future.

Both festivals were initially founded to address 'the real problem of women's representation . . ., which was not the scarcity of work by women, but the scarcity of venues calling for and programming that work' (King, in Cowan et al. 124). Both were also 'anti-fragile' (128), 'actively seeking weirdness, stuff that's subversive, or a bit controversial' (Ginestier, in Cowan et al. 126), both were about 'creating communities' (126), and both addressed and asserted the existence of 'a dyke audience': although both festivals included performers who identified as straight, they 'were talking to straight women and saying, "You're going to be performing for

800 lesbians and their friends"' (Cowan, in Cowan et al. 127). Edgy and Hysteria, then, were intersectional (and therefore intercultural) insofar as they brought together in solidarity various queer, lesbian, and straight genders, sexualities, and cultures, including trans women and 'dyke-adjacent' spectators (128). They also created solidarities across other forms of difference, as is evidenced by the prominence at both festivals over several years of the bilingual (French/English) Afro-Caribbean Canadian playwright/performer Edwige Jean-Pierre, of Congolese and Haitian descent, who 'does not identify as queer, but definitely as feminist' (King, in Cowan et al. 131).

T.L. Cowan effectively summarizes the considerable combined impact of these festivals and is worth quoting at some length:

> In the case of *Edgy + Hysteria*, the festival and cabaret are both forms characterized by variety, by relationality across difference ... [B]oth forms are energized by contiguity, by 'improvisatory *rubbings against* – of performances, of bodies in a small [or large] room' or program (Cowan), by sharing time-space; they exist as assemblages. They are also structured as durational forms through which artists, audiences, volunteers, and organizers endure, stay with it, keep going. They are characterized by a hoped-for horizontalized distribution of fame, fans and fortune, prioritizing connection over division. As artistic genres, performance structures, and platforms of and experiments in relationality, the festival and the cabaret – especially those organized around minoritized, forgotten, neglected, abandoned but nonetheless *existing* cultures – have been and continue to be central to the resilience and perpetual reshaping of queer feminist socialities, aesthetics, and erotic life back and forth between Montréal and Toronto on Via Rail [the main Canadian commuter trainline], and other tracks and times real and imagined ...
>
> *Edgy* and *Hysteria* worked to blow open the limits of the symbolical, gestural, corporeal, relational, and conversational order of queer feminist expressive culture through the co-production of performance, social, and sexual cultures. Both *Edgy* and *Hysteria* were resolutely multi-disciplinary- ... not only in the ways they brought together theatre, performance art, visual art, cabaret, dance, and other artistic forms with queer feminist nightlife, but also in the ways that they pick up on the work of earlier and ongoing festivals, events and political and cultural transformation of queer feminist scenes. The phase here is not discrete but accretive. These festival-relationships do not end so much as be added to, changing and lasting across distance and time. (Cowan, in Cowan et al. 120–2)

Edgy and Hysteria, then, were alternative in developing a festival model, drawing on the cognate form of cabaret, that was, like the Indigenous Festivals I proposed in Chapter 1 as offering an alternative festival paradigm, at once relational, horizontal, and participatory, and both functioned effectively to give priority to connection across respected and acknowledged difference both between and within communities.

Disability Festival Cultures/Disability Culture Festivals

If theatre and performance festivals have proven productive in the constitution of queer communities and the negotiation of intersectional queer cultures, they have also been extraordinarily generative in doing similar things for disability cultures, which are also, as disability theatre scholar Carrie Sandahl says, 'identity based' (qtd in Levitt). Disability theatre and arts festivals are a relatively recent phenomenon, emerging at the community level in the UK in the late1980s, but as truly international events only in the early twenty-first century.[26]

Within disability culture these festivals represent, serve, negotiate, and help to constitute a very capacious community across a wide range of physical and mental disabilities. There have, as with other identity-based festivals, been debates about the value of disability festivals. Some argue that they can create a 'disability ghetto' and preach to the converted (see Muehlemann). Others have questioned whether festivals 'risk usurping the time, money, and other audience and performer resources of more sustained arts programming' throughout the year (Johnston 96). But most point to the value of such festivals in the creation and development of international networks of exchange, not only through performances but through panels, lectures, workshops, and symposia. Kirsty Johnston has argued that festivals also 'provide media engagement, publicity, accessible venues, and targeted, interested audiences' (96). Finally, Johnston, Nina Muehlemann, and others extol the value of events in which no single artist has to bear the burden of representation, and they celebrate the sheer community-building, space-claiming value of festivals for a segment of society that is often stigmatized and quite literally relegated to the margins (like sign language interpreters at the edge of a proscenium). These festivals not only exist as spaces where, in the words of disabled filmmaker Bonnie Klein, 'we can dare to be our most authentic, glorious, courageous selves' (qtd in Kickstart), they also function in part, as Heather Fitzsimmons Frey has argued of festivals for very young audiences, as advocacy.

Not all disability theatre and arts festivals are the same. Some, such as Edmonton's Sound Off, Zagreb's BIT (Blind in Theatre), or Toronto's Rendezvous with Madness, might be considered to be culturally specific, focusing on Deaf, blind and vision impaired, or 'mad' cultures, respectively.[27] Such festivals sacrifice solidarities across broadly intersectional disability cultures in order to acknowledge the specificity of cultures and abilities that have little in common with one another or with, for example, people using wheelchairs or prosthetic devices, or living with chronic illnesses, visible or not. Sound Off, produced by Workshop West Playwrights Theatre and billed as North America's only ongoing Deaf theatre festival, was in its fourth edition in 2020. 'Dedicated to making theatre accessible for both Deaf and hearing audiences and celebrating the stories and talents of Deaf performers' as well as the beauty of American Sign Language, the four-day festival includes discussions, talkbacks, and workshops, and incorporates many free as well as 'Offer-What-You-Will' events ('Sound Off). Sound Off has already had a significant impact, its discussion and networking components having both led to the Awakening Deaf Theatre in Canada conference in Montréal in 2018, and initiated discussions on Deaf and Sign Language theatre across Canada (see Fida).

BIT staged its eleventh biennial festival in 2019 in the Croatian capital city of Zagreb (population ca 1.1 million) in a programme that featured classics of western dramatic literature by the likes of Ionesco, Gogol, and Shaw alongside contemporary plays by Aleš Berger (Slovenia), Dušan Kovačević (Serbia), Vojin Perić (Croatia), and Sarah Houbolt (Australia). But, perhaps remarkably, it also offered, from the UK, the 'queer Crip' couple Amelia Cavallo and Quiplash's *Unsightly Drag, with Workshop* (LiveArt), providing blind and visually impaired performers and audiences access to drag performance in a rare intersectional alliance. The festival features daily roundtables as well as workshops and press conferences to allow opportunities for exchange and networking.

Finally, Workman Arts's multidisciplinary Rendezvous with Madness, the successor to the Madness and Arts World Festival inaugurated in Toronto in 2003, bills itself as 'the first & largest mental health festival in the world' (Workman). Madness and Arts was an ambitious, large-scale event first staged at Toronto's prestigious Harbourfront Centre with a three-quarter-million-dollar budget supporting an international, multidisciplinary programme exploring 'the role of the arts in shaping attitudes toward mental illness in a range of cultures' (Johnston 49–50). A second, expanded festival, inspired by attendance at the first, was held in Münster, Germany, in 2006, and a third in Amsterdam in 2010 (see Johnston 94). Rendezvous with Madness, its successor in Toronto, is now an annual ten-day festival that includes visual art, performance, music, theatre, dance, and media arts, along with panel discussions and in-conversation events.

At the other end of the spectrum from these culturally specific festivals are integrationist ones such as Awakenings, in the small city of Horsham, western Victoria (population ca 16,500), 300 kilometres northwest of Melbourne, Australia, where healthcare is the primary employer. The so-called 'festival of a thousand smiles' (Visit), which addresses disability cultures at large, partnered in 2014 with the 'mainstream' festival, Art Is..., in an experiment to turn it into 'a festival for all abilities' (Coughlan). This apparently integrationist move serves those who do not wish to be identified as people with disabilities, or who argue against the use of 'disability arts' in favour of such terms as 'integrated' or 'inclusive' arts' (see Johnston 99–101). The 'integrated' or 'inclusive' terms are used to suggest 'a kind of thinking with and beyond borders' (Johnston 100) to include Deaf people, the blind and visually impaired, people with various physical and mental health issues, and people who may or may not have disabilities but choose to work with artists who do. 'The term integrated arts is used . . . to suggest inclusion and an unbroken continuum of human behavior and expression' (Johnston 100, quoting Richard Marcuse, et al., *A Legacy for All of Us: A Plan for the Development of Integrated Arts and Culture in British Columbia*).

The majority of the many international disability arts and culture festivals around the world sit somewhere between the culturally specific and the integrationist and feature artists with a wide range of developmental, physical, or sensory disability, mental illness, brain injury, and/or chronic illness. These include such notable events as Crossing the Line, a one-off showcase festival mounted in Roubaix, France (population ca 100,000), in 2018 by a network of seven European disability theatre companies funded by the EU; Unlimited, a biennial festival at the Southbank Centre in London, England launched in 2012 to coincide with the Paralympic Games, notably involving commissioned as well as non-commissioned work by artists with disabilities, and aiming 'to embed work by artists with disability within the cultural sector, reach new audiences and shift perceptions of people with disability' (Unlimited); and the four-day I wanna be with you everywhere performing arts festival at the Performance Space New York in 2019, which

> celebrates the world-making and experimentation that comes from refusing both exclusion and inclusion. At the same time, this gathering is propelled by a refusal of the separation that ableism imposes, starting from the belief and desire that access is a shared commitment to each other. (S. Kim)

I wanna be with you everywhere was inspired by a similar event hosted by Scotland's political arts organization Arika in 2015. Its opening night featured Johanna Hedva, a genderqueer Korean American artist with a chronic illness that at times prevents them from walking or talking; Leah Lakshmi Piepzna-Samarasinha, a queer disabled femme writer, organizer, performer, and educator; and NEVE, a self-proclaimed 'Black punk queer disabled fairy beast' in a wheelchair (S. Kim), together setting the festival's broadly intersectional, intercultural, and politicized tone.

I will close my discussion of disability alternatives by focusing on three of the most significant festivals: Balancing Acts in Calgary, Bodies of Work in Chicago, and NO LIMITS in Berlin and beyond.[28] Balancing Acts was founded in 2002 by Stage Left Productions and ran for a decade as 'the only professional multidisciplinary arts festival in Canada that is dedicated to advancing the concerns of the global disability art and culture movement'. The festival website describes this as:

> an international movement of disabled artists whose objective is to represent the lived experience of disability as complex, dynamic, and infused with a range of experiences that include hopes and dreams, self-worth and autonomy, sexuality and relationships, and social barriers to disability. The artists who are part of this movement use the arts to examine the sociopolitical context of personal and cultural identity. Our collective intention is to advance a creative vision of social equality that embraces the difference of disability, rather than normalizes it or renders it further invisible within mainstream society. (Balancing Acts)

The festival was unique in combining an explicit aspiration to forge transnational links and a transnational disability culture with a practice of commissioning 'challenging, thought-provoking performance work of high artistic merit from emerging and established professional disabled artists whose work aligns with the goals and principles of the global disability arts and culture movement' (qtd in Johnston 95).[29]

The Bodies of Work Festival in Chicago, founded in 2006 and revived in 2013 by disability theatre scholar Carrie Sandahl, herself disabled, has been influential, particularly in the United States, in shifting stereotypical public understandings of disability art as either tragic or inspirational. Work at the festival has dealt with a range of disabilities from depression and PTSD through pain, body image issues, sexuality, and injury to 'how to experience sound without hearing it or dance without using your legs' (Levitt). Bodies of Work is determinedly professional rather than simply community-based or therapeutic, which means that it acknowledges that the responsibility of the artist is to speak beyond the self to larger issues of the human condition, albeit through a personal lens. It regards the unique personal lens of the disability artist as deriving from that artist's unique disability – or unique ability to see the world differently. '[W]e are expressing our perspectives on the world gained by having a unique body, a unique mind, sensory differences, mental health differences', says Sandahl. 'We don't see these as obstacles to overcome, but as experiences to be explored' (qtd in Ise).

> The disabilities civil rights movement has a motto that says: 'Nothing about us, without us'. That is true for the arts as well. I have a physical disability so my experience is very different from someone who is blind or deaf. A lot of the early work was about confronting stereotypes, but the work now – as people will see at the festival – is about trying to enter the mainstream and trying to show how our disabilities give us a particular perspective that's valuable. We're taking charge of how we're represented and we're doing that from our uniqueness. It's not about saying, 'I create art despite my disability.' It's about saying, 'this disability provides me some aesthetic possibilities that have gone unexplored'. (Sandahl, qtd in Kann)

Thus, a dancer in a wheelchair is able to rethink dance and explore new physical possibilities involving arcs, circles, sweeping movements, and spins that are not available to non-disabled dancers (see Ise); performers with mental or cognitive challenges are often able to think in generatively different ways about the world; and blind or visually impaired artists are able quite literally to see the world differently. Festivals such as Bodies of Work that bring such artists together and bring them together with variously disabled and non-disabled audiences, are uniquely positioned to shift the ground of human understanding and capacity, and the festival experience for disabled and non-disabled participants alike can be exhilarating.

I attended my first disability performance festival, Berlin's NO LIMITS, in 2013, and was astonished at the time by the beauty and skill, variety, value, and generative aesthetic difference of theatre and dance that I had previously only given token acknowledgement as intercultural performance. NO LIMITS is Germany's, and I believe Europe's, largest and most important festival for disability and the performing arts. It takes place biennially in the Fall at the three venues of the HAU (Hebbel am Ufer). The eighth edition, in 2017, was dedicated to breaking down conventions and questioning rules of conduct in what it called 'inclusion theatre'. International, intercultural, and integrative, the festival staged artists who refused simply to represent, or be limited by, their disabilities. Deaf and hearing-impaired artists disagreed about hearing aids; shows included multiple spoken, surtitled, and signed languages all of which fought with rather than explained one another; one physically disabled performer snaked sensually in and out of her wheelchair, while another, dressed only

Figure 14 Jo Bannon performs in her mad feminist dance show, *We Are Fucked*, at the NO LIMITS disability arts festival in 2019. Photograph by Paul Samuel White

in a bikini, lasciviously wallowed 'between seduction and repulsion' (Bickel).

In 2019 the ninth edition of NO LIMITS was co-curated (with Marcel Bugieil) for the first time by an artist with a disability, Viennese choreographer Michael Turinsky. As for most editions the featured performers were also disability artists from ten countries and four continents seizing control of their own representation. They included Chiara Bersani, three feet, two inches tall, in a solo performance in which she transformed herself into a unicorn through the course of the show; UK-based live-arts choreographer, dramaturg, educator, and writer Jo Bannon, with albinism, in the mad feminist dance show, *We Are Fucked* (Figure 14); Monster Truck, casting Peter Weiss's *Marat/Sade* with cognitively impaired actors; and Noëmi Lakmaier in a durational piece in which she floated for ten hours on a cushion of 20,000 multicoloured helium-filled balloons. The festival brochure, labelling NO LIMITS 'a laboratory of productive deviations', provides an evocative account:

> Choreographer Michael Turinsky [has moved] the current edition's focus on[to] dance, and thus in turn on[to] bodies: exposed to the gaze of others,

utopian, stigmatized, countered and racialized, poetic and political, sensitive to pain and vulnerable, headstrong, monstrous, full of relish, capti-
vated, animal and plant-like, silent and in dialogue, alone and with others,
as the scene of psychiatric disorders, as a brush and projection screen, full of
unexpected possibilities and impossibilities, with its own kind of memory.
Sometimes unicorn, sometimes plant, sometimes the way they happen to
be at the moment, sometimes extended by assistive devices and set into
motion or lifted by 20,000 helium-filled balloons. (NO LIMITS)

The festival includes a symposium, in 2019 entitled 'Exploding Times,
Displaced Space: Disabilty Art & Crip Spacetime',[30] at which participants,
as in the performances, explore 'strategies on how artists with disabilities
can act politically on stage' (NO LIMITS). This festival is no longer
simply about the everyday barriers faced by people with disabilities; it
moves 'disability' into the category of 'a sociological, system-critical category that concerns everyone' (Bickel).

Disability festivals, then, which not surprisingly attract a specialized
audience, function as transnational sites of activist intervention around
disability rights, deconstruct stereotypes, and build solidarities across disability and other cultures. But they also serve a general audience and
society at large by performing undervalued ways of being and seeing in
often unanticipated, non-normalizing ways, encouraging in everyone the
capacity to experience the world differently. As audience experiences,
moreover, they model an open, welcoming, and non-competitive type of
festival in which the festival gaze of any merely curious onlookers is
consistently and productively encountered and returned.

Political Alternatives

Not all alternative festivals, of course, are identity based. Some festivals,
such as Helsinki's Baltic Circle Festival, have participated directly in public
political debates led by artists in ways that extend the standard festival
format (see Zaiontz, *Theatre & Festivals* 49–52). Others, such as the
Festival international de théâtre pour le développement (FITD) in
Ouagadougou, Burkina Faso, have been about 'asserting the existence
and cultural legitimacy of an entire continent' since 1988 ('Festival international'). But perhaps the most politically alternative festival I have
encountered was the 'manifestival' L'état d'urgence (State of
Emergency), which was founded in Montréal in 1998 by artists Pierre
Allard and Annie Roy and inspired by the fiftieth anniversary of the
United Nations' Universal Declaration of Human Rights. At once

determinedly local and internationally networked, L'état d'urgence was one of many initiatives by ATSA (Action terroriste socialement accept-able – or socially acceptable terrorist action).[31] For its first eight years it took place at Montréal's Place Émilie-Gamelin in the city's Quartier Latin, a regular gathering place for the homeless, where for four to ten days, twenty-four hours a day, the festival offered dormitories, meals, and services to itinerant and homeless people as an expression of resistance to the deterioration of the social fabric. Within and in parallel to this 'homeless spectacle'-cum-'refugee camp' (Zaiontz, *Theatre & Festivals* 94), the festival programmed free theatre, dance, performance art, circus, storytelling, film, visual art, and photography events that drew attention to poverty, homelessness, environmental degradation, and other social ills. But perhaps, as Sylvie St Jacques observed, 'the most interesting spectacle unfolded more in the audience than on the stage. In what other Montreal festival', she asked, 'do we come across a homeless man who fraternizes during a show with a simple party animal?' The homeless (many of them racialized), festival spectators, and passersby were brought together in a festival environment that focused annually on such themes as inclu-sivity, social hygiene, house arrest, and, in the 2009 edition in partnership with Amnesty International, poverty and homelessness as human rights issues.

Four days before the 2010 edition of the festival, Canada's Conservative federal government's Heritage Minister, James Moore, attacked ATSA for its inclusion of 'terroriste' in its name, funding for the festival was with-drawn on that pretext, and the organization changed its name to ATSA quand l'art passe à l'action (When Art Takes Action) (see ATSA). The festival proceeded in 2010 *as* L'état d'urgence for the last time for seven years, operating, as St Jacques says, as a large artistic family outside the realm of 'cultural tourism'. But ATSA continued to operate its manifesti-vals, including, from 2011 to 2013, a one-day Fin Novembre (End of November) event, and in October 2015 Le Temps d'une Soupe (While Having Soup), in which paired strangers, homeless and otherwise, shared soup and conversation on a brightly lit scaffold in Place Émilie-Gamelin. In 2017 Pas d'radis fiscaux: L'état d'urgence featured original interdisciplinary works on the theme of wealth disparity while also pro-viding ATSA's traditional meals and services and hosting a Canada/US/UK arts and homelessness exchange, With One Voice. NGOs, activists, artists, policy makers, and homeless people met together in a series of discussions, presentations, workshops, Legislative Theatre,[32] and other socially engaged art (see 'Quand l'art').

Figure 15   In *The Monument*, by Manaf Halbouni, three burned-out buses stood before the Brandenburg Gate at the Berliner Herbstsalon in 2017 to commemorate the building of a makeshift shield against sniper fire in Aleppo during the Syrian civil war. Photograph by Ric Knowles

In Fall 2017, coinciding with the Pas d'radis: L'état d'urgence and With One Voice events across the Atlantic, I attended the third 'Berliner Herbstsalon' (Fall Salon) entitled 'De-Integrate Yourselves' (Figure 15). The Berlin event is focused, not on poverty and homelessness as such, but on social justice issues emerging from migration, immigration, and cultural difference. The festival is sponsored by the Maxim Gorki Theater, one of the city's state-funded municipal repertory theatres. Since 2013–14 the Gorki has been run by the Turkish-born artistic director Shermin Langhoff, who has brought a new commitment to social justice and cultural difference to the city's state theatres, having popularized the term 'postmigrant theatre' when she was founding artistic director of the Ballhaus Naunynstraße in Berlin's diverse Kreuzberg district.[33] The Herbstsalon took over the Gorki, the Palais am Festungsgraben, the Kronprinzenpalais, and other sites on Unter den Linden, running from the Brandenburg Gate to the Schlossbrücke and Museum Island in the heart of historic Berlin from morning to late at night for two weeks in November. It is described in its brochure as 'a two-week-long public rehearsal for the rebellion against attributions, generalizations, and simplifications' around the construction of identities, unities, purities, and societal integration, incorporation, and homogenization (*3. Berliner Herbstsalon* [5]). The 2017 Herbstsalon featured over 100 interdisciplinary works, installations, and performances by artists from Argentina, Australia, Austria, Bosnia and Herzogovina, Bulgaria, Chile, Croatia, Cuba, France, Greece, Hungary, Iran, Mexico, the Netherlands, Palestine, Poland, Portugal, Romania, Russia, San Marino, Spain, Syria, Turkey, and the United Arab Emirates, as well as artists identified only as Roma. It also included many local Berlin and other German artists, though these were most often also identified as (im)migrants. The theatre pieces in the festival included so-called theatre of the real shows about communism in Germany and immigrant cleaning women in Athens, both featuring non-actors and their real-life experiences;[34] other shows addressed such things as 'whiteness' (racialized), 'the situation' (in the Middle East), the surveillance society, and the European immigration crisis. The installations and performances addressed everything from revenge (blowing up the Parthenon) through freedom of speech and its repression, to the genocide of the Roma and much more, with wit, anger, erudition, invention, and grace. But the real event was no single artwork or show; it was the integration of all of these disparate parts into an extended, cross-cultural collaboration, conversation, and negotiation held in a concentrated space at the heart of Berlin in what constituted a genuinely integrated festival-as-meta-event.

The fourth edition of the Herbstsalon in 2019, subtitled 'De-heimatize it!', directly addressed discourses of 'home' within current neo-fascist and anti-immigrant sentiments in Germany, Europe, and the world. It included a conference and a Young Curators Academy to discuss constructions of identity, nation, and belonging from an intersectional feminist perspective, and it was framed by an impassioned editorial written by Langhoff:

> 'Home' is currently being projected in capital letters on every wall of the republic. But not in the sense of empathy and solidarity with the people who have to flee their homeland. On the contrary, 'homeland' serves the right-wing and right-wing extremists to exclude the expropriated and disenfranchised … What helps against the seemingly unstoppable triumph of male authoritarianism, nationalism and the neoliberal regime? The answer can only be in solidarity. If art wants to oppose these practices of rule, it must think and address the exclusion criteria race, class, gender at the same time … [T]he right of residence has been tightened to an unprecedented degree, the murders [by] right-wing terrorists played down and the affiliation and right to exist of immigrants still seems to be

negotiable again and again. That is why we initiated an international conference and a temporary international academy for the first time in the 4th Berlin Fall Salon to develop theory and exchange practices ... [B]ehind the signature for the 4th Berlin Fall Salon there is an exclamation mark! It is not a question of resigningly closing a chapter, but of opening a new – perhaps angrier – one.

The Berliner Herbstsalon, I suggest and hope, represents the future direction of transnational arts festivals that wish to function effectively to bring cultures together in productive, politically progressive and activist, angrily interventionist ways.

An Alliance of Defiance

Fringe festivals are perhaps the most globally ubiquitous type of theatre, performance, or live-art festival, but it is clear that if their organizers wish to continue to make claims about their status as genuine alternatives or their accessibility to all artists and audiences, and if they want to encourage or enable encounters and negotiations across real, material difference, they need to abandon, or at the very least modify their open access policies and take meaningful, affirmative action. Only by abandoning their modelling of the inequitable alliance between radical democracy and late-stage free-market capitalism will they be able to make credible claims to constitute, as a global movement, the genuine alliance of defiance that the Edinburgh Fringe boasts of being. The experience of attending alternative festivals often involves discomfort quite different from the exhaustion and sensory overload of the 'fringe-binge' or the frustration of failing to get tickets to 'best of the fringe' shows: sharing space with the homeless, finding one's taken-for-granteds challenged, or being confronted by the anger of the dispossessed. But it can also involve engaging with performance in exhil-arating new ways, eschewing the bloatedness of capitalist consumption, and serving across difference as witnesses, allies, participants, and activists.

CHAPTER 5

The Intracultural Transnational

It is January 2018 and I am sitting in the back row of the large conference hall in the Hotel Africa in Tunis, where daily sessions on 'Authority and Knowledge in the Theatre' are held as part of the Arab Theatre Festival. My friend and cultural consultant, Lebanese Canadian director Majdi Bou-Matar, is translating, sotto-voce, all the intricacies and angers of the papers, presenters, and questioners, when, in spite of our deliberately positioning ourselves ten rows behind the closest participants, we're vigorously shushed by someone who has just arrived and perversely chosen to sit close to us. This festival is not intended for translation into English, or any other language. Indeed, unlike city-branding, destination festivals such as Edinburgh, Avignon, and Adelaide, unlike curated, artist-run festivals such as London's LiFT, Vancouver's PuSh, or Toronto's Progress; and unlike the ubiquitous fringes and 'offs'; this festival is not staged for global consumption. The programme exists only in Arabic, the shows do not use surtitles, and in spite of the live streaming of the conference and the opening and closing ceremonies in Arabic throughout the Arab world, the festival has no online presence or publicity in any other language. This festival is for Arabs.

Indeed, the Arab Theatre Festival, sponsored by the Arab Theatre Institute under the patronage of the sovereign ruler of the Emirate of Sharjah, Sheikh Sultan bin Muhammad Al Qasimi, has little live public presence beyond the 600 delegates who constitute the majority of the audience for its (in 2018) thirty-six performances of twenty-seven plays from twenty-three countries in a single week. The fact that a limited number of delegates stay in the same hotel and share meals, attend (some of them) the same conference sessions in the mornings, and see the same three or four shows a day in the afternoons and evenings, enables a frank exchange of views over an intensive week in a different Arab city every January. In spite of the fact that, as one delegate said in Tunis in 2018 (paraphrasing Muammar Gaddafi), 'this room' – the conference room – together with a shared written language, 'is the only thing that brings us together [as Arabs];'[1] and in spite of often fractious debates taking place beyond the

Figure 16   *Fear(s)*, by Jalila Baccar, Fadhel Jaibi, and the Théâtre National Tunisien, epitomized the sense of despair at the Arab Theatre Festival in Tunis in the wake of the hijacking of the Arab Spring. Photograph by Aymen Bachrouch

panoptic gaze of western media, the festival in 2018 evinced a surprising degree of unity. The shows ranged in form from clown and puppetry through productions of western classics to testimonial performance, dance, and physical theatre, but they virtually all shared a sense of loss, outrage, or despair at the hijacking of the hope that had been generated by the Arab Spring, as, in the wake of the European colonizers and the authoritarian regimes, the 'third colonialism', as one conference delegate called it – radical Islam – rushed in to fill the power vacuum after the 2010–12 revolutions (see Figure 16). The performances at the 2018 festival, then – and the festival itself *as* performance – at least in part fulfilled the festival's mandate to 'establish and strengthen intercultural ties between the various countries of the Arab world through a shared passion for theatre' (Amine).[2] The festival also exemplifies an emerging type of festival in the twenty-first century that has developed in reaction to various types of colonialism and neocolonialism, one modelled, not on diplomatic exchange between sovereign nations, but on collaborations within a single transnational community.

The Arab Theatre Festival's general coordinator, Mahmoud Mejri, has defended it from the suggestion that it should be more open to European and western participation, citing its purpose as a celebration of Arab theatre and an opportunity to 'strengthen ties' within the Arab world (see Khlifi). In my experience the festival largely accomplished those goals, working towards the production of an Arab identity and Arab political solidarities while also allowing for fierce political critique and sober self-examination outside of the unsympathetic glare of western headlights. And although there was considerable inter-national squabbling among the scholars, performances at the festival exhibited a greater degree of unity among the artists than even they may have anticipated.

The Arab Theatre Festival is not unique in focusing its attention on a single language group, or on relationships within a cultural formation that crosses national borders. This chapter focuses on 'intracultural transnational' festivals of various kinds that ground themselves in cultural, theatrical, aesthetic, social, and political relations that cross borders *within* cultures, broadly defined, and often also within language groups. It focuses, that is, on festivals serving or supporting specific transnational communities, and asks how such festivals can address, redress, and speak across historical and contemporary cultural and economic inequalities and current political differences. How can intracultural transnational festivals function as decolonizing circles of conversation that stage meaningful dialogues and engage in transnational community-building? How can they avoid the pitfalls of festivalization, eventification, creative city discourse, and the commodification of cultures? How can they sidestep the brokerage of a globally dominant festival marketplace?

Festivals I consider beyond the Arab world include:

- diasporic festivals in Africa and the Caribbean that sprang up in the wake of successful independence movements among former European colonies;
- festivals in the francophone and lusophone worlds that work through (post)colonial relationships among nations united *and* divided by their use of the language of the colonizer;[3]
- regional festivals such as BeSeTo (Beijing, Seoul, Tokyo), which brings together globally regional groups from Northeast Asia *without* a shared language in order to negotiate fraught histories and contemporary identities outside of western brokerage; the Kampala International Theatre Festival, which focuses on sharings and solidarities across East African countries; and Aluna Theatre's RUTAS festival (Panamerican Routes/Rutas Panamericanas) in Toronto, whose reach is hemispheric and whose primary focus is on interdisciplinary Latinx and Indigenous performance.

These festivals struggle to function less as global theatrical marketplaces than as sites of intra*cultural* negotiation, exchange, solidarity, and identity formation across inter*national* differences. They constitute an emerging new festival paradigm that shares some features of 'internation' exchange with the ancient *and* new Indigenous paradigm that I have explored in Chapter 1. And for many such festivals shifting focus away from spectacle, the conference, workshop, and social components are at least as important as the shows.

Festivalizing Diaspora

Perhaps the most socially and geopolitically ambitious of the intracultural transnational festivals are those that bring together vast and geographically dispersed communities, particularly when those communities are scarred by a historical trauma as deep, enduring, and globally impactful as the international slave trade. How can trauma be 'festivalized'? How can festivals dedicated to celebrating the shared cultures of formerly enslaved peoples avoid putting historical trauma on display for touristic consumption? How might diasporic festivalgoers visiting or attempting to constitute a homeland simultaneously (or by turns) play the divided roles of participants, witnesses, and visitors? Unlike other festivals under consideration in this chapter, perhaps *because* they are faced with questions such as these, the reach of both of the festivals treated here goes beyond theatre as a form; it extends, more accurately, to the performance, and the performance-into-being, of newly (re) imagined communities and cultures. The transnationalism of the first festival under consideration, Ghana's PANAFEST, is diasporic, attempting to assemble a scattered African 'nation'; the second, CARIFESTA, rotating among Caribbean nations, employs, in part and problematically, a model of postconial nationalism that emerges out of the decolonizing movement endorsed in 1960 by the United Nations' Declaration on the Granting of Independence to Colonial Countries and Peoples and grounded, initially at least, in the post-war ideology of the sovereignty and 'imagined' cultural homogeneity of nation-states (B. Anderson).

PANAFEST

I will begin with the Pan-African Historical Festival (PANAFEST) on coastal Ghana and its predecessors in Africa, festivals whose outreach has been to a global diaspora and whose histories are fraught in ways that are exemplary of the pressures that accrue in this age of the increasing festivalization of cultures, especially in the so-called 'developing world'. The earliest diasporic African festivals emerged in the virtually immediate wake of African nations' achievements of independence and in the midst of global Pan-African, 'back-to-Africa', and *négritude* movements inspired by the work of leaders such as W.E.B. Dubois (US), Kwame Nkrumah (Ghana), and Marcus Garvey (Jamaica) (see Abaka 349). The Premier Festival Mondial des Arts Nègres was held in Dakar, Senegal in 1966, six years after Senegalese independence from France; the Premier Festival Culturel Panafricain took place in Algiers in 1969, seven years after Algeria gained independence, also from France, after an eight-year war. Both festivals focused on coming to terms with neocolonial European dominance while promoting pan-African solidarities, regenerating African cultures, and charting independent futures. The Dakar Festival, hosted by prominent *négritude* advocate and Senegalese President Léopold Sédar Senghor, assembled artists and scholars from Africa, Europe, and the US – including such art-world luminaries as Langston Hughes, Duke Ellington, Alvin Ailey (US), and Aimé Césaire (Martinique) – in a celebration of African culture and a coming to terms with European colonialism (see Schramm 82). Three years later in Algiers, the festival evinced a more revolutionary spirit and set out to forge solidarities more with political than artistic leaders, and with socialist and anti-imperialist movements globally. There were delegations from the African National Congress (ANC) in South Africa, from Palestine, Vietnam, the Soviet Union, and the GDR (East Germany). Leading an African American delegation which also included Black activist Stokely Carmichael (later Kwame Ture), were Eldridge Cleaver of the Black Panthers and his partner, Kathleen Neal Cleaver, both on the FBI's wanted list at the time (see Schramm 82). Both festivals were highly public challenges to European imperialism, participating in and contributing to global Black resistance movements and functioning as fellow travellers with international socialism.[4]

The second Pan-African Festival of Black Arts and Culture (FESTAC), official successor to the Dakar festival eleven years earlier, was held in Lagos, Nigeria in 1977, in a former British colony with a primarily Muslim poplulation.[5] Ostensibly focused on African cultural resurrection, the impulses driving FESTAC were far from those of Algiers's international socialist humanism. Sponsored by the Nigerian state and held at the lavish National Art Theatre in Lagos (now suffering decay and under threat of sale), FESTAC consisted of a colloquium, a programme of traditional African performing arts, and an exhibition of traditional arts and crafts.

It was characterized by tensions between continental and diasporic delegates and by celebrations of Nigeria's then provisionally successful embrace
of global capitalism; and it was criticized for trading in the commodification of African cultures (see Schramm 82).

These three short-lived festivals laid complicated groundwork for
Ghana's PANAFEST,[6] which, however, takes place in the small university
city of Cape Coast (population ca 170,000) rather than the large mega-
lopolises of the earlier festivals. Cape Coast is a former British colony, a
traditional fishing port with a 50 per cent Christian population that is
more reliant than they are on tourist income, much of it from the diaspora
at its coastal slave castles (or dungeons).[7] PANAFEST has always been less
focused than its predecessors on anti-colonial activism than on bringing
together African diasporic peoples in what François Campana calls 'a big
family reunion' (51) that acknowledges and memorializes the history and
legacy of the transatlantic slave trade.[8] It is not, as Edmund Kobina Abaka
argues, 'merely a carnival over the tragedies, pain and anguish that continue to afflict parts of the continent' (350). Rather its 'core objectives' are:

> to establish the truth about the history of Africa and experience of its
> people, using the vehicle of African arts and culture; to provide a forum
> to promote unity between Africans on the continent and in the Diaspora; to
> affirm the common heritage of African peoples the world over and define
> Africa's contribution to world civilization; to encourage regular review of
> Africa's development objectives, strategies and policies; and to mobilize
> consensus for the formulation and implementation of potential alternative
> options for development. (Victor K. Yankah, qtd in Addo 196)

The idea for PANAFEST was first floated by the foundational Ghanaian
playwright and Pan-Africanist Efua Sutherland in 1980 in her 'Proposal for
a Historical Drama Festival in Cape Coast' (see Schramm 79; and especially Yankah 46 and *passim*). Sutherland's proposal of a drama festival
devoted to examining and remembering the suppressed history of the
transatlantic slave trade, to be held at the Cape Coast Castle at which
enslaved Africans were imprisoned before being dispatched to the Middle
Passage, was not realized until 1991. She had envisioned a festival that
would highlight the 'art of drama as such' (qtd in Schramm 80), but in the
intervening decade politicians had become aware of the tremendous
potential of a festival to attract tourists from the diaspora, particularly
the United States, where it has been vigorously promoted since 1994 (see
Essah), and to reinforce the legitimacy of the Ghanaian state, particularly
the government in charge (see Adrover et al. 157; Schramm 81).[9] The
biennial festival's recurring mottos are 'The Re-emergence of African

Civilization' and 'Uniting the African Family', and it has served both functions reasonably well, contributing to the renewal of African cultures on the continent while convening and celebrating the global African diaspora, albeit through the problematic and potentially coercive discourse of 'family'. The festival has also served as the occasion for generative colloquia among continental and diasporic scholars, held at the University of Cape Coast. In 2003 there was a four-day conference of African traditional leaders from Ghana, South Africa, Nigeria, Sierra Leone, Burkina Faso, Côte d'Ivoire, Benin, and Togo, also involving representatives from the Caribbean and the Americas. The same iteration of the festival featured a massive '1000 Voices Choir' from all participating countries (see Gyan-Apenteng).

Nevertheless, as Lauren Adrover, David Donkor, and Christina McMahon argue about PANAFEST 2009, the festival throughout its history has 'channeled multiple flows of social and political power to promote a shared African heritage that, perhaps inadvertently, pitted the economic and cultural dimensions of emancipation against each other' (163). Sutherland's initial proposal to highlight the art of drama has been overwhelmed by more populist music and dance spectacles that often play into colonialist stereotypes about Africans; by the overarching objective of 'development' as the festival increasingly adopts the coercive globalization rhetoric of the World Bank and International Monetary Fund; and by the commodification of African cultures, crafts, and histories for touristic consumption: 'Ghana's neoliberal economic terrain', that is, 'continues to shape the packaging of African heritage in ways that imbue it with commodity value' (Adrover et al. 163).

Since 1998 the festival has incorporated 1 August Emancipation Day celebrations ('to shore up the country's tourism credentials', Yankah 51),[10] along with various ceremonies staged for African American and Afro-Caribbean visitors that feature the Cape Coast Castle and dungeons and memorialize the slave trade – adhering in this respect to Sutherland's vision, but in ways that have recently been felt to exclude or actively alienate the festival's local Ghanaian publics, who, according to Victor K. Yankah, 'do not completely embrace the festival' (53). The 2019 festival advertised a slave route pilgrimage, atonement ceremonies and memorial wreath-layings, and re-appropriative 'return journey' enactments for dia-sporic Africans through the Castle's famous 'Door of No Return' that had once led to the slaving ships. In my experience PANAFEST is unique among festivals in so directly enacting what Pierre Nora calls a '*lieux de mémoire*' for diasporic Africans for whom, in Nora's terms, 'memory has

Figure 17   A Chief of the Central Region is carried aloft in a palanquin at a special durbar on the grounds of Cape Coast Castle at the Pan African Cultural Festival. Photograph by MyLoupe/Universal Images Group via Getty Images

been torn' (144), besieged by a kind of documentary history that deforms and petrifies it. The ritual reenactments of PANAFEST attempt to restore embodiment for memories that are no longer either direct nor spontaneous, and in doing so perhaps problematically attempt to restore or affirm 'nationhood' – imagined community – to a transnational Africa.

In addition to these memorializing events, the 2019 festival also featured the famous outdoor Akwaaba durbar with traditional Chiefs (Figure 17),[11] which now, however, economically and physically excludes most ordinary Ghanaians (see Adrover et al. 157); an 'International Hip Hop Pan-African Diaspora Family Reunion'; a PANAFEST Village bazaar and expo that includes booths and restaurants selling African fabrics and foods; a fashion show; and a business forum. Well down at number ten on the list are artist workshops and live performances, which are nevertheless said to be 'core to PANAFEST'.[12]

The visitor experience of PANAFEST is certainly celebratory, if overwhelmingly touristic and even voyeuristic. Affect can, of course, be culturally productive when it leads to action rather than merely to cathartic release followed by a return to the status quo. Ultimately, however, the degree to which PANAFEST brings together continental and diasporic Africans beyond the diplomatic or enthusiastic level of temporary catharsis, and for what kinds and quality of exchange or action, is uncertain. Its aspirational rhetoric is ebullient; its achievements are more mixed.

CARIFESTA

Caribbean nations also came together early after achieving independence, in a pan-Caribbean festival designed to promote exchange through the performance of cultures divided by language and national borders but united by shared histories of the enslavement of their African ancestors. It does so, however, in part by employing a problematic postcolonial paradigm of unification grounded in pan-Caribbean nationalism that can problematically elide or exacerbate internal cultural differences. CARIFESTA (Caribbean Festival of the Arts) was founded in 1972 in Guyana, only six years after that country's independence from Britain, and like PANAFEST and its predecessors, it was inspired by Black Power, Pan-Africanist, and decolonizing movements across the Global South and by the writings of Martiniquan intellectuals such as Frantz Fanon and Aimé Césaire (see Bhagirat-Rivera 1025).[13] After an eleven-year hiatus between 1981 and 1992 and in spite of hurricanes and other natural or economic disasters, the festival has been held with increasing regularity in rotating Caribbean nations under the sponsorship of the Caribbean Community (CARICOM), an official United Nations Observer organization of fifteen member states and five associate members, the oldest surviving integrationist movement in the developing world, whose purpose is regional economic integration. CARICOM bills CARIFESTA as 'an embodiment of Caribbean integration' featuring music, dance, theatre, visual arts, folk arts, and literature, as well as regular symposia and workshops (CARICOM).

But CARIFESTA has also had its share of controversy. Saint Lucian poet, playwright, and Nobel laureate Derek Walcott warned against the festival's declining into 'intermittent outbursts of revelry' that through 'the ecstasy of self-gratification' would provide cheap, cathartic release rather than sustained archipelagic identity-building through the arts (qtd in Nettleford 5–6), and this danger remains as I write. In 1995 and again in 2008 Walcott called for a boycott of the festival by artists until such time as governments in the region started supporting artists in a sustained way rather than periodically exploiting them for public display (see Stone; and Anonymous, 'Caribbean').

Nevertheless, partly by containing its global aspirations and partly through serial hosting CARIFESTA has more consistently been able at least partially to fulfill its unifying mandate than have many other such festivals. In 2018 Ramaesh Joseph Bhagirat-Rivera called the first CARIFESTA 'a grandiose yet necessary undertaking of mental decolonization' (1023), one that

> embodied the aspirations of a culturally unified Caribbean grounded in its common African ancestry. Through CARIFESTA, Guyana offered the symbolic and physical space through which to realize the dreams of Caribbean artists and intellectuals to erase Eurocentric cultural prejudices against African-derived cultural forms and embrace a Pan-African cultural heritage that could form the basis of regional unity. (1022)

And indeed, conceived as 'a space to forge diaspora' (Bhagirat-Rivera 1026), CARIFESTA's explicit aspirational goals have been 'to be inspirational, educational, entertaining, and reflect the cultures of "the people"' (1025).[14]

But the festival got into trouble from the start. In the first iteration of CARIFESTA its Pan-Africanist mandate, not surprisingly, alienated its host country's large Indo-Guyanese community, who boycotted the festival in protest that funding dedicated to their community was diverted, without consultation, to a festival addressing the country's African population. Each festival has since attempted to integrate the overall goal of inter-Caribbean unification (largely under the flag of Africa) with each host nation's aspirations to unite their own multiracial and multicultural societies under one *national* flag. They have done so with some success, both through individual performances and through the festival's often high-powered symposium component. In 1972, for example, though the boycott meant that there were no Indo-Guyanese performers featured, Surinamese nationalist poet and politician Robin 'Dobru' Ravales recited his 'I Am a Negro' to the accompaniment of Indian tabla and harmonium, embodying, if perhaps only symbolically, the festival's goals of 'reclaiming Afro-Caribbean identities while simultaneously celebrating multiracial inclusion' (Bhagirat-Rivera 1034). And there continue to be individual performances that feature Caribbean diversity, including such things as regular performances based on Indian classical dance. Nevertheless, the degree to which the Indo-Caribbean and other, particularly East Asian spectators are perceived as being welcome at the predominantly Afro-Caribbean festival still surfaced as a matter of controversy at the festival symposium when I attended it in 2019.

Throughout the history of the symposium, however, celebrated Caribbean intellectuals from different islands and languages – Kamau Brathwaite (Barbados), Édouard Glissant (Martinique), Antonio Benítez Rojo (Cuba), Derek Walcott (Saint Lucia), Rex Nettleford (Jamaica) – have shared the podium and had significant impact on one another and on a developing multilingual pan-Caribbean discourse at a symposium that functions as 'a collective event of Caribbean integration' (Bonfiglio 159). Indeed, the 1976 symposium saw Brathwaite introduce his influential sociology of 'nation language' as 'a strategy of linguistic resistance and cultural decolonization', while in the same year Glissant characterized the festival as 'a concrete manifestation of *Antillanité*' (Bonfiglio 159) – the creation of a specific 'West Indian' identity out of a multiplicity of ethnic, linguistic, and cultural elements. At the 2008 festival, with the theme of 'One Caribbean, One Purpose, Our Culture, Our Life', Nettleford, protesting against the persistence of a binary relationship between each Caribbean nation and its European colonizer, called for 'building bridges across cultural boundaries' (qtd in Allen 51) between peoples within the Caribbean 'who may be part-African, part-European, part-Asian, part-Native American but totally Caribbean' (Nettleford 3). Festival organizers and the governments that support them have, for better and worse, I suggest, embraced a strategy of decolonization that is grounded in resistant postcolonial, pan-Caribbean nationalism that has proven there as elsewhere problematically to sideline internal differences, rather than addressing a more supple form of what Walter Mignolo and others call 'decoloniality' based in the rejection of colonialist epistemologies, including the very concept of the nation-state and its forms of thought and government (Mignolo and Walsh). At the symposium, as at the festival itself, different versions of Caribbean identities emerging from different post-colonies' histories, languages, 'ethnic' communities, and visions of what form Caribbean, West-Indian, or 'créole' nations might take, jostle for position within an atmosphere that is often *made* celebratory by means of the elision of internal differences. In 2019 the festival went outside the Caribbean in featuring as keynote speaker Kenyan scholar Ngũgĩ wa Thiong'o, author of the widely influential *Decolonizing the Mind*, reinforcing the generally Africanist vision in which the festival is grounded.

The relative success of CARIFESTA in achieving its integrative goals, nevertheless, may be understood in part to derive from the festival's mobility among Caribbean nations, which resists its settling in to serve a single national(ist) developmental agenda, and in part from its attracting Caribbean intellectuals rather than simply relying on headline

performances by international superstars (though it increasingly prominently features a popular 'Super Concert' each year, and there is always a
healthy, popular dose of Carnival). The degree to which the festival's
unificatory agenda is successful may also derive from its insistence until
very recently on restricting itself to participation from the Caribbean rather
than, like PANAFEST, from its global diaspora. Only in 2017 in
Barbados, for the first time after an eleven-year struggle, did Trinidadian
Canadian actor and director Rhoma Spencer succeed in convincing organizers to invite a delegation from the active Caribbean theatrical diaspora,
of which Toronto, along with London in the UK, is an epicentre
(Armstrong).[15] Canada remains the only country from outside of the
Caribbean itself officially to participate in CARIFESTA.

Earlier themes for the festival have been such things as 'Rainbow of
Peoples Under One Caribbean Sun', and 'Together is Strength'
(CARIFESTA XIV, 'Archives'). The 2019 edition, however, was somewhat ominously themed 'Connect. Share. Invest'. From the postconial
frying pan to the neoliberal fire, CARIFESTA has not entirely escaped, nor
has it wanted to, World Bank discourses of development, and there is, for
better and for worse, along with the relatively recent goal of increasing
diasporic participation, increased attention to the festival's capacity to
attract tourism from beyond the region. But the discourses of development
at CARIFESTA are at least as concerned with the development of youth
and talent as they are with economics and tourism: each festival includes a
'Youth Village', and youth and children actively participate and perform in
almost all events.

I took part in CARIFESTA XIV in 2019 as part of the official Canadian
delegation led by Spencer, and it was intriguing to observe the ways in
which the festival's unificatory goals were both complicated and advanced
by the presence of a delegation from the diaspora.[16] The rhetoric of the
politicians who addressed large crowds at the festival's opening and
closing ceremonies in Port of Spain consistently celebrated what Dr The
Honourable Nyan Gadsby-Dolly, Minister of Community Development,
Culture and the Arts, called 'cultural integration' across Caribbean nations'
cultural and linguistic differences. Trinidad's acting prime minister, the
Honourable Colm Imbert, expressed his sadness that 'we are still separate
states rather than having a single border', and his hope that 'one day,
politically and economically, we'll be identified as one people'.
Functioning within a governance model that is structurally colonialist
within a primarily British model – Trinidad and Tobago continue to
have a Governor General who represents the monarchy within a

parliamentary system – each of these officials employed a familiar, ideologically coded, and culturally reproductive rather than decolonial discourse of pan-national unification, serving as examples, in Mignolo's phrase, of 'the native elites … doing exactly what the colonizers were doing but in the name of national sovereignty' – or in this case Caribbean unification (qtd in A. Hoffman).

The opening ceremonies, 'The Spirit of Wild Oceans', together with an Indigenous 'snake ceremony' at the closing, posited an imagined creation story for a potentially unified Caribbean nation after the fashion of many postcolonial societies, rather than attempting to imagine a decolonial, postnational culture. There was also considerable emphasis in the speeches on the unification of Caribbean peoples of African, South Asian, East Asian, and (less often) Indigenous heritage, though there was little mention of the descendants of European colonizers. In spite of this aspirational emphasis on a single pan-Caribbean identity, moreover, each of the nineteen participating countries in 2019 marched (and danced) proudly behind its own national flag in the opening parade and the opening ceremony's (perhaps unfortunately titled) 'Parade of Nations', most were featured in nation-specific 'Country Nights' and in booths throughout the festival (suturing the culturally based concept of 'nation' with the geographical, land-based one of 'country' in a familiar ideological formulation), and there were very few collaborative events or, apart from the generally integrative symposium, direct or formal opportunities for exchange as opposed to spectacle.

Although the festival remained dominated by Afro-derived cultural forms, audiences were overwhelmingly Afro-Caribbean, and the degree to which Caribbeans of other than African heritage felt welcome at the largely Afro-celebratory festival was a matter of controversy at the festival symposium, there were frequent performances of Indo-Caribbean dance in the showcases and Country Nights of most nations, including Canada. And there was plenty of 'Chutney SOCA'[17] on offer, including performances by Indo-Caribbean performers Rikki Jai, Nishard Mayrhoo, and Neval Chatelal in the climactic seven-hour 'Super Concert', which featured other Caribbean superstars such as Calypso Rose, Voice, Blaxx, Alison Hinds, Kassav, Machal Montano, and Shaggy. There was also at least one occasion during the epic Trinidad and Tobago Country Night in which Indian and African drummers symbolically 'traded fours' in a spectacle of cross-cultural collaboration. Finally, the theatre programme featured an Indo-Trinidadian 'Best Village Theatre' piece, the collective creation *Temple in the Sea* that treated differences internal to the host nation in somewhat more complex ways.

'Best Village Theatre' is a uniquely Caribbean integrated theatrical form that incorporates music, dance, drama, and traditional folk and mas characters. As articulated by playwright L. Efebo Wilkinson at the festival symposium, the integration is formally mandated by a 'syllabus' – nine songs (including the national anthem), eight dances, a folk character skit, a Carnival character skit, and a fifteen-minute play – applied by the judges to Best Village competitions that were inaugurated throughout Trinidad and Tobago by Prime Minister Eric Williams in 1963 (Wilkinson). Best Village Theatre is now most often written and directed by trained professionals but performed by amateur actors in a region that is still, as I saw advocated on one promotional billboard, 'professionalizing the arts'. Wilkinson's own 'quintessential Best Village play', *Bitter Cassava*, was also featured at the festival. *Temple in the Sea* remounted a 1995 play for the festival, telling the story of a Hindu community's efforts in the 1940s to build a temple for its plantation workers (eventually doing so on the sea because the plantation owners refused to release land – even marshland – for the purpose), and included histories of the arrival of Indian indentured workers in Trinidad between 1845 and 1917, replacing the enslaved Black workers on the plantations in the wake of emacipation. It also told of the Hosay riots and massacre of 1884.[18] The show's prepresentation of complex enmeshed histories of slavery and indenture perhaps provided a ground that was more than merely symbolic for the negotiation and understanding of shared differences.

There were, however, less nuanced examples of Best Village Theatre at the festival in 2019, including one that joyously enacted the celebratory mandate that sets CARIFESTA apart from many other international festivals. Audiences at the elegant National Academy for the Performing Arts in Port of Spain responded raucously to the 'Best of Best Village' theatre presentation of *Salt, No Seasoning*, by emerging playwright Rayshawn Pierre. It's a characteristically Caribbean 'whole-lotta-stuff-goin'-on' kinda show, with music, dance, teeth sucking, a huge cast, child extras, a melodramatic cross-class love story, one villainous politico mother and another who is salt-of-the-earth, and an unapologetic lack of nuance. The audience cheered the good guys, talked back to the bad guys, and gleefully completed sentences along with the actors; they were not there for aesthetic judgement, but to *have a good time*, and they did that.

The Canadian delegation's contribution to the festival included a more complex performance, *Speaking of Sneaking* (Figure 18), a solo show written and performed by Jamaican Canadian Daniel Jelani Ellis and directed by d'bi.young anitafrika that deployed the traditional trickster

Figure 18   *Speaking of Sneaking* was alone at CARIFESTA 2019 in dividing an otherwise
mutually celebratory audience: some cheered, but some left the building when the show
first acknowledged the existence, and persecution or de facto expulsion, of a queer
Caribbean community.

figure of Anansi and incorporated, uniquely in my experience of
CARIFESTA, an acknowledgement of the traditional Indigenous caretakers of the land on which it was created and engagement with issues
around emigration, queer subjectivity, and the relationship between the
two. Acknowledging significant and different *kinds* of difference within the
imagined Caribbean community, the show was alone in my experience of
the festival in dividing an otherwise mutually celebratory audience: some
cheered, but some left the building when the show first acknowledged the
existence, and persecution or de facto expulsion, of a queer Caribbean
community.

But these were not the only exceptional things that the Canadians
brought to the festival. Like others, the Canadian contingent danced with
perhaps *un*characteristic pride behind its national flag at the opening
parade and ceremony, presented at its national 'Country Night', and
generally marched in t- and polo shirts sporting Canada's national colours
and the slogan 'Canadian Pride, Caribbean Vibe'. But together with that
flag and those colours, and uniquely among the national delegations (the

rest of whom tended to promote and celebrate the cultures and geographies of their own countries), the Canadians, familiar with intranational cultural difference in our own country, evinced the spirit of 'one Caribbean' by displaying among the delegation a wide variety of flags from the countries of each of its members' Caribbean heritage marching together. Dancers from Kashedance, the Children and Youth Dance Theatre of Toronto, and Roots and Branches Dance, and members of the Kaiso jazz fusion sextet Kalabash, from islands ranging from Trinidad and Jamaica to Saint Lucia and Cuba, performed, to enthusiastic responses, a critical 'Caribbeanness' that can perhaps only truly exist in diaspora.

Postcolonial Relations

PANAFEST and CARIFESTA are largely government run and are funded largely by governments and internationalist economic organizations such as CARICOM. They are also driven by global cultural and economic imperatives that don't always coincide with the more integrative goals of transnational community-building or cultural resurgence. They struggle against the pressures of globalized festivalization while attempting to unite dispersed or diasporic populations, and work across language as well as cultural differences within their transnational communities. But as Christina S. McMahon argues, 'when festivals interpellate a specific language community, artists and their productions typically have more to say to each other and their spectators because of a shared colonial history and common cultural and linguistic references' (5). Festivals in the francophone and lusophone worlds, moreover, are more able to function outside of the dominance of the overwhelmingly anglophone global festival circuit. Less auspicious for the success of such festivals is the fact that, unlike those in Africa and the Caribbean, these language-based festivals include, and are always in danger of being dominated by, the interests of the European colonizing nations, and increasingly by those of the new colonialisms that are the province of global capital and are centred in the US, China, a resurgent Russia, and the European Union rather than individual Western European nations. For festivals attempting to broker postcolonial and neocolonial relations within the francophone or lusophone worlds, the keys to approaching success seem to rest in location, size, and the strategic circumvention of European brokerage and the dominance of the World Bank, IMF, and global capital.

Francophonie

The francophone world is dominated by France and the influential eighty-eight-member Organisation international de la Francophonie (OIF) with headquarters in Paris, biennial summits, and a global reach. It's motto, 'equality, complementarity, and solidarity', echoes the French 'liberté, égalité, fraternité' and reflects the degree to which French republican universalism, at least in theory and at least in France, continues to hold sway, though festivals in the former French colonies are increasingly deploying global transnationalisms to forge alternative links.

The world of francophone theatre festivals is dominated, if not always well represented, by the Avignon Festival and its symobollically central playing space, the medieval Palais des Papes (Papal Palace). This is particularly true in relation to France's former colonies in Africa and the Caribbean, whose works show up at Avignon rarely, and when they do, have most frequently been assimilated, decontextualized, depoliticized and 'universalized'; that is, they have been stripped of their cultural specificity and local relevance. Emily Sahakian has pointed out that over the festival's first seventy years, to 2016, it programmed fewer than ten works by francophone African playwrights or directors. When it announced an African focus for the 2017 festival, its programming from the continent included only song and dance, perpetuating colonialist stereotypes about African bodies and effectively silencing African voices. The theatre pieces from the African continent that it *has* programmed, Sahakian argues, have either been presented as exceptions to an unstated rule that normalizes universalist French theatrical aesthetics, or selected to avoid any critique of the host country emerging from its former colonies, the peoples of which, of course, are not well represented in the small medieval city of Avignon (population ca 92,000) in the picturesque southeastern region of Provence. 'Avignon, through its mainstage programming and promotional materials, implicitly reaffirms the cultural supremacy of France within a cherry-picked collage of global cultures' (Sahakian 209–10).

As discussed in Chapter 2, iterations of the Avignon festival under Olivier Py since 2014 have evinced increasing interest in staging the experience of immigrants from France's former colonies who live within the metropole. There has been less interest in staging work that emerges from the former colonies themselves, though in 2018 and 2019 Congolese choreographer Faustin Linyekula premiered the first two parts of his testimonial *Histoire(s) du théâtre* at the festival using the story of the

National Ballet of Zaire, including three members of the company's iconic show, *L'Épopée de Lianja*, to probe that country's complex colonial history with – deflecting attention from France – Belgium. Also in 2019 were two shows about (im)migration itself, Salia Sanou's *Multiple-S*, three interconnected dance duets about the divided subjectivities of an immigrant from Burkina Faso; and Yacouba Konaté's autobiographical piece *Young Yacou*, addressed to children and telling the story of his emigration from Côte d'Ivoire. Both shows, characteristically for Avignon, positioned France primarily as a desired destination for migrants, the solution rather than the problem, and avoided disrupting the festival's destination aesthetics.

The International Festival of Francophonies in Limousin (Les Francophonies), held in Limoges, France, itself home to a largely marginalized population within France and a centre of resistance during World War II, extends that city's resistance history by hosting a festival that continues to fight against colonialism within France itself. In many ways Les Francophonies sets out to redress the imbalances of Avignon through its focus on the diversity of francophone cultures rather than on French republican universalisms. Les Francophonies was founded in 1984 by Franco-Belgian director Pierre Debauche, who dreamed of a festival that decentred Paris within France, decentred France within the francophone world, and decentred a single, 'correct' French language. Indeed, Debauche set out to establish contacts and networks that would create what he called a 'South–North pedagogy' (my translation), reversing the dominant colonialist assumption of a North–South flow of knowledge and civilization.

Les Francophonies over the years has focused largely on francophone Africa, establishing South–North dialogues in its early years, and more recently working on the bringing together of francophone 'singularities' and the establishment of horizontal and equal relationships of difference. Under the direction of Monique Blin (1984–2000) the festival established funded residencies for francophone African playwrights at Limoges and was credited with helping to launch the careers of many. It also helped to enable francophone festivals in the Democratic Republic of the Congo and the Côte d'Ivoire, and by fostering collaborations among francophone African nations supported intercultural South–South dialogues and co-productions that to at least some extent bypassed France, if not French brokerage or colonizing festival structures, practices, and epistemologies. In the twenty-first century the festival has established African internships under the directorship of Patrick Le Mauff (2000–6), and since 2006 under Marie-Agnès Sevestre has focused on building a new generation of proactive African artists and shifting from postcolonial resistance to Africanist resurgence, from constructing or critiquing hierarchies to productive cultural juxtapositioning.

Les Francophonies, as Sahakian has pointed out, has been criticized for its discourses of 'discovery' (of African artists) and its use of neocolonialist rhetoric more generally (217), and it has struggled in the twenty-first century because of defunding in 2008 by the French Ministry of Foreign Affairs. Its vision, too, has lost some of its focus because of the inclusion of 'guest' languages and the assumption of a broader transnational reach. Nevertheless, the festival has accomplished many of its decentralizing goals within France, and has made the promising move, in 2018, of appointing actor/director Hassane Kassi Kouyaté, from Burkina Faso, with experience running the national theatre in the French Caribbean 'département' of Martinique, as its new director (see Ministère). In January 2019, Kouyaté changed the name of the festival to 'Les Francophonies – Des écritures à la scène (from writing to the stage) and introduced two annual 'highlights': 'Les Zébrures d'automne' and 'Les Zébrures du printemps'. The first autumn season, in 2019, featured an impressively diverse programme of dance by artists from Burkina Faso, Camaroon, Cape Verde, and Martinique; music from Bénin, Burkina Faso, Canada, Québec, San Salvador, and Sénégal; and theatre and performance from Belgium, Bénin, China, Israel, Mali, Québec, and Taiwan. There were also many 'rencontres', and several iterations of the intercultural 'La Nuit francophone'.[19] The shift in leadership from the colonial centre to the diaspora would seem to have had predictably generative results.

But perhaps the most auspicious way of doing justice to theatre from the former French colonies is to move outside of France 'proper' and focus on festivals held in Africa and the Caribbean. The first and most prominent of such festivals was the Festival culturel de la ville de Fort-de-France in Martinique, founded in 1972 by Martiniquan poet, playwright, politician, and founder of the *négritude* movement in literature, Aimé Césaire. It predates Les Francophonies by over a decade. Sahakian argues that the influence of the Fort-de-France festival and its efforts to 'explore new formulations of interculturalism' have been underestimated. The festival, she contends, has worked hard over the decades to perform and constitute a 'global Caribbeanness' that 'place[s] Martinique and the French Caribbean at the centre of cultural, literary, and knowledge production' in and beyond the francophone world (220). Designed to 'bring the world to Martinique', the festival in the twenty-first century has focused on themes such as plurality (2004), 'Repeating Islands' (2009, linking

Martinique with the world's other islands), and 'The World in the Capital' (2018). Sahakian's account of the 2005 festival, themed 'Insular Imaginaries', emphasizes its generic diversity, its recentring of the world, and its homage to its own 'Three Fires, Three Roots', famous Martiniquans Édouard Glissant, Aimé Césaire, and Frantz Fanon. These moves participate, I suggest, by decentring globalized western festival epistemologies, in the kinds of generative, non-reactionary 'decoloniality' proposed and promoted by Walter Mignolo, Catherine Walsh, and their colleagues in the modernity/coloniality/decoloniality collective. The 'decoloniality' practised by the Fort-de-France and other festivals is not, like the postcolonialism practised at Limoges or indeed CARIFESTA, positioned as resistant, reifying a colonizer/colonized binary. Rather it is a resurgent recentring – in Mignolo's terms, 'an epistemic reconstitution . . . of the ways of thinking, languages, ways of life and being in the world that the rhetoric of modernity disavowed and the logic of coloniality implement' (qtd in A. Hoffman).

Sahakian ends her essay by gesturing towards other, newer festivals in Africa and the Caribbean that create what she calls 'spaces of resistance' in the francophone world (222): Le Festival Mantsina sur scène in Brazzaville, Congo, founded in 2004 by Congolese playwright Dieudonné Niangouna, which functions as a 'crossroads space' for negotiation and debate; Récréâtrales, a biennial festival founded in 2002 in Ouagadougou, Burkina Faso, as a pan-African space of creation, research, and theatrical dissemination (Récréâtrales, my translation); and Univers des Mots, founded in 2012 in Conakry, Guinea by La Muse Company as 'the only theatre festival, or more simply the only international theatre event taking place in Guinea' and dedicated, since the 2017 appointment of artistic director Hakim Bah, to developing encounters between artists from the North and South (Univers, my translation). The Festival Quatre Chemins, founded in Port-au-Prince, Haiti, in 2003 is particularly interesting because of its focus on the Haitian tradition of the 'four paths' (the quatre chemins of its title), and its implications for interculturalism 'from below'. This impoverished country, in the wake of natural and man-made disasters that have between them destroyed festival venues and eviscerated subsidies, nevertheless mounts a festival that, employing only two permanent staff members, has forged transnational links not only with France and Belgium, but also with Québec, the Dominican Republic (with whom Haiti shares the island of Hispaniola and has a violent history and troubled relationship), and other Caribbean countries. Located in a culturally hybrid country at 'a crossroads where various influences mix' and operating 'at the intersection of art and militancy' (Quatre Chemins, 'Dix ans', my translation), the festival, under artistic director Guy Régis Jr, has, both onstage and in festival colloquia, directly confronted urgent political issues ranging from feminism to violence and political corruption. And the festival, I would argue, is more than a 'space of resistance', in Sahakian's formulation; arguably it participates in the less reactionary, less binary movement among the globally marginalized towards the kinds of grounded decoloniality discussed by Mignolo, differently analysed by Leanne Betasamosake Simpson as resurgence (*Dancing*), configured in western terms as a kind of madness or 'heresy' (Peghini and Thérésine 82), and exemplified by the Indigenous festivals discussed in Chapter 1. In an 'editorial' for the 2019 festival Régis laments that 'only 1% of the total health budget of our dear Patrie goes to mental health' and dedicates the festival to 'our mental fragility':

> Of all the madness that is granted
> Of all the follies of which we are capable
> Of all the furious madmen who govern us
> Faced with all the madness that must be exceeded
> We want to talk about the purest madness
> Of the greatest madness of our people: its strength to live against all odds!
>
> (Régis, 'Tout les hommes sont fous')

Each of these small francophone festivals is committed to intensely local conversations within a broadly transnational context. In 2018, for example, Quatre Chemins directly addressed the role of the artist in the earthquake-ravaged country, asking explicitly about the plight of its people and the return of electricity: 'The artist has the right to ask their representative, their senator, the president, why the sun so present in Haiti is not used to create energy for the whole country?' (Quatre Chemins, 'Présentation', my translation). But each of these festivals also addresses transnational issues and relations beyond the local and beyond the postcolonial, they often engage with revisionist adaptations and critiques of western classics, and they all serve as enabling sites of exchange that offer spaces of resurgence and build new, '"heretic" dramaturgies' (Peghini and Thérésine 82) in ways that the imperial centre might have trouble recognizing.

The lesson to be taken from these transnational francophone festivals is perhaps the familiar one that de- or recentring, or better, resurgence, are best and most effectively performed outside of the imperial centre, and that decolonizing, or better, decoloniality, are most likely to be effective when led, not by the colonizer, but by those who have been subjected to colonization. It may be that South–South conversations, negotiations, and solidarities – especially when they are not brokered by the colonizer – need to precede South–North ones, which in turn need to precede the application or invocation of any reconfigured French universalist republicanism, however well-meaning.

The Lusophone World

The same lessons hold true for the lusophone world, including strategic negotiations with a global intergovernmental organization, in this case the Comunidade dos Países de Língua Portuguesa (CPLP), based in Lisbon and formed, like France's OIF and like the British Commonwealth, to deepen mutual friendship and cooperation among its postcolonial members *as* autonomous nation-states. Christina S. McMahon has written well and at length about the complexities of what she calls 'lusophone transnationalism' at festivals in Brazil, Cape Verde, and Mozambique. She explores the ways in which, unlike in francophonie, dominant narratives of nationhood and of the lusophone transnationalism in which these festivals are embedded are disseminated not only from the imperial centre, Portugal, with its racist legacy of 'lusotropicalism', but also, in complicating ways in the newly globalized world, from Brazil.[20] As the current economic powerhouse that has increasingly surpassed Portugal in global influence, Brazil has usurped the imperial centre's key role in defining and controlling what constitutes *lusofonia* (19, 38–42), particularly in Africa, where in spite of a discreditable history it has clear geopolitical ambitions.[21] These national and transnational narratives, McMahon argues, are 'recast' and recoded in various ways and to varying degrees at African festivals both by working within different moulds and empowering different players in ways that can have significant 'aftermath', and by evolving impact beyond the temporalities of the festivals themselves (7, 25–6, and *passim*).

Portugal has no festival that focuses on the lusophone world, though the Festival Internacional de Teatro de Expresión Ibérica (FITEI), in Porto, founded in 1978, features companies from 'the Iberian world', which it defines as 'Portugal, Brazil, Portuguese Africa, Spain and Spanish America' (Arte). Over the years the festival has tended to focus on Portugal, Spain, and Spanish-speaking America, though its 2013 edition featured Brazil due to a lack of funding from Portugal, and the 2018 edition included two productions from Brazil, in both cases designed to show contemporary Portugal in a good light as a desired destination for immigration. The first, a documentary performance, *Passa-porte*, was a Portuguese/Czech show about 'the end of Portuguese colonialism' in Africa and Africans trying to come to Portugal from former colonies (Teatro Municipal do Porto, 'Passa-Porte'). The second, *Libertação*, was another Portuguese/Czech show, this time about the African wars of liberation in Angola, Guinea-Bissau, and Mozambique (see Teatro Municipal do Porto, 'Libertação'). Shows from lusophone Africa itself, however, have never been a feature of the festival.

Festivals such as Brazil's FESTLIP (Festival de Teatro da Língua Portuguesa) in Rio de Janeiro and Festival de Teatro Lusófono (FESTLUSO) in Teresina, however, *have* set out to include the entire lusophone world, and if they inevitably headline shows from Brazil and Portugal, they can also act as 'global casting calls' for African performers, giving them visibility and access to international audiences (McMahon 20), though this tends to be well within a western epistemological festival frame. They can also help to promote dialogue, create what Appadurai calls 'communit[ies] of sentiment' across national borders (8), and promote 'minor transnationalism[s]' (Lionnet and Shih). Indeed, in 2018 FESTLIP live-streamed a good percentage of its programming to Cape Verde, São Tomé and Princípe, East Timor, Angola, Mozambique, and throughout Europe, and in a show called *Poetic Sound* collected actors from all nine lusophone nations (see 'FESTLIP'). But because of global power dynamics and differentials and inequality of access and success between the African, mostly underfunded amateur companies and professionals from Portugal and Brazil, these festivals can also function as 'mechanisms for circulating theatre [that] may ultimately override local epistemologies' (McMahon 7) as well as unequal playing fields in the competition for international presenters, since all performances are measured against western aesthetics and standards.

FESTLIP since its founding in 2008 as a festival dedicated exclusively to work from Portuguese-speaking nations,[22] has demonstrated an unwavering 'Lusophonist zeal' (McMahon 19) and has played a significant role in defining and disseminating the dream of 'a' transnational lusophone culture. In many ways the festival is exemplary: many of its performances are free, there are workshops and panels along with a dozen or more mainstage productions, visiting artists' travel costs and stipends are paid and their venues are provided free of charge, and companies stay for the duration of the festival, often at the same hotel, in order to facilitate exchange (see McMahon 64). The festival, then, is used by African nations to gain recognition on the international scene and remind the world of their complex colonial histories, 'recasting the colonial past' (see McMahon 68–96), if not always the neocolonial present. But FESTLIP's supposed 'empathetic connection to Africa' (65) is also used, at least in part, to justify Brazil's increased presence on the continent today, particularly in the oil-rich former Portuguese colony of Angola. Its vision of lusophone unity and 'family ties' (95), hardly disinterested, can be felt to be coercive and neocolonialist, and local interventions by African theatre companies at the festival are often read as reifying and reductive representations of stereotypical national – or even continental – African cultures aspiring, and inevitably failing, to be more western: in Homi Bhabha's terms, *'almost the same, but not white'* (89, emphasis in original).

African Festivals, including the short-lived Festival de Agosto in Maputo, Mozambique from 1999 to 2005 and the small-scale Mindelact International Theatre Festival, held annually on the island of São Vicente, Cape Verde, constitute a very different strategic recentring of *lusofonia*. Festival de'Agosto, according to McMahon, was 'a rebel in the Lusophone transnation' (52), never explicitly defining itself as lusophone and never really embracing *lusofonia*. Indeed, the non-anglophone country idiosyncratically joined the British Commonwealth in 1995, and the festival associated itself at least as directly with neighbouring Anglophone countries in Africa as with official *lusofonia* as represented by the CPLP, engaging in a productively perverse kind of transnationalism that McMahon calls 'cultural transversalism' (55), and in mutual knowledge exchange in contradistinction to the kinds of one-way colonialist pedagogical model critiqued by Brazilian educational theorist Paulo Freire in his 1968 book, *Pedagogy of the Oppressed*.

Mindelact's relationship to official *lusofonia* is somewhat more complex, and more strategic.[23] Mindelact is a small festival involving a dozen or so mainstage shows over two weeks, with no concurrent performances, allowing artists – including emerging artists at late-night 'Festival Off' presentations – to see each other's work as well as participate with one another in workshops and panels. The festival began in 1995 and went international in 1997 with a focus on recentring Cape Verde as a 'nexus of exchange' within *lusofonia*, a focus that it later dropped as the festival attempted to keep the colonialist aspects of the official *lusofonia* project at arm's length, using it en route to a broader transnationalism but not allowing itself to be contained by it. According to McMahon, 'Mindelact's knack for perpetually recasting its identity ensures that the *lusofonia* project will never completely absorb it' (45). Part of its strategy involves its use, in addition to Portuguese, of the 'Crioulo' languages of Cape Verde's three distinct island cultures, part is a capitalizing on its complex geographical and cultural position between Europe and Africa, and part is its staging of Cape Verdean shows that, in McMahon's terms, 'recast the colonial past', restage class and gender roles, and claim cultural capital for local cultural specificities in resurgent rather than merely resistant ways. In a review of the 2004 festival, Eunice Ferreira speculated about the festival's increasing internationalism, asking, 'Does the growing international nature of the Mindelo theatre festival suggest that interculturalism has replaced African aesthetics and anti-colonial sentiment?' (277). I suggest that the festival has found its own, trans- rather than international ways of deconstructing the postcolonial binaries of imperial/ economic centre-to-periphery that tend to obtain long after a colony gains its independence, and it has done so by tactically deploying its lusophone connections to engage in horizontal, rhizomatic, decolonial networks within a broader, transnational world.

Globally Regional Festivals

Festivals serving a single language-based community, even if it is that of a shared colonizer, can avoid some barriers to communication, and not only those of surtitles or the need for translation. But festivals organized by geographical regions whose histories and contemporary realities are more complex and diverse can also create Appadurai's 'communities of sentiment' across languages and national borders, communities that 'are often transnational, even postnational', and that are capable of 'moving from shared imagination to collective action' (8). The festivals considered in this section vary significantly in scale, sponsorship, and organizational and funding models, but they all in different ways negotiate new and emerging relations across what have historically been virtually impenetrable borders.

BeSeTo

What is perhaps the most politically ambitious of the globally regional festivals is virtually unique in forging its intercultural community directly out of an attempt to redress historical conflict in a region that has relied as heavily on Repressive (military, police, and legal systems) as on Ideological State Apparatuses such as state-sponsored theatre.[24] The BeSeTo Theatre Festival, its name made up of the first two letters of the capital cities of

China, South Korea, and Japan (Beijing, Seoul, and Tokyo), was founded by artists and funded, however inconsistently as allowed for by shifting diplomatic relationships, by the three national governments. The idea was first proposed by Korean playwright Kim Eui-kyung to her Northeast Asian colleagues and fellow International Theatre Institute (ITI) representatives, Chinese director Xu Xiaozhong and Japanese director Tadashi Suzuki, who wanted 'to explore new possibilities in contemporary Asian theatre' outside of the brokerage of the western marketplace (H. Kim 194). Its founding manifesto announced the goal of the festival's becoming a 'cultural meeting that seeks the identity and aesthetic potentials of oriental theatre' (qtd in H. Kim 194) and a site of 'solidarity for autonomous self-discovery in Northeast Asia' (Kim Mun-hwan, qtd in H. Kim 194). The first festival was in Seoul in 1994, and it has been held in a different host city in the region every year since, from five to sixty days in duration, from four to nineteen in number of productions. In a review of the inaugural event, Kim Yun-Cheol summarized its goals: 'Theatrically, the festival aims at discovering and inventing aesthetic potentials of Asian theatre. Politically, it seeks to help the three nations overcome their past history of conflict through cultural communication' (416).

Theatrically, the festival has had remarkable success, including in its first season Suzuki's landmark production of *King Lear* (see J.K. Kim) and many other globally significant shows over the years. But it has perhaps been most notable for addressing, in both creative and scholarly ways, such questions as these, posed by Hayana Kim:

> Is it possible to conceptualize Asian theatrical aesthetics from within? How might one come to an autonomous definition of Asia, a vastly heterogenous entity both geographically and conceptually, without placing it relative to the West? Can one produce Asian theatrical aesthetics that thrive on their own historical and cultural specificities? (194)

One of the most significant ways in which BeSeTo has tackled these questions is to have produced over its history a number of major collaborations among the host countries, most ambitiously, most famously, and most expensively on a lavish production of the Korean classic, *Tale of Chunhyang*, performed in Seoul at the tenth edition of the festival in 2000. This staging, drawing on well-known actors, writers, and directors from all three countries, was divided into three parts using the traditional opera genres of each country: the first, 'Encounter', was performed by Shaobaihua Yue Opera from Zhèjiāng, China drawing on yue opera; the second, 'Parting', was enacted by the Shochiku Kabuki Company of Japan in the style of traditional kabuki dance-drama; and the third, 'Reunion', was performed by the National Changgeuk Company of Korea as ch'ang-geuk/pansori opera (Koo; Moon). According to Koo Ja-hung, the production 'truly reflected the beautiful realization of trans-boundary friendship and passion for art held by the individuals of the theater', though it must be said that it did so in a sequential rather than fully integrated way. Other, often more integrated collaborations have been staged at the festival in 1995, 1998, 2006, 2007, 2010, and 2013. In 2016 in Tottori and Niigata, Japan, there were no less than three such transnational collaborations, including *Macbeth! Macbeth! Macbeth!*, by young Chinese, Korean, and Japanese artists, and *Classroom of Poem*, a collaboration between Japanese actor/director Tori no Gekidan and Korea's Dieda theatre company, set in World War II, a period of critical tension among the three Northeast Asian countries (see Performing Arts Network).

Politically, the challenge has been almost insurmountable. Unlike those of CARIFESTA the goals of BeSeTo have not been regional integration so much as regional acknowledgement and mutual acceptance. In spite of millennia of shared history, there was little shared understanding and considerable hostility among China, Korea, and Japan in the early 1990s when the festival was founded. Western imperialism in the fifteenth and subsequent centuries and Japanese colonialism in the nineteenth left deep rifts that have even now only begun to heal. Indeed, diplomatic relations between Korea and China only began in 1992, two years before the first BeSeTo festival; Japan's failure (or refusal) to acknowledge such things as the 1938–9 massacre in Nanjing, China has negatively impacted relations between those countries; and because of bitterness over the brutality of Japan's 1910 annexation of Korea it wasn't until the late 1990s that the Korean government began to ease its ban on the importation of Japanese media and cultural products. Finally, Hayana Kim suggests that because Japan looked to Europe for its model of modernization, Japanese dominance in Asia led to 'a wholesale disregard of Asian culture as outmoded'. Given this history, Kim argues, BeSeTo has provided an important, Asia-specific public platform 'in which difficult histories and memories are brought forward to be negotiated and reckoned with in a context that is locally specific and culturally informed' (193),[25] and China's current expansionist policies and practices within the region and beyond make this process increasingly urgent as global power relations shift to the east.

Apart from collaborative productions the first area of cooperation in what BeSeTo's founding manifesto calls 'overcoming the past history of conflict' (qtd in H. Kim) is administrative, with circulating leadership and BeSeTo committees in the non-host countries in each iteration recommending festival shows and the final selection being made by a committee in the host country. The festival has also hosted symposia on such topics as creation and distribution, theatre education, promotion and marketing, and stagecraft, as well as reflexive post-festival appraisals of the three countries' theatrical worlds and the status of the festival (Koo). But the main site for the negotiation of troubled histories and Asia-specific theatrical forms is the productions themselves. Hayana Kim cites as one of her examples the 1995 production of Korean playwright Jeong Bok-guen's *The Princess Deokhye* in Tokyo, directed by Korean Han Tae-sook. The play set out, at a moment of renewed tension between the two countries over a Japanese minister's whitewashing of the 1910 annexation treaty, to reclaim the history of the last princess of Joseon, Korea's last imperial dynasty before its, and her, annexation by Japan. The lead-up to the Tokyo production was fraught, the show's director was detained at the airport, an interview with her was withheld from print, the show received little advance publicity, and there were reports of planned actions against it. Nevertheless, the risky production was well received by Japanese audiences who turned out in large numbers, and the show provoked apologies for Japanese colonialism and widespread historical ignorance. Kim argues that this and other successfully daring productions at BeSeTo demonstrate the capacity for the festival to negotiate the complicated histories that structure relationships among the participating nations, while also probing aesthetic differences and promoting inter-Asian theatrical and aesthetic exchange (see H. Kim 197–9).

In recent years, the festival has expanded its vision from mutual understanding to the promotion of Asian theatre globally, it has hosted Asian companies from further afield (including Hong Kong, India, Mongolia, Russia, Taiwan, Vietnam, and Uzbekistan), and, according to Moon Gwang-lip, has served as a catalyst for further exchanges and collaborations, including the founding of the NIB Theatre Festival (Nepal, India, and Bangladesh), inspired by and modelled on BeSeTo. The success of BeSeTo as a globally regional festival operating across linguistic barriers and historical tensions arguably derives from its flexibility in size and format, its having been inspired by artists with the support of a large international arts organization (the ITI), its having rotated among host nations and avoided appropriation by narrowly nationalist agendas, its having actively operated outside of western mediation, and its having successfully aligned its aesthetic and political goals.

Kampala International Theatre Festival

The tiny Kampala International Theatre Festival in Uganda (KITF) is at the opposite end of the spectrum from BeSeTo in terms of ambition (and, so far, duration), in spite of its being the largest international theatre festival in East Africa. The festival was founded in 2014 in the capital of the, as I write, relatively stable former British colony with one of the most traumatic post-independence histories in the world, as an initiative of the US-based non-profit Sundance Institute in collaboration with arts administrator the Bayimba Cultural Foundation and its Artistic director Faisal Kiwewa. Kiwewa and Ugandan playwright Asiimwe Deborah Kawe (Deborah Asiimwe) were its founding directors. Both the size of the festival and its funding model have shaped its vision and been key to its considerable success. As Christina S. McMahon has argued (4–5), most international festivals in Africa, because of their size and their communities' priorities, tend to emphasize community-building over tourism or commercialization, are more conducive to cultural exchange and debate, and are less open to government intervention, interference, or oversight than larger, more visible operations such as PANAFEST. Running for only five days, featuring only ten to twelve productions per year, including readings, and focused exclusively on theatre rather than the arts or performing arts more broadly, KITF is no exception.

The founding of KITF was the culmination of thirteen years of activity in East Africa by the Sundance Institute Theatre Program, and thirteen years of work with Deborah Asiimwe, first as a playwright, then a staff member, and finally as a leader of Sundance's transition to African control (see Sundance). Sundance brought that development experience and funding to partner with local infrastructure and experience provided by the Bayimba Cultural Foundation to offer firm grounding in both the local and transnational for the fledgling festival. Bayimba is a well-respected multi-arts support organization in Uganda whose activities range from education, training, and workshops through audience development to concert and festival sponsorship (see Bayimba). In 2013 Sundance and Bayimba 'resolved to create a platform to develop professionalism among East African theatre practitioners, connect the East African theatre-making community, and broaden access to theatre and develop new audiences by supporting and facilitating the creation and presentation of the best and most relevant theatre productions' (Kampala). Whatever reservations one might have about western discourses of professionalization and development as imported by a US-based NGO in relation to the process of 'decolonizing the mind', to cite one of West Africa's most influential theorists (see Ngũgĩ), KITF would seem to represent a small-scale intracultural success story.

Sundance had invested over the years in artists from Burundi, Ethiopia, Kenya, Rwanda, and Tanzania as well as Uganda, and the first edition of the festival featured – among others, especially from the United States – artists from those countries that they had supported in various regional theatre labs (see Kampala). Many of the shows at the first festival involved international collaboration, as when Ugandan actor Aida Mbowa directed Ethiopian playwright Meaza Worku's *Desperate to Fight* in ways that reflected the social realities of women in both countries (and beyond); when Rwandan dancer/choreographer Wesley Ruzibiza directed American playwright Elizabeth Spackman's *Radio Play*, 'a scathing critique of sur- veillance, censorship, and covert state violence in contemporary East Africa' (Goldstein, 'Kyingi' 537); or when Kenyan director Rogers Otieno supervised a reading of Ugandan playwright Angella Emurwon's *Strings*, which drew on coastal Kenyan and Tanzanian Swahili story chant to explore displacement and generational change in contemporary Uganda. Indeed, most of the shows depicted contemporary East African realities in ways that reflected or promoted regional cultural convergence. Most of the shows were in the colonial language of Uganda, English, or used English surtitles, though one reading, at least, was in untranslated Swahili, almost a lingua franca in much of East Africa but not widely used in Kampala.

According to Julia Goldstein,[26] the first iteration of KITF, under the auspices of Sundance, was notable for four things. The first, the promotion of regional identity and alliance-building across national borders created by European partition in the 1880s and 1890s, was in evidence as delegates at the festival's talkbacks recognized one another's stories about women's circumstances, the dangers of tribalism, the realities of state surveillance and the like as their own. The festival, Goldstein says, 'generated feelings of connection and recognition of similar social and political tensions across national lines' ('Staging' 169), while it also made visible work such as that emerging from Ethiopia, which is virtually unknown in East Africa and elsewhere because it is largely written in Amharic.

The second notable element of the first KITF, the promotion of indigenous (and Indigenous) East African expressive practices, included such things as the use of musical instruments distinctive to East Africa (as opposed to the more widely known West African Kora, Kalimba, Djembe, and Udu). Work such as Sitawa Namwalie's *Room of Lost Names* drew directly on Keynian cosmologies, Luyha creation stories, and a Luo funeral dirge.²⁷ And at talkbacks and post-show discussions Goldstein reports audience applause at Namwalie's expressed intent to take such things seriously.

The third feature of the inaugural festival identified by Goldstein was the cultivation, through exchange and collaboration, of a twenty-first-century East African specifically *theatrical* identity across acknowledged and valued cultural differences, together with the promotion and networking of theatre professionals based in the region. The festival made it known that there was no need to look to Europe or indeed elsewhere in Africa for artists and collaborators.

The final feature and perhaps greatest impact of the festival was the renewal and expansion (to Rwanda, Burundi, and the Democratic Republic of the Congo) of an 'East African discourse' that had developed in the wake of Somalia, Tanzania, Uganda, and Kenya achieving independence in the early 1960s, but had eroded when 'dictatorship and political upheaval in the late '60s and '70s resulted in isolation and inward turning which gave way in the '80s and '90s to the neoliberalization of educational and cultural institutions – circumstances also hostile to the crosspollination of authentic intellectual and artistic discourse across the region' (Goldstein, 'Staging' 171). 'Perhaps', Goldstein speculates, 'the KITF's regional approach can be seen as an alternative mode of stitching together independent states into supranational blocks, not through the logic of global capitalism, but through the affective alliances and discourses that theatrical exchange can facilitate, attending both to affinity and diversity and without erasing difference' ('Staging' 172).

KITF has been held every November since 2014 under the continuing co-direction of Faisal Kiwewa and Deborah Asiimwe, but it has moved out of the Uganda National Theatre, where it was first held, to dispersed sites in Kampala, and in 2018 to the Uganda Museum. The festival no longer features shows developed through Sundance (though the Institute, together with Bayimba, continues to offer core support), and its focus has broadened beyond what Goldstein calls 'cultivating East African regionalism' ('Staging' 168) to a strategic brand of transnationalism, bringing the world to Ugandans who don't have the resources for global travel. If this moves KITF somewhat to the margins of the category of region-based festivals, it does not represent a surrender of autonomy. For it is not the world of the large destination festivals or the global superpowers that the festival provides or mimics; rather, in addition to continuing selective offerings from Uganda and other East African nations, the organizers, without the direct involvement of Sundance, have tended to include artists from, for example, Bulgaria, India, Iran, Iraq, Kosovo, Lebanon, and Senegal, countries not regularly featured on the destination festival circuit but ones sharing with their East African host complex histories of colonialism. As Goldstein argues, rather than capitulation to the cultural flows dictated by global capitalism and the Global North, in 'asserting that global connections need not be limited to the hegemonic and commercial', the festival organizers are 'actively asserting agency over how Uganda globalizes' ('Staging' 172).

In its first half-decade, then, the Kampala International Theatre Festival has used its exclusive focus on theatre, its small size, low profile, relative autonomy, and unique funding model, to broker relationships and cultivate identities and affiliations at local, regional, and globally transnational levels, while simultaneously avoiding many of the instrumentalist pressures of government sponsorship, city branding, tourism, and commercialization that can plague larger festivals' efforts to promote inter- or intracultural negotiation and exchange. In its small, nurturing, and tactical way, KITF is exemplary.

RUTAS

It is October 2018, and I am sitting at Ada Slaight theatre in the Daniels Spectrum in Toronto's Regent Park housing project with my Syrian, Lebanese, Gujarati, Turkish, German, Cree, and white settler Canadian co-creators of Amal, a show by the MT Space Theatre that has just premiered at the Panamerican ROUTES/RUTAS Panamericanas festival (RUTAS). RUTAS is an international hemispheric festival produced by the Latinx Aluna Theatre in partnership with Native Earth Performing Arts, Canada's largest Indigenous theatre company. We are watching the sixty-nine-year-old Wilson Pico, the 'founder of contemporary Indigenous dance in Ecuador', performing his breathtaking but simple solo, cross-dressed triptych about women, Los Materiales de la ira y el amor, and we are weeping. It is only at a festival of transnational solidarity such as RUTAS that powerful, beautiful, and politically charged work such as this can bring such a diversity of artists and audience members together in what the MT Space website calls 'a community of difference'.

RUTAS was founded in 2012 by Beatriz Pizano and Trevor Schwellnus, artistic director and artistic producer, respectively, of Aluna Theatre, with the hemispheric goal of 'connecting the Americas through the arts' (Aluna).[28] The artist-run international festival, funded by municipal, provincial, and federal government funding,[29] alternates every other

October with CAMINOS, a national festival of new work in progress. The aims of both festivals are 'to witness, to experience, and to celebrate the multitude of languages, cultures, and differences that make up . . . the Pan-American experience', and 'to reflect our commitment to human rights, inclusion, and accessibility' (Aluna). RUTAS is a small festival with a budget of only CAD $208,000, produced 'in-house' by Aluna Theatre in conjunction with Native Earth Performing Arts in three spaces across the hall from one another in a single venue over two weeks, with performances Wednesdays through Sundays only.[30] Programming typically involves about twenty performances of eight shows from across the Americas, often in languages other than English. It also includes a couple of films and/or installations, artist workshops, and ten conference sessions (including opening and closing keynotes), plus a community meal, a showcase for emerging artists, and late-night cabarets with different local Latinx, Indigenous, queer and two-spirit performers every night of the festival. The small scale alone helps the festival to fly under the radar of city branders, planners, and politicians in Toronto caught up in festivalizatation and creative city discourses, freeing the organizers to pursue their own transnational networks and politico-aesthetic agendas and giving them the flexibility to respond quickly to global political and theatrical developments.

Most theatre festivals open with flair, with spectacle, or with their most prestigious and internationally known artists. Not RUTAS. In both 2016 and 2018, the organizers opted to open with shows that served above all to consolidate community and forge solidarities. The 2016 opening show, *Antigonas: Tribunal de Mujeres*, by Colombia's Tramaluna Teatro, staged an imaginary tribunal at which seven women, most of whom were not actors but all of whom, including one Nobel Peace Prize nominee, were activists who had lost loved ones to extrajudicial executions and 'disappearances', testified and demanded justice (Figure 19). The Colombian ambassador to Canada sat in the front row as the women told their own stories, with photos of the victims and props – shirts, teddy bears, toys – that had belonged to their lost loved ones. As the show's director, artivist Carlos Satizábal, said during the conference component of the festival, 'Representation is a lie. We work on presentation.' But of course, the show was performed onstage, before an audience, under lights, and as Jiří Veltruský famously said, everything onstage is a sign (if not only that), and will be read, and judged, by a paying audience as representational. It was a courageous show for a festival opening, but it made a very clear statement, and insisted that the audience, instead or also, as in the

Figure 19   The 2016 opening show at the RUTAS festival, *Antigonas: Tribunal de Mujeres*, staged an imaginary tribunal at which seven women who had lost loved ones to extrajudicial executions and 'disappearances' testified and demanded justice. Photograph by The Edisons Media Masters

Indigenous festival paradigm I have proposed in Chapter 1, play the role of ethical witnesses charged with the responsibility to *acknowledge, remember,* and *act accordingly* (see Simon with Eppert 52–3).

If *Antigonas* united the audience to the testimonial stage in 2016 as witnesses, the 2018 opener, Mexican company Sa'as Tún Compañía de Teatro's *Del Manantial del Corazón,* did so through a curious and sometimes discordant combination of theatre and ceremony that was also reminiscent of the Indigenous festival paradigm. Surrounded by audience on four sides, with crosses and candles at all four corners, the stage was constituted as ceremonial space. And the play's central event – framed by the performance of a fictional tale about a midwife, a birth, and a deal with death – was a participatory ritual enactment of Hetzmek, the Mayan baptismal ceremony. Two members from each section of the audience – from the four directions – were invited to present wishes and gifts to the baby of an audience member – bracelets, tobacco, a leather boot. Seeds were distributed to the entire audience, who showered the child with them as it was carried in nine ritual laps around a centre-stage altar, and then the show returned to its framing story and the fictional deal with death. At the curtain call Conchi León, the writer, director, and central performer, stepped forward with a dedication to a young girl and forty-six other children whose deaths in a daycare have gone uninvestigated, and demanded that the Mexican government 'stop killing our children'. Again, the presentation, veering between ritual and testimony on the one hand and representation on the other, was an unusual and brave choice for a festive opening, but it invited solidarities and reflected the core values of a festival that merged the Indigenous with the intracultural transnational.

Once the festivals have opened with such community-based work, subsequent shows tend to consist of ground-breaking work from various performance disciplines and interdisciplines, providing audiences with concentrated windows onto artistic, aesthetic, political, and cultural worlds that are rarely seen on any regular festival circuit in North America/Turtle Island. And they are seen by audiences that have already been constituted, by the opening shows, as communities – communities of difference.

Natalie Alvarez has argued that RUTAS forms 'a theatrical commons grounded in a heterogeneous and intercultural Americas, one that includes Latin American, Latinx, Indigenous, and Afro-Caribbean artists that have historically been excluded from the Eurocentric vision of "Latin America"' ('Roots' 27) – and these increasingly also include artists from other minoritized communities in the northern portions of the hemisphere. And that commons – a 'gathering place to advance transnational coalitional politics' (Alvarez, 'RUTAS' 242) – is grounded in *interculturalidad* (see Imaginario) rather than the internationalization that 'so often characterizes international festivals positioned as windows to the world' (Alvarez, 'RUTAS' 240). The festival, that is, serves to reposition interculturalism as *interculturalidad*, in Walter Mignolo's terms, an '"inter-epistemology" that unravels the logic of colonial thinking' (Alvarez, 'RUTAS' 240', citing Mignolo 138). Part of the festival's signal success in this enterprise derives from re-routing the map of influence in the Americas from (Global) South to North in counterdistinction to the Eurocentric understanding of North–South knowledge distribution. The developmental genealogies of the shows, their 'routes', were explicitly charted in the 2012 festival programme, all leading from the hemispheric South to the northern festival destination of Toronto: Guatemala–Mexico City–Toronto, Bogatá–New York–Toronto, and in one remarkable instance Medellín–Montevideo–Mexico City–Caracas–Bogotá–Edmonton–Ottawa–Toronto (See Alvarez, 'RUTAS' 249). This had the virtue not only of drawing attention to influences moving from Global South to North and complicating national genealogies; it also highlighted some of the complexities of play development networks and practices in a postnational twenty-first century.

An equally significant part of the success of RUTAS derives from the thoughtful organization of the festival's conference component – its 'conversatorios', as they are called (a Spanish neologism combining conversation with conference session). The conversatorios, as Alvarez says, function as 'knowledge sharing opportunities', designed 'to bring a diverse range of people together who might never otherwise be seated at the same table' ('Roots' 29). Their genius, when at their best, is in bringing together artists, activists, and experts, mostly Latinx, Indigenous, queer, two-spirit, trans, or people of colour from the Americas and from different artistic, scholarly, and professional disciplines – frontline workers, lawyers, elders, scholars, artists, and community leaders – to focus on an issue that has been somehow central to a show or shows that everyone in attendance has seen and been moved by. What the panellists have in common are the experience of the shows and what the 2014 festival's keynote speaker, Diana Taylor, calls their 'shared hemispheric reality' (Taylor, 1417, qtd in Alvarez, Kovacs, and Ortuzar 5). In 2014, for example, a panel on 'Femicide in the Americas' was organized around two performances and a public acción. Panel members included Sera-Lys McArthur, a mixed-race actor of Dakota ancestry who performed the previous evening at the Festival in Ntlaka'pamux/Irish playwright Tara Beagan's In Spirit, based on the true story of one of Canada's murdered and missing Indigenous women. The panel also included Brittany Chavez, from Chiapas, Mexico, whose performance of De Eso No Se Habla began the session, and Doris Defarnicio, also from Chiapas, who prior to the In Spirit performance had created a participatory public acción about the violent death of Cheyenne Fox, of Wikwemikong First Nation on Manitoulin Island, Ontario. Panel membership was rounded out by Sandra Spears Bombay, an artist, writer, and educator from the Rainy River First Nation in Ontario; Audrey Huntley, a paralegal, storyteller, and founder of No More Silence, a group in Toronto raising awareness about Canada's missing and murdered Indigenous women; and moderator Pauline Wakeham, co-editor of Reconciling Canada: Critical Perspectives on the Culture of Redress. This variety of perspectives on a tightly focused topic was characteristic of RUTAS's conversatorios, and productive of an exchange that Helene Vosters says 'challenged the containment of narratives of femicide and colonialism within nationalistically inscribed borders [and] cultivated possibilities for the mobilization of transborder resistance' (25). Like the opening shows, too, the *conversatorios* helped to constitute festivalgoers, as in the most generative of the festivals under consideration in this book, including the Indigenous festivals of Chapter 1, as active and responsible participants and witnesses rather than passive consumers of spectacle.

Other panels the same year brought together even more diverse trans-hemispheric panellists for equally unsettling encounters, always including representatives from the shows at the festival that prompt them. These focused on such things as: 'Urban Displacement and Renewal', which took as one of its subjects the very Regent Park neighbourhood, subjected to urban renewal projects, where the festival is held (see James); James Bay Treaty No. 9 in northern Ontario and its historical betrayals by successive governments (see Kovacs); and Indigenous land rights in the wake of the murder in Guatemala of Mayan Q'eqchi' community leader Adolpho Ich while he was protesting against evictions being carried out there by a Canadian mining company (see Schwellnus). The conversations continued in 2016, with diverse and provocative panels on 'Reckoning and Reconciliation, Testimony, and Forgiveness', 'What Do We Remember When We Remember Together?', 'Transcultural Storytelling', 'Decolonizing the Canon', and the outstanding 'Embodying Counter-Histories' panel – one of the most generative I've witnessed at any festival – all circulating around shows at the festival and all featuring hemispheric activists, scholars, frontline workers, and participating artists.

At its best, the conjunction of the performances and *conversatorios*, together with keynote addresses, workshops, ancillary events, and in particular the communal, border-breaking late-night cabarets,[31] comprises a consistent and coherent festival that constitutes '"a space where people come together, to build partnerships and tell their own stories, in their own languages and from their own perspectives" . . . a place where different viewpoints and cultural perspectives converge and collide' (Ortuzar 67, quoting Pizano and Schwellnus). RUTAS is not, of course – cannot be – the perfect model of a festival enabling intercultural encounter and exchange. Its two-week, Wednesday-through-Sunday format means that visiting artist-participants for financial reasons tend to take part in one-week 'shifts' rather than staying for the whole event, and its workshops, rather than serving as places for artists to share approaches and techniques, consist primarily of classes for local artists run by festival visitors. The festival's multilingual nature and small budget, moreover, mean that simultaneous translation, while it is provided, can be awkward or inconsistent, sometimes disruptive, and is generally under-compensated (see Liebembuk). Nevertheless, through strategic and focused transnationalism, tactical deployment of its small physical and organizational footprint, and careful coordination of performances with workshops and *conversatorios*, the festival, as Alvarez argues, is 'maximizing its potential to serve as an agile, responsive structure for Panamerican *interculturalidad* as both a critical practice and a critical consciousness' ('RUTAS' 251).

Places of Encounter

From Tunis to Toronto this chapter has focused on a different festival paradigm that in various ways attempts to forge and negotiate solidarities and cultural identities within transnational communities that have been historically fractured by global imperialism and remain to greater or lesser degrees splintered because of neocolonial economic policies and practices. Some of these festivals first emerged from postcolonial societies aspiring to (inter)national status as symbolized by representation in the United Nations, some first responded directly to the fact of independence/ decolonization in its immediate wake, and some emerged in a twenty-first-century postnational world. Although the International Theatre Institute, sponsored by UNESCO (the United Nations' Educational, Scientific and Cultural Organization), still sponsors festivals, including the successful Theater der Welt, no international festival now credibly serves the diplomatic role of inter-national mediation between sovereign states, but some, such as those considered here, serve to form 'minor' transnational alliances.[32] Like all the festivals in this book, moreover, all of these intracultural transnational festivals operate within an increasingly globalized festival marketplace dealing with the realities and inequalities of global touring and with the urban, national, and global pressures of festivalization, eventification, development, cultural commodification, and tourism. Each of the festivals discussed in this chapter has dealt with the specificities of those pressures in different ways and with different degrees of success. A large-scale festival such as PANAFEST, addressing the global diaspora of a mixed and massive continent with complex histories of colonization, faces different pressures and problems than does a small festival focusing primarily on East Africa, one attempting to bridge violent historical differences in Northeast Asia, or one addressing a single language group in a former colony in Burkina Faso or Cape Verde. But by virtue of each addressing a single transnational community, culturally, linguistically, or regionally defined, the festivals discussed in this chapter manage more successfully than most to make space for productive performative and discursive encounters across acknowledged and valued cultural and other differences, and they offer new ways of thinking about the mediating role of festivals in a globalized, postnational world.

Conclusion
Festival Futures

In mid-March 2020 I was in Wellington, Aotearoa/New Zealand about to fly to Auckland to begin the final leg of a research trip that had taken me to festivals across Australasia. The New Zealand Festival of the Arts in Wellington had just cancelled the planned final show of my visit there because of the global outbreak of COVID-19, the Auckland Festival announced the cancellation of the last half of its 2020 programme for the same reason, and the Canadian government had just issued an advisory asking all travellers to return home and enter a two-week period of self-isolation. Before my confinement was complete, festivals around the world had cancelled their 2020 iterations, and the future of festivals, as of other large gatherings and those involving international travel, was in question. I finished a draft of the manuscript while still observing self-isolation – a far cry from the feeling of *communitas* said to be produced by festivals. Meanwhile, what I had thought was the beginning of an ongoing contemporary investigation into festivals in the twenty-first century seemed to have become a history book about its first two decades, and some of the tenses I had used throughout my first draft had to change from continuing present to past, others from imperfect to perfect. It felt like a moment may have come to an end.

The hiatus brought about by the global COVID-19 pandemic, however, its duration still to be determined as I write, has perhaps given festival stakeholders an opportunity to pause in what had been an exponential increase in the pace of festivalization, to consider what, globally, the effect of that rapid and perhaps not sufficiently considered development had been, and to plan for the future. Festivals have been called upon before to serve as agents of both cultural and economic renewal, including in Europe after the Second World War and, in a startling parallel, in Toronto after the 2003 outbreak of another coronavirus pandemic, Severe Acute Respiratory Syndrome (SARS). One of the purposes of this book's Conclusion, then, is to ask how, apart from the turn to digital festivals that has become, at least, a temporary measure for most of the festival world, live festivals might be recreated, not to participate in further city branding, creative city discourse, neoliberal entrepreneurialism, or late capitalist globalization but to best contribute to the formation of alliances across difference in order to serve as spaces of intercultural negotiation and exchange. How can festivals rise from the ashes of the pandemic to serve, as James Clifford says of museums, as 'risky, contested sites of socio-cultural activity', spaces for negotiating 'the opportunities and constraints created by powerful and overlapping cultural, economic, political and historical forces, and shifting political alignments ... mediating insides and outsides, [and] imperfectly negotiating social factions' (qtd in Papastergiatis and Margin 52–3).

'We must look beyond the presentation of our registered cultural trademarks', maintained Ricaerd ten Cate as early as 1992 in an argument that equally obtains today. 'We must find connections to the local and national culture, all the time poking and stirring the ant heap' (87). And crucially, we must take the current opportunity to fill the void pointed to by Bernadette Quinn in 2005, 'the absence of any sort of dialogue between those who theorise about arts festivals within performing arts and theatre studies domains and those who strategise around them in urban planning contexts' (939). This conclusion therefore begins with a practical attempt to distil some 'wise practices'[1] from my analyses throughout this volume, practices that might be useful beyond theorists of theatre and performance studies to planners, funders, artists, audiences, and other stakeholders in the intercultural potential of future festivals.

Shifts in the focus and form of many festivals that I have examined in this volume, and the emergence of different festival paradigms, have come about in response to changing global economic and political conditions in the first two decades of the millennium, in which the old model of nation-to-nation cultural and diplomatic exchange has proven no longer to be effective or purposeful in a postnational world. Festivals that emerge in the wake of the current pandemic will inevitably continue to be responsive to shifting contexts and conditions, including the increased attention to, turmoil over, and changes already being brought about because of inequities and injustices globally that the pandemic has both exacerbated and exposed. The Black Lives Matter movement, a decentralized and non-hierarchical social movement originating in the US in 2013, has gone global during COVID-19 in response to an increase in and the increased visibility, because of technology, of police killings of Black people in the US and Indigenous and racialized people everywhere. The pandemic has impacted poor and racialized communities disproportionately, making graphic structural and systemic injustices that undergird an increasingly rapacious and white supremacist capitalist system. Protests against race-based injustices perpetrated on Black and Indigenous people and people of colour have become commonplace throughout the globe, including within Hollywood, élite professional sports, and celebrity culture, perhaps replacing festivals themselves as forms of live social gathering and the negotiation of cultural values. All of this makes yet more more urgent the need for new ways of thinking about festivals as intercultural mediators, where artists and others can come together in generative ways in live, performative dialogue across real and respected differences. This conclusion, then, considering festival futures, returns at last to questions I asked in the volume's opening chapters. Can we find, in ancient and contemporary Indigenous practices, a new, generative, decolonial, and culturally responsive festival paradigm?

Wise Practices

One of the most difficult things in planning a festival is getting the timing right, at once making sure that everything is in place early *and* maintaining sufficient flexibility to stage an event that is relevant, up to date, and capable of responding to changing social and political circumstances. Even before programming begins it's necessary to line up support networks, backers, and stakeholders. This means, first, making sure that local, regional, and national governments and the relevant embassies are on side, not only as funders or writers of welcoming messages in promotional brochures and programmes, but as supporters of an intercultural, decolonial mandate. At many festivals, featured international shows from non-western countries have been cancelled, or at best recast, because artists' visas have been denied, often at the last minute, so festivals that wish to include a healthy component of international, intercultural programming from off the beaten festival track need to have appropriate people on board early – and ideally *on* their Board – that can advise and, when necessary, intervene in such cases.

Corporate funders, and especially individual community donors, even of small amounts, must also be in place early, and this needs to be done opportunistically to match shows with local communities' cultural connections and interests. For the purposes of engaging across difference, many small donors are often better than one or two large ones, especially corporate sponsors with questionable human rights and extractivist environmental records. Diasporic communities and businesses in festival cities will often be eager not simply to see but to support work from their ancestral or more recent homelands. But local supporters – councillors, members of government, NGOs, business and community leaders – are crucial to having and maintaining a level of support that drowns out cynics and helps to attract broad community backing and, eventually, audiences, particularly for work that might be culturally or aesthetically unfamiliar, challenging, or unsettling. Garnering such support needs to start early and needs to be maintained. Community good will, as Peter Sellars learned at the Adelaide Festival in 2002, can never be assumed.

One of the key things that has surfaced in relation to almost every type of festival researched for this book, is that it is incumbent upon festivals engaging in de- or recentring, in orchestrating sometimes uncomfortable encounters across difference, or in decoloniality, to place at the tops of their creative and organizational teams leaders from non-dominant, minoritized groups. The fundamental principle is that of 'no about us without us', and particularly not without the 'us' being represented. These key people need to be in place at top leadership levels from the beginning, participating fully in visioning and planning rather than being brought in at the last minute as window-dressing. This means their being involved at the outset in determining the overarching mandate of the festival and the themes of individual iterations: what is this festival about, what is its purpose, what are its goals? A festival without a more specific mandate, like many of the destination festivals examined in my second chapter, often falls back on the universalist mantra of 'excellence', which most often serves whatever cultural standard is currently dominant and excludes the unfamiliar, unsettling, or 'other'; or it simply sets as its de facto goals the attraction of tourists and the promotion of its brand.

The decentring of leadership can also often be generative. It can involve assembling intercultural teams rather than appointing individuals, while always keeping in mind any groups who, inevitably, are *not* in the room and engaged in the conversation. The team approach also has the advantage of accumulating larger bodies of knowledge and experience with theatrical cultures intranationally and around the world, allowing team members to fan out more broadly than is often possible when a single artistic director or curator is charged with trolling for shows at the world's large festivals with no knowledge of, or time to visit, more ex-centric performances or performance cultures. And of course the leadership team must be fully familiar and informed about local developments, particularly local experimental and intercultural work and work from marginalized communities at home. Flying in star guest directors or curators can often have the unintended effect of marginalizing or excluding important local work.

It's also clear from my analysis throughout this book that the festivals that are most interculturally generative are in no real sense open-access – at least not without some form of affirmative action programming. Difference must be mandated and can never be assumed. It's clear, too, that the most progressive festivals think of their leadership practices as curation rather than programming, and that those practices are undertaken by artists (rather than managers) with clear artistic and cultural visions for festivals that therefore move beyond the cafeteria-style programming model that has become a barrier to the evolution of the destination festival circuit. One of the key jobs of the curator or curators is to put artists productively into conversation with other artists as well as with audiences, to generate opportunities for exchange and encounter across cultural as well as disciplinary and aesthetic differences, and to be self-reflexive about the nature and work of festivals themselves.

Among the ways of avoiding stultification and the 'decline' stage in 'the destination lifecycle' (Robertson and Wardrop 118), is to change leadership often, which also avoids the endless reproduction of limited, quixotic, or coercive worldviews over time. The Progress festival in Toronto goes so far as to involve multiple guest curators in every iteration of the festival. The Ruhrtriennale in Duisburg maintains its flexibility by appointing its artistic directors for three-year limited terms; The New Zealand Festival of the Arts used three different guest curators serially in 2020, supplemented by central programming; and other festivals, such as Malta, LiFT, and TBA have revolving guest curators, new ones in each iteration of the festival.

Germany's Theater der Welt, sponsored by the ITI, goes one step further: not only does each iteration of the festival occur in a different city under different creative leadership, but the festival is scheduled triennially to avoid the never-ending pressures of sustainability that face annual festivals. This gives curators and creators time for commissions and relationships to develop and avoids the situation of directors having the need unthinkingly to fill slots in the programme with whatever shows are available from the touring menu. Each iteration of BeSeTo and CARIFESTA, though the former is annual, is hosted not only in a different city under different leadership, but in a different country in Northeast Asia and the Caribbean, respectively. Other of the world's most interculturally generative festivals, such as London's LiFT, Toronto's

RUTAS, and Kitchener, Ontario's IMPACT occur biennially. All of these strategies can help festivals avoid some of the pressures from city planners and marketers to serve primarily as promoters of their cities' brands and allow festivals more flexibility in programming difference and engaging with local cultures rather than merely staging the latest attraction doing the rounds. The logical extreme of this, of course, is that often a one-off or very occasional festival such as Living Ritual, which frames my discussion in Chapter 1, can have a significant impact, particularly through the judicious bringing together of artists for purposeful exchange rather than display.

Living Ritual was also a small, carefully contained event, and many other festivals that have been most effective at staging difference have avoided the temptation to expand. As I have argued of the Kampala International Theatre Festival and of RUTAS in Toronto, 'The small scale alone helps the festival to fly under the radar of city branders, planners, and politicians caught up in festivalizatation and creative city discourses, freeing the organizers to pursue their own transnational networks and politico-aesthetic agendas and giving them the flexibility to respond quickly to global and theatrical developments.' Size matters.

Size can matter in other ways as well. Festivals such as Bogotá's Iberoamericano and Toronto's Luminato that are dispersed throughout a large city can often serve that city's tourist and creative city agendas well. They are, however, less able to orchestrate sustained exchanges among visiting and local artists and their audiences than are festivals, such as Under the Radar or Progress, that are contained within the walls of a single building (including a comfortable cafeteria or bar) or, such as IMPACT or TBA, are within easy reach of one another on foot or by public transit. In Chapter 3 I have quoted Norman Frisch on the notable benefits of this type of proximity among venues in Portland, particularly for artist interaction and the generation of new ideas. That said, however, it is also often useful, especially at curated live-arts festivals, to get a festival out of theatre buildings to engage directly with its host city in site-specific ways, and this can be particularly productive in engaging with cultural communities in specific city neighbourhoods whose residents don't normally go to the theatre.

Related to the question of location is the sometimes-overlooked element of hospitality. Fringe festivals often do this well through communal beer tents and central gathering places where artists and audiences can casually congregate and engage in productive exchanges. Other festivals have used other strategies. Artists at the IMPACT festival have a designated breakfast location, and in each of its iterations the festival has also had a restaurant sponsor where artists and audiences can dine together on specially made and named festival pizzas or beer. Festivals might want to consider providing food vouchers for specific festival restaurants rather than per diem payments in order to encourage mingling. But the best examples in my experience have been in Tunis, where at both the Arab Theatre Festival in January 2018 and the Journées théâtrales de Carthage in December of that year, festival delegates saw the same shows and stayed and shared all of their meals at the centrally located Hotel Africa, in easy walking distance of all festival venues. Not surprisingly, these festivals generated the most intense and engaged conversations of any I have attended. As Norman Frisch says,

> I think most festival curators will agree that the greatest festivals are where the interaction among the artists is as intense as the interaction of artists and audience. That happens, but it's not the norm; it really has to be constructed, thought through in a very deliberate way. It generally doesn't happen by accident. A lot of that has to do with the economics of festivals; it's cheaper to present artists alongside one another without making opportunities for them to interact. It's less efficient to allow the time and space for artists to be able to see one another's work and to spend time together outside of the venue in which they're performing. That actually takes a lot of effort, and I think the greatest festivals are the festivals where that effort is expended, and the artists *themselves* come away with an expanded awareness and experience; they learn something about their own work. (50)

Scheduling requires careful consideration at both the macro and micro levels of time of year, duration, and programming shows and venues. Most festivals, of course, benefit from good weather, usually in summer or, in hot countries, spring or fall, particularly if the programme involves travelling between venues, on foot or otherwise. Some, however, such as New York's Under the Radar or Toronto's Progress, staged under a single, cozy roof, benefit from January timeslots in the northern hemisphere. Under the Radar is particularly well positioned to take advantage of the annual meeting of the Association for Performing Arts Professionals after the holiday season, drawing interested and invested audiences. Equally important, however, in the promotion of generative encounters between artists *and* between artists and audiences, is a programme that is temporally condensed to allow visitors to stay for the duration, and carefully scheduled to allow artists to see one another's work.

A festival that extends over many weeks and uses only evening timeslots may reward local audiences who are not able to set festival time apart from their daily lives, but it is less convenient for visitors and not conducive to artists sticking around or encountering the work of others. It's not, in short, very festive. I found it frustrating, as an international visitor, to find that the Adelaide Festival and Fringe both scheduled most of their shows in the evenings and on weekends, against one another, limiting the amount of work I could see during my two-week visit, and generally keeping artists apart. In Edinburgh I was seeing four or five shows each day, in Adelaide one or two. The Edinburgh Fringe's month of all-day scheduling, with most shows in a constant slot each day throughout the festival, is much more festively frenetic for audiences, of course, but also much more likely to bring artists together at one another's shows and in intense conversations and exchanges in the city centre's pubs and restaurants and along the High Street. Short, intense festivals lasting four days to a week, like many in the Arab world, in which everyone is able to see and discuss the same shows, create ideal conditions for debate and exchange. In a perfect world, festivals could avoid parallel programming altogether, as at Romania's Interferences.

More important than scheduling, of course, is what is scheduled, so programming is key. There are many different models, some more conducive to intercultural encounter than others, but there are some simple guidelines, some of them having to do with artists, some with audiences. First, festivals need to programme as much genuine rather than merely cosmetic difference as possible, and to do so intersectionally across as many *kinds* of difference as possible, including ethnicity, gender, sexuality, ability, generation, and genre. Any genuine interest in intercultural communication, negotiation, and exchange, moreover, is not served by inviting shows under the creative control of dominant-culture artists that draw on or represent minoritized cultures and cultural texts without the explicit permission or active participation of people from the cultures in question. As we have seen in examples for almost all different types of festival in this book, however, if a festival or network has the funding for it, commissioning collaborations can be pivotal, not simply among like-minded artists and companies but among artists from different social and cultural positions, paying attention to using commissioning money to support artists who most need it. Curators need actively to seek out work that is *not* everywhere, not the festival flavour of the week, but happening in the globe's off-the-beaten-festival-path's nooks and crannies and addressing the performance of real and respected difference.

Interculturalism and interdisciplinarity go hand in hand. As my discussion in Chapter 3 suggests, live-art festivals are often better able than purely disciplinary ones to schedule work that cuts across cultural as well as disciplinary difference. Interdisciplinary work can have among its proper-ties the capacity to denaturalize generic determinants and bring disciplin-ary and other cultures together in conversation. Interdisciplinary work also often uses languages other than the spoken or written, which tend to silo cultures. And it can effectively use the materiality of languages (their sounds, their visuals, the shapes of their symbols and so on) rather than just their meanings, to serve as cross-cultural mediation. Finally, interdis-ciplinarity at festivals can be transformative for artists as well as audiences. As I've quoted Norman Frisch saying of Portland's TBA, a festival signif-icantly dedicated to 'time-based arts' rather than simply to theatre:

> it encompasses installation work, all kinds of media work, new media work, site-specific performance, dance, theater, and so on. It's creating a context in which all these different kinds of artists are seeing and connecting with one another, and it's opening up the possibilities of these various art forms to one another. Over and over again I've met artists at that festival who began as one kind of artist and became another kind of artist because their eyes and senses were opened by encountering other artists at this festival over many years. (51)

The quality of conversation and interaction staged at any festival, no matter how enabling the arrangements are, depends on who is taking part. One of the most important roles of the curator is not just bringing good shows to a festival, but staging dialogue among interesting and provocative artists, local and international, who, through their work and through their conversation, challenge one another and challenge audiences. This can mean curators visiting local theatrical (inter)cultures in places where art is engaging with social and political realities in specific communities rather than staging shows created for a generic international festival audience. And it can mean putting socially engaged artists from those communities strategically into dialogue with one another and with artists and audiences from the various local communities that constitute global, increasingly diverse festival cities.

Many festivals include as ancillary events 'talkback' sessions with artists, press conferences, or other paratheatrical activities designed, usually, to enhance audience engagement. Most of these, especially in this neoliberal age of the artrepreneur, involve artists, drawing on their experience as self-publicists, simply describing and promoting what they do and answering audience questions. The best, however, include conferences and panels that purposefully bring artists whose work is being performed at the festival into conversation with one another and with audiences, but also with critics, scholars, historians, activists, politicians, and community members. The conference component of the Arab Theatre Festival is a lively example of the kinds of exchange that can be generated, though its congregation is mainly scholars and critics. The *'conversatorios'* at the RUTAS festival, however, as discussed in Chapter 5, uniquely and generatively link panels thematically, often on human rights and other political issues, to shows at the festival, and put their creators directly into dialogue with one another and with stakeholders who are deeply informed about the issues covered. One of the most important roles of conference coordinators at these festivals is also to choose experienced chairs and facilitators who can, through advance planning and key interventions, push panellists beyond their familiar publicity scripts into publicly listening and sharing in productive and informative ways. It works best if the panels are kept small – three or four people at most – the topics tightly focused, and the panelists asked to prepare in advance answers to specific, focused questions and then allowed time to interact. Even more productive than panels, if they are well organized, are workshops, in which artists can get on their feet in studio and share skills, techniques, and cultural forms, with – or often preferably without – audience members as witnesses or participants.

In addition to productive exchange, one of the most important functions of panels and workshops, and one that they share with lobby displays, programming material, and the careful matching of festival shows, is to provide social, cultural, and historical context that allows access to and understanding of the full meaning of work that might otherwise sit simply as exotic, strange, or titillating, positioning audiences as voyeurs or consumers. Working across cultures in performance often requires finding ways to re-embed work within the understandings, epistemologies, cosmologies, and cultural practices from which they derive their meaning and use. One festival that positions itself to do this well is Poland's Malta, through its 'Idioms' laboratory programme that addresses urgent social issues, stages a two-day Forum, and supports a publication programme designed to provide rich intellectual context for the performances they present. Another is Interferences in Romania, where 'transcending borders' is an explicit focus (Komporaly 550), and where there are daily post-performance discussions that focus on such things as language, cultural translation, heritage, and belonging. Inteferences also stages public workshops/demonstrations by the performers to explicate and contextualize culturally specific performance forms. This kind of work can be supported, in part, by staging complementary shows from the same or similar source cultures in the same festival, which has the added benefit of relieving any one show from the burden of representing an entire people or social group.

In addition to scheduling and programming, and part of the process of contextualization, are issues of the procedures around the presentation and management of the festival itself once it is underway. It is healthy, and increasingly common, for festivals to avoid presenting performances under their national banners, for example, tacitly suggesting that they play an ambassadorial, or representative role promoting implicitly homogeneous national cultures. Chapter 2 provides the example of the Festival Internacional de Buenos Aires (FIBA) in 2009, unusual among destination festivals in listing its events by city rather than nation of origin – and few of those cities were recognizable global capitals. Similarly, some festivals have resisted labelling shows as theatre, dance, performance art, or music, relying on more flexible programme descriptions to characterize shows and resisting generic labels that can sometimes unhelpfully shape audience expectations. In the programme for its 2012 iteration, the RUTAS festival took the unusual but very generative step of tracing the routes by which shows had arrived at the festival, sometimes complex, and almost always South to North.

The day-to-day management of a festival – also, of course, requiring advance planning – involves attention to a few things that have significant impact on its role in enabling generative intercultural encounter. One of these is obvious: all the artists must be paid, and none should be expected to be rewarded as second-class citizens. Some shows, of course, are more expensive than others for entirely practical reasons. But when in recent years, for example, the cash-strapped Festival Iberoamericano in Bogotá, continuing to pay significant sums for large international shows, stopped paying local artists who were expected to participate for the sake of the exposure, it ran into well justified boycotts, and the image of the festival was significantly damaged. Elsewhere, on the other hand, at festivals such Brazil's FESTLIP, organizers attempt admirably to level the festival playing field by providing impoverished theatre companies from African countries equitable stipends, travel, accommodation, and venue rental costs, while also housing artists in the same accommodation to enable intercultural dialogue. Beyond considerations of equity, it's ideal, where possible, to book and reimburse artists for the duration of a festival rather than only for the days on which they set up, perform, strike, and travel. With appropriate accommodation, fees, and tickets to the shows, artists can justifiably be expected not only to see one another's work, but also to attend and participate in panels, workshops, and other activities that can otherwise be seen as ancillary. To talk to one another and to audiences.

More complex arrangements around any international festival involve taking into account different procedures, practices, traditions, and regulations in participating countries, particularly when schedules are tight and understandings may be different around such things as working conditions, the timing of breaks, and the definition and regulation of jobs and contracts by professional associations and unions. The fact that artists and their technical support teams are working with in-house managers and technicians across differences in language, technology, and theatrical cultures can lead to misunderstandings, delays, and in at least one case that I have encountered, the last-minute cancellation of shows and the bad feelings that accompany such eventualities.

Crucial to the running of festivals across different cultures is the question of accessibility, broadly understood. The first principle is economic: if organizers want participation from any but élite communities to attend their festivals, and if they want to stage conversations that cross cultural barriers between peoples and classes, they need to avoid the élite ticket prices that plague many large destination festivals. Many fringe and live-arts festivals do keep costs down, Under the Radar normally capping at USD $35, which is reasonable for New York, others managing to stay within the $15 to $25 range, and the Toronto Fringe, for example, charging CAD $13 per ticket, or $50 for a five-show pass. Some festivals stage loss leaders free of charge to attract attention and serve the widest communities possible, and at some, admirably Fusebox in Austin, Texas and ANTI in Kuopio Finland, admission to all performances is free and economic considerations for audiences are obliterated.

Physical accessibility for both artists and audience members is essential, not simply for shows representing and hailing people with disabilities, and while this has historically been an issue for older buildings, most spaces in recent years have worked to install ramps and elevators as well as accessible seating, though this is more often the case for audience members than for artists. The Toronto Fringe (and others), however, have admirably modified their 'unbiased' lottery processes to include special categories for artists who identify as culturally diverse, those who identify as artists with disabilities, and seniors,[2] and of course there are many disability arts, queer, and culturally specific festivals. Even some of the large-scale destination festivals have begun to be cognizant of the need for more than token representation of non-dominant groups, but this type of awareness requires ongoing vigilance, and as I indicated at the outset of this section, representation from those groups at a leadership level. It is also good practice to include, wherever possible, 'relaxed', or sensory-friendly performances to accommodate people with autism spectrum disorder or other sensory sensitivities.

But accessibility goes beyond questions of physical access and comfort, and moves us into the essential realm, for cross-cultural encounter, of translation. This requires festivals to address the thorny issues of surtitles, of untranslated non-dominant languages onstage, of signing, and of audio interpretation. Apart from providing the necessary projection equipment for titling, most festivals leave questions of translation up to the visiting artists, and this is unfortunate. Festival organizers would do well to take whatever measures they can to ensure that artists are well served and audiences are saved the neck-wrenching experience of pivoting from side-to-centre stage between the main action and hard-working signers, or from the drama on floor level to the (often jumbled) surtitles high above the stage. Most festivalgoers have also had the disconcerting experience of watching signers who haven't been provided with copies of a script or a conference paper in advance and are struggling to keep up, or of trying to follow surtitles run by non-native speakers of the show's dominant language, surtitles that anticipate, lag behind, or misrepresent the onstage action.[3]

Wise practices, which involve integrating whatever form of translation is necessary into the design of the show from the outset, are the provenance of the show's creators, not directly of festival organizers – though festival organizers could let it be known that this is among the criteria they use in show selection. Signing does not have to be relegated to the sidelines, and some of the best work I've seen involves signers *as actors*, or in other cases signers shadowing actors on the stage and taking full part in the action. In all cases, however, signers should be rehearsed and full, active participants in the show. Two shows that have appeared recently at multiple festivals provide other kinds of models. Jan Derbyshire's *Certified*, when I saw it at the Progress Festival in 2020, included audio interpretation for blind and vision-impaired audiences that was fully integrated, served all audiences well as a full part of the planned experience of the show rather than an afterthought, and involved the otherwise solo performer addressing the audio interpreter directly. Jaha Koo's *Cuckoo*, at OzAsia, PuSh, Progress, and elsewhere in the same festival season made the sensible but simple provision of providing onscreen surtitles behind the stage for video sequences but used subtitles on the façade of a centre-stage table, well within the range of the audience's peripheral vision, for translations of the onstage action. A performance of Diano Tso's *Red Snow*, by Toronto's Red Snow Collective and Aluna Theatre at the Shanghai International Contemporary Theatre Festival in 2012, incorporated translations of the English text into Chinese ideograms and the Chinese text into English throughout the set as a full part of Trevor Schwellnus's design.[4] Finally, sometimes there is no need of translation, as in the Toronto Fringe production of *In Sundry Languages*: 'what happens', asks the show's creator, 'when we don't hide the fact that things are not really translatable?' (Art Babayants, qtd in Karas).

But translation should ideally be at the heart of any festival that wishes to stage generative intercultural encounters, as it was at the Interferences Festival in 2014. Interferences provides surtitles or simultaneous translation in three languages, but crucially, as I've quoted Jozefina Komporaly saying in Chapter 2, 'There was no such thing as a primary language for this festival' (551), a fact that decentres English or any other would-be lingua franca, destabilizes the normalization of linguistic equivalence, and puts languages into active and problematized interaction. 'Translation', Komporaly argues, 'was not a subsidiary facet, but [the festival's] central focus' (551).

Many festivals, as an adjunct to their programme that has the side benefit of attracting presenters, include variations on the showcase, or 'industry series', closed to the general public but providing artists with the opportunity to try to market their work for potential touring, and international presenters with the opportunity to network. These are sometimes appalling occasions, meat markets at which artists are paraded in brief timeslots before a room of 'experts' in order to display truncated slices of their work, usually with little or no tech support, often in small non-theatrical spaces with low ceilings and/or poor acoustics. In some instances, the artists only have the chance to show short video clips and provide brief elevator pitches. These are rarely satisfactory occasions for any artist, but they are particularly inappropriate for showcasing work that is unusual, durational, complex, or culturally unfamiliar. If a festival chooses to include an industry series in its programme, it would benefit from providing artists with enough lead time for preparation, enough time to both present and contextualize their presentations appropriately at the festival itself, and enough tech support to provide a good sense of the work's strengths – particularly when the work is interdisciplinary or intercultural. The event, too, should be contextualized though such things as an introductory meet-and-greet, a casual opportunity for follow-up that doesn't feel like an interrogation, and, as there are now at many festivals such as Vancouver's PuSh, a conference, workshop, or seminar component and relaxed opportunities for informal exchange.

Festival Futures

I have been discussing practicalities, but perhaps a more significant issue around how we might think about festivals as the post-pandemic twenty-first century proceeds would be conceptual. In Chapter 1 of this book, I asked what it would mean 'to see theatre and performance festivals, not as having begun within the competitive framework of ancient Greece but among the relational frameworks of Indigenous communities globally? What would it mean to understand festivals as conferring cultural capital through the dispersion rather than accumulation of worldly goods? To consider festivals as sites of the exchange rather than the commodification of cultures? To consider them as being grounded in the land and in Indigenous knowledge systems rather than in deterritorializing and decontextualizing programming practices?' These questions all centrally involve the question of festival space, place, and the lands they occupy.

Many festivals in the Global West and North since the mid twentieth century have quite literally 'taken' place, and occupied territory. That is to say, many festivals have moved in for a period of time, to the considerable chagrin of many of the locals, and populated (or overrun) a designated festival space with visitors, tourists, artists, and others, occupying the place as if it were *terra nullius*, echoing the land-grabs of global colonization, if only temporarily. This has generally also involved reproducing international and objectifying viewing technologies and performer–audience relationships, and imposing ways of seeing and being on a site to which they may be neither natural nor welcome. I have suggested that international festival circuits – anglophone, lusophone, and francophone – often replicate earlier colonial trade routes – 'circuits of empire' (Hutchison 158) – through which Europe's colonies were despoiled of their natural resources through the labour of enslaved or colonized peoples for the enrichment of European coffers. These festivals themselves similarly emulate the ways in which European settlers from the sixteenth century onwards imposed European imaginings of theatrical space onto landscapes considered to be culturally empty and therefore open to colonialist inscriptions, building replicas of European theatres throughout the colonies to which touring companies travelled without unsettling their own ways of thinking, working, or seeing (see Carter, Davis-Fisch, and Knowles 95). More recent, post-1989 circuits of power are similarly reflected in more recently evolving networks that move outward from imperial centres in the US, Russia, and China. And many artists at international festivals today, imagining themselves to be global citizens, stage what I have called transnational/local performances that (sometimes clumsily) adapt to the cities that host them in much the same way colonial theatre architects decoratively adapted their prosceniums and fire curtains to acknowledge changed spaces and circumstances without fully accommodating to them.

In the twenty-first century the same festivals also participate in and support a globalized creative culture of nomadism that is promoted by French curator, critic, and theorist Nicolas Bourriaud in his influential book, *The Radicant*. In his celebration of the migratory artists whose work populates so many twenty-first-century festivals and who are, he argues, liberated from identity categories such as race, ethnicity, and culture, Bourriaud offers the Aboriginal Australian 'walkabout' as 'a wonderful metaphor for the contemporary art exhibition as the prototype of the journey form' (121). But as I have argued elsewhere, rather than drawing on any Indigenous source in his reference to the walkabout, Bourriaud cites English travel writer Bruce Chatwin, he ignores the fact that walkabouts are durational ceremonial practices tied to very specific landscapes to which the people have very specific and grounded relationships, and he fails to acknowledge the fact that many of the nomadic artists he celebrates have for decades appropriated Indigenous cultural practices without permission or acknowledgement (Knowles, *Performing* 14). And they have done so in the deterritorialized space of festivals.

As this book has demonstrated, many festivals have begun to engage with space in less appropriative and sometimes more generative ways, often moving outside of objectifying Vitruvian theatrical spaces, reconfiguring or multiplying the options for audience–stage relationships and taking the immediately local (and locally intercultural) as their subject matter. Some have also begun to renegotiate their relationship to late capitalist modes of festival production and consumption, recognizing the inequities and dangers of free-market neoliberal models. To return more fully to a reconsideration of the origins of festivals, however, and to replace the Festival of Dionysus with the corroboree, the potlatch, and other performances of negotiation and exchange as origins and sources, I suggest that festivals could go further than they have to date, and this might begin with a deeper reconsideration of place and the performative negotiation of internation relationships. This does not mean appropriating Indigenous performance forms and ceremonial practices, nor does it mean appealing to them metaphorically, as Bourriaud does; it means, rather, learning from them as models of wise practices of participation and ethical witnessing, of protocols of welcome and ceremonies of mutual acknowledgement, of negotiation and exchange, of relational accountability, and of respect for the land on which festivals occur and its human and non-human inhabitants.

In Chapter 1 I described the use, at the Living Ritual Festival in Toronto, of the reciprocal, relational Onkwehon:we Edge of the Woods ceremony to open the festival outdoors on the grounds of the Harbourfront Centre at the shores of Lake Ontario. I also wrote there about the 'nest of welcomes', including the traditional Māori pōwhiri, that preceded the performance of Te Rēhia Theatre's *SolOthello* at the RUTAS festival at Native Earth Performing Arts's Aki Studio, constituting the public as guests. And I wrote about the welcome to the Vancouver Olympics extended to the world by the Four Host First Nations chiefs through a traditional Coast Salish U'tsam (witness) ceremony, a ceremony also used by Quelemia Sparrow for her own show, *Skyborn*, at the PuSh Festival in 2020, constituting the public as neither consumers nor guests, but witnesses-of-record holding responsibility for the collective memory of the event. Each of these occasions modelled Indigenous ways of thinking about internation encounter as Michi Saagiig Nishnaabeg scholar Leanne Betasamosake Simpson describes it, and as it might usefully apply to all festivals. For Simpson, the traditional Anishinaabe were not wanderers, as Indigenous peoples are often depicted in popular culture and as Bourriaud's artist-nomads purportedly are. Rather they were purposefully moving outward from a territorial centre, not to borders or boundaries, but to places of encounter 'where one needs to practice good relations with neighboring nations' (*Dancing* 89). Using Indigenous festivals as models, curators beyond the Indigenous world in the twenty-first century might also generatively begin to consider festivals as places of encounter, places in which to constitute new relationships, and to institute negotiations through reciprocal and respectful protocols of welcome. Indigenous festivals have always been about learning how to share territory and resources – how to live together 'in a good way'. Might future festivals beyond the Indigenous world come to serve the same purposes? Might performances at such festivals come to be thought of as participating in a process of exchange, of making offerings, of sharing territory?

Indigenous festivals and festivals led by Indigenous curators have also extended those festivals' engagement with place beyond the built environment, beyond the harbours of Hamburg, the multicultural

Figure 20   Festival artistic director Tekaronhiáhkhwa Santee Smith in her solo show *NeoIndigenA*, produced by Kaha:wi Dance Theatre at the Living Ritual Festival in Toronto in 2017. Photograph by Erik Zennström

neighbourhoods of London, or the industrial buildings of Duisburg. I have described the opening of The Festival of the Dreaming in 1997 under the leadership of Koori performer and director Rhoda Roberts (Bundjalung Nation), which was choreographed by Bangarra Dance Theatre's artistic director Stephen Page (Yagambeh), as a trans-Indigenous corroboree and cleansing ceremony bringing all the clans together outside of theatrical space and acknowledging the land and its human and non-human inhabitants. I have also described the opening of the Adelaide Festival in 2004 under the directorship of Page, when the opening ceremony assembled 500 members of the Kaurna, Narrungga, and Nagarrindjeri peoples, not in the Festival Theatre, but on the riverbank, where a fire was lit 'designed to reawaken the spirit ancestors, ignite the energies of contemporary indigenous groups and cleanse the site to shape a healthier future for generations to come' (Gilbert and Lo 127). And Noonuccal-Nughi playwright and director Wesley Enoch, as artistic director of the Sydney Festival since 2017, has extended this practice, holding a WugulOra ('one mob') morning ceremony on Australia day, not in the Sydney Opera House but on the Walumil Lawns in riverside Barangaroo Reserve as part of the festival, including a smoking ceremony involving the medicinal burning of the leaves of local, native plants.

Like the openings of the Living Ritual (see Figure 20), Weesageechak Begins to Dance, and Talking Stick Festivals in Canada, and like the buŋgul dance/ceremony that is performed by the Yolŋu peoples every evening outdoors on the festival grounds in Gumatj clan country during the Garma Festival on North Arnhem Land, these events are not merely symbolic. They encode law, language, genealogy, tradition, and cosmology. And they signal a different, new *and* ancient way of relating to the land on which festivals are held, one that extends well beyond the built environment to include and acknowledge the territory, the water, and all human and non-human life that inhabits them as relationships that must be acknowledged, nurtured, and sustained. It may well be that a reconsideration of the creation story of festivals globally could issue in collaborative, relational, and newly generative festival futures all around the world.

Notes

Introduction

1 The show was directed by Catherine Fitzgerald and Pat Rix of Tutti Arts.
2 For a more detailed analysis of the George Town Festival in these terms see Knowles, 'Between the Flag'.
3 Throughout I follow Daphne Lei (571) in using 'East' to indicate the ideological East, and 'Asia' to indicate the geographical East.
4 For a range of current essays on 'the new interculturalism' see Lei and McIvor; McIvor and King.
5 See the 'Aardvark in the Park' festival in St. Paul, Minnesota (http://publicartstpaul.org/aardvark-in-the-park-festival-july-27th-2019), and the Zorilla Fest in Mumbai, India (www.facebook.com/events/981940448616220).
6 I exclude from consideration International Online Theatre Festivals, such as the one run by *The Theatre Times* and *Digital Theatre+* for one month in April 2019 and again in 2020, screening the work of thirty international artists and companies, and including an Open Fringe component (see *Theatre Times*). Since the outbreak of COVID-19, of course, many festivals have gone online, including the global 'Social Distancing Festival', curated by actor and playwright Nick Green (see Low). These festivals raise questions about virtual space and mediatization that are beyond the scope of this book, which is interested in gatherings at which the negotiation of cultural values happens in real time among live, interacting bodies.
7 I understand 'trans-Indigenous' to be a form of transnationalism that invokes a different kind and meaning of 'sovereignty' than that invoked by internationalism. I explore this in more detail in Chapter 1.
8 I am distinguishing recent understandings of 'critical cosmopolitanism' from the 'universal cosmopolitan existence' articulated by Immanual Kant in 1784, which excluded Black and Indigenous peoples from 'proper personhood'. See Kant 51; Knowles, *Theatre & Interculturalism* 56–8; and Gilbert and Lo 4–5 on various kinds of 'new cosmopolitanism'.

9 The term 'eventification' and its cognates were coined in theatre studies in 1999 by the IFTR (International Federation for Theatre Research) working group on The Theatrical Event. See Hauptfleisch 'Festivals' 46, n.1.

10 Marjana Johansson and Jerzy Kociatkiewicz define the experience economy as 'a socioeconomic system where aesthetic experiences, rather than goods or services, form the basis for generating value' (392). See also Zherdev 7, 10–12.

11 My account of Litt's intervention and the True North Festival is indebted to Houston 113–15.

12 I am using 'deterritorialized' in Deleuze and Guatarri's semiotic sense of the deterritorialization of the sign, leaving it open to capitalist recoding, or reterritorialization. See Deleuze and Guatarri 240–62.

13 For the relationship between decoloniality and resurgence, see Chapter 1, note 5.

14 These include Majdi Bou-Matar, Beatriz Pizano, Bruce Gibbons Fell, Torsten Jost, and Christel Weiler, as well as the anonymous translators at the Performing Tangier Festival and conference, and the signers and audio interpreters at many festivals.

15 I use 'creation story' to signify primary cosmogonies, told and retold in ways that provide foundational ontologies for Indigenous cultures. A festival creation story, then, relates directly to what festivals are understood to be.

16 I use decolonization here to refer to nations gaining legal, political independence from their former colonizers, in counterdistinction to 'decoloniality' as theorized by Walter Mignolo and his colleages in the modernity/coloniality/decoloniality collective (see Mignolo and Walsh; Mattison; A. Hoffman).

17 See, for example, the 'Fungus Among Us Mushroom Festival' in Whistler, British Columbia, Canada (Whistler Naturalists).

18 In considering 'wise practices' rather than 'best practices', I am following an Indigenous Community Development model. 'Wise practices' are defined as 'locally-appropriate actions, tools, principles or decisions that contribute significantly to the development of sustainable and equitable conditions' (Cynthia Wesley-Esquimax and Brian Calliou qtd in Calliou 17). Rather than aspiring to be universal, wise practices are 'idiosyncratic, contextual, textured, and notstandardized' (O.L. Davis, qtd in Calliou 17). I am grateful to Yvette Nolan (Algonquin and Irish) for drawing my attention to this distinction.

Chapter 1

1 Storyweaving is a play creation method invented by Muriel Miguel and employed by Spiderwoman in all their work. It is used, according to Miguel, 'to entwine stories and fragments of stories with words, music, song, film, dance and movement, thereby creating a production that is multi-layered and complex; an emotional, cultural, and political tapestry' (qtd in Mojica 165). Miguel and Aanmitaagzi's artistic director Penny Couchie (Mohawk and Anishinaabe) led a workshop on the technique at the festival.

2 'Internation', referring to Indigenous nations, is a term used by Penny Couchie in a panel at the festival on Indigenous collaboration in contradistinction to 'international'. The terms invoke different understandings of both nation and sovereignty (see note 25 below).

3 Indeed, Plains Cree director Floyd Favel calls theatre (in an unfortunately gendered phrase) 'the younger brother of tradition', which, arriving relatively recently on Turtle Island, shares with ceremony the capacity 'to connect us to our "higher self"' (31). Theatre, however, 'has a social and cultural function and it serves the society while Tradition is at the service of spirit and spiritual forces' (31). Favel situates Indigenous theatre in a 'Shadow Zone' between the two.

4 For a nineteenth-century anthropological account by a white settler scholar of the scroll and the Midē'wiwin see W.J. Hoffman, and for a late twentieth-century account that attempts to encapsulate both European and Anishinaabe views of the ceremonies, see Angel. Henceforth, unless they are identified by Indigenous nation, all scholars cited are understood to be non-Indigenous.

5 In citing 'decoloniality' I am invoking the term both as it is used by Argentinian scholar Walter Mignolo to discuss the epistemic 'delinking' and 'dewesternization' of knowledge systems (see Mattison), and as it is explicated and explored by Michi Saagig Nishnaabe scholar Leanne Betasamosake Simpson as 'decolonial love' (a term coined by Dominican American writer Junot Díaz – see Moya), a non-reactionary, non-binary aspect of Indigenous resurgence, as discussed below (see Simpson, 'decolonial', *Islands*, and *Dancing*).

6 'Potlatch', according to Clutesi, is an early European distortion of the Nuu-chah-nulth words 'Pa-chitle', to give, and 'Pa-chuck', gift, which would have been heard frequently enough during the occasion to have been mistaken for the name of the event itself (10).

7 For a discussion of Indigenous relationality, including relational ontologies, epistemologies, axiologies, and 'relational accountability', see Opaskwayak Cree scholar Shawn Wilson 62–125.

8 Simpson refers to 'Indigenous internationalism' in a chapter that is more specifically focused on 'Nishnaabeg Internationalism' (*As We Have* 55–70), in which she explores the relational basis of her culture's encounters with other human and non-human nations.

9 Mino-bimaadiziwin, Anishinaabemowin for 'the good life', is the result of living 'in a good way', according to the teachings of the ancestors. For the Anishinaabe this involves Anishinaabemowin (the language, ways of communicating), Inendamowin (ways of thinking), Gikendaasowin (ways of knowing), Inaadiziwin (ways of being), Izhichigewin (ways of doing, or taking action), Enawendiwin (ways of relating to all of creation, human and non-human – all our relations), and Gidakiiminaan (ways of relating to the earth and the environment). This is specific to the Anishinaabe, but most Indigenous nations, particularly on Turtle Island, have similar concepts that

guide the people towards living 'in a good way', and the phrase has been widely adopted. See 'Anishinaabe Mino Bimaadzimwam'; 'Anishinaabe'.

10 The four host Nations – the Tsleil-Waututh, Musqueam, Lil'wat, and Squamish – also jointly hosted the Four Host First Nations Aboriginal Pavillion, with events ranging from concerts to educational presentations.

11 Except where otherwise indicated information on The Festival of the Dreaming is drawn from Hanna 64–89, and from Roberts.

12 Gamarada is a Dharug word meaning 'friend'.

13 Higgins-Desbiolles argues that 'one of the important lessons to be learned from the experience of the 2000 Olympics, [was] that instead of being a site of ugly indigenous protests before the international spotlight, the Olympics instead showcased what Australia could and should be' (42).

14 For an account of hobbyists in a US context see Philip Deloria (Anishinaabe) 128–53.

15 Although the closest translation of 'whakapapa' in English is 'lineage', as I understand it the Te Reo Māori word is more about ancestry than linear descent (which in English has to do with the property rights) and is central to locating oneself in a larger context of land, sea, and *iwi* (tribe).

16 *DECLARATION* has been staged in different cities and different contexts. In each incarnation Moro builds a site-specific design frame involving set pieces and video projections, and the company invites Indigenous guest artists to collaborate in creating new work throughout each day before spectators who are invited to drop in, and then in the evening to attend a collaborative formal presentation that has emerged from the day's work. In the interests of disclosure, I worked on the installation as a dramaturg for guest artist Monique Mojica (Guna and Rappahannock) at Ottawa's National Arts Centre in 2015.

17 Perhaps in part because of ARTICLE 11's intervention and those of others, the repatriation of Demasduit's and Nonosbawsut's remains was approved in 2019 and completed in March 2020.

18 In the interests of disclosure: I have worked with MT Space as a dramaturg and have served on the IMPACT Festival's programming and conference committees.

19 'Arrivant' is Chickasaw scholar Jodi Byrd's term for non-Natives who live in Indigenous territory but share the experience of racialization and colonialism. In Canada this often means refugees and immigrants of colour as well as the descendants of enslaved peoples.

20 The festival circuit has always sought out the 'cutting edge', which elsewhere has often involved western artists appropriating and decontextualizing the traditional performance forms of Indigenous and other cultures. What has been much less common is the presentation of cutting-edge work by Indigenous and immigrant artists themselves.

21 For more on RUTAS see Chapter 5. In years alternating with RUTAS, Aluna and Native Earth co-produce CAMINOS, a smaller-scale intra-national festival within Canada dedicated to developing new work from the same communities in diaspora.

22 Again, full disclosure: I was a member of the Aluna Theatre Board of Directors and also served as co-creator and dramaturg for *Amal*. Another of its creators was Cree actor and musician Nigel Irwin.

23 Many Indigenous people in referring to the city of Toronto use the Mohawk 'Tkaronto', meaning 'where there are trees standing in the water', which is presumed by some to be the origin of the name (see https://katerynabarnes .com/indigenous-word-of-the-day). Others argue that Toronto derives from the Wendat 'Toronton', referring to fishing weirs, and others argue that to privilege either of these is to fail to acknowledge other Indigenous Nations and naming practices.

24 'Aki' means earth, land, or place in Anishinaabemowin (the language of the Anishinaabe peoples).

25 Arguing that 'the challenge for indigenous peoples in building appropriate postcolonial governing systems is to disconnect the notion of sovereignty from its Western, legal roots and to transform it' (468), Kanien'kehá:ka (Mohawk) scholar Taiaiake Alfred provides a history and critique of 'state sovereignty as applied to the Indigenous peoples of Turtle Island'. For other Indigenous scholars on sovereignty see Anaya (Apache and Purépecha), Joleme Rickard (Tuscarora), and on the 'doing', 'reading' (or interpreting), and experiencing of sovereignty as a practice, see Robinson ('Welcoming', and 'Public Writing'). Robinson argues that 'sovereignty is not held within documents/ objects but instead within "doing"' ('Welcoming' 6): 'sovereignty is not a thing, but an action' ('Public Writing' 85).

26 I'm indebted to Māori Canadian theatre artist David Geary for this interpretation of a word and concept that might otherwise be rendered in English as 'self-respect'. The online Māori dictionary indicates that mana is 'a supernatural force in a person, place, or object', and that it includes 'an element of stewardship' when used in relation to resources such as land or water.

27 The dish-with-one-spoon wampum records a treaty between the Anishinaabe and Haudenosaunee nations in which they agreed to share custodianship of the land and water resources of the St Laurence and Great Lakes basins in eastern Canada and the United States, with no wasting of resources. It is now widely understood to apply to all who occupy that territory. See 'The Dish with One Spoon'.

28 I place 'reconciliation' in scare quotes because in Australia, Canada, and elsewhere, it has currency in government documents on 'truth and reconciliation', is questioned by many, in that it presupposes an original state of harmony to which these societies might return, and it imagines responsibility for 'conciliation' as being mutual. Most Indigenous peoples would prefer to see a goal of reparation as the responsibility of settlers.

29 'Free settler' is used to distinguish Adelaide, which was settled by wealthy colonialists who paid their own passage, from other Australian cities that were first settled overwhelmingly by forcibly transported convicts.

30 Bangarra's long-time Yugambeh musical director David Page, brother of Stephen, passed away in 2016; Steve Francis's score paid tribute to his legacy.

31 Enoch was recognized for this work in January 2020 when he was made a member of the Order of Australia. In acknowledging the award Enoch said, 'This appointment recognises not just my achievements but the contribution of all Indigenous artists working in Theatre. The soul of our nation is reliant on artists stepping up to tell the stories that reflect and challenge us to be better human beings. The storytelling of our nation has often overlooked Indigenous narratives and there are many who have gone before me and will come after me who will assist all Australians to connect to the 60,000+ history of this continent' (qtd in 'Sydney Festival Director').

32 'Blak out', according to Enoch, 'is actually a term we use for ourselves: when there's a whole lot of black fellas around, we say, 'It's a blak out tonight'' (qtd in Boon).

33 Garneau identifies 'irreconcilable spaces of Aboriginality' as 'intellectual spaces that exist apart from a non-Indigenous gaze and interlocution. The idea is to signal to non-Indigenous spectators the fact that intellectual activity is occurring without their knowledge; that is, "without their knowledge" as in without their being aware, and "without their knowledge" in the sense of intellectual activities based in Native rather than Western epistemologies' (26–7).

34 Indeed, other Aboriginal communities within Australia who have lost many of their performance traditions draw upon and adapt those of the Yolŋu as part of their own process of reconstruction and growth (see Magowan 313–14), to the point that 'the dance traditions of Arnhem Land have played, and continue to play, a key role in the construction of indigeneity in Australia today' (Magowan 309).

35 The Uluru proposal of 2017, 'Uluru Statement from the Heart', in which Aboriginal and Torres Strait Island people proposed constitutional reforms that would enshrine a place for them in the constitution within a representative advisory body on Indigenous issues, was rejected as divisive by the Conservative government of the time (see Referendum Council).

36 'Pasifika' is a term unique to Aotearoa, roughly equivalent to 'Oceania' or 'the Pacific Islands'. 'Pacific peoples', and 'Pacific Islanders', refer to the diverse Indigenous peoples of this vast region; 'Polynesians', 'Melanesians', and 'Micronesians' are colonially imposed regional trans-Indigenous designations.

37 I use 'intra-National' to refer to festivals representing work from a single nation-state (in this case Canada), though Talking Stick works across many Indigenous Nations. This is in contradistinction to 'intranational' as discussed in Chapter 5.

38 A fourth type of Indigenous festival is in the planning stages in Peterborough, Ontario, where Nogojiwanong Indigenous Fringe Festival – 'the first and only Indigenous *Fringe Festival* in the known world' (Nogojiwanong) – was planned for June 2020 but was postponed because of the COVID-19 pandemic.

39 For the early history of Weesageechak Begins to Dance see J. Preston.

40 'Two-Spirit', coined in Winnipeg in 1990, is an umbrella term that brings together terminology from various Indigenous peoples. It refers to people who

are 'blessed by the creator to see life through the eyes of both genders', and serve their different communities in different ways, often as 'balance keepers' (Enos).

41 The show was written by Miria George, Hone Kouka (Māori), and Yvette Nolan (Algonquin and Irish), choreographed by Michelle Olson (Tr'ondëk Hwëch'in First Nation) and Te Hau Winitana (Cook Islands), and directed by Hone Kouka.

42 For a more complete treatment of the Living Ritual Festival see Knowles, 'Because'.

Chapter 2

1 *Flight* was commissioned by the EIF and adapted from Brothers's novel by Oliver Emanuel, incorporating poetry by Rumi (Jalāl ad-Dīn Muhammad Rūmī). It was directed by Jamie Harrison and Candace Edmunds.

2 Ironically, the show was framed by a discourse of risk for *audience* members: in the pre-show lobby there were signs reading: 'For your own safety, please don't touch the set at any point; you will be wearing head phones throughout; please leave large coats and bags at coat check; you will be entering a dimly lit space for the duration; if you need assistance press the button and wait for 45 seconds … In case of emergency we will alert you, front of house lights will come up: wait in your seat.' We were escorted individually to our separate cubicles, and 'rescued' from them individually at the end.

3 For a detailed review of my experience of the 2017 Edinburgh International Festival and Fringe see Knowles, 'Festivals'.

4 The Ruhrfestspiele Recklinghausen was also founded in 1947 when a group of actors from Hamburg gave a guest performance in gratitude for the miners there having saved their winter season by smuggling coal past the military police to keep their theatres going. The festival has a major international profile, but unlike Edinburgh and Avignon is organized around annual themes (a playwright, a particular country) and has never had the same influence on the international festival model as they have (see 'Ruhrfestspiele'). Edinburgh, Avignon, and Recklinghausen are also destination festivals in the sense that they are not located in the large urban centres of their respective nations, and, like Wagner's Bayreuth and many other festivals, not only reward but require travel – or what has often been called pilgrimage – for most of their audience base.

5 See Temple Hauptfleisch on the 'colonial' quality that 'shaped, coloured, and affected the reputations of all the events' at the Grahamstown Festival, referring to 'a sense of nostalgia rooted in a romanticized vision of the British Empire' that obtained there ('Eventifying' 186). The National Arts Festival (better known as the Grahamstown Festival) is undoubtedly a destination event, but for historical and cultural reasons has develop differently than others. See Kruger for an excellent current account.

6 The controversy revolved around the fact that 'Luminato's windfall cut directly into the funds available for numerous other, lower-profile initiatives' (Levin and Solga 159), and much of the money was used to fund out-of-province, out-of-country work selected by Luminato, bypassing the arts councils' peer-juried system. See also Michèle Anderson, who speculates about 'Luminato suddenly becoming the belle of the arts and culture ball after only showing up at a quarter to midnight' (33–4).

7 The information in this paragraph is drawn from the *Luminato 2018 Annual Report* and from the festival's website (Luminato).

8 In 2009, as many as 80 per cent of Luminato events were free (see M. Anderson 20, 25–30, and 67–8); by 2019 the only free events were one waterfront concert, one small exhibition, and three panels attached to film screenings. For consideration of the festival's neighbourhood initiatives, creative participation, and outreach programmes in its early years see M. Anderson 44–7. For a detailed analysis of the top-down problematics of its most prominent neighbourhood initiative, 'Streetscape: Living Space at Regent Park', see McLean, 'Cracks'.

9 The festival programme lists a fourth commission, *Obeah Opera*, but this was a somewhat reductive revisioning of a show first co-produced in 2012 by Toronto's Theatre Archipelago and b current.

10 Canada was the first country in the world to legislate, beginning in a 1971 policy document, entrenched in the Charter of Rights and Freedoms in 1982, and passed into law in 1988, a policy of official multiculturalism. For analysis and critique of the policy see Bannerji; Bissoondath; and Gunew (who also deals with Australia's policies), and, as it relates to theatre and performance, particularly in Toronto, see Knowles, *Performing* 23–43.

11 Among the very few exceptions are productions of familiar canonical works, such as the surtitled German-language production of *Richard III* directed by Thomas Ostermeier at the EIF in 2016, and the surtitled Dutch Internationaal Theatre Amsterdam production of *Oedipus* in 2019, directed by the British Robert Icke. In these cases, 'élite' audiences for the most part already know the story and can ignore or merely scan the surtitles.

12 *Anything that Gives Off Light*, in 2016, a co-production by the EIF with the TEAM (based in Brooklyn) and the National Theatre of Scotland, about a Scottish man and a woman from Appalachia, was billed as 'bridging the cultural divide'. In 2017 the Festival co-produced Ionesco's *Rhinoceros* with the Royal Lyceum Theatre in Edinburgh and DOT Theatre in Istanbul. Its programme billed the production as 'a cross-cultural dialogue' between the adaptor, Scottish playwright Zinnie Harris, and Turkish director Murat Daltaban, but the focus was on the classic European source text.

13 For an extended discussion of *Ganesh* as 'reflexive interculturalism' see Tan.

14 The New Zealand Festival of the Arts and the Auckland Festival are Associate members.

15 The Perth Festival in Western Australia, formerly the Perth International Festival of the Arts, founded in 1953, has surpassed Adelaide in terms of

attendance and box office receipts, but has never equalled it in prestige, and its numbers are bolstered by large popular musical and other events. When I attended in 2020, after an exciting first week dedicated to Indigenous performance (as discussed in Chapter 1), the festival relied on a combination of local fare, an extensive film programme, an extensive series of classical and popular music including headliners such as Phillip Glass, Rufus Wainwright, Amanda Palmer, Kate Tempest, and Mavis Staples plus a late-night 'City of Lights' concert series and a literary series that saw celebrity author Neil Gaiman fill the 2000-seat Perth Concert Hall. The relatively limited number of theatre offerings was dominated by high-profile revivals of the decades-old blockbusters, *Bran Nue Dae* and *Cloudstreet*, both of which are set in Western Australia and the latter of which I discuss below.

16 Lutton also cast neuroatypical actor Benjamin Oakes to play Fish Lamb, the character who suffers neurological trauma early in the play and the novel it is based on.

17 The unnamed reviewer for *Culture Whisperer* argued that the casting practice was 'a clever move, making the audience focus on the ethics behind the arguments being presented rather than the physical identity of the person making them' ('Doctor').

18 Throughout this book I use 'white' and other terms designating racialization not in any essentializing ways – I recognize that race is a social construction – but to indicate the ways in which skin colour is read and accrues different degrees of privilege, power, or oppression in real material terms at this historical moment.

19 The production's semiotics were explicated in a bilingual sixteen-page illustrated brochure given to the audience to supplement the programme. The iconic vocabulary, however, neither provided reductive decodings nor explained away the show's complexities; rather it focused on key Buddhist concepts and iconographies that the production employed or evoked.

20 For an excellent account of *Kiinalik* see V.K. Preston, 146–54.

21 The name change occurred after Montréal's Festival international de nouvelle danse (FIND) ceased operations in 2003 and FTA expanded its mandate to include dance, theatre, performance, and live art more generally, explicitly eschewing rigid categorization by genre.

22 A book-length celebration of the FTA was published in 2018, including photographs, manifestoes, debates, stories, anecdotes, and testimonies by forty artists and others who have participated in the festival over its history. See Mill and Parent.

23 The exception to this, in 2020, was the housing of the Laurie Anderson/Hsin-Chien Huang virtual reality installation, *To the Moon*, at the Dowse Art Museum in Lower Hutt, a 45-minute bus ride from city centre. The installation was housed in more central locations at the Adelaide and Under the Radar (New York) festivals in the same year.

24 These included *Trois Grandes Fugues*, an assemblage by the Lyon Opera Ballet of three major female choreographers' takes on Beethoven's *Die Grosse Fuge*;

Dimanche, a charming gestural- and object-theatre piece by the Belgian Cie Chalisaté and Cie Focus about climate catastrophe; and *Strasbourg 1518*, a dance piece by New Zealand's Borderline Arts Ensemble based on an historically recorded dance-plague-as-revolution (or 'choreomania') in the post-medieval French city.

25 This has not changed. In the Fall of 2019, against the objections of Indigenous peoples on Turtle Island who had unsuccessfully offered to serve the show as cultural consultants, Lepage, in collaboration with Ariane Mnouchkine, premiered his *Kanata* at the Festival d'Automne in Paris, representing a history of Indigenous peoples in what is now Canada with no Indigenous involvement.

26 The information in this paragraph is drawn from Graham-Jones.

27 The population also includes a sprinkling of Romani and a significant unregistered 'floating' population.

28 Although its last official iteration under ITI endorsement was in Nanking, China, in 2008, and in spite of current plans to revive it, in real terms Théâtre des Nations ended as a regular event in 1998 in Zürich, Switzerland.

Chapter 3

1 In a different taxonomy, Joyce Rosario, former Associate Artistic Director of the PuSh Festival in Vancouver, calls these festivals 'a kind of third wave', after the post-War and Fringe festivals (qtd in Zaiontz, 'Festival' 162), while Marjana Johansson and Maria Laura Toraldo use the term 'boutique festival' to designate small festivals with many very similar characteristics, including what they call 'participatory activities' (221).

2 Ferguson provides some valuable accounts of what some curators actually do on the ground in these capacities. See especially his account of the work of curator Mirna Zagar in Zagreb and Vancouver (106–9).

3 Festivals in Transition (FIT) was initiated by Munich's SPIELART and was originally made up of eight European festivals. The partners, in addition to SPIELART, currently include Alkantara (Lisbon); Baltic Circle Festival (Helsinki); Downtown Contemporary Arts Festival, or D-CAF (Cairo); Drodesara (Centrale Fies, Italy); Drugajanje (Maribor, Slovenia); Homo Novus (Riga); LiFT (London); Reykjavík Dance Festival and Lókal (both in Reykjavík); SAAL Biennaal (Tallin); and SPRING (Utrecht). FIT developed the four-year Urban Heat, not itself a festival, but a typical second-wave project that brought together artists, academics, faith leaders, political scientists, and technologists to enable artists 'to develop their understanding of fundamental issues and challenges facing cities' (Japan Foundation).

4 The seminar included Britta Marakatt-Labba (artist and member of Sámi Artist Group, 1978–83), Raisa Porsanger (artist and curator), Rauna Kuokkanen (Research Professor of Arctic Indigenous Studies, University of Lapland), Pauliina Feodoroff (director and Sámi activist), Sini Harkki

(programme manager, Greenpeace) and others. It was moderated by film-maker and storyteller Suvi West.

5 Both 'LIFT' and 'LiFT' are used, by others and by the festival itself. I have chosen to use the more common LiFT, except, of course, when quoting.

6 My account of the partnership between LiFT and Mammalian Diving Reflex follows Zaointz, 'From' 30–3.

7 The partners, in addition to ANTI, are Savona University in Kuopia, Finland; Seconde Nature in Aix-en-Provence, France; ID Lab in Sainte-Étienne, France; Public Art Lab in Berlin, Germany; Citilab in Cornellà, Spain; BEK Bergen Centre for Electronic Arts in Bergen, Norway; Kontjener, in Zagreb, Croatia; Liepaja City Council in Liepaja, Latvia, and La Chambre Blanche, in Québec City, Canada.

8 IN SITU partners are Artopolis Association/PLACCC Festival (Hungary), Atelier 231/Festival Viva Cité (France), CIFAS (Belgium), Ctyri dny/4+4 Days in Motion (Czech Republic), FAI-AR (France), Freedom Festival (United Kingdom), Kimmel Center (US), Metropolis (Denmark), La Paperie (France), La Strada Graz (Austria), Les Tombées de la Nuit (France), Lieux publics (France), Norfolk & Norwich Festival (United Kingdom), Teatri ODA (Kosovo), Theater op de Markt (Belgium), On the Move (Belgium), Østfold kulturutvikling (Norway), Oerol Festival (Netherlands), Terni Festival (Italy), and UZ Arts (United Kingdom).

9 This quotation, from the translation provided on the Malta website by way of Google translate, has been adjusted to use more idiomatic English.

10 In addition to Malta, the members of HoF are: LiFT (London), HAU Hebbel am Ufer (Berlin), Kaaitheater (Brussels), brut Wien (Vienna), Archa Theatre (Prague), Teatro Maria Matos (Lisbon), Frascati (Amsterdam), Théâtre Garonne (Toulouse), BIT Teatergarasjen (Bergen). It was funded from 2007 to 2013 by the individual partners and by the Culture Programme of the European Union.

11 This, of course, is partly a result of the ways in which neoliberalism promotes individual entrepreneurialism, partly because such shows are both inexpensive and portable, and partly because they adjust easily to almost any venue.

12 I have seen both TBA and T:BA used. I have chosen to use TBA except when quoting because it is the version used on the Festival's website.

13 Venues within the Public Theater in 2020 included LuEsther Hall (capacity 160), Martinson Hall (199), Neuman Theater (299), Shiva (99, hosting the six-show 'Incoming' series), The Classroom at the Public (hosting Laurie Anderson and Hsin-Chien Huang's short VR performance, *To The Moon*), and, in the case of the four-show 'In Concert' series, Joe's Pub (a dinner theatre environment). Nothing was scheduled in 2020 for the larger Anspacher space (275). Off-site locations included the Ellen Stewart Theatre at La MaMa (299), Japan Society (260) (both in Manhattan), and the flexible BRIC House (in Brooklyn).

14 As explained in Chapter 1, 'grounded normativity' is a term coined by Dene scholar Glen Coulthard to refer to a 'place-based foundation of Indigenous

decolonial thought and practice', 'the modalities of Indigenous land-connected practices and long-standing experiential knowledge that inform and structure our ethical engagements with the world and our relationships with human and nonhuman others over time' (13).

15 The approximately USD $500,000 budget for Under the Radar comes from the Doris Duke Foundation, the Mellon Foundation, other foundations, the Public Theater, ticket sales, and individuals (Martin 129).

16 In an Executive Order in 2017 President Donald Trump restricted travel to the US by citizens of Iran, Iraq, Libya, Somalia, Sudan, Syria, and Yemen. A second order removed Iraq from the list, and later a Presidential Proclamation removed Sudan from the list but added restrictions on Chad, North Korea, and Venezuela. Most of the listed countries are predominantly Muslim, and the travel ban has often been referred to as the 'Muslim ban'. President Joe Biden rescinded the ban on his first day in office in January 2021.

17 If audience members register for a show and fail to turn up, however, all of their bookings are cancelled. For details about the Free Range Art Initiative see Fusebox, 'Fusebox Festival 10th Anniversary'. For a list of the festival's current sponsors, including those making free admission possible, see 'Fusebox 2020'.

18 For sophisticated reviews of *Estado Vegetal* see Cotter; Ripp.

19 Since 2014 Goldcorp has worked hard at its reputation, in 2018 signing an 'impact and benefit agreement' with Brunswick House, Chapeau Cree, and Chapleau Ojibwe First Nations in Northern Ontario in which 'Goldcorp recognizes and respects the rights and interests these First Nations have around the Borden project site [in Chapleau, Ontario], and the three First Nation communities recognize and support Goldcorp's rights and interests in the development and future operation of the mine' ('Goldcorp').

20 The Downtown Eastside was the site at which a notorious sexual predator confessed to the murder of forty-nine women, most of them Indigenous, in the 1990s and early 2000s.

21 First Nations peoples officially constitute 6 per cent of the population of the province, though that percentage is steadily rising. These figures for both the city and province may not include many mixed-race or unregistered off-reserve people.

22 The participants were Dara Culhane as chair; Daina Ashbee (Euro-Cree-Métis); Cris Derksen (Euro-Cree); Lindsay Lachance (Anishinaabe); Michelle Olson (Tr'ondëk Hwëch'in First Nation), artistic director of Raven Spirit Dance; and Wesley Enoch (Noonuccal-Nughi), playwright, director, and artistic director of the Sydney Festival, Australia.

23 'Crip' is a short-form reclamation of the offensive labelling of people with disabilities as 'cripples'. It is used inclusively to refer to all disability cultures (see Mirk).

24 This did not reflect a major change at PuSh. Before Franco Boni took over from Norman Armour as artistic director in 2019, then Associate AD Joyce

Rosario talked about the importance to the festival of relationships, of the curatorial role as one of 'caretaker and custodian', and the festival's commitment to 'feed a city' (qtd in Zaiontz, 'Festival' 163–4). Both Boni and Rosario left the festival, not without controversy, in July 2020, after the manuscript of this book was submitted to the press.

25 Immediately before departing from Toronto to take up his position at PuSh, Boni had directed Métis writer, actor, puppeteer, and filmmaker Jani Lauzon's deeply relational environmentalist show, *Prophecy Fog*.

26 Indigenous futurism, a term coined by Anishinaabe scholar Grace Dillon in the Introduction to her anthology, *Walking The Clouds*, as an analogue to Afrofuturism, weaves traditional knowledges into futuristic settings and ideas, using science fiction and other forms of speculative arts in the service of decoloniality. See Dillon 10.

27 Stó:lo scholar Dylan Robinson describes the role of the official witness as 'central to the longhouse work undertaken … in all Northwest Coast First Nation communities', where, 'Because audiovisual and written recordings of the proceedings are prohibited, witnesses act as our books.' 'Witnesses', he says, 'know that they may be called on in the future to recall what they have seen accurately and truthfully', bearing history 'within the collective memory, and within the mind and the body' (*Hungry Listening* 224).

28 According to the 2016 Census, Chinese is the largest ethnic group in Vancouver, representing 20.6 per cent of the city's population (see 'Demographics'). The city's population is ca 42 per cent ethnically Asian.

29 Portland is second only to San Francisco in the US in the percentage of its population reporting as gay, lesbian, bisexual, or transgender.

30 It is projected that by the time of the 2036 census visible minorities will represent 63 per cent of the population.

31 SummerWorks does not identify as a fringe festival, and it differs from such festivals in several ways. In addition to being curated, it involves itself, sometimes over several years, with works in development; it provides more resources – dramaturgical, technical, marketing, fundraising, grant-writing, finding venues for site-specific work – than most fringes do; it provides more tech hours, more flexible formats, and more design and technical options than most fringes; and it does not charge participation fees to artists. Although it is true that the work presented is 'mostly new, mostly local', in the past four years 30 per cent of the work presented has come from outside of Toronto, and there are now one or two projects by international artists each year. I am grateful to Laura Nanni and Sue Balint for information on SummerWorks and Progress.

32 In 2020, for example, there was a consistent general festival audience throughout the two weeks with the partial exceptions of *Certified*, a show about mental illness that attracted a disability arts audience that was not as apparent during the rest of the festival, and of the screening, on a Monday evening when most theatres are dark, of a series of short dance films, *Screen:Moves*, which seemed to attract a primarily dance crowd. This last was ironic, in that

the films were generally cross-disciplinary, consisting of dancers making films, the most interesting of which might best be described as film *as* dance – incorporating the spatial, rhythmic, and movement vocabularies and sensibilities of dancers and choreographers into the filmic genre through choreographic editing and post-production.

33 The Rhubarb Festival is Canada's longest-running new works festival, held every February at Toronto's Buddies in Bad Times, the largest queer theatre in North America. It tends to overlap with Progress by a few days each year. In 2019 the Performance Bus included live performances as it escorted patrons between the festivals.

34 Canadian Heritage, or the Department of Canadian Heritage, funds initiatives that support 'Canadian identity and values'. Unlike the arts councils, which operate through peer assessment by juries of artists, Canadian Heritage is a direct branch of government.

35 Contributing to *Good Morning Mr Orwell* were such art world luminaries as George Plimpton, as host, Laurie Anderson, Joseph Beuys, John Cage, Merce Cunningham, Peter Gabriel, Allen Ginsberg, Phillip Glass, Charlotte Moorman, Oingo Boingo, Peter Orlovsky, and the Thompson Twins.

36 I'm thinking in particular of large-scale festivals such as Festival/Tokyo, the Hong Kong Arts Festival, and the Singapore International Festival of Arts; the Perth, Adelaide, Melbourne, and Sydney Festivals; the Delhi International Arts Festival; Iberoamericano in Bogotá, Colombia, Santiago a Mil in Chile, and the Festival Internacional de Buenos Aires in Argentina. Apart from the National Arts Festival in Grahamstown, South Africa, African festivals tend either to be diasporic or developmental, often through the support of western NGOs, and festivals in the Arab world are almost exclusively intracultural (see Chapter 5).

Chapter 4

1 The other co-creators were Michael Marinaccio and Tod Kimbro.

2 I will use EFF or 'the Fringe' when talking about the Edinburgh Festival Fringe and 'the Fringe' when talking about other specific fringe festivals with Fringe in their titles; I will use 'fringe' when talking about fringe festivals more generally.

3 For a succinct history of the founding and early years of Avignon 'Off' see Wehle 34–5.

4 The examples given here are from the 'PuShOFF' and 'Club PuSh' series that are part of Vancouver's PuSh Festival, and from the 'Nouvelle Scène' that featured young innovative local work at the Festival du théâtre des Amériques (FTA, now Festival TransAmériques) from 1997 to 2004. The Nouvelle Scène, as I have written elsewhere, was a worthy initiative 'because of the ways in which international festivals tend to delocalize and dehistoricize work, to privilege work created for the international circuit, and to reward

established works resulting from long gestation periods – as it showcased a group of younger, newer, or more experimental local work' ('Festival' 94; see also Knowles, 'Urban'; Morison). PushOFF operates in part as an industry mechanism for 'getting a group of international programmers into a room to see people's work' (Deborah Pearson, qtd in Zaiontz, 'Festival Sites' 155), while Club PuSh, 'a festival within a festival … programmes a multidisciplinary spread of experimental performance, music acts, film, and cabaret by national and local artists' (Zaiontz, 'Festival Sites' 164 n6).

5 There are curated fringe festivals, primarily in Europe, Asia, and the United States, that I don't consider here because they are not significantly different, structurally, from festivals discussed elsewhere in this volume, and most of them are not significantly international.

6 In 2019 the EFF topped 3 million in tickets sold, for 3,841 shows from 63 countries. There were also over 1,000 street performers.

7 Although my summary here is accurate as far as it goes, the distribution of and relationship between curated and uncurated, corporate and independent venues at the EFF is complex. For a detailed understanding see the 444-page document, 'The Fringe Guide to Choosing a Venue' (Edinburgh Festival Fringe Society).

8 I am indebted to Harvie, 'International', throughout my discussion of the EFF. Most of the world's fringe festivals function as neoliberal marketplaces in the ways Harvie describes, but most disguise this through the rhetoric of radical democracy or creative anarchy. The New Zealand Fringe, in Wellington, however, in its 2020 incarnation, used programme notes by Tim Brown, the Chair of one of its sponsors, explicitly to celebrate the fact that 'each Fringe production is an entrepreneurial experiment. The artistic equivalent of a start-up.'

9 By my estimation, during festival time on any given day each August there are well over 1,200 performances to choose from in what is, by world standards, a relatively small city (2017 population ca 540,000).

10 There was also a serially intercultural breakfast-time series of readings, the 'B!RTH Project', hosted at the Traverse Theatre, by women from the US, UK, India, and Syria on the subject of birth, said to be the world's 'sharpest moment of inequality'. See also Waterfield, for an account by a theatre-maker of 'social' plays at the EIF and EFF in 2014.

11 For a more complete account of the 'international intercultural' at the 2017 Edinburgh Fringe Festival see Knowles, 'Seeking'. See also Knowles, 'Festivals' and 'Not Just Counting Sheep'.

12 One of the major barriers to addressing these problems and inequities is that the Festival Fringe Society that runs the event receives only 6.5 per cent of its turnover from public subsidy – the equivalent of 1 per cent of the Fringe's box office intake. The EIF, by comparison, receives 25.3 per cent, while large European festivals receive 35.2 per cent government subsidy on average (Thomasson, 'Producing' 199).

13 According to Sarah Thomasson, Adelaide receives 18 per cent of its turnover from public subsidy, compared to the the EFF's 6.5 per cent ('Producing' 199).

14 Thomasson provides a long list of festivals of various kinds that take place in Adelaide in 'Mad March' ('Producing' 199). Although Edinburgh and Adelaide are among the world's best-known festival cities, they are so synchronically, primarily during their festival seasons, unlike (say) Montréal or Toronto, whose festivals span the calendar diachronically. Toronto's weekly alternative arts magazine, *Now*, includes among its events listings a regular listing of ten to twenty festivals of one kind or another virtually every week of the calendar year.

15 In addition to CAFF, there are the United States Association of Fringe Festivals (www.usaff.org), with 19 members; the World Fringe Alliance (www.worldfringealliance.com) with 10 members; and World Fringe: International Fringe Festival Association (www.worldfringe.com), with 263 members. Only CAFF restricts membership through the guiding principles outlined here.

16 This distinguishes CAFF fringe festivals from many others such as the Adelaide Fringe, which takes an administration fee from box office receipts.

17 See Knowles, *Performing*, for an account of Toronto's intercultural performance ecology.

18 For the festival's full 'Accessibility Manifesto' see Toronto Fringe, 'Accessibility Manifesto'.

19 Participation fees for those selected in the lottery range from CAD $551 to $760 depending on the house capacity throughout the run, and on participation category (Ontario, National, International, Dance, Kidfest, Teen, or Senior), which covers the venue rental. The information on the lotteries at the Toronto Fringe is drawn from Toronto Fringe, 'Lottery'.

20 The Toronto Fringe also supports various year-round programmes for youth, theatre artists, and the theatre community, and runs a Creation Lab with fully equipped creation spaces that can be rented for as little as CAD $6/hr.

21 In addition to Pizano, Schwellnus, and myself the delegation consisted of Sue Balint and Bruce Gibbons Fell (Aluna Theatre), Franco Boni and Aislinn Rose (The Theatre Centre), Majdi Bou-Matar (MT Space Theatre and the IMPACT Festival), Kelly Read (Why Not Theatre), Laura Nanni (the SummerWorks and Progress festivals), Naomi Campbell (the Luminato Festival), Keith Barker (Native Earth Performing Arts), Mark Hammond (the Sony Centre), and Denise Bolduc (independent producer).

22 FITB lost some of its original spirit after the death of its founder, Fanny Mikey, in 2008 (see Gener) and in more recent years has struggled financially and lost much of its local reputation because of a recurring failure to recompense local artists, who in 2018 were boycotting the festival. I did see good shows in 2018 from Slovenia, Argentina, Colombia, and Italy, but for the most part the line-up was from the International circuit's B-list and was dominated by populist spectacle, circus (always a prominent feature of Latin American festivals), and solo shows.

23 Although I have treated the street scene in Edinburgh here as a-fringe-of-a-fringe, I have not in this book included discussions of the many international festivals of street theatre, particularly in Europe, that have alternative status. A leading one is the Street Theatre Festival of Aurillac which, perhaps ironically, has its own 'off', or fringe festival of buskers (see Harris).

24 For details about the Forest Fringe microfestivals in Thailand and Japan, see Field, 'Forest Fringe Goes International;' for Toronto see Zaiontz, *Theatre & Festivals* 77–8.

25 I consider these festivals, taken together, to be international as well as intercultural, not only because of the intersectionality of queer nations at the events, but also because of the relationship they establish between Québec, a distinct nation with its own National Assembly within the nation-state of Canada, and 'ROC' (Rest of Canada).

26 The earliest disability arts festivals of which I am aware were in London in 1987; the first large international festival was the High Beam Festival in Adelaide, Australia in 1998. High Beam hosted many of the world's earliest disability theatre and dance companies but didn't survive the millennium's first decade. It was followed in Australia by the inaugural Awakenings Festival in Melbourne in 2007, which was attended by members of Aotearoa/New Zealand's Interacting Theatre Company, who returned to their Auckland base and in turn founded the ongoing InterAct Disability Arts Festival, which features both professional and community disability arts. Disability festivals in Canada also began early, with Art with Attitude at Toronto's Ryerson University in 2000 and the KickstART Festival in Vancouver in 2001, followed in short order by Calgary's Balancing Acts in 2002, Toronto's Madness and Arts World Festival in 2003, and the Abilities Arts Festival (now Tangled Art + Disability) in 2005, also in Toronto. In the UK the Liberty Festival, a Mayor of London event, was launched in 2003 and had its heyday in the mid-2000s but has recently been scaled back in both size and subversive attitude (see Pring). In the US, the Bodies of Work Festival was founded in Chicago in 2006, and in Europe Berlin's NO LIMITS Festival began in 2005 and the BIT festival was founded in Zagreb in 2009.

27 Many find the use of 'mad' offensive, but there is also a 'mad pride' movement among mental health services users, former users, and their allies to reclaim the word (see 'Mad Pride'). It is in this latter sense that it is used by Rendezvous with Madness, and that I quote it here.

28 In 2020 NO LIMITS festivals were planned for Barnsley, the biggest disability festival to date in the UK, and in Hong Kong.

29 For summaries of each of the festival's iterations see the 'archives' link on the website (Balancing Acts).

30 'Crip', too, as indicated in Chapter 3, is a short-form reclamation of the offensive labelling of people with disabilities as 'cripples'. It is used inclusively to refer to all disability cultures (see Mirk).

31 I am indebted to Keren Zaiontz for drawing my attention to *L'état d'urgence* and to her accounts of the 'manifestival' and of ATSA in her *Theatre & Festivals* (93–7) and 'Human Rights'.

32 Legislative Theatre is a variation on Augusto Boal's Forum Theatre, in which a short, issue-based play is staged, audience intervention is invited to 'solve' the issue, and discussion follows that often involves the establishment of mock legislatures who draft bills based on the solutions provided by the audience as 'spect-actors' (see Boal).

33 'Postmigrant theatre', what Lizzie Stewart calls a kind of 'pre-emptive self-labelling', refers to theatre in which immigrant and racialized characters and performers are not limited to their position *as* 'others'. See Stewart.

34 The shows referred to here are *Atlas des Kommunismus*, by Argentine actor-director Lola Arias and ensemble, directed by Arias; and *Clean City*, text and direction by Prodromos Tsinikoris and Anestis Azas (Greece).

Chapter 5

1 The comment drew attention to the lack of ethnic, cultural, religious, national, historical, or geographical commonalities across an 'Arab world' that extends geographically across artificially imposed borders from the Levant to Sudan and Somalia and from Mauritania to Oman. It extends culturally, moreover, from historic Syria to Egypt, Saudi Arabia, and the Emirates, united only by a language, classical Arabic, many of whose spoken dialects are virtually inscrutable to one another.

2 For a review of the 2018 iteration of the festival see Knowles, 'Arab'.

3 Although well worthy of consideration, apart from Toronto's hemispheric RUTAS festival, this chapter does not discuss the many and various festivals both within 'Latin America' and beyond that are dedicated to the Ibero-American world, which, because they include both Portuguese- and Spanish-speaking countries (though not always Spain or Portugal), are organized by somewhat different principles. For an overview of these see Graham-Jones.

4 International socialism (or proletarian internationalism), in counterdistinction to nation-reifying economic and diplomatic internationalisms, signifies a global class struggle against capitalism working toward a world revolution and leading to a stateless socialist world.

5 Another successor to the Dakar festival is the third World Festival of Black Arts (FESMAN) in 2010, the extensive programme for which is published in Gibbs, 'Theatre' 42–4. FESMAN, too had ambitions of uniting the diaspora and 'conveying a new vision of Africa as free, proud, creative and optimistic' (Niang 30, quoting President Abdoulaye Wade). And according to Amy Niang, 'At its best the festival was a unique moment of pure art, of Pan-African communion, during which time was frozen to let African genius shine and radiate to the rest of the world' (30). But it was also seen as Senegalese President and festival founder Abdoulaye Wade's extravagant attempt to leave

a personal legacy, costing the country £52 million at a time when it was rife with poverty and in social and political crisis. 'Ordinary people felt alienated from the festival' according to Niang (30), and it prompted Ghanaian novelist Ayi Kwei Armah to conclude that festivals were 'wasteful demonstrations of intellectual bankruptcy' (qtd in Gibbs, 'Theatre' 41).

6 They may also be seen as the predecessors of Marché des Arts du Spectacle Africain (MASA), a biennial festival founded in 1993 in Abidjan, Côte d'Ivoire as a platform for promoting African performing arts. MASA continues to serve as a meeting and networking place for professional and non-professional artists but has never had the profile or global impact of either its predecessors or PANAFEST.

7 Dakar has a largely Muslim population of ca 2.5 million, Algiers a largely Arab-Berber population of ca 5 million, many of whom are Sunni Muslim, and is located on the Mediterranean rather than the Atlantic Coast, and Lagos is the most populous city on the continent with a population of between 8 and 21 million. It is a major financial and government centre, a major port, and a traditional 'melting pot' for European and African cultures with a majority Christian but major Muslim population.

8 For a useful annotated bibliography of PANAFEST organized chronologically to 2012 see Gibbs, 'PANAFEST'.

9 Katharina Schramm refers to 'the appropriation of the festival by the state' (266).

10 Emancipation Day – 'the day set aside for the celebration of emancipation of slaves in the Americas and the Caribbean' ('Celebrating') – began to be celebrated in Ghana in 1998 – the year it became part of PANAFEST – after encouragement to do so came from diplomatic sources in Trinidad. Thanks to Rhoma Spencer for drawing my attention to this.

11 A durbar, loosely, is a kind of public reception, with the Chiefs holding court.

12 This information and prioritization are taken from the programme for the 2019 festival. See Panafest.

13 CAIFESTA also had a predecessor, the first Caribbean Festival of the Arts, held in San Juan, Puerto Rico in 1952 (see CARIFESTA CIV, 'History'), the year that Puerto Rico was proclaimed a Commonwealth, though it remained (and remains) a territory of the United States.

14 More detailed 'objectives' of the festival are more fulsomely laid out on the current web page (see CARIFESTA XIV, 'History') as follows:

> To establish and celebrate the arts as the most important dynamic force for reflection on our dreams and visions in the process of self-affirmation of the Caribbean personality
> To maximize people's participation in the arts, promote integration and intensify the interaction between the people and the artists of the Region
> To deepen the awareness and knowledge of the diverse aspirations within the Caribbean Community through an on-going process of exposing the peoples of the Region to each other culturally by means of the development of our creativity

To embrace developments in communications technology and the media – while accepting the challenge this technology poses – to positively advance our culture at home, throughout the diaspora and the world, despite the fact that that same technology appears to be challenging established traditions

To foster a vision of Caribbean unity and possibility by facilitating the documenting and disseminating of artworks as highlights of the ongoing historical and cultural development of our people

To expose children and Caribbean youth to the arts and traditions of the Region as a basis for building vibrant and dynamic institutional support for their development as citizens of the future Caribbean

To encourage excellence by bringing masters and youth together to initiate systems of apprenticeship for young artists

To promote the development of cultural industries and merchandising in order to maximize the economic potential of CARIFESTA and the arts, for the benefit of the artists and Caribbean societies as a whole.

15 For an account of the development of 'a womban-centred Afro-Caribbean diasporic performance aesthetic' in Toronto, see Knowles, *Performing* 109–26.

16 For a more detailed account of CARIFESTA XIV in 2019 see Knowles, 'Canada Comes'.

17 SOCA ('Soul of Calypso'), is a popular form of up-tempo music driven by bass and drum that developed out of a fusion of calypso, funk, soul, and zouk in Trinidad in the early 1970s. 'Chutney SOCA' is one of the original styles that features the influence of East Indian musical forms and includes lyrics in Hindi.

18 Indentured workers arrived from India to replace enslaved Africans in the wake of emancipation in 1834, and faced conditions little better than they had been for the Africans (see Singh). The Hosay riots (or the Jahaji or Muharram massacre) took place on 30 October 1884, when British colonial police fired on participants in the annual Hosay procession (the Shi'a Festival of Muharram). See Caribbean Muslims.

19 Information on the Zébrures d'automne 2019 programme is from Les Francophonies.

20 Lusotropicalism is a discredited theory of 'racial democracy' first proposed by Brazilian sociologist Gilberto Freyre in the mid twentieth century. It argued that Portuguese imperialism was fundamentally benevolent because Portuguese colonizers were themselves ethnically hybrid, adapted well to tropical conditions, and married local women. The theory persists in the myth that there is no racism in Brazil. See McMahon 16–17, 36–8, 60.

21 Brazil's historical relationship to Portugal's former colonies in Africa includes its active participation in the transatlantic slave trade. For Brazil's recent economic ambitions in lusophone Africa see Vinícius de Freitas. Jair Bolsonaro's ascendancy to the presidency in January 2019 has deepened concerns about Brazilian imperialism aboad and at home, particularly in relation to Brazil's Indigenous poplulation.

22 These are Portugal, Brazil, Cape Verde, Angola, Mozambique, Guinea-Bissau, East Timor, São Tomé and Principé, Equitorial Guinea (since 2007), and Macau (a special administrative region of China). Fifteen per cent of Uruguay's population speaks Portuguese, but it is not an official language.

23 My account of Mindelact follows McMahon 68–129.

24 For the disctinctions between Repressive and Ideological State Apparatuses as mechanisms of control see Althusser.

25 I am indebted to Kim's essay throughout my discussion of BeSeTo.

26 I am directly indebted to Goldstein's 'Staging East Africa through Global Exchange' throughout my discussion of KITF.

27 The Luyha are a group of Bantu tribes that constitute the second largest ethnic group in Kenya; the Luo are a Nilotic (Nile Valley) ethnic group in western Kenya and northern Tanzania. Goldstein points out that 'Namwalie's embrace of performance traditions from multiple Kenyan ethnic groups eschews the narrow promotion of her own ethnic identity, emphasizing, rather, expression of the diversity of the region's ethnic groups – an act with particular political significance after the ethnically-charged post-election violence that flared up in Kenya in 2007 and 2008' ('Staging' 170).

28 I have attended RUTAS not only as an audience member and as a member of the creative team of the MT Space production of *Amal* but also as a member of the board of directors of Aluna Theatre, which produces the festival.

29 The company also runs fundraising campaigns inviting individual donors to contribute to bursary programmes for underprivileged artists and students to participate in the festival, including the artist workshops, helping to fulfill the mandates of accessibility and inclusiveness.

30 Budget figures are for the 2018 festival. 76 per cent of RUTAS funding comes from three levels of government in Canada, 9 per cent from donors and sponsors, and 14 per cent from earned income (box office, co-productions, and workshop fees). 27 per cent is spent on artist fees, 20 per cent on labour, 9 per cent on production expenses (supplies, running costs, etc.), 6 per cent on venue rentals, 14 per cent on travel and hospitality, 10 per cent on marketing, and 9 per cent on administration fees. The festival broke even in 2018, with a surplus of CAD $1,710.11. Budget figures were generously provided by Trevor Schwellnus.

31 According to Alvarez and in my own experience, 'these social nights have been pivotal to the realization of Aluna's larger aims to build a community of Latinx-Indigenous alliances' ('Roots' 31).

32 For 'minor transnationalism' see Lionnet and Shih.

Conclusion

1 For 'wise practices' as opposed to 'best practices' in the discourses of Indigenous community development see the Introduction to this volume, note 18.

2 I am focusing here on intercultural issues. For a discussion of ways in which other problems with the open access model are being or might be addressed at the Edinburgh Fringe, see Harvie, 'International', 112–16.

3 For an article addressing 'the politics informing the act of interpretation' through translation (26) that asks such questions as what happens when 'the invisibility of the act of translation' is disrupted (27) see Liebembuk.

4 Again, full disclosure: I served this production as dramaturg.

Work Cited

3. Berliner Herbstsalon. Progamme, 11–26 November 2017.

Abaka, Edmund Kobina. *House of Slaves and Door of No Return: Gold Coast/ Ghana Slave Forts, Castles and Dungeons and the Atlantic Slave Trade.* Trenton, NJ: Africa World Press, 2012.

Addo, Edward. 'The Golden Jubilee of Independence and Panafest in Ghana: "All that Glitters Is Not Gold."' *Controversies in Tourism.* Ed. Omar Moufakkir and Peter M. Burns. Wallingford and Cambridge, Mass.: CABI, 2012. 186–200.

Adelaide Fringe. 'Annual Review 2019.' https://adelaidefringe.com.au/2019-annual-review. 26 June 2021.

'Manifesto.' https://adelaidefringe.com.au/manifesto. 12 December 2019.

Adrover, Lauren, David A. Donkor, and Christina S. McMahon. 'The Ethics and Pragmatics of Making Heritage a Commodity: Ghana's PANAFEST 2009.' *TDR (The Drama Review)* 54.2 (2010): 155–63.

Alfred, Taiaiake. 'Sovereignty.' *A Companion to American Indian History.* Ed. Philip J. Deloria and Neal Salisbury. Malden, Mass.: John Wiley & Sons, 2002. 460–74.

Allen, Chadwick. 'Decolonizing Comparison: Towards a Trans-Indigenous Literary Studies.' *The Oxford Handbook of Indigenous American Literature.* Ed. James H. Cox and Daniel Heath Justice. Oxford: Oxford UP, 2014. 377–94.

'Performing Serpent Mound: A Trans-Indigenous Meditation.' *Theatre Journal* 67.3 (2015): 391–411.

Trans-Indigenous: Methodologies for Global Literary Studies. Minneapolis: U of Minnesota P, 2012.

Allen, Rose Mary. 'Music in Diasporic Context: The Case of Curaçao and Intra-Caribbean Migration.' *Black Music Research Journal* 32.2 (2012): 51–65.

Althusser, Louis. 'Ideology and Ideological State Apparatuses (Notes towards and Investigation).' *Lenin and Philosophy and Other Essays.* Trans. Ben Brewster. New York: Monthly Review Press, 1971. 127–86.

Aluna Theatre. 'Connecting the Americas through the Arts.' Programme Note. panamerican ROUTES | RUTAS panamericanas 2016, Daniels Spectrum, Toronto. 1.

Alvarez, Natalie. 'Roots, Routes, RUTAS.' *Theatre Research in Canada/Recherches théâtrales au Canada* 30.1–2 (2019): 27–41.

'RUTAS | ROUTES: A Festival Commons of Hemispheric *Interculturalidad.*' Knowles (ed.), *Cambridge Companion*, 239–53.

Alvarez, Natalie, Sasha Kovacs, and Jimena Ortuzar. 'Performance and Human Rights in the Americas.' *Canadian Theatre Review* 161 (2015): 5–8.

Amine, Khalid. 'Theatre Festivals in Post-Arab Spring Countries.' Knowles (ed.), *Cambridge Companion*, 147–61.

Anaya, S. James. *Indigenous Peoples in International Law*. New York: Oxford UP, 1996.

Anderson, Benedict. *Imagined Communities: Reflections on the Origin and Spread of Nationalism*. Revised Edn. London: Verso, 1983.

Anderson, Michèle. 'Democratizing *Luminato*: Private-Public Partnerships Hang in Delicate Balance.' Report of the Toronto Culture Working Group, Robarts Centre for Canadian Studies, 15 September 2009. http://robarts.info.yorku .ca/archives/toronto-public-culture-working-group. 20 November 2019.

Angel, Michael R. *Discordant Voices, Conflicting Visions: Ojibwa and Euro-American Perspectives on the Midewiwin*. PhD Dissertation, University of Manitoba, 1997.

'Anishinaabe Mino Bimaadizwin: Principles for Anishinaabe Education.' www .renaud.ca/public/Aboriginal/Mino-Bimaadizwin-Principles-for-Education .pdf. 7 March 2019.

Anonymous. 'Caribbean Artists Kept in "State of Deprivation" – Nobel Laureate.' *Caribbean Today* 19.10 (2008): 15.

ANTI. https://antifestival.com/en. 14 January 2020.

'Maria Cruz Correira (BE): Voice of Nature: The Trial.' https://antifestival .com/en/tapahtuma/maria-lucia-cruz-correia-be-voice-of-nature-the-trial/ #more-4264. 1 February 2020.

Appadurai, Arjun. 'Disjuncture and Difference in the Global Cultural Economy.' *Public Culture* 2.2 (1990): 1–23.

Modernity at Large: Cultural Dimensions of Globalization. Minneapolis: U of Minnesota P, 1996.

Arestis, Stefan. 'The 10 Best Gay Theatre Festivals around the World.' *Nomadic Boys* 28 July 2019. https://nomadicboys.com/gay-theatre-festivals-around-the-world. 2 January 2020.

Armstrong, Neil. 'Canada Sends First Caribbean Diaspora Delegation of Performers to Carifesta; Seeks Community Support.' Pride 27 June 2017, http://pridenews.ca/2017/06/27/canada-sends-first-caribbean-diaspora-dele gation-performers-carifesta-seeks-community-support. 26 June 2021.

Arte Institute. 'FITEI:International Theatre Festival of Iberian Expression.' www .arteinstitute.org/posts/view/384/34. 21 January 2019.

'ATSA.' https://fr.wikipedia.org/wiki/ATSA. 8 January 2020.

Australian Government. *Guidelines: Major Festivals Initiative*. www.arts.gov.au/ sites/default/files/FINAL%20Major%20Festivals%20Initiative%20Guide lines.pdf?acsf_files_redirect. 9 March 2020.

Balancing Acts: Calgary's Annual Disabilty Arts Festival. www.balancing-acts.org/ about.htm. 7 January 2020.

Baltic Circle. https://web.archive.org/web/20160213142230/https://balticcircle .fi/en/info. 26 June 2021.

'About Us.' Web content no longer available. Accessed 11 January 2020.

'Bangarra Dance Theatre Performance of "Bennelong." www.youtube.com/ watch?v=DEqfQhVhb1U. 20 March 2020.

Bannerji, Himani. *The Dark Side of the Nation: Essays on Multiculturalism, Nationhood, and Gender.* Toronto: Canadian Scholars, 2000.

Barker, Clive. 'The Possibilities and Politics of Intercultural Penentration and Exchange.' *The Intercultural Performance Reader.* Ed. Patrice Pavis. London: Routledge, 1996. 247–56.

Barron, Zoe. 'Cloudstreet, Perth Festival (WA).' *Performing ArtsHub* 24 February 2020. https://performing.artshub.com.au/news-article/reviews/performing-arts/zoe-barron/review-cloudstreet-perth-festival-wa-259847. 10 March 2020.

Bayimba. 'About.' http://bayimba.org/about. 23 February 2019.

Bergman, S. Bear. 'Review: How I Learned to Serve Tea (Progress Festival/Why Not Theatre.' *Mooney on Theatre* 16 February 2020. www.mooneyontheatre .com/2020/02/16/review-how-i-learned-to-serve-tea-progress-festival-whynot-theatre. 17 February 2020.

Berlant, Lauren. *Cruel Optimism.* Durham, NC: Duke UP, 2011.

Beyond Calligraphy. 'Flying White.' www.beyondcalligraphy.com/flying_white_script.html. 26 January 2020.

Bhabha, Homi. *The Location of Culture.* London: Routledge, 1994.

Bhagirat-Rivera, Ramaesh Joseph. 'Between Pan-Africanism and a Multiracial Nation: Race, Regionalism, and Guyanese Nation-Building through the Caribbean Festival of Creative Arts (CARIFESTA), 1972.' *Interventions* 20.7 (13 July 2018): 1022–36.

Bickel, Julika. 'Wedding with Obstacles.' *Nacht kritik.de.* https://translate.google .com/translate?hl=en&sl=de&u=https://nachtkritik.de/index.php%3Foption %3Dcom_content%26view%3Darticle%26id%3D14629:8-no-limits-festival-2017-das-festival-fuers-inklusionstheater-in-berlin-zeigt-als-schwerpunkt-diesmal-auch-arbeiten-mit-gehoerlosen-performern-und-verabschiedet-sich-von-jerome-bels-disabled-theater%26catid%3D53%26Itemid%3D83&prev= search. 8 January 2020.

Billington, Michael. 'The Doctor Review – Robert Icke Offers Brilliant Diagnosis of Modern Ills.' *The Guardian* 21 August 2019. www.theguardian.com/ stage/2019/aug/21/the-doctor-review-robert-icke-juliet-stevenson-almeida. 11 March 2020.

Bishop, Nancy. 'Review: *Andares* at Chicago Shakes Introduces Indigenous People of Mexico with Stories and Song.' *3CR Third Coast Review* 28 October 2019. https://thirdcoastreview.com/2019/10/24/review-andares-at-chicago-shakes-intro duces-indigenous-people-of-mexico-with-stories-and-song. 15 February 2020.

Bissoondath, Neil. *Selling Illusions: The Cult of Multiculturalism in Canada.* Toronto: Penguin, 1994.

Blair, Kelsey. 'The Body Labours Sonorously in Foxconn Frequency (no. 3) (PuSh Festival).' *Theatre Times* 7 May 2018. https://thetheatretimes.com/

review-body-labours-sonorously-foxconn-frequency-no-3-push-festival. 26 June 2020.

Blood on the Dance Floor. Programme. By Jacob Boehme. Prod. ILBIJERRI Theatre Company at the Progress Festival, Toronto, 30 January–17 February 2019.

Boal, Augusto. *Legislative Theatre: Using Performance to Make Politics.* Trans. Adrian Jackson. London: Routledge, 1998.

Bold, Christine. 'Princess White Deer's Show Blanket: Brokering Popular Indigenous Performance across International Borders.' *Theatre Research in Canada/Recherches théâtrales au Canada* 41.1 (2020): 39–63.

Bonfiglio, Florencia. 'Notes on the Caribbean Essay from an Archipalegic Perspective (Kamau Brathwaite, Édouard Glissant and Antonio Benítez Roho).' *Caribbean Studies* 43.1 (2015): 147–73.

Boon, Maxim. 'Wesley Enoch Unpacks His Sydney Festival Blak Out Season.' *Audrey Journal: Sydney's Arts Journal* 8 January 2018. www.audreyjournal.com .au/arts/wesley-enoch-unpacks-sydney-festival-blak-season. 10 September 2018.

Bourriaud, Nicolas. *The Radicant.* Trans. James Gusson and Lili Porten. New York: Lucas & Sternberg, 2009.

Bradby, David, and Maria Delgado. Editorial. *Contemporary Theatre Review* 13.4 (2003): 1–4.

Bramwell, Murray Ross. 'Festival Fractured by Chaos. Adelaide Festival 2002 [review].' *The Australian* 15 March 2002. https://dspace.flinders.edu.au/ xmlui/bitstream/handle/2328/280/AdFestAust12March02v2.pdf?sequence= 1&isAllowed=y. 10 March 2019.

Brantley, Ben, Jesse Green, and Laura Collins-Hughes. 'At Under the Radar, Avant Garde Shows Leap Outside Reality.' *New York Times* 17 January 2020. www.nytimes.com/2020/01/17/theater/under-the-radar-festival.html. 7 April 2020.

Brave Festival. www.bravefestival.pl/en. 29 August 2018.

Brissenden, Alan. 'Festival Review: *Black Velvet.*' *The Adelaide Review* 1 March 2020. https://web.archive.org/web/20200804001356/https://www.adelaidereview .com.au/arts/performing-arts/2020/03/01/festival-review-black-velvet. 26 June 2021.

British Council Australia. 'Unlimited Festival and Symposium 2018.' www .britishcouncil.org.au/unlimited-festival-and-symposium-2018. 7 January 2020.

Brown, Tim. 'Fringe 2020; The Biggest Yet.' *Wellington NZ Fringe Arts Festival Event Programme.* 28 February–21 March 2020. 7.

Budde, Antje, and Sebastian Samur. 'Making Knowledge/Playing Culture: Theatre Festivals as Sites of Experiential Learning.' *Theatre Research in Canada/Recherches théâtrales au Canada* 40.1–2 (2019): 83–101.

Burkett, Ronnie. 'Illuminating Thoughts: Ronnie Burkett on Forget Me Not.' Luminato, 26 April 2019. https://web.archive.org/web/20200811102442/ https://luminatofestival.com/Blog/April-2019/Illuminating-Thoughts-Ronnie-Burkett-on-Forget-Me. 26 June 2021.

Byrd, Jodie A. *The Transit of Empire*. Minneapolis: U of Minnesota P, 2011.

Byrne, Tim. 'Cloudstreet Review.' *Time Out Melbourne* 13 May 2019. www
.timeout.com/melbourne/theatre/cloudstreet-review. 10 March 2020.

Cade, Rosana. 'The Radical Art of Holding Hands with Strangers.' *The Guardian*
18 August 2016. www.theguardian.com/artanddesign/2016/aug/18/radical-
art-of-holding-hands-with-strangers-rosana-cade-walking-holding. 1 January
2020.

Calliou, Brian. 'Wise Practices in Indigenous Community Economic
Development.' *Inditerra: Revue internationale sur l'Autochtonie* 4 (2012):
14–26. https://ccednet-rcdec.ca/sites/ccednet-rcdec.ca/files/wise_practices_
in_indigenous_community_economic_development.pdf. 27 August 2020.

Campana, François. 'The Africa of Festivals: Bringing People Together.' Trans.
Joel Anderson. *Contemporary Theatre Review* 13.4 (2003): 48–56.

Capelle, Laura. 'At Avignon Festival, Lots of Imagination on Show, but Few
Women.' *New York Times* 19 July 2018. www.nytimes.com/2018/07/19/
theater/france-avignon-festival-theater.html. 3 May 2019.

Caribbean Muslims: News, History, Culture & Religion. 'The Hosay or
Muharram Massacre of 1884 in Trinidad.' 4 November 2012. www
.caribbeanmuslims.com/the-hosay-or-muharram-massacre-of-1884-in-trinidad.
17 November 2017.

CARICOM Caribbean Community. 'CARIFESTA.' https://caricom.org/cari
festa. 21 February 2019.

CARIFESTA XIV. 'CARIFESTA Archives.' https://2019.carifesta.net/carifesta-
archives. 26 June 2021.

'History of the CARIFESTA.' https://2019.carifesta.net/history-of-carifesta. 26
June 2021.

Carter, Jill. '"It's About Becoming": Indigenating Research Practice at the
CDTPS.' *Theatre Research in Canada/Recherches théâtrales au Canada* 39.1
(2018): 242–51.

Carter, Jill, Heather Davis-Fisch, and Ric Knowles. 'Circulations: Visual
Sovereignty, Transmotion, and Tribalography.' *A Cultural History of
Theatre in the Modern Age*. Ed. Kim Solga. London: Bloomsbury, 2017.
95–116.

Carter, Jill, Karyn Recollet, and Dylan Robinson. 'Interventions into the
Maw of Old World Hunger.' *Canadian Performance Histories and
Historiographies*. Ed. Heather Davis-Fisch. Toronto: Playwrights Canada P,
2017. 205–31.

Catanese, Brandi Wilkins. *The Problem of the Color[blind]: Racial Transgression
and the Politics of Black Performance*. Ann Arbor: U of Michigan P, 2011.

Caust, Jo. 'A Festival in Disarray: The 2002 Adelaide Festival: A Debacle or
Another Model of Arts Organization and Leadership?' *Journal of Arts
Management, Law, and Society*, 34.2 (2004): 103–18.

Caust, Jo, and Hilary Glow. 'Festivals, Artists and Entrepreneurialism: The Role
of the Adelaide Fringe Festival.' *International Journal of Event Management
Research* 6.2 (2011): 1–14.

'Celebrating Ghana's Emancipation from Slavery.' GhanaWeb 28 July 2018. www.ghanaweb.com/GhanaHomePage/entertainment/Celebrating-Ghana-s-emancipation-from-slavery-672661#. 22 August 2019.

Chalcraft, Jasper, Gerard Delanty, and Monica Sassatelli. 'Varieties of Cosmopolitanism in Arts Festivals.' *The Festivalization of Culture*. Ed. Andy Bennett, Jodie Taylor, and Ian Woodward. Farnham, Surrey: Ashgate, 2014. 109–29.

Chalcraft, Jasper, and Paolo Magaudda. '"Space Is the Place": The Global Localities of the Sónar and WOMAD Music Festivals.' Giorgi et al. (eds.), *Festivals*, 173–89.

Clifford, James. *Routes: Travel and Translation in the Late Twentieth Century*. Cambridge, Mass.: Harvard UP, 1997.

Clutesi, George. *Potlatch*. Sidney, BC: Gray's Publishing, 1969.

Commanda, Erica. 'Spiderwomen Theatre's Muriel Miguel on Material Witness.' *Muskrat Magazine* 25 July 2017. http://muskratmagazine.com/spider woman-theatres-material-witness. 18 September 2018.

Communitech. 'True North Festival.' https://web.archive.org/web/20180303130828/http://truenorthwaterloo.com/festival. 26 June 2021.

Cotter, Lucy. 'Plants as Other: Manuela Infante's Estado Vegetal.' *Mousse Magazine*. http://moussemagazine.it/manuela-infante-lucy-cotter-2019. 3 February 2020.

Coughlan, Matt. 'Awakenings Festival, Art Is. . . Festival to Team Up.' *Wimmera Mail-Times* 14 May 2104. www.mailtimes.com.au/story/2282111/awaken ings-festival-art-is-festival-to-team-up. 6 January 2020.

Coulthard, Glen Sean. *Red Skin, White Masks: Rejecting the Colonial Politics of Recognition*. Minneapolis: U of Minnesota P, 2014.

Cowan, T.L. 'Cabaret at Grunt: Up Your Community.' *Queer Intersections: Vancouver Performance in the 1990s*. 2012. https://performance .gruntarchives.org/essay-cabaret-at-grunt.html. 4 January 2020.

Cowan, T.L., Moynan King, and Miriam Ginestier '*Edgy + Hysteria*: Not Like Sisters, Like Lovers, Comrades, Peers; or, How Montreal's Edgy Women Festival and Toronto's *Hysteria Festival* Got It on across Space and Time.' *Theatre Research in Canada/Recherches théâtrales au Canada* 40.1–2 (2019): 118–34.

Dakin, K.J., and Trina Moyles. 'Indigenous Farmers Confront Canada's Goldcorp.' *Briarpatch* 1 September 2014. https://briarpatchmagazine.com/articles/view/indigenous-farmers-confront-canadas-goldcorp. 20 January 2020.

Davidson, Helen. 'Garma Festival: Indigenous Sovereignty Would Be a "Gift for All Australians".' *The Guardian* 3 August 2018. www.theguardian.com/australia-news/2018/aug/04/garma-festival-indigenous-sovereignty-would-be-a-gift-for-all-australians. 12 September 2018.

Delaney, Brigid. 'Ganesh Versus the Third Reich: "Do We Have the Right to Perform This?"' *The Guardian* 8 August 2014. www.theguardian.com/stage/2014/aug/08/ganesh-versus-third-reich-edinburgh-festival-2014. 25 April 2019.

Delanty, Gerard. 'Conclusion: On the Cultural Significance of Arts Festivals.' Giorgi et al. (eds.), *Festivals*, 190–8.

Deleuze, Gilles, and Félix Guattari. *Anti-Oedipus: Capitalism and Schizophrenia.* Trans. Robert Hurley, Mark Seem, and Helen R. Lane. Minneapolis: U of Minnesota P, 1983.

Deloria, Philip J. *Playing Indian.* New Haven, Conn.: Yale UP, 1998.

'Demograhics of Metro Vancouver.' *Wikipedia.* https://en.wikipedia.org/wiki/ Demographics_of_Metro_Vancouver. 12 February 2020.

'Deportation with a Layover: Failure of Protection under the US-Guatemala Asylum Co-operative Agreement.' *Human Rights Watch* 19 May 2020. www.hrw.org/report/2020/05/19/deportation-layover/failure-protection-under-us-guatemala-asylum-cooperative. 27 September 2020.

Dickinson, Peter. 'PuSh.' Email to Ric Knowles 22 January 2020.

'PuShing Performance Brands in Vancouver.' *Theatre Research in Canada/ Recherches théâtrales au Canada*, 35.2 (2014): 130–50.

'Waka/Ciimaan/Vaka Workshop at SFU Woodwards.' *Performance, Place, and Politics* blog 21 August 2016. http://performanceplacepolitics.blogspot.com/ 2016/08/wakaciimaanvaka-workshop-at-sfu.html. 17 November 2019.

Dillon, Grace (ed.). *Walking the Clouds: An Anthology of Indigenous Science Fiction.* Tucson: U of Arizona P, 2012.

'The Dish with One Spoon.' *Indian Time* 5 August 2010. www.indiantime.net/ story/2010/08/05/cultural-corner/the-dish-with-one-spoon/7510.html. 10 April 2020.

'The Doctor, Duke of York's Theatre.' *Culture Whisper.* www.culturewhisper .com/r/theatre/the_doctor_almeida_theatre/13912. 11 March 2020.

Doğan, Evinç. 'City as Spectacle: The Festivalization of Culture in Contemporary Istanbul.' *Young Minds Rethinking the Mediterranean* (2011): 69–93.

Duffy, Michelle. 'The Emotional Ecologies of Festivals.' *The Festivalization of Culture.* Ed. Andy Bennett, Jodie Taylor, and Ian Woodward. Farnham, Surrey: Ashgate, 2014. 229–49.

Edinburgh Festival Fringe. 'Fringe Central Events Programme 2017.' Edinburgh Festival Fringe Society, 2017.

Edinburgh Festival Fringe Society. 'The Fringe Handbook for Choosing a Venue.' http://edfringe.s3.amazonaws.com/uploads/docs/venues/Fringe-guide-to-choosing-a-venue.pdf. 7 August 2019.

Edinburgh International Festival. *Edinburgh International Festival 2–26 August 2019.* Programme. Edinburgh International Festival, 2019.

Ellis-Peterson, Hannah. 'Arab Arts Showcase at Edinburgh Fringe Beset by Visa Difficulties.' *The Guardian* 17 August 2017. www.theguardian.com/uk-news/2017/aug/17/arab-arts-showcase-at-edinburgh-fringe-beset-by-visa-difficulties. 23 February 2018.

English, James F. 'Festivals and the Geography of Culture: African Cinema and the "World Space" of Its Public.' Giorgi et al. (eds.), *Festivals*, 63–78.

Enoch, Wesley. 'If You Remove Language, You're Also Removing Knowledge of Landscape.' British Council 13 August 2018. www.britishcouncil.org/

voices-magazine/wesley-enoch-sydney-festival-edinburgh-international-cul
ture-summit. 2 September 2018.

'That's a Wrap on #sydfest 2018!' https://2019.sydneyfestival.org.au/stories/
2018-thanks-wesley. 7 April 2020.

Enos, Tony. '8 Things You Should Know about Two Spirit People.' *Indian
Country Today* 28 March 2017. https://indiancountrytoday.com/archive/8-
misconceptions-things-know-two-spirit-people. 26 June 2021.

Essah, Patience. 'Slavery, Heritage and Tourism in Ghana.' *International Journal
of Hospitality & Tourism Administration* 2.3–4 (2001): 31–49.

Exhale Dance Tribe. http://exhaledancetribe.com. 14 March 2020.

Falassi, Alessandro (ed.). *Time Out of Time: Essays on the Festival.* Albuquerque: U
of New Mexico P, 1967.

Falconi, Jorge Perez. 'Space and Festivalscapes.' *Platform* 5.2 (2011): 12–27.

Favel, Floyd. 'Theatre: Younger Brother of Tradition.' *Native Theatre, Native
Earth: Celebrating Twenty-Five Years of Native Earth Performing Arts, Inc.*
Toronto: Native Earth Performing Arts, 2007. 30–4.

Fenton, Rose, and Lucy Neal. *The Turning World.* London: Calouste Gulbenkian
Foundation, 2005.

Ferdman, Bertie. 'From Content to Context: The Emergence of the Performance
Curator.' *Theater* 44.2 (2014): 5–19.

Ferguson, Alex Lazardis. 'Symbolic Capital and Relationships of Flow: Canada,
Europe, and the International Performing Arts Circuit.' *Theatre Research in
Canada/Recherches théâtrales au Canada* 34.1 (2013): 97–124.

Ferreira, Eunice. 'Mindelact. The Tenth Annual International Theatre Festival of
Mindelo.' *Theatre Journal* 57.2 (2005): 272–7.

'Festival international de théâtre pour le développement (FITB) à Ouagadougou.'
routard.com. www.routard.com/guide_agenda_detail/7898/festival_interna
tional_de_theatre_pour_le_developpement_(fitb)_a_ouagadougou.htm. 9
January 2020.

'FESTLIP Arrives at the 10th Edition and Honors in Rio's Portuguese Theatre
Company.' *Portugal Digital* 25 October 2018. https://vaaju.com/portugal/
festlip-arrives-at-the-10th-edition-and-honors-in-rios-portuguese-theater-
company. 7 February 2019.

Fida, Kashmala. 'Sound Off: Canada's Only Deaf Theatre Festival Returns with
More Performances' *The Star* 3 February 2019. www.thestar.com/edmon
ton/2019/02/03/sound-off-canadas-only-deaf-theatre-festival-returns-with-
more-performances.html. 7 January 2020.

Field, Andy. 'Forest Fringe Goes International.' British Council 24 May 2013.
https://theatreanddance.britishcouncil.org/blog/2013/05/forest-fringe-goes-
international. 1 January 2020.

Field, Andy, Tania El Khoury, Farah Saleh, Christopher Haydon, Alice Yousef,
Henry Bell, Rachel McCrum, and Harry Giles. 'Welcome to the Fringe.'
Contemporary Theatre Review – Interventions February 2016. www
.contemporarytheatrereview.org/2016/welcome-to-the-fringe/. 10 September
2019.

Finkel, Rebecca. 'A Picture of the Contemporary Combined Arts Festival Landscape.' *Cultural Trends* 18.1 (2009): 3–21.

Fischer-Lichte, Erika. 'European Festivals.' Knowles (ed.), *Cambridge Companion*, 87–100.

The Routledge Introduction to Theatre and Performance Studies. Ed. Minou Arjomand and Ramona Mosse. Trans. Minou Arjomand. London: Routledge, 2014.

Tragedy's Endurance: Performances of Greek Tragedies and Cultural Identity in Germany since 1800. Oxford: Oxford UP, 2017.

Flight. Programme note. Edinburgh International Festival 2017.

Florida, Richard. *Cities and the Creative Class.* New York: Routledge, 2005.

The Rise of the Creative Class and How It's Transforming Work, Leisure, Community and Everyday Life. New York: Basic Books, 2002.

Forest Fringe. https://forestfringe.co.uk. 31 December 2019.

'Paper Stages.' https://forestfringe.co.uk/project/paper-stages-2012. 31 December 2019.

Foucault, Michel. 'Of Other Spaces.' *Diacritics* 16.1 (1986): 22–7.

Preface. *The Order of Things: An Archaeology of the Human Sciences.* New York: Vintage, 1973. xv–xxiv.

Les Francophonies en Limousin. 'Projet artistique: Missions' www.lesfrancophonies.fr/Missions. 23 November 2018.

Free Festival. 'August 6–30 2020.' www.freefestival.co.uk. 31 December 2019.

'Perform with Us.' https://freefestival.co.uk/Perform_With_Us.aspx. 31 December 2019.

'Theatre Shows.' www.freefestival.co.uk/Genre.aspx?GenreID=2&GenreName=Theatre. 31 December 2019.

Freire, Paulo. *Pedagogy of the Oppressed.* Trans. Myra Bergman Ramos. New York: Bloomsbury Academic, 2018.

Frew, Elspeth A., and Jane Ali-Knight. 'Creating High and Low Art: Experimentation and Commercialization at Fringe Festivals.' *Tourism, Culture & Communication* 10.3 (2010): 231–45.

Frey, Heather Fitzsimmons. 'A Small Festival for Small People: The WeeFestival as Advocacy.' *Theatre Research in Canada/Recherches théâtrales au Canada* 40.1–2 (2019): 64–82.

Fricker, Karen. 'Tourism, the Festival Marketplace and Robert Lepage's *The Seven Streams of the River Ota*.' *Contemporary Theatre Review* 13.4 (2003): 79–93.

Friedman, Sam. 'The Hidden Tastemakers: Comedy Scouts as Cultural Brokers at the Edinburgh Festival Fringe.' *Poetics* 44 (2014): 22–41.

Fringe Festivals. 'About Caff.' https://fringefestivals.com/about-caff. 10 September 2019.

Frisch, Norman. 'Creative Interactions: Norman Frisch Interviewed by Tom Sellar.' *Theater* 44.2 (2014): 47–61.

FTA. 'Historique.' https://fta.ca/historique-2. 26 June 2021.

Full Circle First Nations Performance. 'About the Talking Stick Festival.' https://fullcircle.ca/festival/about. 26 June 2021.

'Headliners.' https://fullcircle.ca/festival/events-2018/headliners. 24 September 2018.

'Fusebox 2020.' https://schedule.fuseboxfestival.com/sponsors. 7 April 2020.

'Fusebox Festival 10th Anniversary.' www.kickstarter.com/projects/fusebox/fuse box-festival-10th-anniversary-free-range-art. 21 January 2020.

'Fusebox Festival 2019.' Web content no longer available. Accessed 21 January 2020.

Future Divercities. 'Project Context.' http://futuredivercities.eu/index.php/about. 14 January 2020.

Ganambarr, Don Wininba. 'The Directors of Buŋgul discuss Gurrumul and Country.' *Buŋgul* programme, Adelaide Festival. 2–3 March 2020.

García, Beatriz. 'Urban Regeneration, Arts Programming and Major Events: Glasgow 1990, Sydney 2000, Barcelona 2004.' *International Journal of Cultural Policy* 10.1 (2004): 103–18.

Gardner, Lyn. 'Forest Fringe: 10 Years of Risk-Taking Theatre that Reinvented Edinburgh.' *The Guardian* 16 August 2016. www.theguardian.com/stage/ theatreblog/2016/aug/16/forest-fringe-edinburgh-festival-theatre. 31 December 2019.

Garneau, David. 'Imaginary Spaces of Conciliation and Reconciliation: Art, Curation, and Healing.' *Arts of Engagement: Taking Aesthetic Action in and Beyond the Truth and Reconciliation Commission of Canada.* Ed. Dylan Robinson and Keavy Martin. Waterloo: Wilfrid Laurier UP, 2016. 21–42.

Gener, Randy. 'In Bogotá, an Homage to a Diva of Iberoamericano.' *American Theatre* 27.5 (2010): 24.

George Town Festival. Programme booklet, 2018.

Gibbs, James. 'Introduction.' *African Theatre* 11 (2012): xi–xv.

'PANAFEST through the Headlines: An Annotated Bibliography.' *African Theatre* 11 (2012): 56–67.

'Theatre Programme for FESMAN and Commentary.' *African Theatre* 11 (2012): 39–44.

Gilbert, Helen, and Jacqueline Lo. *Performance and Cosmopolitics: Cross-Cultural Transactions in Australia.* Basingstoke: Palgrave Macmillan, 2007.

Giorgi, Liana, and Monica Sassatelli. 'Introduction.' Giorgi et al. (eds.), *Festivals*, 1–11.

Giorgi, Liana, Monica Sassatelli, and Gerard Delanty (eds.). *Festivals and the Cultural Public Sphere.* London: Routledge, 2011.

Gleaden, Henry. 'Review: Cuckoo at Attenborough Centre for the Creative Arts, Brighton.' *Exeunt Magazine* 15 February 2019. http://exeuntmagazine.com/ reviews/review-cuckoo-attenborough-centre-creative-arts. 13 February 2020.

'Goldcorp Signs Impact and Benefit Agreement with Indigenous Communities.' *Northern Ontario Business* 6 June 2018. www.northernontariobusiness.com/ industry-news/mining/goldcorp-signs-impact-and-benefit-agreement-with- indigenous-communities-946091. 26 January 2020.

Goldstein, Julia. 'Kiyingi Kampala International Theatre Festival.' *Theatre Journal* 67.3 (2015): 535–40.

'Staging East Africa through Global Exchange: The Kampala International Theatre Festival.' Knowles (ed.), *Cambridge Companion*, 162–77.

Graham-Jones, Jean. 'International Festivals in Latin America: Festival Santiago a Mil and Festival Internacional de Buenos Aires.' Knowles (ed.), *Cambridge Companion*, 224–38.

Graver, David, and Loren Kruger. 'Locating Theatre: Regionalism and Interculturalism at Edinburgh.' *Performing Arts Journal* 15.2 (1993): 71–84.

Grundy, Kenneth. 'The Politics of South Africa's National Arts Festival: Small Engagements in the Bigger Campaign.' *African Affairs* 93 (1994): 387–409.

Gunew, Sneja. *Haunted Nations: The Colonial Dimensions of Multiculturalisms.* London: Routledge, 2004.

Gyan-Apenteng, Kwadwo. 'Panafest Set to Thrill!' *Michigan Citizen* 2 August 2003: B1.

Hanna, Michelle. *Reconciliation in Olympism: Indigenous Culture in the Sydney Olympiad.* Petersham, NSW: Walla Walla P, 1999.

Harris, Sue. '"Dancing in the Streets": The Aurillac Festival of Street Theatre.' *Contemporary Theatre Review* 14.2 (2004): 57–71.

Harvie, Jen. 'Cultural Effects of the Edinburgh International Festival: Elitism, Identities, Industries.' *Contemporary Theatre Review* 13.4 (2003): 12–26.

Fair Play – Art, Performance, and Neoliberalism. Basingstoke: Palgrave Macmillan, 2013.

'International Theatre Festivals in the UK: The Edinburgh Festival Fringe as Model Neoliberal Market.' Knowles (ed.), *Cambridge Companion*, 101–17.

Staging the UK. Manchester: Manchester UP, 2005.

Hauptfleisch, Temple. 'The Culture Bazaar: Thoughts on Festival Culture after a Visit to the 2003 Klein Karoo Nasionale Kunstefees (KKNK) in Oudtshoorn.' *South African Theatre Journal* 17.1 (2003): 258–75.

'The Eventification of Afrikaans Culture – Some Thoughts on the Klein Karoo Nasionale Kunstefees (KKNK).' *South African Theatre Journal* 15. 1 (2001): 169–77.

'Eventifying Identity: Festivals in South Africa and the Search for Cultural Identity.' *New Theatre Quarterly* 22.2 (2006): 181–98.

'Festivals as Eventifying Systems.' *Festivalising! Theatrical Events, Politics and Culture.* Ed. Temple Hauptfleisch, Shulamith Lev-Aladgem, Jacqueline Martin, Willmar Sauter, and Henri Schoenmakers. Amsterdam: Rodopi, 2007. 39–47.

Hetherington, Kevin. *The Badlands of Modernity: Heterotopia and Social Ordering.* London: Routledge, 1997.

Higgins-Desbiolles, Freya. 'Reconciliation Tourism: Healing Divided Societies.' *Tourism Recreation Research* 28.3 (2003): 35–44.

Hill, David. 'Welcome to Guatemala: Gold Mine Protester Beaten and Burned Alive.' *The Guardian* 12 August 2014. www.theguardian.com/environment/andes-to-the-amazon/2014/aug/12/guatemala-gold-mine-protester-beaten-burnt-alive. 26 January 2020.

Hoffman, Alvina. 'Interview – Walter Mignolo/Part 2: Key Concepts.' *E-International Relations* 21 January 2017. www.e-ir.info/2017/01/21/inter view-walter-mignolopart-2-key-concepts. 18 September 2020.

Hoffman, W[alter] J[ames]. *The Midë'wiwin or 'Grand Medicine Society' of the Ojibwa.* Seventh Annual Report of the Bureau of Ethnology to the Secretary of the Smithsonian Institution, 1885–6. Washington: Government Printing Office, 1891. 143–300. www.gutenberg.org/files/19368/19368-h/19368-h .htm. 26 June 2021.

Holledge, Julie, and Joanne Tompkins. *Women's Intercultural Performance.* London: Routledge, 2000.

Holledge, Julie, Sarah Thomasson, and Joanne Tompkins. 'Rethinking Interculturalism Using Digital Tools.' McIvor and King (eds.), *Interculturalism*, 89–111.

'Hotel Shabby Shabby: Pop-up Hotel Offers Recycled Rooms Built for Under €250.' https://inhabitat.com/clever-pop-up-hotel-in-germany-features-recycled-rooms-built-under-320/raumlabor-hotel-shabby-shabby-122. 23 July 2019.

House, Stephen. 'Adelaide Festival: Doku Rai.' *atAussietheatre.com* 2 March 2013. https://aussietheatre.com.au/reviews/adelaide-festival-doku-rai. 9 March 2020.

House on Fire. www.facebook.com/pg/houseonfire.eu/about/?ref=page_internal. 15 January 2020.

Houston, Andrew. 'Majdi Bou-Matar's Impact: An Examination of the IMPACT Festival and Its Survival in the Waterloo Region.' *Theatre Research in Canada/ Recherches théâtrales au Canada* 40.1–2 (2019): 102–17.

Huffman, Shawn. 'On and Off: A Tour of Theatre Festivals in Canada and the United States.' *Contemporary Theatre Review* 13.4 (2003): 57–65.

Husband, Dale. 'Lemi Ponifasio: I'm on the Stage because I Want to Change the World.' *E-Tangata* 13 August 2016. https://e-tangata.co.nz/arts/lemi-ponifa sio-im-on-the-stage-because-i-want-change-in-the-world. 29 August 2018.

Hutchison, Yvette. '"Zones of Occult Instability": A South African Perspective on Negotiating Colonial Afterlives through Intercultural Performance.' McIvor and King (eds.), *Interculturalism*, 153–79.

Imaginario, Andrea. 'Significado de Interculturalidad.' *Significados.* www .significados.com/interculturalidad. 26 June 2021.

Indigenous Corporate Training. 'First Nation Talking Stick Protocol.' 20 January 2015. www.ictinc.ca/blog/first-nation-talking-stick-protocol. 15 September 2020.

Interferences International Theatre Festival. 'About the Festival.' www .interferences-huntheater.ro/2018/en/about-the-festival/mission-history. 21 July 2019.

Irmer, Thomas. 'Theater der Welt in Berlin.' *PAJ: A Journal of Performance and Art* 22.2 (2000): 123–31.

Ise, Claudine. '"Bodies of Work" Is All About Art and Ability.' *Chicago Tribune* 9 May 2013. www.chicagotribune.com/entertainment/ct-xpm-2013-05-09-ct-ott-0510-bodies-of-work-20130509-story.html. 7 January 2020.

James, Ryan K. 'Urban Redevelopment and Displacement from Regent Park to El Cartucho.' *Canadian Theatre Review* 161 (2015): 17–21.

Jamieson, Kirstie. 'Edinburgh: The Festival Gaze and Its Boundaries.' *Space & Culture* 7.1 (2004): 64–75.

Japan Foundation. 'Arts Organization of the Month: Urban Heat.' 6 November 2017. https://performingarts.jp/E/society/1710/1.html. 26 June 2021.

Jarque, Michael. 'Nick Power's "Between Tiny Cities": The Power of Two.' *Dance Informa: Australian Edition* 5 July 2019. https://dancemagazine.com.au/2019/07/nick-powers-between-tiny-cities-the-power-of-two. 7 March 2020.

Johansson, Marjana. 'City Festivals and Festival Cities.' Knowles (ed.), *Cambridge Companion*, 54–69.

Johansson, Marjana, and Jerzy Kociatkiewicz. 'City Festivals: Creativity and Control in Staged Urban Experiences.' *European Urban and Regional Studies* 18.4 (2011): 392–405.

Johansson Marjana, and Maria Laura Toraldo. '"From mosh pit to posh pit": Festival Imagery in the Context of the Boutique Festival.' *Culture & Organization* 23.3 (2017): 220–37.

Johnston, Kirsty. *Stage Turns: Canadian Disability Theatre*. Montreal: McGill-Queen's UP, 2012.

Jones, Chris. 'Moving "Andares" at Chicago Shakespeare Has Stories of Rural Mexico, Without Any Romantic Gloss.' *Chicago Tribune* 24 October 2019. www.chicagotribune.com/entertainment/theater/reviews/ct-ent-andares-destinos-review-1025-20191024-fhlqsap7fbdlbgvmxd7xu3wv44-story.html. 15 February 2020.

Kann, Drew. 'Bodies of Work Festival.' *WTTW News* 15 May 2013. https://news.wttw.com/2013/05/15/bodies-work-festival. 7 January 2013.

Kant, Immanuel. *Political Writings*. Ed. Hans Siegbert Reiss. Trans. Hugh Barr Nisbet. 2nd ed. Cambridge: Polity, 1990.

Karas, James. 'In Sundry Languages – Review. Toronto Laboratory Theatre Production.' 6 July 2019. https://jameskarasreviews.blogspot.com/2019/07/in-sundry-languages-review-toronto.html. 13 September 2019.

Kavass, I.I. 'Adelaide Festival of Arts.' *The Australian Quarterly* 32.2 (1960): 7–16.

Khlifi, Roua. 'Arab Theatre Festival Draws a Large Audience in Tunis.' *The Arab Weekly* 21 January 2018. https://thearabweekly.com/arab-theatre-festival-draws-large-audience-tunis. 9 February 2019.

Kickstart Disability Arts and Culture. 'Our History So Far.' www.kickstartdisability.ca/about-us/history. 7 January 2020.

Kiinalik: These Sharp Tools. Programme. Luminato Festival, Toronto. 12–16 June 2019.

Kim, Hayana. 'Reckoning with Historical Conflicts in East Asian Theatre Festivals: The BeSeTo Theatre Festival and the Gwangju Media Arts Festival.' Knowles (ed.), *Cambridge Companion*, 192–206.

Kim, Jae Kyoung. '*King Lear* by William Shakespeare.' *Theatre Journal* 66.3 (2014): 452–4.

Kim, Ju Yon. 'Between Paper and Performance: Suspicion, Race, and Casting in *The Piano Teacher.*' *Modern Drama* 63.2 (2020): 127–53.

Kim, Sarah. 'One of the Kind Performing Arts Festival, by and for the Disability Community.' *Forbes* 26 April 2019. www.forbes.com/sites/sarahkim/2019/04/26/i-wanna-be-with-you-everywhere/#3f6ce41d4176. 7 January 2020.

Kim Yun-Cheol. 'The First BeSeTo Theatre Festival.' *Theatre Journal* 47.3 (1995): 416–19.

Knowles, Ric. 'Adapting to Shakespeare.' *The Shakespeare's Mine: Adapting Shakespeare in Anglophone Canada.* Ed. Ric Knowles. Toronto: Playwrights Canada P, 2009. iii–ix.

'The Arab Theatre Festival.' *Theatre Journal* 71.2 (2019): 220–3.

'"Because It's Ritual, and We're Living": Living Ritual International Indigenous Performing Arts Festival.' *Canadian Theatre Review* 174 (2018): 83–8.

'Between the Flag and the Hungry Ghosts.' *Canadian Theatre Review* 181 (2020): 86–8.

'Canada Comes to CARIFESTA: The Caribbean International Festival of the Arts, Trinidad and Tobago, August 2019.' *Canadian Theatre Review* 182 (2020): 72–81.

'Festival de Théâtre des Amériques.' *Canadian Theatre Review* 92 (1997): 90–5.

'Festivals: What Good Are They? What Are They Good At? The Case of Edinburgh 2017.' *Theatre Journal* 70 (2018): 369–82.

'Not Just Counting Sheep: Canada Hub at the Edinburgh Fringe.' *Canadian Theatre Review* 179 (2019): 85–90.

Performing the Intercultural City. Ann Arbor: U of Michigan P, 2017.

Reading the Material Theatre. Cambridge: Cambridge UP, 2004.

'Seeking the International Intercultural: The Seventieth Edinburgh Fringe Festival.' *Canadian Theatre Review* 177 (2019): 90–3.

Theatre & Interculturalism. Basingstoke: Palgrave Macmillan, 2010.

'Urban Dreams, Native Rites, and Rural Pleasures.' Rev. of Festival de théâtre des Amériques 1999. *Canadian Theatre Review* 102 (2000): 72–80.

(ed.). *The Cambridge Companion to International Theatre Festivals.* Cambridge: Cambridge UP, 2020.

Komporaly, Jozefina. 'Interferences International Theatre Festival.' *Theatre Journal* 67.3 (2015): 550–4.

Koo Ja-hung. 'The BeSeTo Festival and China-Korea Theatre Exchange.' Performing Arts Market in Seoul (PAMS): The Future of Asian Performing Arts – China Now. National Theatre of Korea. 7–12 October 2014. www.gokams.or.kr/artnews_upload/[PAMS%202014]THE%20FUTURE%20OF%20ASIAN%20PERFORMING%20ARTS_CHINA%20NOW.pdf. 11 February 2019.

Kovacs, Sasha. 'Performance as Treatment in the James Bay Treaty No. 9.' *Canadian Theatre Review* 161 (2015): 43–7.

Kruger, Loren. 'The National Arts Festival in Grahamstown: Culture, Economics, and Race in South Africa.' Knowles (ed.), *Cambridge Companion*, 178–91.

Lachance, Lindsay, and Selena Couture. 'Transformational Kinstellatory Relations and the Talking Stick Festival.' *Theatre Research in Canada/ Recherches théâtrales au Canada* 40.1–2 (2019): 10–26.

La Flamme, Michelle. 'BC Aboriginal Theatre History in the Making: Talking with Margo Kane about the History of Full Circle and the Talking Stick.' *Canadian Performance Histories and Historiographies* Ed. Heather Davis-Fisch. Toronto: Playwrights Canada P, 2017. 93– 114.

Langhoff, Shermin. 'Editorial.' 4th Berlin Fall Salon: De-Home It!' https://translate .google.com/translate?hl=en&sl=de&u=https://www.berliner-herbstsalon.de/ &prev=search. 2 January 2020.

Latif, Shaista. House Program. *How I Learned to Serve Tea.* Progress Festival. Toronto February 2020. http://progressfestival.org/wp-content/uploads/ 2019/11/howilearnedtoservetea-houseprogram.pdf. 17 February 2020.

Lei, Daphne. 'Interruption, Intervention, Interculturalism: Robert Wilson's HIT Productions in Taiwan.' *Theatre Journal* 63.4 (2011): 571–86.

Lei, Daphne, and Charlotte McIvor (eds.). *The Methuen Drama Handbook of Interculturalism and Performance.* London: Bloomsbury, 2020.

Les Francophonies: Des écritures à la scène. 'Les Zébrures d'automne 2019 Programmation/Calendrier.' www.lesfrancophonies.fr/Programmation-Calendrier. 9 April 2020.

Levin, Laura. 'Ecology and Site-Specificity in Festival Production: A Conversation with Laura Nanni.' *Theatre Research in Canada/Recherches théâtrales au Canada* 40.1–2 (2019): 135–52.

Levin, Laura, and Kim Solga. 'Building Utopia: Performance and the Fantasy of Urban Renewal in Contemporary Toronto.' *Theatre and Performance in Toronto.* Ed. Laura Levin. Toronto: Playwrights Canada P, 2011. 156–75.

Levitt, Aimee. 'The Art of Disability on Display at Bodies of Work.' *Chicago Reader* 7 May 2013. www.chicagoreader.com/chicago/bodies-of-work-festi val-disability-arts-culture/Content?oid=9562482. 7 January 2020.

Liebembuk, Shelley. 'The Interpreter Made Visible: The Politics of Translation across the panamerican ROUTES/RUTAS panamericanas Festival.' *Canadian Theatre Review* 161 (2014): 26–30.

Lim, Alvin Eng Hui. 'Routes and Routers of Interculturalism: Islands, Theatres and Shakespeares.' McIvor and King (eds.), *Interculturalism*, 61–87.

Lin, Kuan-Wen, Patrick Stein, and Joe Goldblatt. 'New Investment: An Exploratory Case Study of Three Mature Edinburgh Festivals and Their Future Funding Opportunities.' *Event Management* 15.2 (2011): 179–95.

Lionnet, Françoise, and Shu-mei Shih (eds.). *Minor Transnationalism.* Durham, NC: Duke UP, 2005.

Litt, Michael. 'Southern Ontario's Silicon Valley: Unleashing Waterloo's Tech-Innovation Sector.' *Globe and Mail* 28 March 2018. www.theglobeandmail .com/business/commentary/article-southern-ontarios-silicon-valley-unleashing-waterloos-tech. 31 October 2019.

286   *Work Cited*

Live Art Development Agency. 'DIY: 2019 – Quiplash: Unsightly Drag.' www
.thisisliveart.co.uk/opportunities/diy16-2019-quiplash-unsightly-drag. 7 June
2020.
Living Ritual Festival. Programme. Toronto. 25–7 July 2017.
'Lookout.' https://aplacetolookout.co.uk. 23 July 2019.
Low, Stephen. 'In Conversation: Nick Green on the Social Distancing Festival.'
Intermission 25 September 2020. www.intermissionmagazine.ca/in-conversa
tion/in-conversation-nick-green-on-the-social-distancing-festival. 25 September
2020.
Loyer, Emmanuelle, and Antoine de Baecque. *Histoire du Festival d'Avignon*.
Paris: Éditions Gallimard, 2016.
Luminato. https://luminatofestival.com. 19 November 2019.
   Luminato 2018 Annual Report. https://issuu.com/luminato/docs/luminato_
2018_annual_report_for_web. 26 June 2021.
Mackley-Crump, Jared. 'The Festivalization of Pacific Cultures in New Zealand:
Diasporic Flow and Identity within Transcultural Contact Zones.'
Musicology Australia 35.1 (2013): 20–40.
'Pacific Festivals in Aotearoa.' *Spasifik* 51 (July/August 2012): 58–61.
'Mad Pride.' https://en.wikipedia.org/wiki/Mad_Pride. 9 January 2020.
Magowan, Fiona. 'Dancing with a Difference: Reconfiguring the Poetic Politics of
Aboriginal Ritual as National Spectacle.' *Australian Journal of Anthropology*
11.3 (2000): 308–21.
Malone, Gavin. 'Ways of Belonging: Reconciliation and Adelaide's Public Space
Indigenous Cultural Markers.' *Geographical Research* 45.2 (2007): 158–66.
Malta Festival Poznań. 'MALTA Short History.' https://malta-festival.pl/en/festi
val/about/history. 14 January 2020.
Mammalian Diving Reflex. https://mammalian.ca/about/who-we-are. 13 January
2020.
Marcus, George E. *Ethnography through Thick and Thin*. Princeton, NJ: Princeton
UP, 1998.
Martin, Carol. 'Under the Radar Festival, New York: Experimental, Urban, and
Global.' Knowles (ed.), *Cambridge Companion*, 118–31.
Martin, Jacqueline E., Georgia K. Seffrin, and Rodney C. Wissler. 'The Festival Is
a Theatrical Event.' *Theatrical Events: Borders, Dynamics, Frames*. Ed. Vicky
Cremona, Peter Eversmann, Hans van Maanen, Willem Sauter, and John
Tulloch. Amsterdam: Rodopi, 2004. 91–110.
Massie-Blomfeld, Amber. 'Interview: New Yorker David Binder on the Local-
Global Hybrid of Lift 2018'. *Run Riot* 1 May 2018. www.run-riot.com/
articles/blogs/interview-new-yorker-david-binder-local-global-hybrid-lift-2018.
26 June 2021.
Mattison, Christopher. 'Delinking, Decoloniality, and Dewesternization:
Interview with Walter Mignolo (Part II).' *Critical Legal Thinking: Law and
the Political* (2 May 2012): https://criticallegalthinking.com/2012/05/02/
delinking-decoloniality-dewesternization-interview-with-walter-mignolo-part-
ii/. 13 September 2020.

Maurin, Frédéric. 'Still and Again: Whither Festivals?' *Contemporary Theatre Review* 13.4 (2003): 5–11.

McIvor, Charlotte. 'Introduction: New Directions?' McIvor and King (eds.), *Interculturalism*, 1–26.

McIvor, Charlotte, and Jason King (eds.). *Interculturalism and Performance Now: New Directions?* Cham: Palgrave Macmillan, 2019.

McLean, Heather E. 'Cracks in the Creative City: The Contradictions of Community Arts Practice.' *International Journal of Urban and Regional Research* 38.6 (2014): 2156–73.

'Hos in the Garden: Staging and Resisting Neoliberal Creativity.' *Environment and Planning D: Society and Space* 35.1 (2017): 38–56.

McMahon, Christina S. *Recasting Transnationalism through Performance: Theatre Festivals in Cape Verde, Mozambique, and Brazil.* Basingstoke: Palgrave Macmillan, 2014.

McRobbie, Angela. *Be Creative: Making a Living in the New Cultural Industries.* Cambridge: Polity, 2016.

Meerzon, Yana. 'Avignon 2019: Seeking the Other: Staging the Paroxysms of Orientalism.' *Theatre Times* 10 August 2019. https://thetheatretimes.com/ avignon-2019-seeking-the-other-staging-the-paroxysms-of-orientalism. 26 June 2021.

Menza, Carla, and Laurent Lapierre. 'Company Profile: Fanny Mikey and the Ibero-American Theatre Festival of Bogotá.' *International Journal of Arts Management* 6.2 (2004): 66–77.

Metropolis. www.metropolis.dk/en/about-metropolis. 14 January 2020.

'About Metropolis 2019.' www.metropolis.dk/en/about-metropolis-2019. 6 April 2020.

'In Situ.' www.metropolis.dk/en/in-situ. 14 January 2020.

Mignolo, Walter. *The Idea of Latin America.* Hoboken, NJ: Blackwell, 2005.

Mignolo, Walter, and Catherine E. Walsh. *On Decoloniality: Concepts, Analytics, Praxis.* Durham, NC: Duke UP, 2018.

Mill, Jessie, and Marie Parent (eds.). *FTA: Nos jours de fête.* Montréal: Les Éditions Somme Toute, 2018.

Ministère de la Culture, République française. 'Nomination d'Hassane Kassi Kouyaté à la direction du Festival des Francophonies en Limousin.' www .culture.gouv.fr/Presse/Communiques-de-presse/Nomination-d-Hassane-Kassi-Kouyate-a-la-direction-du-Festival-des-Francophonies-en-Limousin. 24 November 2018.

Mirk, Sarah. 'Let's Talk about Crip Culture.' *Bitchmedia* 17 July 2015. www .bitchmedia.org/post/lets-talk-about-crip-culture. 9 January 2020.

Mojica, Monique. 'Chocolate Woman Dreams the Milky Way.' *Indigenous Women in Canada: The Voices of First Nations, Inuit, and Métis Women.* Spec. Issue of *Canadian Women's Studies* 26.3–4 (2008): 160–8.

Money, Laura. 'Perth Festival 2020 | Hecate | 5 Stars.' *The Fourth Wall* 10 February 2020. https://fourthwallmedia.wordpress.com/2020/02/10/perth-festival-2020-hecate-5-stars. 10 March 2020.

Moon Gwang-lip. 'NE Asian Theatre Takes Center Stage.' *Korea JoongAng Daily* 6 September 2012. http://koreajoongangdaily.joins.com/news/article/article .aspx?aid=2959042. 24 February 2019.

Morison, Thomas. 'Domestic International Festivals.' *Canadian Theatre Review* 125 (2006): 120–4.

Moses, L.G. 'Indians on the Midway: Wild West Shows and the Indian Bureau at World's Fairs, 1893–1904.' South Dakota State Historical Society 1991. www.sdhspress.com/journal/south-dakota-history-21-3/indians-on-the-midway-wild-west-shows-and-the-indian-bureau-at-worlds-fairs-1893-1904/vol-21-no-3-indians-on-the-midway.pdf. 23 April 2020.

Moya, Paula M.L. 'The Search for Decolonial Love: An Interview with Junot Díaz.' *Boston Review: A Political and Literary Forum* (26 June 2012): http:// bostonreview.net/books-ideas/paula-ml-moya-decolonial-love-interview-junot-d%C3%ADaz. 13 September 2020.

MT Space. 'About MTSpace.' http://mtspace.ca/about-mt-space. 4 March 2019.

MT Space Theatre. *Amal.* Unpublished script. 11 October 2018.

Muehlemann, Nina. 'Why We Need Disability Arts Festivals, Now and in the Future.' Disability Arts Online 11 June 2018. https://disabilityarts.online/ magazine/opinion/need-disability-arts-festivals-now-future. 7 January 2020.

Munro, Iain, and Silvia Jordan. '"Living Space" at the Edinburgh Festival Fringe: Spatial Tactics and the Politics of Smooth Space.' *Human Relations* 66.11 (2013): 1497–525.

Nanni, Laura. Telephone conversation with Ric Knowles, 14 April 2020.

Neilson, Brett. 'Bodies of Protest: Performing Citizenship at the 2000 Olympic Games.' www.uws.edu.au/__data/assets/pdf_file/0009/365742/Neilson_ Bodies_of_Protest_ICS_Pre-Print_Final.pdf. 26 June 2021.

Nettleford, Rex. 'Keynote Address: The Caribbean Artist's Presence and Education for the Third Millennium.' *Caribbean Quarterly* 45.2–3 (1999): 1–9.

Ngũgĩ wa Thiong'o. *Decolonizing the Mind: The Politics of Language in African Literature.* London: James Curry, 1981.

Niang, Amy. 'African Renaissance between Rhetoric & the Aesthetics of Extravagance.' *African Theatre* 11 (2012): 30–8.

Nicol, Emily. 'Sydney Festival's Strong Indigenous Program Is Heartening and Unflinching.' *The Guardian* 24 January 2017. www.theguardian.com/cul ture/2017/jan/24/blood-song-and-language-reconnecting-with-sydneys-origins-through-art. 3 September 2018.

Nightingale, Andrea W. *Spectacles of Truth in Classical Greek Philosophy: Theoria in Its Cultural Context.* Cambridge: Cambridge UP, 2004.

Nogojiwanong Indigenous Fringe Festival. https://indigenousfringefest.weebly .com/?fbclid=IwAR1I-AJZFmaYK4E1RYRFaqJMed12CFF8p9HT67auO18 sunHlkw_PJcaUVqA. 6 February 2020.

'NO LIMITS: Disability & Performing Arts Festival Berlin.' www.no-limits-festival.de/media/nolimits2019-programmbuch.pdf. 8 January 2020.

Nora, Pierre. 'From *Between History and Memory*: Les Lieux de Mémoire.' *Theories of Memory: A Reader*. Ed. Michael Rossington and Anne Whitehead. Baltimore: Johns Hopkins UP, 2007. 144–9.

Nygren, Christina. 'Festivals in Religious or Spiritual Contexts: Examples from Japan, China, India, and Bangladesh.' *Festivalising! Theatrical Events, Politics and Culture*. Ed. Temple Hauptfleisch, Shulamith Lev-Aladgem, Jacqueline Martin, Willmar Sauter, and Henri Schoenmakers. Amsterdam: Rodopi, 2007. 261–80.

O'Bonsawin, Christine M. 'Indigenous People and Canadian Hosted Olympic Games.' *Aboriginal Peoples and Sport in Canada: Historical Foundations and Contemporary Issues*. Ed. Janice Forsyth and Audrey Giles. Vancouver: UBC Press, 2013. 35–63.

Okareka Dance Company. 'Okareka Dance.' https://vimeo.com/okarekadance/about. 5 April 2020.

Ortuzar, Jimena. 'Aluna Theatre: Building Pan-American Communities.' *Canadian Theatre Review* 157 (2014): 64–7.

Panafest Pan African Historical Festival. 'Draft Programme for Panafest 2019.' www.panafestghana.org/page/?nid=10. 21 February 2019.

Papastergiatis, Nikoa, and Meredith Martin. 'Art Bienalles and Cities as Platforms for Global Dialogue.' Giorgi et al. (eds.), *Festivals*, 45–62.

Paré, Michel F. 'Queer West Art and Film Festivals.' https://artsfestival.queerwest.org/festival-2/international. 2 January 2020.

Parker, Brenda. 'Beyond the Class Act: Gender and Race in the "Creative City" Discourse.' *Gender in an Urban World: Research in Urban Sociology*. Ed. Judith N. DeSena. Bingley: Jai Press/Emerald, 2008. 201–33.

Pavis, Patrice. *Theatre at the Crossroads of Culture*. Trans. Loren Kruger. London: Routledge, 1992.

Peck, Jamie. 'Struggling with the Creative Class.' *International Journal of Urban and Regional Research* 29.4 (2005): 740–70.

Peghini, Julie, and Amélie Thérésine. 'Les Récréâtrales (Ouagadougou)/Mantsina sur Scène (Brazzaville): Des espaces où s'inventent des dramaturgies résistantes.' *Horizons/Théâtre* 6 (2016): 82–99.

Performing Arts Network Japan. 'Japan Topics.' 4 October 2016. www.performingarts.jp/E/topics/archive/2016/j20160802.html. 25 February 2019.

Phipps, Peter. 'Indigenous Festivals in Australia: Performing the Postcolonial.' *Ethnos* 81.4 (2016): 683–96.

'Performances of Power: Indigenous Cultural Festivals as Globally Engaged Cultural Strategy.' *Alternatives: Global, Local, Political* 35.3 (2010): 217–40.

'Performing Culture as Political Strategy: The Garma Festival, Northeast Arnhem Land.' *Festival Places: Revitalizing Rural Australia*. Ed. Chris Gibson and John Connell. Bristol: Channel View, 2011. 109–22.

Pizano, Beatriz, and Trevor Schwellnus. Interview with Jimena Ortuzar. Toronto. 18 August 2013.

Portland Institute for Contemporary Art. 'TBA.' www.pica.org/tba. 29 January 2020.

Portmann, Alexandra. 'International Festivals, the Practice of Co-production, and the Challenges for Documentation in a Digital Age.' Knowles (ed.), *Cambridge Companion*, 36–53.

Preston, Jennifer. 'Weesageechak Begins to Dance: Native Earth Performing Arts Inc.' *TDR (The Drama Review)* 36.1 (1992): 135–59.

Preston, V.K. 'Queer and Indigenous Art: Performing Ice Times in Climate Crisis.' *Theatre Journal* 72 (2020): 143–62.

Pring, John. 'Disappointment at Mayor's Scaled-back Plans for Liberty Arts Festival.' *DNS: Disability News Service* 17 October 2019. www.disabilitynewsservice.com/disappointment-at-mayors-scaled-back-plans-for-liberty-arts-festival. 7 January 2020.

Pringle, Lyne. 'NZ Festival Review: In Jerusalem Disparate Elements Come Together in a Plea for Peace.' *Stuff* 23 February 2020. www.stuff.co.nz/entertainment/stage-and-theatre/119743413/nz-festival-review-in-jerusalem-disparate-elements-come-together-in-a-plea-for-peace. 12 March 2020.

Prismatic Arts Festival. http://prismaticfestival.com. 31 August 2018.

Progress. Press release. 19 December 2019. http://progressfestival.org/wp-content/uploads/2020/04/Progress2020-Press-Release-Dec-10.pdf. 21 April 2020.

The Public. 'Under the Radar 2020.' https://publictheater.org/programs/under-the-radar/under-the-radar. 16 January 2020.

PuSh International Performing Arts Festival. 'About & History.' https://pushfestival.ca/about-the-festival/about-the-festival. 25 January 2020.

'Fall Update.' [2020] Publicity Flyer.

'Programme.' Vancouver. 16 January – 4 February 2018.

'Quand l'art passe à l'action.' www.atsa.qc.ca/en/eu-2017-home. 9 January 2020.

Quatre Chemins. 'Dix ans d'histoires.' www.festival4chemins.com/about. 26 November 2018.

'Présentation de l'édition 2018.' www.festival4chemins.com/copie-de-presentation-1. 26 November 2018.

Quinn, Bernadette. 'Arts Festivals and the City.' *Urban Studies* 42.5–6 (2005): 927–43.

Rancière, Jacques. *Dissensus: On Politics and Aesthetics*. London: Connections, 2010.

Rasmussen, Tom. 'The Reality of Edinburgh Fringe When You're a Working Class Performer.' *Dazed* 9 August 2019. www.dazeddigital.com/life-culture/article/45522/1/edinburgh-fringe-when-youre-a-working-class-performer?fbclid=IwAR1CNowdIfaep3CAMvzxdnCiuSF2_MR_t94By5X8L2GOzoXO_giZ8OEkQJU. 14 August 2019.

Récréâtrales. 'A propos.' http://recreatrales.org/?page_id=2096. 26 November 2018.

Referendum Council. 'Final Report of the Referendum Council.' 30 June 2017. www.referendumcouncil.org.au/final-report.html#toc-anchor-ulurustatement-from-the-heart. 14 September 2020.

Regev, Motti. 'International Festivals in a Small Country: Rites of Recognition and Cosmopolitanism.' Giorgi et al. (eds.), *Festivals*, 108–23.

Régis Jr, Guy. 'Tous les hommes sont fous.' http://lenational.org/post_free.php?elif=1_CONTENUE/culture&rebmun=4140. 26 June 2021.

Remshardt, Ralf. 'Theater Der Welt Festival.' *Theatre Journal* 70 (2018): 229–32.

Rickard, Jolene. 'Visualizing Sovereignty in the Time of Biometric Sensors.' *South Atlantic Quarterly* 110.2 (2011): 465–86.

Rimini Protokoll. 'Ciudades Paralelas – Parallel Cities.' www.rimini-protokoll.de/website/en/project/ciudades-paralelas-parallele-staedte. 30 January 2020.

Rine, Natalie. 'New York Review: Makuyeika Colectivo Teatral's "Andares" Presented by Under the Radar Festival at the Public.' *On Stage Blog* 24 January 2020. www.onstageblog.com/reviews/2020/1/24/new-york-review-makuyeika-colectivo-teatrals-andares-presented-by-under-the-radar-festival-at-the-public. 15 February 2020.

Ripp, Alexandra. 'Estado Vegetal.' *Theatre Journal* 71.3 (2019): 382–4.

Roberts, Rhoda. 'A Passion for Ideas: Black Stage.' *Australasian Drama Studies* 32 (1998): 3–20.

Robertson, Martin, and Kenneth MacMillan Wardrop. 'Events and the Destination Dynamic: Edinburgh Festivals, Entrepreneurship and Strategic Marketing.' *Festival and Events Management: An International Arts and Culture Perspective.* Ed. Ian Yeoman. New York: Routledge, 2004. 115–29.

Robinson, Dylan. *Hungry Listening: Resonant Theory for Indigenous Studies.* Minneapolis: U of Minnesota P, 2020.

'Public Writing, Sovereign Reading: Indigenous Language Art in Public Space.' *Art Journal* 76.2 (2017): 85–99.

'Welcoming Sovereignty.' *Performing Indigeneity.* Ed. Yvette Nolan and Ric Knowles. Toronto: Playwrights Canada P, 2016. 5–32.

Roche, Maurice. 'Festivalizataion, Cosmopolitanism, and European Culture: On the Sociocultural Significance of Mega-Events.' Giorgi et al. (eds.), *Festivals*, 124–41.

Rogers, Amal. 'Can She Dig It? Amal Rogers on Dana Michel's *Mercurial George.*' *Walker* 12 January 2018. https://walkerart.org/magazine/overnight-review-dana-michel-mercurial-george. 1 February 2020.

Ronström, Owe. 'Four Facets of Festivalisation.' *Puls – Journal for Ethnomusicology and Ethnochoreology* 1.1 (2015): 67–83.

Rößler, Maria. 'Of Lonely Humans and Loving Rice Cookers. Performance Review of *Cuckoo* by Jaha Koo, Presented at MMCA Performing Arts: Asia Focus, Seoul.' December 2017. https://mariaroessler.work/Of-lonely-humans-and-loving-rice-cookers. 13 February 2020.

'Ruhrfestspiele Theatre Festival in Recklinghausen.' www.nrw-tourism.com/ruhr festspiele-theatre-festival-in-recklinghausen.13 April 2019.

RUTAS. 'Unearthed.' www.alunatheatre.ca/festival/rutas-2018/?gclid=CjwKCAj wzqPcBRAnEiwAzKRgS-3H_pxQ2BN2JNTQpjR3RV-RZjOuNITwbouY qh6JcWcjQjTUJVIwJhoCLRgQAvD_BwE. 31 August 2018.

Sahakian, Emily. 'Festivals in the Francophone World as Sites of Cultural Struggle.' Knowles (ed.), *Cambridge Companion*, 207–23.

Schoenmakers, Henri. 'Festivals, Theatrical Events and Communicative Interactions.' *Festivalising! Theatrical Events, Politics and Culture*. Ed. Temple Hauptfleisch, Shulamith Lev-Aladgem, Jacqueline Martin, Willmar Sauter, and Henri Schoenmakers. Amsterdam: Rodopi, 2007. 27–37.

Schramm, Katharina. *African Homecoming: Pan-African Ideology and Contested Heritage*. Walnut Creek, CA: Left Coast P, 2010.

Schwellnus, Trevor. 'Retracing *The Last Walk of Adolfo Ich*.' *Canadian Theatre Review* 161 (2015): 64–73.

Search Party. 'Growing Old with You.' http://searchpartyperformance.org.uk/project/growing-old-with-you. 1 January 2020.

Sellar, Tom. '"A Change Has Totally Taken Place." Interview with Matthias Liliental.' *Theater* 44.2 (2014): 73–9.

'The Curatorial Turn.' *Theater* 44.2 (2014): 21–9.

Shahriari, Sara. 'Human Zoo: For Centuries, Indigenous Peoples Were Displayed as Novelties.' *Indian Country Today* 30 August 2011. https://newsmaven.io/indiancountrytoday/archive/human-zoo-for-centuries-indigenous-peoples-were-displayed-as-novelties-xzic286HEEiwgWX6P4wn7A. 28 August 2018.

Shields, Rob. *Places on the Margin: Alternative Geographies of Modernity*. London: Routledge, 1991.

Sieg, Katrin. *Ethnic Drag: Performing Race, Nation, and Sexuality in West Germany*. Ann Arbor: U of Michigan P, 2009.

Simon, Roger I. with Claudia Eppert. 'Remembering Obligation: Witnessing Testimonies of Historical Trauma.' *The Touch of the Past: Remembrance, Learning, and Ethics*. Ed. Roger I. Simon. New York: Palgrave Macmillan, 2005. 50–64.

Simpson, Leanne Betasamosake. *As We Have Always Done*. Minneapolis: U of Minnesota P, 2017.

Dancing on Our Turtle's Back: Stories of Nishnaabeg Re-Creation, Resurgence and a New Emergence. Winnipeg: Arbeiter Ring, 2011.

'Decolonial Love: Building Resurgent Communities of Connection.' EMMA Talks: Messages from Below. SFU Woodward, Vancouver BC. 8 April 2015. Web. 10 March 2019.

Islands of Decolonial Love. Winnipeg: Arp Books, 2013.

Singh, Sherry-Ann. 'The Experience of Indian Indenture in Trinidad: Arrival and Settlement.' *Caribbean Atlas*. www.caribbean-atlas.com/en/themes/waves-of-colonization-and-control-in-the-caribbean/waves-of-colonization/the-experience-of-indian-indenture-in-trinidad-arrival-and-settlement.html. 17 November 2019.

Slater, Lisa. '"Our Spirit Rises from the Ashes": Mapoon Festival and History's Shadow.' *Festival Places: Revitalizing Rural Australia*. Ed. Chris Gibson and John Connell. Bristol: Channel View, 2011. 123–35.

'Sovereign Bodies: Australian Indigenous Cultural Festivals and Flourishing Lifeworlds.' *The Festivalization of Culture.* Ed. Andy Bennett, Jodie Taylor, and Ian Woodward. Farnham, Surrey: Ashgate, 2014. 131–46.

Smith, Janet. 'At the PuSh Festival, Cuckoo Uses Talking Rice Cookers to Unpack Tragedy.' *Georgia Straight* 15 January 2020. www.straight.com/arts/1347061/push-festival-cuckoo-uses-talking-rice-cookers-unpack-tragedy. 12 February 2020.

Smith, Linda Tuhiwai. *Decolonizing Methodologies: Research and Indigenous Peoples.* London: Zed Books, 1999.

Smith, Saphora, and Andy Eckardt. 'Germans of Turkish Descent Struggle with Identity, Seek Acceptance.' *NBC News* 14 August 2018. www.nbcnews.com/news/world/germans-turkish-descent-struggle-identity-seek-acceptance-n886961. 16 September 2020.

SolOthello. By Regan Taylor. Dir. Craig Geenty. Prod. Te Rehia Theatre Company at the Aki Studio, Toronto, 6–8 October 2016.

'Sound Off: A Deaf Theatre Festival.' www.soundofffestival.com. 7 January 2020.

Stallybrass, Peter, and Allon White. *The Poetics and Politics of Transgression.* Ithaca, NY: Cornell UP, 1986.

Stevenson, Karen. *The Festival of Pacific Arts: Celebrating 40 Years.* Suva, Fiji: Secretariat of the Pacific Community (SPC), 2012.

Stewart, Lizzie. 'Postmigrant Theatre: The Ballhous Naunynstraße Takes on Sexual Nationalism.' *Journal of Aesthetics & Culture* 9.2 (2017): 56–68. www.tandfonline.com/doi/full/10.1080/20004214.2017.1370358. 2 January 2020.

St Jacques, Sylvie. 'A Final State of Emergency Call.' *La Presse* 26 November 2010. https://translate.google.com/translate?hl=en&sl=fr&u=http://www.lapresse.ca/vivre/societe/201011/26/01-4346517-un-dernier-appel-detat-durgence.php&prev=search. 9 January 2020.

Stone, Rosemary. 'Carifesta – Straight from the Artist's Lips.' *Caribbean Today* 6.10 (1995): 24.

Sundance Institute. 'Theatre Program.' www.sundance.org/programs/theatre-program. 23 February 2019.

Sydney Festival. 'About.' www.sydneyfestival.org.au/about. 2 September 2018.

'Bayala – Baraya: Sing Up Country.' https://2018.sydneyfestival.org.au/baraya. 4 September 2018.

'Innovate: Reconciliation Action Plan 2015–2017.' 25 May 2015. https://issuu.com/sydneyfestival/docs/sydneyfestival_reconciliationaction. 8 March 2020.

'Sydney Festival Director Wesley Enoch Awarded Order of Australia.' *Broadway World Sydney* 25 January 2020. www.broadwayworld.com/sydney/article/Sydney-Festival-Director-Wesley-Enoch-Awarded-Order-Of-Australia-2020 0125. 5 February 2020.

Sykes, Jill. 'Stones in Her Mouth: A Terrifyingly Beautiful Performance.' *The Sydney Morning Herald* 29 May 2014. www.smh.com.au/entertainment/

dance/stones-in-her-mouth-a-terrifyingly-beautiful-performance-20140529-zrrl8.html. 26 June 2021.

Tan, Marcus Cheng Chye. 'Elephant Head on White Body: Reflexive Interculturalism in *Ganesh Versus the Third Reich*.' *Contemporary Theatre Review* 26.4 (2016): 416–28.

Taylor, Diana. 'Remapping Genre through Performance: From "American" to "Hemispheric" Studies.' *PMLA* 122.5 (2007): 1416–30.

Taylor, Timothy D. 'World Music Festivals as Spectacles of Genrefication and Diversity.' *Music in the World: Selected Essays*. Chicago: U of Chicago P, 2017. 114–26.

Teatro Municipal do Porto. 'André Amálio/Hotel Europa: Libertação. www.teatromunicipaldoporto.pt/EN/evento-destaque/fitei-2018/andre-amalio-hotel-europa-libertacao-no-ambito-do-fitei-2018/. 2 February 2019.

'André Amálio/Hotel Europa: Passa-Porte. www.teatromunicipaldoporto.pt/EN/evento-destaque/fitei-2018/andre-amalio-hotel-europa-passa-porte-no-ambito-do-fitei-2018/. 2 February 2019.

ten Cate, Ricaerd. 'Festivals: Who Needs 'Em?' *Theatre Forum* 1 (1992): 85–7.

Te Rehia Theatre. 'About/Kaupapa.' https://terehiatheatre.com/about-us-te-kaupapa. 3 January 2017.

Theatre Times. 'The International Online Theatre Festival.' https://thetheatretimes.com/iotfestival and https://thetheatretimes.com/iotfestival2020. 14 April 2020.

Thomasson, Sarah. 'The Australian Festival Network.' Knowles (ed.), *Cambridge Companion*, 132–46.

'The "Jewel in the Crown"? The Place of the Adelaide Festival in the Australian Festival Ecology.' *Performance Research* 17.4 (2012): 145–8.

'Producing the Festival City: Place Myths and the Festivals of Adelaide and Edinburgh.' PhD Dissertation, Queen Mary University of London, 2015.

'"Too Big for Its Boots"? Precarity on the Adelaide Fringe.' *Contemporary Theatre Review* 29.1 (2019): 39–55.

Thompson, Jessie. 'LIFT Festival 2018: From Glow-in-the-Dark Pigeons to Political Parties, 8 Shows Not to Miss.' *Go London* 23 May 2018. www.standard.co.uk/go/london/theatre/lift-festival-2018-from-glowinthedark-pigeons-to-political-parties-8-shows-not-to-miss-a3846846.html. 13 January 2020.

Thompson, Selina. 'Excerpts from the Diary of a Black Woman at the Edinburgh Fringe.' *Exeunt* 21 August 2017. http://exeuntmagazine.com/features/excerpts-diary-black-woman-edinburgh-fringe. 26 February 2018.

Tonkin, Maggie. 'Cloud Gate Dance Theatre: Water Stains on the Wall.' *Dance Australia* 20 March 2012. www.danceaustralia.com.au/review/cloud-gate-dance-theatre-water-stains-on-the-wall. 9 March 2020.

Toronto Fringe. 'Accessibility Manifesto.' https://fringetoronto.com/accessibility/manifesto. 10 September 2019.

'The Lottery and Site-Specifics.' https://web.archive.org/web/20191120143950/https://fringetoronto.com/lottery-and-site-specifics. 26 June 2021.

Turk, Edward Baron. *French Theatre Today: The View from New York, Paris, and Avignon.* Iowa City: U of Iowa P, 2011.

'Turning Point Ensemble & Wen Wei Dance Present the Premiere of FLYING WHITE.' *Broadway World* 7 January 2020. www.broadwayworld.com/bwwdance/article/Turning-Point-Ensemble-Wen-Wei-Dance-Present-The-PremiereOf-FLYING-WHITE-20200107. 28 January 2020.

Ugavule, Emele. 'Black Ties: A Reflection.' *Witness: Performance, Discussion, Community* 6 February 2020. https://witnessperformance.com/black-ties-a-reflection. 30 March 2020.

Um, Hae-Kyung. 'Introduction: Understanding Diaspora, Identity, and Performance.' *Diaspora and Interculturalism in the Performing Arts.* Ed. Hae-kyung Um. London: Routledge, 2005. 1–15.

UNESCO. 'The Kampala International Theatre Festival.' n.d. https://en.unesco.org/creativity/policy-monitoring-platform/kampala-international-theatre. 26 June 2021.

Univers des mots. 'Le Festival Univers des Mots, une fabrique des écritures contemporaines.' https://universdesmots.weebly.com/festival.html. 26 November 2018.

Varney, Denise, Peter Eckersall, Chris Hudson, and Barbara Hatley. *Theatre and Performance in the Asia-Pacific.* Basingstoke: Palgrave Macmillan, 2013.

Veltruský, Jiří. 'Man and the Object in Theatre' (1940). *A Prague School Reader on Esthetics, Literary Structure, and Style.* Ed. and trans. Paul L. Garvin. Washington, DC: Georgetown UP, 1964. 83–91.

Vinícius de Freitas, Marcus. 'Brazil and Africa: Historic Relations and Future Opportunities.' The German Marshall Fund of the United States 8 February 2016. www.gmfus.org/publications/brazil-and-africa-historic-relations-and-future-opportunities. 7 February 2019.

Visit Horsham Region. 'Local Arts Festivals.' https://visithorsham.com.au/activities/local-arts-festivals. 6 January 2020.

Vizenor, Gerald. *Manifest Manners: Narratives on Postindian Survivance.* Hanover, NH: Wesleyan UP, 1994.

Vosters, Helene. 'Cultivating a Cross-Border, Extra-Theatrical Assemblage in Resistance to Femicide in the Americas.' *Canadian Theatre Review* 161 (2015): 22–5.

Waterfield, Carran. 'Social Theatre at the Edinburgh Festival: A Report from a Theatre-Maker.' *Research in Drama Education: The Journal of Applied Theatre and Performance* 20.2 (2015): 237–41.

Waterman, Stanley. 'Carnivals for élites? The Cultural Politics of Arts Festivals.' *Progress in Human Geography.* 22.1 (1998): 54–74.

Wehle, Philippa. 'Avignon, Everybody's Dream.' *Contemporary Theatre Review* 13.4 (2003): 27–41.

Werry, Margaret. Response to American Society for Theatre Research panel, 'Performing Transnationalisms through Festivals.' Minneapolis, Minn., 6 November 2016.

Whistler Naturalists. 'Fungus Among Us.' www.whistlernaturalists.ca/fungus-among-us-mushroom-festival. 30 March 2020.

Wilkinson, L. Efebo. 'Best Village Theatre: Compelling Presence, Emerging Form (the Evolution of a Caribbean Theatrical Genre)' CARIFESTA Symposium. University of the West Indies, Port of Spain, Trinidad. 16–25 August 2019.

Willems-Braun, Bruce. 'Situating Cultural Politics: Fringe Festivals and the Production of Spaces of Intersubjectivity.' *Environment and Planning D: Society and Space* 12.1 (1994): 75–104.

Wilson, Shawn. *Research Is Ceremony: Indigenous Research Methods.* Halifax, NS: Fernwood, 2008.

Workman Arts. 'Rendezvous with Madness Festival.' https://workmanarts.com/rendezvous-with-madness. 7 January 2020.

Wunderbar. 'About Us.' https://wunderbar.org.uk/about/about-us. 14 January 2020.

'Xuntian He.' Schott. https://en.schott-music.com/shop/autoren/xuntian-he. 5 July 2019.

Yankah, Victor K. 'The Pan-African Historical Theatre Festival (PANAFEST) in Ghana, 1992–2010: The Vision and the Reality.' *African Theatre 11* (2012): 45–55.

Younis, Madani. 'Black, Asian and Other Artists from Marginalised Groups Have Fought Their Way onto the Programmes of Edinburgh Festival Fringe and I Want to Shout about It.' *Bush Theatre*, 22 August 2017. www.bushtheatre.co.uk/bushgreen/black-asian-and-other-artists-from-marginalised-groups-have-fought-their-way-onto-the-programmes-of-edinburgh-festival-fringe-and-i-want-to-shout-about-it. 23 February 2018.

Zaiontz, Keren. '"Festival Sites: The Civic and Collective Life of Curatorial Practice." An Interview with Deborah Pearson and Joyce Rosario.' *Theatre Research in Canada/Recherches théâtrales au Canada* 40.1–2 (2019): 153–65.

'From Post-War to "Second-Wave": International Performing Arts Festivals.' Knowles (ed.), *Cambridge Companion*, 15–35.

'Human Rights (and Their Appearances) in Performing Arts Festivals.' *Canadian Theatre Review* 161 (2015): 48–54.

Theatre & Festivals. London: Palgrave, 2018.

Zarrilli, Phillip B. 'Religious and Civic Festivals: Early Drama and Theatre in Context.' *Theatre Histories: An Introduction.* Phillip B. Zarrilli, Bruce McConachie, Gary Jay Williams, and Carol Fisher Sorgenfrei. New York: Routledge, 2006. 53–98.

Zherdev, Nikolay. 'Festivalization as a Creative City Strategy.' IN3 Working Paper Series (2014). https://cercles.diba.cat/documentsdigitals/pdf/E140137.pdf. 26 June 2021.

Zukin, Sharon. 'Urban Lifestyles: Diversity and Standardization in Spaces of Consumption.' *Urban Studies* 35.5–6 (1998): 825–39.

Index

Milton Keynes UK
Ingram Content Group UK Ltd.
UKHW021637041123
431941UK00015B/62